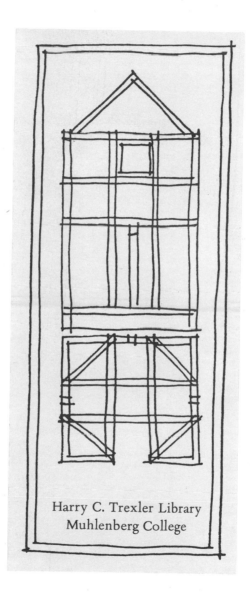

World Savings

World Savings

An international survey

Introduction by Nobel Laureate
Franco Modigliani

Edited by Arnold Heertje

BLACKWELL
Oxford UK & Cambridge USA

In association with the Dutch Savings Banks Association

Copyright © De Echte Kern, BV. 1993

First published 1993

Blackwell Publishers
238 Main Street
Cambridge
MA 02142
USA

108 Cowley Road
Oxford OX4 1JF
UK

Library of Congress Cataloging-in-Publication Data

World savings: An International Survey / edited by Arnold Heertje.
   p. cm.
  Includes bibliographical references and index.
  ISBN 0–631–18521–6
  1. Saving and investment. I. Heertje, Arnold, 1934–
HC79.S3W675 1993
339.4'3 – dc20   92–27435 CIP

British Library Cataloguing in Publication Data

A CIP catalogue record for this book is available from the British Library.

Typeset in 10 on 12 pt Ehrhardt
by Graphicraft Typesetters Ltd., Hong Kong
Printed in Great Britain by T.J. Press Ltd., Padstow, Cornwall

This book is printed on acid-free paper

Contents

Contributors

Professor Franco Modigliani is Institute Professor Emeritus at the Massachusetts Institute of Technology, Cambridge, USA

Dr Barbara Kauffmann is a member of the Directorate-General for Economic and Financial Affairs, Brussels, Belgium

Professor Willem H. Buiter is Professor of Economics in the Department of Economics at Yale University, USA

Dr Jeffrey Owens is Head of the Fiscal Affairs Division in the Directorate for Financial, Fiscal and Enterprise Affairs at the OECD, Paris, France

Professor Lawrence J. Lau is Professor of Economics in the Department of Economics at Stanford University, USA

Professor Dr Jean-Paul Fitoussi is President of Observatoire Français des Conjonctures Economiques (OFCE)

Dr Jacques Le Cacheux is Acting Director in the Research Department at the Observatoire Français des Conjonctures Economiques (OFCE)

Professor Barry W. Ickes is Professor of Economics in the Department of Economics at The Pennsylvania State University, USA

Professor Charles Yuji Horioka is Professor of Economics in the Institute of Social and Economic Research at Osaka University, Osaka, Japan

Dr W. F. Duisenberg is President of the Dutch Central Bank, Amsterdam, The Netherlands

Professor Dr A. H. E. M. Wellink is Director of the Dutch Central Bank, Amsterdam, The Netherlands

Preface

This book is the result of an initiative by the Dutch Savings Banks Association. Its aim is to compare and to analyze, both theoretically and empirically, the volume of savings in the USA, Western Europe, Eastern Europe and Japan. Differences in savings rates are often substantial between these regions and this phenomenon is part of the imbalance in the world economy.

We are fortunate that so many eminent scholars have been willing to contribute to this volume and it is a great honour that the Nobel Laureate, F. Modigliani, agreed to write the introduction. We are also grateful to the President of the Dutch Central Bank, Dr W. F. Duisenberg, and to his co-author, Professor Dr A. H. E. M. Wellink, Director of that institution, for writing the final chapter on a global savings policy. We hope that this book will prove to be a major contribution to the international discussion on savings.

J. F. T. Vugts
Chairman of the Board of the Dutch Savings Banks Association

Introduction

Franco Modigliani[*]

INTRODUCTION

This volume deals with the broad subject of World Saving. What makes this issue a topical one is the combination of a declining trend in national saving, from the 1960s to the 1970s and even more markedly from the 1970s to the 1980s, and a growing need for investment funds to reverse the declining trend in investment in the developed countries and to finance developing countries, including Eastern Europe.

The volume collects together eight essays. Only one chapter is essentially theoretical in nature. All the remaining ones are concerned with empirical issues: what determines saving behavior? What caused the widespread contraction in aggregate saving in the last decade or two? What are the implications for policy? Three of the chapters deal with the issue or a part thereof in general terms, while the other four focus on the experience of selected countries: three market economies – the United States, Western Europe, and Japan – and the socialist countries of Eastern Europe. The last chapter draws policy conclusions, building on the other chapters.

THE ROLE OF THE "LIFE-CYCLE HYPOTHESIS"

All chapters, with the exception of the first, share in common their reliance in some degree on the analytical framework provided by the so-called Life-Cycle Hypothesis, or LCH for brevity (Modigliani & Brumberg 1954a and 1954b; Modigliani 1986, 1991). According to this model, individual consumption reflects the preferred allocation of available life resources to consumption over life, while saving and dissaving perform the function of bridging the gap between the life-cycle of income and the desired path of consumption, taking into account their uncertainty. In this view, individual saving arises primarily from "hump saving," transitory accumulation of wealth destined for later expenditure. In addition, some of the accumulation may end up (by miscalculation or by design) in the form of bequests. This basic foundation is common to the so-called Permanent Income Hypothesis of Milton Friedman (PY), in that both LCH and PY rely on the rational postulate that consumption is based on permanent income or life resources. But the permanent income hypothesis has very little to offer toward an understanding of *aggregate* saving, because, through its assumptions of an infinite life, it cannot deal with the critical role of the life-cycle of income and consumption. In LCH, on the other hand, aggregate saving results from the interaction of hump wealth (and bequests) with the rate of growth of the economy. If income grows steadily (whether because of population and/ or productivity growth), then each age group will enjoy more life resources than the same age group the period before. Under plausible assumptions about preferences and their stability, saving and wealth of each age group, and of the economy as a whole, will then also increase at the rate of growth of income. But since the growth of wealth is saving (aside from the transitory effect of capital gains), it follows that the rate of growth of assets is equal to the ratio of saving to wealth and with a stable growth this ratio must be equal to the rate of growth of income. But this implies that the saving/income ratio will be equal to growth times the wealth/income ratio.

Note that this basic LCH relation implies that, in a stationary economy, saving tends to zero, independently of the income of the country. The saving rate will be positive only if growth is positive and will increase with the rate of growth; on the other hand, it will tend to be unaffected by how rich or poor the country is, except, possibly, for very poor countries which are not part of this study.

MACROECONOMIC ASPECTS, SAVING AND ENDOGENOUS GROWTH

Willem Buiter is concerned in principle with the macroeconomic aspects of saving. But his contribution, in contrast to the others, is entirely theoretic: he sets up a number of hypotheses without much regard for their realism, and proceeds to derive logical implications, including some about economic policies, without asking whether they are supported by empirical observations. One further characteristic of his paper is that the problem he is concerned with is rather specific: what are the macroeconomic implications, particularly the dynamic ones, of recent contributions which have endeavored to endogenize (productivity) growth? Since the endogenization of growth is achieved by making growth a function of investment which, in a closed economy, is the same as private saving, except for government, he is interested in analyzing the problem in the context of a model in which saving is also endogenous.

In order to keep the modeling of endogenous growth to a minimum he chooses an extremely simplified formulation. Specifically, he assumed that the aggregate co-production function has the property that output is proportional to capital input (in other words there is constant return to scale to capital rather than to a set of factors, as in the traditional approach). He shows that this assumption has the remarkable implication that the rate of growth of the economy, both capital and output, is proportional to the rate of national saving. There is of course absolutely no evidence to support this extreme model as against the long-established standard one.

As for the modeling of saving, in contrast to all other papers in this volume, it bears little relation to the life-cycle model except for relying on an overlapping generation model and rational behavior (assumptions which are common also to the permanent income hypothesis).

In this model, individual consumption is obtained by maximizing expected utility, assuming the popular additive isoelastic utility function, subject to the lifetime budget constraint. The resulting path of consumption is smooth, rising or falling at a constant rate, till the random time of death. Everyone expects that same labor income (except for an assumed predictable decay of earning power) until death. Accordingly, there is no retirement and no retirement hump. And there is also no room for bequests. Aggregate consumption is the sum of individual wealth plus human wealth net of taxes.

It is unclear under what conditions this model of consumption will generate positive or negative saving, and how aggregate saving will respond to the growth rate.

A particularly interesting question is whether the model implies that the saving rate is a monotonically increasing function of growth (at least in the relevant range). If so, the consumption function and the growth function would form a closed system of two equations in two unknowns. Such a formulation would help to make the exposition more transparent.

Despite these qualms, it must be admitted that the application of his model to issues in public finance gives pretty intuitively sensible answers, as far as they go. For instance, the model rejects debt neutrality as long as some of the new taxes fall on later generations, and that would be excluded only if there are no births (but this result holds only because his model does not allow for the Barro possibility of people saving more now to pay for the later taxes). Similarly, an unfounded social security system is found to lead to an increase in aggregate consumption and a fall in saving; but again this conclusion holds because in his model people do not retire and therefore he excludes Feldstein's retirement effect. In this and other similar cases examined – like that of deficit-financed tax cut – the reduction in saving has a magnified effect on the economy through his production function, as it also reduces the growth of capital and consumption. However, one interesting unexpected result is that the path resulting from such deficit-increasing and growth-reducing policies "WILL NOT be Pareto dominated" by one with the higher growth rate. This result, which had been partially anticipated by others, is not likely to disappear as a result of more realistic assumptions about production and saving.

MICROECONOMICS OF SAVING

We may begin by reviewing the "general" paper of Barbara Kauffmann. Its purpose "is to analyze households' decision-making processes in accumulating wealth," i.e., the determinants of the (hump) path of wealth discussed above.

The Behavior of Saving in Recent Decades

Figure 1.1 and Table 1.1 provide an idea of the nature of the decline in saving in the last three decades, focusing on the G7 countries, which enjoy the largest per capita income and make a very large contribution to the pool of world savings. It is seen that between the 1960s and 1980s gross saving declined in every country by substantial amounts. For four out of five countries, the decline is between 5 and 12 percentage points. It is interesting to observe that the United States, the country whose low level and persistent decline in saving has been the source of so much concern and blame by the entire world, shows in fact between the 1960s and 1980s a middling decline of some 3.5 percentage points. The table also reveals that most of the decline in saving occurred between the 1970s and the 1980s though, with very minor exceptions, the trend had already begun between the 1960s and 1970s.

Actually the gross saving figures in the table tend to underestimate the magnitude of the decline. In the first place saving should be measured net of depreciation. The difference is important because, for a variety of reasons – some having to do with a shift in the composition of capital toward shorter-lived investments – the share of the depreciation to gross output increased just about everywhere. It is therefore more useful to look at net saving, even allowing for the possibilities of defects in the depreciation figures. One then finds that the decline in net saving between 1960 and 1980 is uniformly higher and amounted to at least 5 percent for all but one country, reaching around ten points for two.

The figures just reviewed contain some "surprises" for the student of saving behavior. Until the 1970s it had been widely held that the saving ratio of a country would be a pretty stable number – except for cyclical effects and other disturbances, which however should wash out in averaging over ten periods. In addition, the difference in saving ratios across countries was thought to be modest, at least within the set of developed economies. The second view was abandoned between the 1960s and 1970s as a result of new statistical data, and their interpretation in the light of the LCH. But the instability within a country still remains a puzzle. This volume should contribute toward resolving that puzzle.

Figure 1.1 shows for each decade a breakdown of the national saving between the three component sectors: the government, the household and the corporate sector. One important fact brought out by the chart is the universal and mostly large deterioration in the fiscal budget of each country. However, these figures are unfortunately systematically biased because they are not corrected for the effect of inflation. As explained by Kauffmann (*Inflation*, pp. 48–50) when there is inflation the income and saving of any creditor must be reduced by the extent of the inflation-induced loss in the purchasing power of his claim; similarly for debtors whose real debt is reduced by inflation, one must add to his income and saving the amount of depreciation from inflation. Of course, within the private sector, creditors and debtors offset each other. But the private sector as a whole is a net creditor toward the public sector (through its holding of the private, domestic national debt). Therefore the figures for the public sector should be corrected by adding the (ex post) rate of inflation multiplied by the privately held debt, and the same figure should be added to the private saving. Clearly for the period under consideration this inflation correction both reduces the level of saving and increases the extent of the decline relative to what is shown in Figure 1.1.

In a recent paper (Modigliani, 1990) I have actually estimated this correction for a sample of 22 OECD countries and find that it is negligible for the 1960s, when there was little inflation, but amounts to 1.7 percentage points of the 1970s. For the 1980s it is even higher, 2.4 percentage points, due largely to two countries, Belgium and Italy, with a large debt and relatively high inflation. In the case of Italy in particular, the correction to the deficit and the saving ratio is 8 points in the 1970s and 9 in the 1980s, large enough to turn the large deficit in Figure 1.1 into a surplus, and the highest rate of private saving into a middling one.

Motives for Saving

Next the author reviews the motives that lead households to save in order to accumulate wealth before spending it:

Retirement and social security The first motive is to provide for the period of retirement when consumption can no longer be financed out of a withering income. The extent of private accumulation for that purpose depends on various circumstances. For instance, it will increase with the length of the retirement period (a point stressed in the original formulation of LCH). It will also be affected by social security and its retirement provisions.

Unfortunately, this effect turns out to be rather complex, as explained by Kauffmann (*Social Security*, pp. 39–42), because it has two contrasting component effects on household saving. First the government pension obviates the need for private accumulations. However, there is a second, more subtle, effect called the "induced retirement" effect. The availability of a pension encourages an earlier and longer retirement which, by LCH, should mean more saving. Kauffmann reports a number of empirical results which point to contradictory conclusions about the overall effect of social security. Actually, a study of mine (Modigliani and Sterling, 1983) finds clear evidence of both effects, but also finds that when taken together, they roughly offset each other. On the whole the available evidence suggests that the effect of social security on saving is uncertain but unlikely to be large, except, indirectly, by decreasing labor-force participation.

Return on capital It is widely held that the return that can be obtained on accumulated wealth should be an important inducement to saving. In fact, it may result in more or less saving, again because of contrasting effects. The conventional wisdom of course holds that a higher return must unequivocally lead the rational man to save more or postpone consumption (the substitution effect). But this answer is wrong since a rise in return will make creditors and other owners of wealth better off, and this must work in the direction of raising consumption now as well as later (the income effect). The magnitude and balance between the two responses will depend on taste and on the importance of wealth relative to present and future consumption.

Kauffmann refers to a type of negative income effect, frequently mentioned in the literature, based on the consideration that a rise in the interest rate reduces the "present" or discounted value of life labor income. Actually this independent effect is an error. By an income effect, we mean that as a result of the change in the interest rate, the initial budget constraint is changed as to allow the consumer to increase his consumption. Now while a rise in interest rates reduces the present value of labor income it also reduces the present value and possible wealth of future consumption. The balance can be shown to depend on whether the person holds positive wealth – which should be generally true according to the LCH – and on the maturity structure of the assets and the consequent change in market value. Provided the portfolio is sufficiently short the income effect will be positive, making for less saving. But whether or not this effect will outweigh the substitution effect is an empirical question. Many tests have been performed with strikingly contradictory results. Kauffmann suggests that the evidence "more often indicates that the interest elasticity of saving is positive." But the two latest careful studies with which I am acquainted, one by Hall (1988) and one by Bosworth (1991), as well as that by Lau included in this volume, support the view that I have long held, namely that the elasticity is not negative or systematically appreciably different from zero. This conclusion has important implications with respect to the feasibility of increasing saving through tax incentives which are considered below.

Inflation As already shown, inflation distorts major statistics. Since few among the public or the politicians seem to be able to see through these fallacies they are potentially serious, particularly with respect to government deficit, in that they direct attention to the wrong remedies. But inflation has much more serious effects on saving. When inflation lifts interest by the inflation premium, interest income and income will also increase. If the consumer was rational and understood fully the cause of his higher income, he would realize that it merely compensates for the loss in purchasing power suffered by his assets. Accordingly, he should not increase his consumption, but instead save the whole premium, thus offsetting the inflation loss. But it is conceivable that some households may initially fail to see the necessity to save more so as to offset the loss. In this case, consumption will rise and so true savings will fall by at least some fraction of the inflation premium. Modigliani (1990) finds for 22 OECD countries strong evidence to support the hypothesis that households consume a substantial fraction of the inflation premium estimated at 40–50 percent. With the average inflation premium declining by 2 percentage points between the 1960s and the 1980s, the estimated decline in savings, adjusted for inflation, can be placed around 0.9–1 percent. This is a large effect compared with a decline in the saving rate of 2.5 percentage points. If saving is not adjusted for inflation, then the saving ratio can be expected to rise. Kauffmann mentions a few other effects such as inflation-induced uncertainty, but these effects are probably unimportant empirically.

Other motives impacting on individual behavior Several other motives are discussed by Kauffmann. Among these, of particular interest are those related to uncertainty and credit rationing (liquidity constraint). They are expected to lead to more saving, especially in combination and particularly among the young. Credit rationing per se means that a feasible consumption path must have the property of giving rise at all times to a non-negative net worth. Especially for the young with lower income this must typically lead to cumulating consumption less saving (or more dissaving). If there were credit rationing on the other hand, there would be no reason for saving more other than uncertainty about how to allocate resources over life. But uncertainty of future resources and needs gives an incentive to save and accumulate a reserve against contingencies sparing to future accumulation thus justified by retirement or other motives.

Bequests   There remains one more important motive to which Kauffmann pays little attention – namely the bequest motive. Traditionally this motive was regarded as the most important source of saving and of the existing stock of wealth. But the LCH some 40 years ago called attention to the role of hump wealth, which can account for wealth without need for bequests. In fact, in a simulation using the simplest life-cycle pattern – constant income while working, and constant consumption through life – it was shown that hump wealth could amount to some five times income – a ratio of the order of magnitude that was actually observed for the US. But clearly bequests do exist and their transmission from one generation to the other will add to the stock of wealth generated by the other motives. It can be shown that under some plausible assumptions, that have some empirical support, one might expect the flow of bequests to be proportional to income, and the stock of bequeathed wealth to be proportional to total wealth. Under these conditions, bequests do not change the fundamental property of LCH, namely that saving depends on growth.

One interesting question that has been intensely debated is just how large a fraction of wealth is due to bequests, in contrasts to the life-cycle. While some authors have claimed that it might be as high as four fifths (Kotlikoff and Summers, 1981), I have come to the conclusion, using several different methods and sources, that for the US, that proportion does not exceed one quarter to one fifth. This means that by far the major component of saving is "life-cycle" saving – accumulation for later expenditure. Furthermore, even that portion that may come from inheritances may have quite different origins and implications. As Horioka points out (chapter 7), one may usefully distinguish five bequest motives. The first, and probably the most important, is the result of the precautionary holding of wealth together with uncertainty of the date of death and about medical expenses. Two other motives result from the endeavor of parents to use bequests to secure the children's economic support. These three types of bequests all fit the life-cycle model in the sense that they are motivated by desired, retired consumption, and that the accumulation to which they give rise will tend to be proportional to life resources. Only the truly altruistic types of bequests

– whether due to the subjective utility of bequests or the inclusion in one utility with the utility of heirs – do not directly fit the life-cycle paradigm. There is little information on the relative importance of these true bequest motives, though Horioka provides some interesting information (see below); however they seem unlikely to be large and in any event, as shown above, they need not change the aggregative properties of the pure life-cycle model.

Forces that affect saving without (necessarily) having an impact on individual behavior

Under this heading there are two variables to consider, both of which are mentioned by Kauffmann but not singled out as major influences on saving, and especially on the recent decline in saving.

Public saving Since national saving is the sum of private and public saving, budget surplus in principle increases national saving dollar per dollar. Thus during the last two decades for the sample of 22 OECD countries the decline in (inflation-adjusted) surplus reduced national saving by 3.8 percentage points, or nearly two-thirds of the total decline of 6.3 percentage points. However this conclusion, that would have been widely accepted some years ago, is questionable since it assumes that public saving does not influence private saving. The LCH however suggests that an increase in deficit signals an increase in future taxes to service the debt and that therefore the private economy, to smooth consumption, should increase its saving enough to cover those taxes. Given that life is finite, the additional saving should be but a fraction of the deficit (Modigliani, 1990), which has been estimated as falling within the range 0.2 to 0.6 (Sterling, 1977).

Barro (1974) has suggested that the fraction should instead be one, on the grounds that those currently living should be expected to take into account also the interest that will be levied on the heirs. But this view suffers from serious shortcomings on theoretical and empirical grounds (Modigliani, 1990). A test based on the 22 OECD countries supports the LCH prediction that government surplus should have a strong influence on private saving; but its coefficient, although somewhat variable in alternative formulation and sub-periods, is mostly around −0.4 and below. If we accept 0.4 as a reasonable estimate, we can say that the decline in surplus of about 4 percentage points increased private saving by 1.6 percentage points and therefore produced a *net* decline in national saving by only 2.4 points or 40 percent of the total.

Income growth This plays a critical role in LCH, which implies that saving cannot be maintained without maintained growth. Kauffmann discusses the impact of population growth – how saving depends on the demographic structure which in turn depends on growth. But she suggests that in the case of productivity the "effect of growth is no longer unambiguous." This is a commonly held view, first stated by Milton Friedman; it rests on the consideration that the expectation of a higher future income will lift current consumption relatively to current income. But this conclusion neglects two very important points. The first is the so-called Bentzel effect: when productivity is growing steadily, each generation is richer than the preceding one. Therefore the savings of the young are based on larger life resources than the dissaving of the old, leading to net saving. One can show that, for modest rate of growth, the Bentzel effect will dominate the expectation effect. But this might not be true for high growth, because at high growth the young would choose to consume more than their income, thus starting life by accumulating a debt. Beyond some point more rapid growth would cause this negative net worth to increase fast enough to reduce saving. But this view neglects a fundamental fact of life in our societies, namely that it is rather infeasible for a person to borrow substantial amounts unless he has some net worth to provide security. Hence, as a rule, the young cannot start out dissaving. In fact, as pointed out earlier as well as by Kauffmann (*The life-cycle hypothesis of saving*, pp. 35–6), they will typically start out saving, in order to provide a precautionary cushion and for bulky purchases when they cannot be acquired on reasonable credit terms. The evidence confirms that young people save (Kauffmann, pp. 35–6). Once the possibility of negative saving is eliminated, more productivity growth must mean more saving.

There is abundant evidence to support the role of income growth as much recent empirical work, especially that based on country cross-section, has successfully used a measure of growth. In principle the two components of growth, population and productivity, effect the saving rate through different channels, one through the age structure and age differences in the propensity to save, the other through the Bentzel effect. However their quantitative effect can be expected to be quite similar and many studies have used the total growth rate as one of the explanatory variables. It appears that the recent large and widespread decline in growth may be a major source of the decline in saving.

One noteworthy implication of the growth effect is that it can account for differential saving rates between countries without recourse to traditional explanations, such as differential thriftiness, reflecting different cultural values. Two countries in which individual households have identical thrift habits, in the sense of identical allocations of resources over life, may exhibit different saving ratios, depending on growth. Thus differential growth may go a long way toward explaining the low saving of the slow-growing US versus the high saving of fast-growing countries like Japan and Italy. This conclusion is consistent with Kauffmann's somewhat cryptic concluding remarks: ". . . it would be wrong to jump to the conclusion that households in a particular country or period are relatively impatient or less thrifty just because their observed overall saving rate is relatively low."

SAVING IN WESTERN EUROPE

Recent Developments

Fitoussi and Le Cacheux begin by presenting some basic facts about saving in Western Europe in the last couple of decades, focusing on five main countries, members of the EC (figures 5.1–5.3). Their facts are consistent with those of Kauffmann, namely a pretty universal decline in gross national saving since the 1960s. Fitoussi's annual data shows a turn-around in some countries at the beginning of the 1980s (not visible in household saving – Kauffmann, figure 1.2) but in every case the average for the 1980s remains below that of the 1970s and 1960s. The author recalls that according to LCH this decline could be related to the household saving rate being positively correlated with the rate of growth of the economy, and indicates that "This conclusion conforms with the general observation of the reduction in saving – and investment – ratios as being broadly in line with that of real growth rates in most countries." He also notes that LCH also implies a negative association between the private saving rate and the wealth/income ratio and concludes "On this point too, there is ample evidence: although reliable and comprehensive households' wealth accounts are not available over long time periods for all European countries, all indicators reflect a marked increase in households' wealth/income ratios everywhere." There is also a brief discussion of the life-cycle implications of demographic structure, namely that saving should tend to be reduced by a large share of retired population (which is characteristic of low growth) and also by larger pre-working-age population (characteristic of faster growth). But in steady state growth the retired effect should dominate over the dependency effect so that faster growth and a younger population should, on balance, increase saving. This seems to be the opposite of the authors' conclusion, which does not appear to receive any support from the evidence adduced.

Inadequacies of LCH

Despite pointing out these areas of agreement between models of the LCH variety and observed behavior, the authors claim that "models built upon the life-cycle hypothesis do not seem to perform very well in empirical applications" (p. 200). But in my view they do not succeed in building a strong case in support of this blanket indictment. Thus they complain that individual households do not behave according to the prediction of the hypothesis, citing Bosworth (1991). Not only do I read Bosworth differently, but they also ignore a lot of evidence that, in major respects, household behavior is consistent with LCH, especially allowing for precautionary wealth and bequests (Modigliani, 1986). They also lament the "representative agent framework" yet, by its very nature, the LCH does not rely on the representative agent, but on heterogeneous populations.

But the most unwarranted of their complaints is that according to the data, government deficit is not offset fully by higher private saving whereas, according to LCH, the private sector should see through the government veil and thus offset the deficit (the so-called Barro hypothesis).

But the Barro hypothesis does not rest at all on rationality or on seeing through government veils. It depends instead on *all* existing households choosing to insulate totally *all* their heirs, forever after, from *any* unfavorable consequence of the current deficit in terms of future taxes. As mentioned earlier, LCH rejects this most improbable behavior and corresponding inference. It suggests instead that saving might rise enough to cover the present value of future taxes following on those presently alive. This is a fraction of the deficit, possibly up to some 30 to 40 percent, and this conclusion is actually well supported by the evidence (Modigliani, 1990).

An Alternative Explanation

Ostensibly because of the inadequacies of LCH, Fitoussi proposes an explanation of what happened to Western Europe during the last decade different from the "often alleged one, to wit" that the initial drop in saving – presumably arising from the smaller growth and appreciation of wealth – has caused the increase of real interest rates, which in turn triggered the sharp downward adjustment in domestic investment. He rejects this explanation which "may help to understand medium and long run developments," but "is not appropriate to account for observed variations in Western Europe." Two reasons are given. First, that "real interest rates appear to be heavily influenced by monetary policy," and second, that "Europe is not a closed economy." He then proceeds to tell his alternative story which centers on the role of the second oil-price shock followed by the US shock in the form of sharply higher interest rates. These high rates spread to Europe through a German policy of very tight monetary and fiscal policy aimed at preventing devaluation and the accompanying threat of inflation. The other EC countries in turn had to toe the tight line in an endeavor to maintain their parity with the Mark; and the economies had to adjust painfully to this situation which lasted until oil prices and American interest rates came down.

I have no major difference with this account, but it does not seem inconsistent with the role of the life cycle. To begin with, the high US interest rates, that reflected initially the endeavor to end monetary accommodation of inflation, were maintained and even increased in real terms for a few years as a result of the huge federal deficit that reduced national saving and through dollar appreciation drew capital from the rest of the world. While the effects of this policy on US unemployment and investment were not dramatic, as a result of the loose fiscal policies offsetting the tight fiscal policy, they were disastrous in Europe which, understandably, refused to follow the US in its irresponsible fiscal policy. There was accordingly a large rise in unemployment and fall in the growth rate, which in turn reduced saving.

Fitoussi ends his contributions on a rather pessimistic note concerning the future of saving and interest rates. His major worry is public dissaving and the small likelihood of improvement because of many developments, including a tendency to less progressiveness and to reduced taxation of capital income. He seems to be more optimistic about household saving but he does not tell us whether this is because he expects more vigorous growth and or less appreciation of assets, working through an LCH mechanism, or independently of such developments.

SAVING IN JAPAN

Saving and Growth: a Historical Perspective

Mr Horioka again begins with some basic facts about saving in Japan, covering most of the postwar period. For the person not steeped in the economy of Japan, they are highly instructive. First they confirm that the Japanese have saved a lot – at times. In 1970 *net* national saving rose as high as 31 percent. But one should not jump to the conclusion that the high rate is a stable feature of the Japanese economy reflecting their inborn thriftiness or virtue, as is so frequently done. Instead, their saving ratio has fluctuated a lot and largely in sympathy with the equally unstable rate of growth.

Estimates for the period 1885 to 1940 (Ando, Guiso, Terlizzese, and Dorsainvil, 1940) reveal that the growth rate is very volatile but averaging only something short of 3 percent per year. During this period the saving rate was mostly below 5 percent and averaged below 10. The high growth rate begins in the mid 1950s, moving rapidly above 5 percent. The saving ratio starts at 15 percent of which, however, 3.7 is due to government surplus. The private rate at 11.5 percent is by no means extraordinary. But after 1960, when growth really takes off, reaching a high plateau of nearly 10 percent for over a decade, private saving becomes impressive – from 17 percent to a peak of 23 percent. This extraordinary level is furthermore supplemented by a huge government saving – mostly between 6 and 7½ percent – lifting national saving to the record 31 percent. After 1970 growth declines quite rapidly for a few years, averaging only about 1.5 percent between the mid 1970s and 1980s, and private saving also tends to decline, though more gradually. Finally growth settles at a new plateau, around 3 percent, and private saving stabilizes around a level of 16–17 percent, eventually falling to 14 percent. Thus the decline from peak comes to over 8 percentage points or 40 percent. Somewhat surprisingly the government surplus also contracted sharply after the mid 1970s and till the mid 1980s, with the result that national saving declined to around 19 percent in the mid 1980s – a loss of 12 percentage points. However, a late sharp recovery in government surplus brought national saving back to 23 percent.

These figures are striking when one recalls that in the US and worldwide there was serious concern about the decline in US saving, which was taken as an indication of lax habits and loss of moral fiber. Actually the decline in the private saving rate between the 1960s and 1980s was only 2 percent for the US and 2.5 for the average of the OECD countries. These figures pale in comparison with the decline reported for Japan.

Horioka gives some consideration to the possibility that the high rate of saving of Japan in comparison with the US and other countries might reflect different methods of measurement or omissions, such as the treatment of the purchase of durable goods. But he finds little support for that hypothesis except for a modest upward bias in Japanese saving estimates growing from the fact that, in the official statistics, depreciation has been computed at original rather than at reproduction cost.

Life Cycle versus Bequests

The rest of Horioka's contribution is largely devoted to the question of whether the Japanese experience can best be accounted for by the life-cycle framework or instead by the so-called "dynasty model" in which saving and wealth arise primarily from accumulation intended for bequests. He points out that the questions of which explanation is more nearly relevant is of considerable interest. To the extent that saving behavior reflects the life-cycle, it should be affected by any number of life-cycle variables, including age structure, length of retirement, government deficit, social security and the like. But if the dynasty paradigm is the relevant one, then, at least under the Barro version, these variables should have little effect on aggregate national saving.

His main conclusion is that, despite the widespread practice of inter-generational bequests, which seems to be much more common in Japan than in the US, "the life-cycle model" is far more applicable to Japan than the dynasty model is (p. 269). This conclusion would have been reinforced had he not relied on a very narrow definition of life-cycle accumulation, namely for and only for supporting retired consumption, and had instead included all hump wealth. Hump and bequest saving represent a comprehensive set of motivations, except for a few motives which seem to be of no empirical relevance.

Horioka's conclusion is supported by evidence with respect to a variety of phenomena. First, the LCH implies that saving should be positive till retirement, and then become negative, i.e., wealth should decline thereafter. Unfortunately, there are serious difficulties in measuring saving and wealth of the old because of a widespread practice of children doubling up with their father's family. As a result the father, particularly if less affluent, disappears as an independent household. For this and other reasons some households will not be reported, causing an upward bias in the measured wealth of the old. Making allowances for these biases, as far as possible, it appears that both dependent and independent aged households dissave, though in some cases the dissaving begins at a rather advanced age. Similarly there is evidence that wealth tends to decrease beyond some age, though that age may again be fairly advanced. However, Ando and Kennickell (1987) have shown that if income and saving are corrected for capital gains or losses on money fixed assets due to inflation, and/or social security benefits, are treated as a transfer, rather than as an income, as they really should, then dissaving may begin as early as the first half of the 1970s.

Second, there is evidence from many studies, including some by Mr Horioka, that the two major variables that are the essence of the life-cycle – age structure of the population and the rate of growth of income – are in fact important determinants of Japanese saving. The role of social security also receives some support, especially with respect to its unfavorable effect on the labor supply of the aged.

Another way of measuring the importance of life-cycle versus dynasty is to estimate the fraction of aggregate wealth that can be attributed to bequests received, the remaining portion being presumably life-cycle wealth (with proper allowance for wealth that may be currently accumulating for future bequests). Japanese survey data reveal a widespread desire to leave bequests to children. In one survey over half of the respondents expressed this view. This is a lot larger than seems to be the case in the US. However attempts at estimating life-cycle and non-life-cycle wealth along the lines pursued in the US and several other countries produces, for Japan, mostly fairly low estimate for inherited wealth, below 30 percent, though a couple reach in the 40 percent range. What is interesting however is that the results obtained for Japan are broadly similar to those obtained in other countries.

However the cited estimates of inherited wealth must be regarded as very much of an overestimate of the "dynastic bequests" because bequests, according to Horioka, may also arise from other life-cycle motives. The most obvious case is bequests arising, unintentionally, from the holding of wealth for precautionary reasons. In addition, Horioka distinguishes four kinds of bequests, two of which may be regarded as life-cycle motivated because their aim is to provide for retired consumption. One is an "implicit contract" in which children commit themselves to support their parents in exchange for a bequest. The other is a "strategic bequest motive," where the threat of disinheritance is used by parents to induce children to care for them.

In an endeavor to secure information on the importance of these various sources of saving and bequests, Horioka turns to some survey data which appear to be unusually rich in Japan. These data serve to confirm in the first place that financing of retirement and other life-cycle motives are overwhelmingly cited by the respondents as reasons for saving. At the same time, and somewhat surprisingly, relatively few of the aged report dissaving – less than 20 percent even of those aged over 70. Horioka tries to reconcile the two results, though not entirely convincingly, The proportion of respondents that envisages a truly altruistic bequest is only about one third in one survey and 16.5 percent in another (which however is somewhat suspicious as it fails to give the respondents a choice of "no bequests").

However, further support for the dynasty model comes from other findings, e.g., that the level of wealth-holding as well as labor-force participation of the aged increases with the number of living children. At the same time a few other findings strengthen the implicit contract hypothesis: for instance, the finding that children's support payments increase with the parents' holding of wealth or that the parents' bequeathable wealth increases the probability of doubling up with children.

Thus, the overall survey evidence indicates that both kinds of motivation play a role, but suggests that the larger component of an apparently large bequest flow can be attributed to the implicit contract and is thus consistent with life-cycle. This consideration, together with the success of the basic life-cycle variables in explaining aggregate saving, lead the author to conclude that in Japan, "the bulk of saving is, directly or indirectly, for life-cycle purposes" (p. 269).

SAVING IN EASTERN EUROPE
Determinants of aggregate saving

Ickes offers an analysis of the private and national saving process in the planned or non-market economy of Eastern Europe and the former Soviet Union. The basic difference, of course, is that in a planned economy national saving is, basically, targeted by the government as part of the overall national economic plan. The target is achieved through retained earning of enterprises and through direct and especially indirect taxation. It is augmented by a contribution from individual decisions of the households, which can be affected only indirectly through incentives. But that contribution is, typically, relatively small. By contrast, in the market economy private saving is the result of individual decisions of household and firms and provide the bulk, while government savings are typically small and primarily motivated by budget pressures and the desire to avoid deficits, rather than by the desire to achieve some overall savings target (though there certainly are instances of aiming for a surplus in order to raise national saving).

In general the investment targets that underlie the saving flow reflect, it is suggested, a balancing between the additional output that can be obtained through investment, and the cost to consumers, as seen by the planner, of squeezing current consumption. However the planners must in addition take into account the disincentive effects of low availability of consumption goods. The overall rate of investment actually chosen by Russia and the other communist countries in the Russian sphere turns out to be almost universally in the 25 to 30 percent range. Compared with OECD market economies this range corresponds to that observed for the half a dozen highest saving countries but is clearly higher than the average for OECD. Of course, recent information on the state of production facilities in Eastern Europe has lead to serious questions about whether investments were economically chosen and efficiently executed.

An interesting issue is how do investment targets respond to unavoidable shocks in output? Does the planner choose to sacrifice the consumption or the investment target? The data presented clearly suggest that investment absorbs much of the shock but it would appear that consumption also absorbs some, as income is found to be somewhat smoother than consumption (with a single exception); this is, of course, the opposite to what one typically finds in market economies.

Motives for Private Saving

What motivates families to save in a socialist system and how strong are the various motives? If one went by the model of an "ideal" socialist economy one might conclude that there is very little incentive to save, at least for the motives which were seen as important in a market economy. As the author points out, the availability of pensions, apparently with a high replacement ratio, provides little incentive to save for retirement; until recently neither houses nor durable goods nor a business could be readily acquired, implying no incentive to accumulate in order to acquire them; similarly, there would be little reason for precautionary balance given the stability of employment and the availability of free medical care, and transfers by bequest or intra vivos cannot have much appeal in an equalitarian society with free education. Last but not least, there was practically only one way to accumulate wealth, namely in the form of nominal assets like cash or deposits, subject to the risk of inflation.

In fact, there are indications that household savings were more important than this picture might suggest, especially in more recent times. Durable goods and even houses became available, and their purchase would require more accumulation than in OECD countries, both because they are more expensive (relative to income) and because of the non-existence of credit from financial institutions. Also in a system in which the availability of goods is uncertain, people tend to hold balances to enable them to take advantage of opportunities and to buy in the free market.

A different explanation that has been offered for the relatively high flow and stock of saving is the so-called "saving overhang" hypothesis: because the income that people receive exceeds the value of goods allocated to consumption at official prices, people have no choice but to accumulate the difference in cash or deposits. This hypothesis has generated heated exchanges which the author reviews. I tend to share his basic doubts concerning the overhang argument. The main reason for doubt is that in the socialist economy with extensive rationing, an economically significant parallel economy develops alongside the official one. But when a household is free to spend its resources in this second market it can no longer be said to hold cash and deposits because it has no way to spend them. On the contrary it would seem that the price level in the free market would tend to be determined by the supply and demand for "overhang balances," reflecting also the expectations of future prices and supply. In any event, one conclusion seems safe, namely that the overhang must affect the relation between official and black market prices which in time should lead the authorities to be concerned with continuing the overhang to prevent it from causing growing leaks from the official to the black market.

Saving during the Transition

Ickes extends his analysis to consider the behavior of saving during the transition to a market economy. Since according to the overhang theory people are supposed to hold liquid balances because of the unavailability of goods through official channels, it follows that if goods become freely available they will rush to buy them, liquidating their assets for cash to be spent on the goods. This would generate high inflation which in turn might reinforce the desire to buy goods now. But this conclusion is most questionable. The existence of black markets implies that at the outset, balances were held voluntarily; what then happens to liquid balances with liberalization must depend on prices, price expectations and the course of actual and expected real income. Suppose, for example, that free prices begin at or above the initial black-market level and are expected to fall because of rising availability. Then there will be obviously no tendency for a significant net liquidation of balances. More generally, it would seem that even though saving might be initially reduced, only the expectation of rapidly rising prices could generate a stampede out of nominal assets and even this danger could be minimized by offering a generous real interest rate (e.g., by indexation).

It is also widely held, even by the author, that saving will tend to decline because of a higher income together with the expectation of future rises. But this conclusion is wrong; it can be shown that provided that households are prevented from having a negative net worth, even though consumption may rise, it will rise proportionately less than income, basically because older cohorts cannot increase their consumption, or only to a limited extent.

One more argument against the fear of massive dissaving is that – as pointed out earlier – in the market economy households will find that they need substantially higher balances at each stage of the life-cycle than in the socialist economy.

While these considerations invite hope with respect to the behavior of private saving in the short and longer run, as the author points out, it is most doubtful that private saving can make up for the unavoidable decline in government saving to be expected from many causes, among which the author includes privatization. Hence, the conclusion that these economies will be major importers of capital in the near term.

TAXATION AND SAVINGS

Effects of Taxation on Saving

Jeffrey Owens' assignment is to deal with the effect of taxation on saving. He reminds us of the fact that taxation affects saving basically by changing the after-tax return. This means that while there are many ways of impinging on the rate of return, such as taxing labor income and property income at different rates, or taxing consumption rather than income, the effectiveness of any approach must finally depend on the response of consumers to the rate of return. This point is important because the response to the rate of return is basically uncertain, as noted earlier. One can therefore not be sure that a tax measure raising returns will have favorable effect, especially if in detaxing interest the government loses revenue. Proposed measures have to be scrutinized very carefully and designed to minimize the income effect. The substitution of an income tax with an equal revenue consumption tax (say through indirect taxation) may on balance not have a very marked net income effect and thus succeed in raising saving. Still opponents point to the unfavorable distributional aspect, as between income classes and age classes, resulting from the substitution, though it must be remembered that a sales tax can easily be made progressive through variation in rates by type of goods and through a rebate offered to all.

Another way taxation affects saving is through the deductibility of interest on debt. In principle, tax deductibility should tend to encourage borrowing for consumption. The author also claims that the evidence (tables 3.1 and 3.3) supports the effectiveness of interest non-deductibility in increasing savings, as the countries with the most generous treatment of interest deductibility also have some of the lower saving ratios. But this conclusion does not seem consistent with his evidence: in table 3.3 there are six countries that are reported as allowing full deductibility of interest incurred for consumer purchases. Of these six only two have relatively low saving (Denmark and Sweden), while the remaining ones are medium to very high savers (Netherlands, Norway, Luxembourg, and Switzerland). In addition it must be remembered that much of the borrowing may be spent for investment goods (houses, durable goods). If those goods are recognized as investment rather than consumption, then the tax deductibility may actually encourage saving.

Unfortunately the outcome of the analysis is not too encouraging in terms of current and broadly accepted policy recommendations to raise saving. One suggestion is a shift from direct to indirect taxes, which has already been tried for a while. The second, but very doubtful in my mind, is to shift some of the tax burden from corporations to households. In a market of rational investors it should really make little difference and we really have no sound basis for predicting how much more corporations might get and how much less households would save. The last suggestion is to limit the deductibility of consumer's debt. Such measures would probably have some effectiveness in reducing consumer expenditures and investment, though at the expense of consumer's welfare, especially that of younger households.

Taxation and Portfolio Composition

The rest of the chapter examines the effect of taxation not on the aggregate but on the composition of household portfolios. Such effects arise because tax systems differ extensively, within a country and between countries, in the way in which different financial instruments and different sources of income are treated by the tax code. In many countries even the same instrument, say a nominal debt, may be taxed differently depending on the exact nature of the issuer (e.g., private firms, the government, development banks, foreigners) and who owns them (domestic households, financial intermediaries, foreigners). This gives rise to a whole tax rate matrix, which incidentally is very conducive to tax arbitrage.

This discrimination by the tax code is usually justified by the desire to give incentives to certain types of saving or investment or types or financing. Thus, tax advantages are given quite frequently for the purpose of encouraging saving, especially accumulation for retirement. They take the form of tax postponement of contributions to pension reserves by the employer and/or employee. The favorable treatment may include the tax exemption of earnings on the accumulation. Similar treatment is sometimes granted to small savers to encourage, in particular, the holding of equities, or for saving directed to a special purpose, like buying a house (*epargne maison*, in France).

Three tables illustrate the enormous variety with which various sources of income are treated within a country and across countries. One finds that tax laws distinguish over 30 different types of income, and that for less than half of these is the taxation uniform within and across countries. One type of property income where the differences are particularly striking is dividends and capital gains. In particular, in the case of capital gains one finds that within the OECD countries eight do not tax them at all, while for the remaining 15 countries the top rate of taxation goes from 10 to nearly 60 percent. Similarly in the case of interest: in many countries interest income is taxed at flat and relatively low rates and not lumped with other income and taxed at the progressive rate, as would be appropriate in a truly progressive system.

The taxation of interest earned by foreigners is typically also handled by withholding, and frequently at a rate even smaller and established by international agreement. These provisions reflect in part the fact that, with high capital market mobility differentials, tax rates can result in large swings in capital movements. Thus, the competition for capital results in low or altogether no taxation on interest incomes.

The author concludes with the suggestion that tax reforms, in course or contemplated by the OECD, hold some promise to "increase somewhat the level of saving."

US SAVING IN THE POST-WAR PERIOD

The Model

The next chapter examines the behavior of saving in the US from the late 1940s to 1980. The author relies on a novel formulation first developed in a joint paper with Professor Michael Boskin, and the results hold some surprise and challenge.

The foundation of their approach is a demand for consumption. But their demand differs from the customary type of consumption function in that it comes out of the simultaneous solution of two equations. One is the demand for (nominal) consumption. The other is an equation modeling the nominal demand for leisure and having the same formal structure as the consumption equation.

The consumption demand equation is unconventional in that it does not depend explicitly on income. Instead both demands are assumed to depend on wealth and to be proportional to it, but with a proportionality factor depending on a number of variables. The most important are three prices: the price of consumption, and the wage rate, both current and expected future (discounted), and the interest rate which are taken as exogenous. But the interest rate enters the equation not only to measure the substitution effect between present and future consumption but also to capture the effect of a change in interest on the present value of future prices and wages.

From the demand for leisure and the available endowment of time, one can derive a nominal labor income. Adding to it an estimate of nominal non-labor income derived from non-human wealth (exogenous) and the value of nominal interest, one can obtain the estimate of total income. Finally subtracting consumption from income one obtains aggregate saving.

In addition to prices the authors the authors introduce a set of other variables designed to throw light on the distributional effect as distinguished from the aggregate effect of certain variables. In particular they add variables to measure the distribution of wealth across five age classes. Other variables are designed to measure the effects of the distribution of wealth between the cohort born before 1939 (the pre-depression vintage) and those born thereafter – a relative distribution that the authors hold to be of great significance (see below). Finally one variable provides a measure of the inequality in the distribution of wealth across cohorts.

The specification is completed by two more "aggregate variables," the prime-age white male unemployment rate, and, unfortunately, a time trend. Finally the left-hand side of each equation is divide by (the same) function of the real wages and the interest rate, a step whose rationale is left somewhat vague, and both equations are scaled by wealth.

As the authors point out, the two behavior equations are not derived from an assumed utility-maximizing, or rational, behavior – except for imposing a priori homogeneity of zero degree in prices and wages on the demand equations.

The large number of parameters of the model is estimated by appropriate techniques and according to the authors the model fits the data quite well. This statement is hard to evaluate closely because of their unusual (though understandable) procedure of scaling by wealth; offhand the fit would seem to be within the range of other studies, though not as good as some. The parameter estimates thus obtained are then used to derive important behavioral parameters and to test a number of significant hypotheses.

Before looking at the results one should remember that the authors have made a large number of assumptions and simplifications, because they had to or because they chose to. A few examples are given below with some indication of how they might bias or limit the analysis.

1   Although current consumption depends on future wages, future wages are expected to differ from current wages only because of inflation: real wages are a function of age, but not of time; yet according to the LCH there should be some effect from growth of real wages.

2   Prices, wages, interest, and wealth are all treated as exogenous. The treatment of wealth is particularly to be regretted since in principle it could be built from saving, possibly taking capital gains as exogenous.

3   All households are assumed to retire at the same age (65). This leads to a very improbable behavior of consumption and saving and probably to an underestimate of saving after age 65 (see figures 3.4 and 3.2).

4   No distinction is made between permanent and transitory taxes; this failure may help to explain why the fitted equation underestimates consumption in the years 1968–9.

The Effect of Interest Rates

Coming now to the results, one of the most interesting relates to the highly controversial issue of the effects of a change in interest rates (r) on consumption, an effect which cannot be deduced from rational behavior but is essential for an understanding of the effect of taxes on saving. The estimated effect is positive, contrary to conventional wisdom. This result might appear surprising in that, ostensibly, the coefficient measures the pure substitution effect (since wealth is kept constant), and that effect should be negative. But actually that coefficient measures also the effect on current consumption of a decline in the present value of all future prices, which should increase consumption, and all future wages, which should decrease it. Therefore, the coefficient of r clearly reflects much of the income effect, and therefore its sign is indeterminate.

Next, the authors compute an elasticity of saving with respect to interest rates allowing for the effect on income of a higher return on non-human wealth. That elasticity is still negative, numerically large, and highly significant.

This is remarkable in that their addition to income through property income is certain to be upward biased. Indeed, how much income rises when there is a rise in interest rates depends on the origin of the rise. If, for instance, net of tax interest rises at the expense of labor, or through government subsidies, then the favorable effect on property income will be offset by losses elsewhere, or by government dissaving. In general the relevant issue is what happens to consumption.

Finally, the authors present a third calculation in which they allow for the fact that a rise in r reduces wealth and hence consumption (through the present value of labor income, as non-human wealth is assumed to be invested in short-term instruments). With this correction the consumption and saving elasticity declines (in absolute value) but retains the initial sign and remains highly significant. But note that it is not obvious that this revaluation of human wealth is warranted because as noted, at least to some extent, the correction for wealth effects is already incorporated in the estimated coefficient of r.

In summary, their results clearly support the view that a rise in interest is more likely to reduce than to increase saving.

The Role of Wealth and Age

Another interesting finding bears on the question of the effect of wealth on consumption; according to their results *aggregate* consumption is proportional to *aggregate* wealth (i.e., unit elastic), but individual consumption has a much lower elasticity, and is very significantly different from 1, only about two thirds. This result rejects the permanent income hypothesis as well as the elementary form of the life-cycle hypothesis, which postulate saving proportional to permanent income or life resources. But it supports the generalized version of LCH which allows for bequests of a fraction of resources depending on the relative wealth position of the household.

Note also that an aggregate consumption function which is linear and homogeneous in wealth implies the LCH proposition that, in steady growth, the saving rate is an increasing function of income growth (with value zero at zero).

The estimated effects of the age structure on consumption is another significant result. In the model it appears to have an important effect because essentially the propensity to consume with respect to wealth is found to depend on age and to increase continuously with age, which is a major implication of LCH. Thus an ageing of the population, and consequent rise in the share of wealth held by older cohorts, should tend to reduce saving. This effect seems to play an important role, especially since the 1960s.

Of the two remaining variables, unemployment has the expected negative and very significant effects. The time trend is positive and unfortunately significant even though there is no ready interpretation for its role; since the 1960s it contributes as much as 0.5 percent to the annual growth of consumption.

The Post-depression Cohorts

One final result to which the authors attach great significance is the finding of a large difference in the propensity to consume between the cohorts born before 1939 (pre-depression) and those born thereafter. It is the larger propensity to consume of the former group as it comes to constitute a growing fraction of the total population that, according to the author, is responsible for the rising trend of consumption and decline in saving in recent years. It is estimated that, in the period since 1963, this vintage effect more than accounts for the growth in real per capita consumption.

It is hard to know just what to make of this result. Certainly the idea of a sudden large change in preferences affecting only cohorts born after a certain year runs contrary to the common assumption of "continuity"; tastes change slowly, if at all. The depression was a traumatic experience but it is hard to believe that it could have affected tastes permanently. Furthermore we don't yet have a complete understanding of the implication of their findings. Clearly, given the budget constraint, the post-depression generation must either consume a smaller fraction of resources after retirement – whether by design or by lack of foresight – or must be bequeathing a smaller fraction of their life resources than was prevalent historically. In the first case the decline in saving may be stopped or reversed as the improvident generation finds that it cannot afford to dissave as much as its elders; and the example may instruct later generations. But if the program is less bequests, then the reduction of saving and capital may be permanent. The future of saving and bequests should help clarify the role of the post-depression generation. It may be noted that saving has continued to drift down during most of the 1980s, as the authors expected, because of the growing share of the "high living" generation. However it seems to have reached bottom in 1987 and has been very modestly drifting up ever since.

On the whole, Lau's paper is a significant one; an interesting, innovative and stimulating contribution. I trust this judgement is not biased by the fact that the results are so supportive of the LCH!

REFERENCES

Ando, A., Guiso, L., Terlizzese, D. and Dorsainvil, D. 1940: "Saving, Demographic Structure, and Productivity Growth: The Case of Japan," Paper presented at "Conference on Saving Behavior: Theory, International Evidence, and Policy Implications," Savings Bank Research Foundation, Finland.

Ando, A. and Kennickell, A. B. 1987: How Much (or Little) Life Cycle is There in Micro Data? The Cases of the US and Japan. In R. Dornbusch, S. Fischer, and J. Bossons (eds).

Barro, R. J. 1974: Are Government Bonds New Wealth? *Journal of Political Economy* 82.

Bosworth, B. 1991: The Global Decline in Saving: Some International Comparisons. *Brookings Papers on Economic Activity 1.*

Friedman, Milton 1957: *A Theory of the Consumption Function.* Princeton: Princeton University Press.

Hall, R. E. 1988: Intertemporal Substitution in Consumption. *Journal of Political Economy 95.*

Kotlikoff, L. J. and Summers, L. H. 1981: The Role of Intergenerational Transfers in Aggregate Capital Accumulation. *Journal of Political Economy 89.*

Modigliani, F. 1986: Life cycle, Individual Thrift, and the Wealth of Nations. *Les Prix Nobel,* Stockholm: The Nobel Foundation, 260–81.

Modigliani, F. 1988: The Role of Intergenerational Transfers and Life Cycle Saving in the Accumulation of Wealth. *Journal of Economic Perspectives 2.*

Modigliani, F. 1990: Recent Declines in the Saving Rate: A Life Cycle Perspective. *Rivista di Politica Economia 12* [English version], 5–32.

Modigliani, F. 1991: Life Cycle Hypothesis. In Peter Newman, Murray Milgate and John Batwell (eds), *The New Palgrave Dictionary of Money and Finance,* London: Macmillan (1992).

Modigliani, F. and Brumberg, R. 1954a: Utility Analysis and the Consumption

Function: An Interpretation of Cross-section Data. In K. K. Kurihara (ed.), *Post-Keynesian Economics*, New Brunswick, NJ: Rutgers University Press.

Modigliani, F. and Brumberg, R. 1954b: Utility Analysis and Aggregate Consumption Functions: An Attempt at Integration. From a 1945 manuscript, *The Collected Papers of Franco Modigliani*, Vol. 2 (A. Abel, ed.), Cambridge MA: MIT Press (1980), 128–97.

Modigliani, F. and Sterling, A. 1983: Determinants of Private Saving with Special Reference to the Role of Social Security – Cross-country Tests. In F. Modigliani & Hemming, R. (eds), *The Determinants of National Saving and Wealth*, London: Macmillan Press, Ltd.

Sterling, A. 1977: An Investigation of the Determinants of the Long Run Savings Ratio. Bachelor's thesis, Cambridge, MA: Massachusetts Institute of Technology.

Part I

Economic Analysis of Saving

1

Microeconomic Aspects of Saving

*Barbara Kauffmann**

INTRODUCTION

The past decade has been marked by relatively low national saving in the industrial countries. The net national saving rate in the OECD countries declined from an average of around 14 percent of GNP in the preceding two decades to roughly 9 percent; in the 1980s, the corresponding figures were 13.5 percent and 10 percent for the major seven industrial countries (table 1.1). This relative decline in funds available for financing investment needed to support growth and welfare improvement has raised much concern. On the one hand, the declining supply of global funds is faced with a large demand for global savings – enhanced recently by the transition process in Central and Eastern Europe and in the Soviet Union. On the other hand, despite higher capital mobility there is still a link, even though it may be declining, between a country's saving and investment performance.[1]

One important cause of low national saving has been the dissaving of the government sector in various countries (figure 1.1). Certainly most of the attention has been attracted by the US federal budget deficit which relative to GNP is lower than that of Canada and Italy but stands out in absolute terms and with respect to its impact on the world's capital market. This has led to the call for a reduction in budget deficits by many economists, followed by declarations at the political level, e.g., at the latest Economic Summits of the G7. So far the consolidation process has been successful only in some countries. However, this seems more a problem of political feasibility than a lack of clarity about the necessary steps to be taken since they are, at least as far as the expenditure side is concerned, unambiguous.

* I would like to thank Arnold Heertje, Franco Modigliani, Javier Santillán, Stefan Sinn, Patrick Steimer, and Marian Kane for helpful comments and Pierre Baut and Ierotheos Papadopoulos for technical assistance. The views expressed by the author are not necessarily those of the Commission of the European Communities.

Barbara Kauffmann

Table 1.1 National saving ratios[a]

	USA	Japan	Germany	France	Italy	UK	Canada
1960–9							
gross	19.7	34.8	27.3	25.6	28.3	18.8	21.9
net	10.7	25.5	19.8	18.0	19.9	11.3	11.5
1970–9							
gross	19.6	35.6	24.4	25.9	26.0	18.8	22.6
net	9.2	25.6	15.2	17.1	16.3	9.2	13.0
1980–9							
gross	16.2	32.4	22.9	20.3	21.6	16.6	20.2
net	3.8	21.6	12.0	8.9	10.8	5.6	9.6

[a] As percent of GDP and NDP, respectively.

Source: Eurostat.

Private saving has also generally been lower in the 1980s than in the preceding decades, with the exception of Canada where it has been noticeably higher. The role of business saving in the general decline of private saving and hence national saving has been relatively minor compared to that of household saving. Not only do businesses provide a much smaller share (about one third) of net private saving than households, they have also increased their saving propensity in the course of the 1980s (despite a lower period average) as opposed to the downward movement of overall private saving until the late 1980s. Perhaps it is decisive that households are the ultimate owners of businesses and hence do, at least to a considerable extent, take into account the savings of businesses (of which they own shares) when deciding how much to save out of their disposable income.[2]

Thus, the other important cause of low national saving in the 1980s has been the decline in the saving rate of the household sector in many countries, after an increase during the 1960s and early 1970s (figures 1.1 and 1.2).[3] In particular, the US household saving rate has attracted considerable attention since it has declined from an already relatively low level. However, it has been shown that the difference in the household saving ratios between the US and other countries is reduced considerably if the data are corrected for statistical differences.[4] The causes and possible remedies for the generally low level of household saving in the past decade are far less clear than those for government saving. The saving rate of the household sector is the result of the behavior of a large number of individual household units which are influenced in their decision to accumulate capital

Figure 1.1 Saving in the G7 countries (as a percentage of national income)

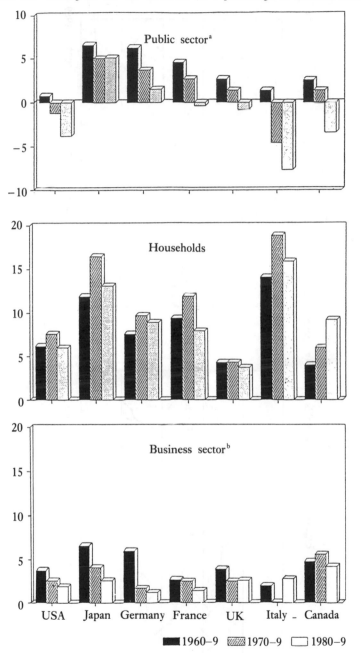

^a General government
^b Including public enterprises
Source: *BIS Report*, June, 1991; based on OECD data.

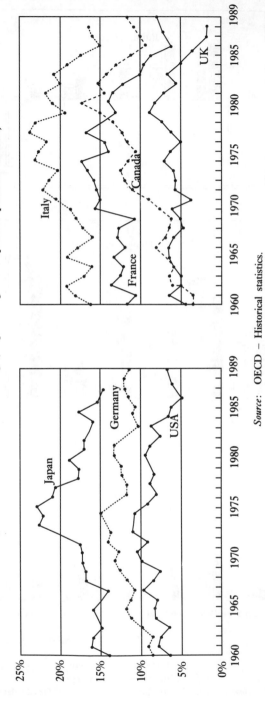

Figure 1.2 Net households saving (as percentage of disposable personal income)

Source: OECD – Historical statistics.

by various factors. In order to understand the level and movement of a country's overall saving rate it is necessary to study the saving behavior of the household units.

Broadly speaking there are two main reasons why households save. The first, the long run, reason is provision for the period after life-time employment. People save in order to be able to maintain their consumption after they stop working and possibly to leave behind a bequest. The second reason for saving arises from uncertainty either due to exceptionally low income or high necessary expenditures (precautionary saving). The common element is the maximization of the (extended) household's expected life-time utility. When making their saving plans households are affected by various variables such as the age of household members, household wealth, and corporate saving, as well as by interest and inflation rates, tax and financial regulations.

The purpose of this chapter is to analyze households' decision-making processes in accumulating wealth and in particular, how they are influenced by these variables. Furthermore, it will be shown, drawing on the existing theoretical and empirical literature, which role such variables may have played in determining observed saving patterns of the household sector of various countries. The next section addresses the dependence of the household's saving rate on age and on retirement conditions in the context of the life-cycle model and the implication of demographic changes for the aggregate saving rate. The role of the return on savings and how tax policy interferes with the saving decision are discussed in the following section. Finally, the impact of changes in wealth, corporate saving, inflation and income as well as the role of uncertainty and liquidity constraints in this process, are analyzed.

SAVING FOR OLD AGE

The Life-Cycle Hypothesis of Saving

Saving is the household's decision to forgo consumption at a particular moment in time to be able to consume at a future date. It is the result of the fact that households prefer a smooth consumption path, but are faced with an income stream which is not smooth – be it due to the sharp drop in income with retirement or to short-run fluctuations. The simple life-cycle hypothesis of saving (assuming no bequest, no social security and no un-certainty) is a useful point of departure for analyzing this process with emphasis on the long run.[5] It starts from a typical household's income stream of low income at the beginning of the employment period, rising thereafter to drop sharply when retirement starts (in the simplest case, income is constant over the full employment span, zero thereafter). The decision of how much to save or to consume in each period is furthermore affected by the household's initial wealth, rate of time preference,[6] and the prevailing market interest rate. According to the life-cycle hypothesis, the saving pattern resulting from the household's attempt to maximize lifetime utility subject to its income stream is hump-shaped, rising from low levels in early years of economic life to high levels in later years and then falling to negative levels after retirement.

Positive *aggregate* personal saving rates (which are observed in most countries) are explained in the simplest case of no productivity growth and constant income by positive population growth that gives younger households with relatively high saving rates a higher weight than older households. If productivity growth is taken into account, one argument put forward has been that the combination of positive population growth and income growth from one age cohort to the next explains positive aggregate household saving.[7] However, if intra-generation income growth is taken into account in addition to income growth from one generation to the next, the effect is no longer unambiguous; as the young household which takes this future income stream as given saves less in early years or even dissaves, the overall rate can easily be negative given positive population growth. Hence the additional assumption is needed that income profiles of a given generation are relatively flat, which is not always true.

Another possible explanation for a positive overall saving rate is that people save not only for consumption at old age but also to leave a bequest.[8] In a growing economy the bequest left behind would be greater than that received and hence at any moment the overall saving for the bequest would be positive. Such a bequest term can quite easily be incorporated into the life-cycle model.[9] It would at the same time help to explain why generally observed saving rates of retired people are, although lower than average, not negative as implied by the simple LCM.[10] Furthermore, it would provide one possible but barely sufficient explanation for the observation that young households save in a growing economy (even though less than average) despite an (expected) steep rise in future income.[11] Household surveys generally not only confirm that saving rates are lower than average for old-age households and for very young households; they also reveal that the presence of children tends to dampen the household's measured saving performance.[12]

Population Structure

The primary usefulness of the simple life-cycle model of saving, with or without bequest, is to explain how demographic factors affect the aggregate

Table 1.2 Old-age dependency ratios[a]

	USA	Japan	Germany	France	Italy	UK	Canada
1960	15.5	9.5	16.0	18.8	13.3	17.9	12.9
1965	15.8	9.2	18.3	19.4	14.7	18.9	13.0
1970	15.8	10.2	20.7	20.7	15.8	20.7	12.9
1975	16.3	11.6	22.6	21.5	17.6	22.4	13.1
1980	17.1	13.4	23.4	21.9	19.3	23.3	14.1
1985	18.0	15.0	21.2	19.7	18.6	23.0	15.3
1989	18.9	16.6	22.0	21.1	21.4	23.9	16.7
2005[b]	18.0	26.0	29.0	24.0	25.0	22.0	19.0
2025[b]	29.0	32.0	37.0	33.0	32.0	28.0	34.0

[a] Population aged 65 and over, divided by population aged between 15 and 64.
[b] OECD projections.

Source: OECD, Labour force statistics; Eurostat; IMF, *World Economic Outlook*, May 1991.

household saving rate. As the individual saving rates vary with age, the overall saving rate depends on the population structure. If, for example, the share of the older population is relatively low, this should have, ceteris paribus, a positive effect on the overall personal saving rate. If, and this is slightly more complicated, life expectancy increases such that retirement at a given age leads to a longer expected retirement period, the young household's effort to accumulate wealth is expected to increased the aggregate saving rate; once the generation with increased life expectancy reaches retirement age, there will be a higher share of people above a given age, and consequently a lower aggregate saving ratio.

Widely used indicators for the population structure are dependency ratios. Table 1.2 shows the old-age dependency ratios (ratio between population aged 65 years and older and that from 15 to 64 years) in the G7 countries for selected years between 1960 and 1989. All countries have experienced considerable ageing of their populations which certainly had a dampening effect on saving. This development is expected to continue.[13]

Regarding the period average, it is possible to group broadly the data into those with relatively high dependency ratios (the four European countries) and those with relatively low ratios (Japan, Canada, and the United States), with Italy and the United States at less extreme positions. The dependency ratios in the four European countries increased strongly in the period from 1960 and 1975 and stabilized thereafter at high levels (only Italy's ratio kept increasing by the same amount); their 1989 ratios range from 21.1 percent in France to 23.9 percent in the United Kingdom. On the other hand, for

Table 1.3   Young age dependency ratios[a]

	USA	Japan	Germany	France	Italy	UK	Canada
1960	52.0	47.1	31.5	42.5	34.6	35.8	57.5
1965	50.8	37.8	34.5	41.1	34.4	36.3	56.6
1970	45.6	34.7	36.4	39.9	34.5	38.3	49.1
1975	39.1	35.8	33.5	38.2	34.6	37.3	40.7
1980	34.0	35.0	27.4	35.1	30.7	32.8	34.0
1985	32.7	31.7	21.6	32.2	25.3	29.3	31.8
1989	32.9	27.4	21.5	30.6	22.1	28.9	31.0
2005[b]	29.0	28.0	22.0	28.0	25.0	31.0	27.0
2025[b]	30.0	27.0	23.0	28.0	24.0	31.0	28.0

[a]   Population aged under 15, divided by population aged between 15 and 64.
[b]   OECD projections.

Source: OECD, Labour force statistics; Eurostat; IMF, *World Economic Outlook*, May
1991.

the United States, Japan, and Canada, the first half of the period under
consideration saw stable rates and strong increases in the second half.
Particularly Japan's ratio, which started from a relatively low level, has increased by 5 percentage points since 1975 to 16.7 percent in 1989. Presently,
Canada's old age dependency ratio is the lowest with 15.3 percent; the US
ratio has reached 19.3 percent.

Hence, as far as the share of the older population is concerned, the
population structure of the three non-European countries, especially Japan
and Canada, seems to have been more conducive to higher saving rates
than that of the European countries considered here. However, after
widening prior to 1975, the gap has since diminished. That the share of
the older population plays a role in explaining intercountry differences has
been confirmed by Feldstein (1980) and Koskela and Virén (1983) among
others.

A quite different picture is presented by the young age dependency ratios
(the ratio between the population aged under 15 and that between 15 and
64) as shown in table 1.3. They play a role because households with
dependent children tend to save less. As a general trend all dependency
ratios have declined considerably. The US and Canada, and also Japan for
the average of the period considered, have the highest dependency ratios
with strong declines by around 20 percentage points over time, whereas the
European countries, especially Germany and Italy, are at the lower range
with more moderate declines ranging from 6 percentage points (United Kingdom) to 12 percentage points (France and Italy).

It is likely that this dependency structure and its change has at least partly offset the effect of old age dependency and its increase over time. Furthermore, the international comparison indicates that the lower young age dependency ratios in the European countries are conducive to higher saving ratios there; but the gap has recently diminished, and for Japan it has almost disappeared. A confirmation of the importance of young age dependency ratios in explaining international household saving differences can, be found, for example, in Graham (1987).

Social Security

A very important and at the same time complicated issue in this context is the effect of a social security system on household saving. Social security replaces at least partially individual retirement saving. It takes away a part of the household's income, lowering its disposable income, and transfers a regular sum to the retired household, increasing its disposable income. With population and productivity growth the impact on the overall saving rate depends on how the social security system is funded.[14]

In a fully funded system where the government invests the contribution of taxing a generation to pay that generation's old-age benefits at a later date, the decline in personal saving of the younger (growing) generation caused by the social security tax is not fully matched by the lower dissaving (higher saving) of the older generation if people behave rationally. Hence with such a system we would expect a lower overall household saving rate than without it, but no change in the national saving rate since government saving should increase by the same amount. Furthermore, there would be no change in the consumption profile.

With the so-called pay-as-you-go system, the social security contributions raised from the working population are immediately redistributed to the older population. Its effect on aggregate saving depends crucially on the way people form their expectations about future benefits. If the young anticipate the same benefits which they would receive under the funded system, the fall in their saving will exactly match the lower dissaving of the old with no change in the overall rate of household saving. When the system is introduced, aggregate consumption increases due to the positive wealth effect in-curred by the old who benefit from the system without having contributed.

If, however, the young generation expects to gain from the social security system, anticipating the same relative benefits to lifetime income which the old generation currently receives,[15] then it would – according to the life-cycle hypothesis – reduce its saving by more than the amount deducted by social security taxes from its income. Hence, with a given retirement age, the introduction or expansion of the pay-as-you-go system would be expected to lower the aggregate household saving in a growing economy. This decline in aggregate household saving would not be compensated by a change in government saving, and the proportion of income devoted to consumption would increase permanently through the increase in lifetime wealth (see Kotlikoff, 1979, for further discussion). On the other hand, if households fully understand that this intergenerational redistribution will ultimately have to be financed and lead to higher taxes, and if they altruistically take future generations' wellbeing into account as assumed for the Ricardian Equivalence Theorem, then neither the young nor the old may perceive a positive wealth effect. Instead, they will be induced to leave larger bequests such that aggregate saving remains unchanged.[16]

If, on the other hand, the young generation perceives that it will not benefit from the social security system the way the currently old are benefitting since there will only be a relatively small number of people working to support an increasing number of old, they may start saving more than under a funded system.[17] In this context Tabellini (1991) and Auerbach and Kotlikoff (1991) have argued that a growing share of the old will be able to influence through the democratic process the level of benefits they will receive. However, as national economies become more and more interwoven and multinational corporations play a larger role, mobility is also likely to increase. It can therefore be argued that the generation who would then be forced to pay the extremely high taxes might decide to emigrate. Under these considerations it would not be optimal for the social security receivers who compete globally for the young contributors to vote for a very high level without taking into account this possible emigration effect.

What has been omitted from the previous discussion is the effect that the social security system can have on retirement age. It is important for the determination of the overall effect of the system on household saving. The social security system may induce people to retire earlier than otherwise for two reasons. First, if social security benefits are not or only partly paid to older persons who continue working, this is an implicit tax on labor supply that will discourage many people from working after they become eligible for retirement. Second, the positive wealth effect inherent in the social security system causes people not only to want more consumption goods but also more leisure.[18] But the expansion of retirement (leisure) requires a larger saving effort during this shortened period of employment. Since this retirement effect works in an opposite direction to the wealth effect discussed above, the overall impact of the social security system on saving is unclear from a theoretical point of view.

Table 1.4 Social security transfers (as a percentage of GDP)

	USA	Japan	Germany	France	Italy	UK	Canada
1960	5.0	3.8	12.0	13.5	9.8	6.8	7.9
1965	5.2	4.7	12.4	16.4	12.5	7.5	6.0
1970	7.5	4.6	12.7	14.8	12.4	8.7	7.9
1975	11.1	7.7	17.6	17.4	15.6	10.2	10.0
1980	10.9	10.1	16.5	19.2	14.1	11.7	9.9
1985	11.0	11.0	16.2	22.1	17.1	14.0	12.2
1989	10.3	11.1	15.6	21.4	17.7	11.9	11.8

Source: OECD, Historical statistics.

Table 1.5 Old age participation ratios[a]

	USA	Japan	Germany	France	Italy	UK	Canada
1965	16.9	36.8	14.1	17.8	10.7	13.0	15.5
1970	16.0	31.7	11.1	12.8	7.1	11.6	12.9
1975	13.1	27.9	6.9	9.0	5.7	10.0	10.9
1980	11.9	26.3	4.5	4.9	7.5	6.2	8.9
1985	10.2	24.3	3.3	3.4	4.8	5.0	7.7
1989	11.1	23.8	2.7	2.9	4.6	5.5	6.9

[a] Working population aged 65 and over, divided by total population aged 65 and over.
Source: OECD, Labour force statistcs; Eurostat.

Social security payments have increased considerably relative to GDP since 1960, which cannot simply be explained by the fact that the share of the older population has increased (table 1.4). This is particularly true for Japan, whose ratio of social security benefits to GDP, starting from a low 13.5 percent, has doubled since then. Overall, with a given retirement age, the past improvement of relative retirement benefits would suggest, according to the life-cycle hypothesis, a dampening of the saving ratio since it can be assumed that households have in the past expected a similar positive wealth effect as that observed for older people. However, table 1.5 reveals that the improvement in social security benefits has moved in line with a decline in the labor force participation of the old,[19] making the overall effect difficult to determine.

The empirical evidence has been contradictory (see Dean et al., 1990).

Numerous studies have found evidence that the social security system has depressed savings in the past (see, e.g., Feldstein (1974) for the US,[20] Shibuya (1987) for Japan, and Feldstein (1980) for international data). On the other hand, there has been a considerable number of studies which found no such effect (e.g., Kotlikoff (1979) who did, however, find that social security tax contributions in the US have reduced private savings of the younger group in his sample, and Koskela and Virén (1983) who found indications that the induced retirement effect may have been at work).

To summarize, a household's savings propensity varies considerably with age as the household tries to accumulate assets to provide for retirement and therefore saves most when income is high. Forced retirement saving through the social security system alters the flow of income; in particular, it raises old-age income. Therefore the perceived need to save personally in the pre-retirement period and to dissave during retirement is decreased since social security replaces part of the deliberate saving. It is likely that these two effects may have been at work in the industrial countries, where the population has aged and the social security system has expanded. However, their impact has been counterbalanced by the decline in young-age dependency ratios and a decrease in retirement age. Whereas the on-going ageing of the population structure is expected to have a dampening effect on overall household saving rates, individual households will probably save more for a retirement period which may bring only relatively low benefits. The increase in the retirement age that should have a dampening effect on savings will probably be compensated by an increase in life expectancy which would increase savings.

THE RETURN ON SAVING

The Real Interest Rate

A crucial element in the household's intertemporal decision-making process is the real interest rate. It signals the extra consumption that can be afforded in the future per unit consumption given up at the present. How and in what direction the interest rate affects household saving has been a heavily debated issue (see, e.g., Boskin, 1978, Summers, 1981, and Evans, 1983). Probably the main reason for this ongoing debate is that the answer to the question whether or not households respond to increases in interest rates by saving more (positive interest elasticity) has major implications for the impact of tax policies on households' saving behavior and ultimately on the question whether changes in the tax policy could increase welfare.

The problem of determining the sign and size of the interest elasticity of saving arises from the fact that an interest rate change affects the household's saving process through different channels which, taken separately, lead to opposite reactions. An increase in the interest rate makes current consumption relatively more expensive, inducing the household to postpone consumption ("substitution effect"). In addition, due to the higher interest rate the household's future labor income now is worth less in present terms, which should increase the household's saving effort ("human wealth effect," which is one particular type of income effect).[21] On the other hand, the household now receives more interest income for the same amount of saving, allowing it to consume more in all future periods if it is a net creditor.[22] This direct "income effect" would induce higher consumption in the present as well as in all future periods, lowering current saving. Hence, in order for the household's overall saving reaction to an interest rate increase to be positive, it is necessary that the substitution and human wealth effects dominate the income effect.

Clearly, the household's reaction to an interest rate rise depends on which stage of economic life the household is moving through (see also Evans, 1983, on this point). For example, if the household had just reached retirement and was expecting no or only very negligible social security payments, intuitively it can be expected that the possibility of buying more in future periods due to the income effect may induce him to consume more today in response to an interest rate increase. There would be no or only a very small human wealth effect, and the substitution effect would most likely be dominated by the income effect. On the other hand, in the case of a young household, the human wealth effect is more important; given the long economic life ahead the gain to be made from saving to broaden the range of consumption paths may seem more worthwhile.[23]

It should be kept in mind that the discussion of these effects is based on the assumption that the interest rate change observed is expected to be permanent. If uncertainty is taken into account, it is less likely that a risk-averse household would be induced by an interest rate increase to save less on the basis of increased future consumption possibilities which he may in fact never reach if the interest rate declines again because of the irreversibility of his choice for more current consumption today. The issue of uncertainty will be addressed below but it seems worth mentioning it here because it has an effect on the interest elasticity of saving that we expect to observe in reality.

Real interest rates have been considerably higher in the 1980s than in the previous two decades.[24] However, it would be wrong to jump to the conclusion that this observation, together with an unusually low saving performance of households, does signify a negative interest elasticity. On the contrary, the evidence is quite mixed and more often indicates that the interest elasticity of saving is positive (cf. Smith, 1989). But there are considerable differences with respect to the estimated size of the interest elasticity of saving. While some, e.g., Boskin (1978), Summers (1981), and Tullio and Contesso (1986), find large positive effects, others as, e.g., Evans (1983), do not find any significant effect of interest rate changes on aggregate household saving.

Taxes[25]

Of the three types of taxation, consumption tax, wage tax, and capital income tax, only consumption tax – if it is linear – is completely neutral with respect to the savings rate; i.e., it does not distort the household's intertemporal decision. This indirect tax is raised when consumption takes place, but it does not burden future consumption any differently from current consumption. On the other hand, both wage and capital income taxes do influence the household's intertemporal saving decision. The wage tax extracts income only during the pre-retirement period and therefore shifts the household's saving activity backwards, leading to lower saving rates in earlier years. The tax on interest income drives a wedge between the household's intertemporal substitution in consumption and the firm's intertemporal substitution in production.[26] With positive interest elasticity, a tax on interest income induces the household to save less than without the tax. The firms then have to pay higher (before tax) interest rates in order to induce households to increase their saving, ultimately leading to a situation where less is saved and invested and consequently per capita income is lower than without the tax (or with the consumption tax).[27]

The different implications for saving and welfare of income-based as compared to expenditure-based taxes have been pointed out by Summers (1981), Kotlikoff (1984), Smith (1989), and many others and have led to a call for a move in the direction of expenditure-based taxation.[28]

In considering how the household's saving process is distorted in different countries a first measure one might look at is the marginal income tax rate. This could lead to the conclusion that saving is much less discouraged in the United States and Canada, with maximum marginal tax rates around 30 percent, than in most European countries where rates range from a "low" 40 percent in the United Kingdom to 60 percent in Italy. However, there are reasons to believe that this does not characterize the situation correctly. If the ratio of direct to indirect taxes is compared, the United States and Canada have, together with Japan and Italy, relatively high ratios (table 1.6).[29] This ratio has been very similar in the United States and Japan in the 1980s, with relatively high 1.7 and 1.6 respectively, followed by Italy which has seen a continuous rise in direct taxes as a share of GNP, with

Table 1.6 Taxes as percent of GNP

	USA	Japan	Germany	France	Italy	UK	Canada
A. Direct tax							
1970–9	13.3	9.3	12.3	7.3	6.5	14.0	14.9
1980–9	13.3	12.8	12.2	9.0	12.6	13.9	15.6
B. Indirect tax							
1970–9	8.4	6.9	13.0	14.3	9.1	14.1	13.1
1980–9	7.7	7.8	12.6	14.6	9.6	16.2	12.7
(A)/(B)							
1970–9	1.6	1.3	0.9	0.5	0.7	1.0	1.1
1980–9	1.7	1.6	1.0	0.6	1.3	0.9	1.2

Source: EC Commission, internal publication; Bank of Canada.

Canada as well as Germany, the United Kingdom, and France at the lower end. It is likely that the Canadian ratio will drop in response to the introduction of the value-added tax at the beginning of 1991; similarly, the increases in consumption tax in 1990 in Japan and in various excise taxes in the United States may have contributed to a lower ratio.[30]

Important in this context is the interaction between taxation and inflation. The reduction in real wealth caused by inflation is compensated for, as far as it is expected, by higher nominal interest rates. Since these interest payments generally are counted fully as income, the effective taxation of the amount actually saved is increased. First, the part that compensates only for income losses is taxed as well as the real return on saving. Secondly, the progressiveness of the tax system may imply a higher marginal and average tax rate if the tax system is not fully indexed as is usually the case. Thus, in combination with a tax system, especially if it is progressive, inflation causes the effective real rate of interest to decline (which is usually only partially compensated for by an increase in the rate paid by the investor). These effects may discourage saving (in inflation-adjusted terms) in countries with relatively high inflation such as Italy and the United States.[31]

If we focus on the capital income tax which is the type of income tax that, given a positive interest elasticity of saving, discourages saving most, the picture changes even more. Besides the official income tax rates, the issue of how tax collection is actually insured and whether there are exemptions or deductions play an important role. In Germany, for instance, where this has been the subject of a recent ruling of the German Constitutional Court,[32] presently there is neither a source tax[33] nor reporting of banks to the revenue offices.[34] In most of the other countries, including the other six

Table 1.7 Measures to ensure tax collection on capital income: source taxes and control messages (R)

	USA	Japan	Germany	France	Italy	UK	Canada
Interests on savings accounts	R	20	–	R	30	23.25	R
Interests on bonds	R	20	–	R	12.5	25	R
Dividends	R	20	25	R	10	0	R

Source: Drucksache Nr. 11/2599 des Deutschen Bundestags.

of the G7 nations, there are measures that ensure tax collection (table 1.7). Japan, the United Kingdom, and Italy have source taxes varying from 20 percent (Japan) to 30 percent (Italy) for deposits, whereas in the United States, Canada, and France, banks are obliged to report on capital income to ensure tax compliance. For dividends the conditions are about the same, but in this case there is also a source tax of 25 percent in Germany.

Of course, it is not suggested here that the measures taken in these countries are able to prevent tax evasion altogether. It is well known that banking accounts in countries where capital income is neither taxed nor reported, e.g. Luxembourg, are quite common. So the explanatory power of the difference in effective rates of taxation and possibilities for evasion among countries should not be overestimated. But it is quite possible that the lack of tight control on capital income taxation in some countries such as Germany may have distorted less against the saving process than in other countries.

Tax Exemptions and Saving Incentives

Governments have created a variety of tax exemptions with the goal of promoting domestic savings. The understanding that this will have the desired effect rests, of course, on the presumption that the interest elasticity of saving is indeed positive. Interest income from certain government bonds is very commonly exempted.[35] In addition, there has been a tradition in some countries, including Japan and France, to exempt income earned on personal saving accounts. This has been particularly important in Japan where about 70 percent of interest income earned on personal saving was exempt until the tax reform of 1988.[36] It had the effect that the average tax rate paid on this type of income was below 10 percent in the 1980s (Bovenberg et al., 1989). The comparable average ratios for the same years were much higher in the United States, ranging from 28.5 percent in 1980 to 22.4 percent in 1987.

Two forms of saving are often treated very generously. One is saving explicitly tied to the provision for retirement (private pension plans or special accounts), the other is saving for and in the form of private housing. Such preferential treatment may merely cause households to shift assets into those forms that benefit from such measures without increasing households' overall saving propensity. Undoubtedly there will be such a shift. But there is also evidence that these incentives may well have a positive overall impact on households' saving activity, as, e.g., in Carroll and Summers (1987) who examined the difference in saving rates between the United States and Canada.[37] The US and Canadian saving rates were very similar until the early 1970s when they started to diverge. One of the factors Carroll and Summers identified as contributing to these divergences is the treatment of retirement saving which became increasingly more generous in Canada, as compared to the United States, through various increases in the ceilings of tax-sheltered contributions to pension plans (employer-sponsored Registered Pension plans and individual Registered Retirement Savings Plans).[38] In the United States, there have also been sheltered saving opportunities (Individual Retirement Accounts (IRA's) and Keogh plans), but they were much more limited.[39] In his FY 1992 budget proposal, the President proposed enhancing IRA's again as well as creating so-called Family Savings Accounts (see US-Japan Working Group, 1991).

In the context of housing it is again not the United States that has the most generous treatment of saving. In some countries, e.g., Germany and France, there are bonus and deduction schemes for saving that is tied to housing construction or purchase, thus prior to the acquisition of a house; in Germany, where various programs were started after WWII to cultivate household wealth and home ownership, they have been slowly cut back.[40] Once a house has been purchased, this asset generally receives preferential treatment relative to other forms of wealth because neither the implicit rental income nor the capital gains from an increase in the value are taxed.[41]

Another measure that certainly does induce the shift of assets into housing is the deductibility of mortgage interest payments which is possible in all G7 countries except for Canada.[42] This is an especially beneficial scheme for households in those countries where tax rates and/or inflation and hence nominal interest rates are high. It may, however, dampen the household's overall savings propensity mainly in cases where it is possible to use some of the mortgage credits for consumption purchases. The extreme case of explicitly deducting interest payments for consumption goods which was until recently the practice in the United States certainly had a dampening effect on the consumer's saving propensity.

To conclude, apart from social security, various other government policies influence households' saving process. How important this impact is depends to a large extent on the interest elasticity of saving. If it is, as suggested by some studies, significantly positive, then taxes discourage households from saving the amount that would be optimal for the economy as a whole. Although marginal tax rates are relatively low in the United States as compared to other countries, a closer examination of generous exemption schemes, e.g., in Japan and Canada, and looser enforcement of tax collection, e.g., in Germany, indicate that the effective taxation of capital income in the United States may have been higher than in other countries, particularly if the interaction between taxation and inflation is taken into account.

It may be a coincidence that countries with relatively high saving rates, such as Japan and Germany, either have little control of tax collection or generous tax exemption rules. For instance, it has been argued that those countries which have a "tradition of saving" are those which are most likely to use saving incentives; this would lead to the conclusion that the observed coincidence of generous tax treatment and a high saving ratio would not prove any positive effect from those measures. But the experience in the United States and Canada seems to indicate that tax deductions and saving incentives can make a difference.

CHANGES IN WEALTH AND INCOME

Inflation

The impact of inflation on household saving is ambiguous since the process involves various short-run as well as the long-run channels which have opposite effects. One effect which has already been mentioned is more of a measurement problem than a real impact on households' behavior in accumulating assets: if inflation is anticipated, the erosion of wealth that it causes is compensated for by a corresponding inflation premium on the real interest rate. The household that accumulates wealth will consider this part of interest payments as a necessary contribution to keeping real wealth constant and will only count the remaining part to actual saving.[43] Measured saving, on the other hand, does include these inflation-premium payments. Therefore it generally overstates (for years with positive inflation) the real saving activity of the household sector which is a net creditor. It understates at the same time the actual saving of the business and government sectors that tend to be net debtors.[44] The difference between actual and measured saving is, of course, particularly high in periods and countries of high inflation.

During the 1970s when the two oil shocks drove up inflation rates (figure 1.3), the measured saving rates overstated the actual saving activity of households markedly while understating actual business saving. Consequently, the actual fall in household saving during the early 1980s when inflation declined was less pronounced than indicated by measured saving rates. However, Dean et al. (1990), who compared the original to adjusted saving rates, found that the inflation adjustment does not generally change the fact that saving was higher in the 1970s, nor does it affect the position of saving rates in the 1980s as compared to the 1960s.

A related and already mentioned channel through which expected inflation affects saving is the interaction between the tax system and inflation. It leads to a lower effective rate of return because the "compensation payments" discussed above are counted as taxable income; assuming a positive interest elasticity of saving, the household's saving rate declines.

As for unanticipated inflation, there are several channels that may play a role in the shorter run. When inflation is unexpected, compensation for the erosion of wealth does not take place and the real return on wealth declines (at first). This has the various effects (substitution, human wealth, income) discussed above in connection with real interest rate changes. In addition, the household may be induced to shift from financial wealth into real assets which are now relatively more attractive. Since these real assets include consumer durables which are part of the consumption measure despite the fact that they are not fully consumed during the current period, the saving rate declines.[45] Furthermore, two opposite effects of money illusion are conceivable: first, if households mistakenly perceive income growth at least partly as real income growth (although it is not), then they may decide to increase real consumption which will lower their saving rate (Branson and Klevorick, 1969). Second, if households mistakenly take observed price increases for increases in relative prices, they may buy fewer consumption goods than under perfect information (Deaton, 1977).

The empirical evidence on the saving-inflation link is mixed (cf. Sturm, 1983, and Koskela and Virén, 1985). When the "compensation effect" is captured by a "real wealth variable," the estimated sign and significance of the remaining effect of inflation on saving varies considerably from study to study. Whereas a negative sign is generally taken as a reasonable result, those who find a positive sign most often attribute it to the fact that inflation is positively correlated with uncertainty and that higher uncertainty causes higher saving (see discussion below). In that case the lower inflation of the 1980s (if it is separated from the related decline in uncertainty) may well have been a factor encouraging households to save more than in the previous decade.

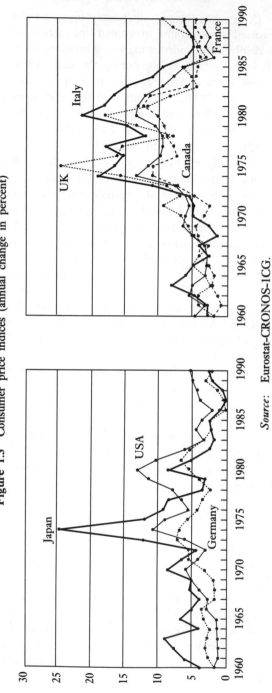

Figure 1.3 Consumer price indices (annual change in percent)

Source: Eurostat-CRONOS-1CG.

Increases in Current Wealth

The life-cycle and permanent-income hypotheses predict that with given expected income an increase in current real wealth decreases the share of current disposable income saved, since it renders possible a higher lifetime consumption level. Conventional income and saving measures do not include revaluations of real wealth. Therefore measured saving rates decline when households incur a positive wealth effect and raise current consumption accordingly. For example, an increase in the real value of housing, which is an important form of household wealth, may decrease the saving propensity of those, mostly older, households who own a house. Clearly, these households can now afford a higher level of lifetime consumption despite the fact that their labor income streams are unchanged. Those households who neither own nor want to buy a house may save more to finance the rent payment or they may opt for a smaller apartment or house and maintain their saving rate.

The impact on the savings behavior of a young household which does not yet own a house but has purchasing plans is less straight forward. If we assume that it expects to derive some utility from living in its own house, the household may increase savings in order still to be able to purchase it. This is the so-called target saving argument. However, this argument fails to consider that the choice for owner-occupied housing is price elastic, with higher prices likely to discourage the choice for housing purchase.[46] Although the implication for the young household's saving behavior is not clear a priori, it is likely that the overall effect of the increase in the real value of housing is negative.[47] However, the reaction of savings to an increase in housing wealth should be less pronounced than that caused by increases in most other sources of wealth since it is related to higher rent payments (consumption expenditures) and may also not be sold as easily at the end of life as other forms of wealth. See Thaler (1990) for a discussion of the fungibility of wealth.

Household wealth and particularly housing wealth increased considerably in the 1980s. Wealth increases were exceptionally high in Japan where housing and land prices have sky-rocketted; increases in housing wealth were also considerable in the United Kingdom and Canada.[48] It seems therefore, likely that this increase in housing wealth dampened household savings, particularly in Japan, and possibly also in other countries. Similarly, during the 1980s, stock prices rose rapidly until 1987, and especially so in Japan. This long-run movement certainly stimulated consumption during the 1980s. In the short run, on the other hand, consumption generally reacts only partially to stock price increases since they will – given their high variance – at first be considered mostly temporary. This is probably the reason why the stock market crash in 1987 did not dampen private consumption as much as was generally expected.

Corporate Saving

The ownership of business assets is a particular form of household wealth. It gives rise to current and future income streams from the business to the household sector. This link between both sectors of the economy makes it impossible to explain corporate and household saving independently of each other.

A part of the relation between the two savings ratios is more of a measurement problem, as mentioned earlier, than a structural link: since the household is a net creditor of the business sector (including the financial sector), it is compensated for the erosion of its net wealth position if inflation is positive and expected. This inflation premium is counted in the statistics as income and saving (if it is reinvested to keep real net wealth constant) and leads to an overprediction of actual household saving and an underprediction of actual business saving. The effect is that with changing inflation both sectors' saving rates move in opposite directions. Poterba (1987) gives a detailed study of this relationship in the United States.

Much more interesting is the structural relation between the two sectors' saving rates. The discussion has mainly centered around the question: "To what extent do households pierce through the corporate veil?" Shareholders receive a part of their current income in the form of dividends from the firms that are left with "retained after-tax profits" to invest. As these investments produce future income flows, a household which completely "pierces the veil" takes business saving fully into account in its lifetime consumption strategy. In particular, with perfect capital markets it displays the same consumption behavior whether or not business profits are distributed. This can also cause corporate and household saving rates to move in opposite directions. With given profits, higher dividend payments would lower business saving, causing the household's measured income to decline. Since the household would perceive the compensating increase in future income (indicated by capital gains which are not included in the measured current income), its consumption should remain unchanged even though its measured saving rate would decline.

That household and business sector saving rates move in opposite directions resulting in a relatively stable private saving rate was first observed by Denison (1958) and since then confirmed by many others, including David and Scadding (1974). However, some studies such as Poterba (1987) found that household saving offsets movements in the corporate saving rate only partially; this implies that tax policy affecting the firm's payout decision has an impact on the private saving rate.

Corporate saving was relatively low in the 1970s, as a result of several factors, including lower profit shares and higher inflation and interest rates as a result of the oil price shocks. During the 1980s, measured corporate saving picked up again as profit shares increased and inflation declined. However, households have had more liquid financial means available for consumption during the past decade than the dividend payments included in measured disposable personal income may suggest. Share repurchases spurred by takeover threats and tax considerations, as well as leveraged buyouts (both affecting neither measured personal income nor saving), have played an important role. For instance, Summers and Carroll (1987) found that corporate repurchases and takeovers may have lowered the US private saving rate by 1 to 2 percentage points.

Uncertainty and Short-run Movements in Income

Most life-cycle/permanent-income models of saving are based on the assumption that the present value of lifetime wealth is given since it is assumed either that future income flows are certain or that the individual behaves as if the expected value of future income were indeed a certain income (certainty equivalence). In reality, uncertainty is one of the major problems the household faces. Uncertainty about the time of death which causes the individual to save more and to leave a higher bequest than under certainty is only one aspect. There are other, mostly shorter run, aspects of uncertainty which can have a major impact on the household's saving strategy, changing the long-run profile of wealth accumulation and the reactions to fluctuations in income.

Looking first at the individual's lifetime saving profile, uncertainty causes a typical risk-averse household[49] to save more at young age and less at old age than under certainty equivalence (Caballero, 1990). The household derives a higher disutility from the risk of having to decrease future consumption in response to a lower-than-expected income than the utility associated with the (same) probability of being able to increase future consumption in response to a corresponding lower-than-expected income. To diminish the potential impact of such a low income on future consumption, the household is willing to forgo some of its current consumption (which it would not do if future income were certain). If income is realized as expected, the household will stick to its original saving plan, which will allow it after a lower consumption level in earlier periods to consume more in later periods than under certainty equivalence. Otherwise, the household can readjust its savings strategy every time income (or necessary consumption) is different

Table 1.8   Participation rate of women[a]

	USA	Japan	Germany	France	Italy	UK	Canada
1965	45.7	55.8	48.8	45.7	31.0	50.0	35.3
1970	50.4	55.4	48.1	49.8	29.1	53.5	41.1
1975	54.9	51.7	49.7	52.9	29.9	58.6	50.5
1980	61.3	54.9	50.0	55.6	39.2	61.7	57.9
1985	65.5	57.2	50.3	56.4	40.6	62.6	63.5
1989	69.4	59.3	54.7	57.6	44.0	66.0	68.2

[a]   Share of women at work.

Source: OECD, Labour force statistics.

from what had previously been expected. Overall, this "prudent" behavior of a typical household faced with income uncertainty is one explanation why very young households do have positive saving ratios despite their high expected income, and consequently also helps to explain a positive aggregate household saving rate in a growing population.

A consequence of this relation between uncertainty and the household's intertemporal choice is that an increase in uncertainty will induce a prudent household to accumulate more wealth, whereas a decrease will lower the saving rate. For example, it is likely that such forces were at work during the 1970s when the world economy was hit by major up- and downswings following expansive economic policies and the two oil crises. Households perceived the higher possibility of being unemployed or suffering a cut in real income through high inflation and may have tried to form a buffer against possible income losses.

As the 1980s brought a long expansion which was only recently inter-rupted by recessions in the Anglo-Saxon countries, the perceived income risk declined and consequently the perceived need for precautionary savings did too. This may be one important explanation for the decline in household saving during the greater part of the 1980s (and the recent pickup). As pointed out earlier, the movement in inflation rates coincided with the change in uncertainty and may therefore mistakenly have been identified as a factor with a positive impact on household saving (besides the real wealth effect). Other longer-run factors that may have contributed to a decline in uncertainty are the expansion of the social security net, which has made the loss of income through unemployment less dramatic, and the evolution of various insurance schemes. Finally, it is also conceivable that the entrance of women into working life which can be seen from table 1.8 may have dampened households' perceived uncertainty.[50]

Uncertainty may also help to shed some light on observed responses to short-run income changes. For example, the life-cycle/permanent-income theories predict that the household's consumption pattern will be smooth at the moment of a sudden and previously announced increase in income; i.e., the household's savings rate would increase in response to such a change but consumption would not since the increase in consumption is predicted to take place at the moment of the announcement. However, as shown by Flavin (1981) and Wilcox (1989), consumers do react quite strongly to announced increases in current income with increases in consumption ("excess sensitivity of consumption"). Furthermore, consumers respond less to unannounced changes in labor income than under the certainty equivalence ("excess smoothness of consumption"). Caballero (1990) has shown that if specific assumptions are made about the form of the utility function, uncertainty and prudent behavior can explain both these interrelated phenomena. In the longer run saving is not affected by these phenomena.

Liquidity Constraints

Another possible explanation for the excess smoothness and sensitivity of consumption as well as positive overall savings is the presence of liquidity constraints. The typical model of the consumer's utility maximization subject to a lifetime budget constraint is based on the assumption that capital markets are perfect. This implies that a household cannot only borrow against currently held assets such as housing or stocks, but that it is also able to borrow against expected future lifetime income. This leads to the model prediction that a household with no current assets and a low current income but with high expected future labor income will be a net borrower in early years. In reality, however, capital markets are far from perfect and there are borrowing constraints that prevent the household from borrowing as much as would be optimal. As a result, current wealth plays a much more important role for the young household's consumption level than would be implied by the standard models without a liquidity constraint. Evidence for such an effect for a considerable number of households has generally been found by Zeldes (1989), Koskela and Virén (1984), and Ogawa (1990).

Whereas borrowing constraints may have played an important role in the past by preventing very young households from being net borrowers and inducing them consequently to expand consumption in response to income increases more than would be warranted without such a constraint, developments in financial markets are likely to have led to a decrease in the importance of this factor. New financial instruments have been created and constraints have been reduced. An important development in this area is the reduction of the percentage down-payment needed for the purchase of a house. Similarly, car makers, for example, have developed their own credit instruments. This, together with the rapid expansion of credit card use, may have contributed to lowering the credit constraint in recent years. This factor may also have dampened household saving during the last decade. However, it certainly also had the beneficial effect of enabling households to choose a consumption and savings path which is closer to their optimum and at a lower cost of financial intermediation.

CONCLUSION

Saving remains a complicated and only partly understood issue even after decades of intensive and excellent research. A major difficulty is that saving is a forward-looking activity and involves households' formation of expectations about future developments in an uncertain future. It is not only future income from labor and capital or the expected lifetime of the household members that has to be anticipated. Other important parameters include population growth, implied social security benefits, and future taxes.

The saving rate, especially that of households in each country, is the result of a multitude of factors ranging from demographic characteristics to those influencing individual households in different ways. The simple life-cycle model is useful for explaining the long-run impact of changes in the population structure on the saving propensity of the household sector as a whole. In the past, the population has aged in industrial countries and this has, taken separately, dampened saving behavior. As this ageing process continues, saving of the overall household sector can be expected to be depressed further. The individual household is influenced by expectations about future income, including retirement benefits and corporate profits, and their uncertainty, as well as by inflation, taxation, and incentive schemes which change the expected flow of income and therefore affect saving decisions. This chapter discussed some of these channels affecting a household's saving behavior and may have been relevant for the determination of the overall housing rates observed. It should be clear from the above discussion that it would be wrong to jump to the conclusion that households in a particular country or period are relatively impatient or less thrifty just because their observed overall saving rate is relatively low.

NOTES

1 See Feldstein and Horioka (1980) and Feldstein and Bacchetta (1989) for empirical evidence and Santillán (1991) for a survey of the general discussion.

2 This issue is discussed further on pp. 48–56.

3 It should be noted that the saving rates are not corrected for the inflation effect that usually entails an overestimation of the actual saving of households and an underestimation of that of government and business sectors, as discussed on pp. 48–50.

4 See Blades and Sturm (1982). Hayashi (1989) found that most of the difference between the US and the Japanese personal saving rates is a statistical illusion. Similarly, the US-German household savings gap can be reduced if statistical differences are taken into account (Kauffmann, 1990).

5 See Ando and Modigliani (1963). The closely related Permanent Income Hypothesis introduced by Friedman (1957) has been used more often to study short run fluctuations of income and consumption. For a brief discussion of the difference between the two models see Modigliani (1990).

6 The rate of time preference is generally assumed to be positive. This is, e.g., confirmed by Lawrance (1991) who derived from a sample of 1513 US households a rate of time preference of 13 percent for the sample mean, with lower values for higher income and educational levels, and vice versa.

7 See Ando et al. (1991a) for an extensive discussion of this point, and Shibuya (1987).

8 Cf. Kotlikoff (1988).

9 See, for example, Evans (1983).

10 Another explanation for the positive saving ratio of the old is that the time of death is uncertain. Cf. Mirer (1979).

11 Other more powerful explanations are uncertainty about future income and liquidity constraints (see pp. 48–56) and the desire to maintain flexibility for future decisions (Ando et al., 1991b).

12 This is confirmed by Ando et al. (1991a), based on microdata on Japanese households.

13 Shibuya (1987) found a dampening effect of ageing, raising the share of the retired people, on Japan's saving rate. Using simulations he predicted a further decline of the Japanese household saving rate. Similarly, Auerbach et al. (1990), Auerbach and Kotlikoff (1991), and Cutler et al. (1990) project declines in US aggregate saving rates during the first decades of the 21st century.

14 In an economy without productivity and population growth, the life cycle hypothesis would predict no overall change of aggregate household saving. Saving ratios for younger households would be lower (both saving and income decline by the same amount, but the ratio declines), and the older households' saving ratios would rise (even if benefits are fully spent, the dissaving relative to a higher income becomes smaller).

15 I.e., there is a higher benefit than under the funded system made possible by the payments of future generations (with higher income).

16 See Barro (1974), Carroll and Summers (1987), and Wilcox (1989) whose findings of consumption increases in the US in response to the rise in social security benefit payments cast doubt not only on the validity of the Ricardian Equivalence Theorem, but also on that of the Life Cycle Hypothesis.

17 In view of the ageing problem, several countries have started to run surpluses

(transforming the former pay-as-you-go systems into partly funded systems). But despite these efforts there may still be a negative wealth effect embedded in the social security system for those currently young. On the other hand, there is the possibility of a major inflow of potential social security contributors, particularly from Eastern European countries and Soviet republics in the coming decade(s), which may partially compensate this effect.

18 Assuming both are normal goods. In addition, the social security tax distorts the household's choice in favor of leisure.

19 It probably has been partly caused by the increase in relative income of the old, but may also have been affected by increases in other forms of wealth which will be discussed later.

20 In his 1982 paper Feldstein obtains broadly similar results, but does point to the limitations of using time series data to study this "inherently dynamic process."

21 It should also increase the incentive to work.

22 If it is a net debtor, saving should be increased. The household sector generally is a net creditor of the business and public sectors. In a closed economy the aggregate income effect may be unimportant if the household's ownership of businesses and future tax payments are fully considered in the saving decision. However, as countries generally either are net debtors or creditors (see, e.g., Sinn, 1990), the income effect cannot be ignored.

23 Summers (1981) pointed out in a footnote that the terminology of the "human wealth effect" might be somewhat misleading since it has this positive effect ("broadening the set of feasible consumption paths") in addition to the effect of "reducing the value of consumers' endowment in terms of first-period consumption."

24 It is problematic to calculate the real interest rate correctly since it depends on expectations about future inflation rates and not actual values.

25 For a more detailed discussion of this subject see Owens' contribution in this book.

26 See Bovenberg et al. (1989); this paper also addresses the effects of different treatment of income earned by residents and non-residents in the US and Japan.

27 Apart from the direct effect of taxation on household saving, there is also the indirect effect via business saving. Higher corporate tax rates dampen after-tax business profits and hence the dividend payments received by households. Furthermore, as Poterba (1987) shows, higher dividend tax rates tend to lower the payout to households and to increase corporate saving (from which households ultimately benefit as well).

28 Of course, it is recognized that the consumption tax is more regressive than a progressive income tax and may therefore be rejected on equity grounds. Furthermore, it does distort the decision between leisure and consumption, taxing the latter heavily, but not the former.

29 Certainly it is not possible to decide on this basis alone as to whether one tax system is more distorting than another since it does not take into account the tax incidence, as can be seen from the shares in GDP.

30 For a list of such increases in the United States, see, e.g., the Structural Impediments Initiative (SII) Report (1991).

31 There are other effects of inflation on saving which will be discussed later.

32 Urteil des Zweiten Senats des Bundesverfassungsgerichts vom 27. Juni 1991.

33 A 10 percent source tax was introduced in 1990 and abolished only six months later due to massive capital flight.

34 On the contrary, the banking law of 1979 does specifically ask local tax authorities to respect the "relation of trust" between banks and customers. As a result of the legal situation which has to be changed by January 1, 1993 practically only those who declare their capital income have to pay taxes since those cases where nothing is declared are extremely unlikely to be investigated. According to the Court, no more than half of the taxable capital income is declared in Germany (based on estimates of the German authorities). The Bundesrechnungshof (General Accounting Office) even found during its examinations (of a very limited number of households) that the quota of declaration varied between 3.7 percent and 47.7 percent from one revenue office to the other. As a reaction to the ruling there are now plans to introduce a 25 percent source tax for residents and to revise upwards substantially the exemption levels.

35 Byrne's (1976) list of countries with such a custom included all countries currently belonging to the G7.

36 Since 1988, most income in Japanese savings accounts is subjected to a 20 percent source tax (cf. Hayashi et al., 1988).

37 This is a particularly good case for comparison since the two countries have much in common not only geographically and institutionally but also demographically.

38 In addition, a $1,000 deduction of investment income was introduced in 1974.

39 For example, the IRA's were first restricted to a small number of people, then extended to all taxpayers in 1981, and subsequently capped in 1986.

40 In 1975, government bonuses were restricted to medium- and low-income earners; cf. Kauffmann (1990).

41 In addition, it is common that the real estate property is largely undervalued when an inheritance asset is estimated.

42 As pointed out by Dean et al. (1990), in terms of efficiency it would make sense if interest payments were tax-deductible as long as the income on housing investment was taxed. But as they are not it is likely that the various measures lead to a distortion of investment in favor of housing and at the expense of business.

43 Von Ungern-Sternberg (1981) showed in an empirical study for Germany and the United Kingdom that households do indeed behave as if they would not consider the compensation for wealth erosion through inflation as part of their income.

44 Modigliani (1990) found an underestimation of government saving (corresponding broadly to an overestimation of private saving) in the order of 0.4 percentage points in the 1960s and around 2 percentage points in the 1970s and 1980s for the average of the 21 OECD countries. See Elmeskov et al. (1991) and Barro (1974) on this issue.

45   The former effect depends on a positive elasticity of saving.
46   Yoshikawa and Ohtake (1989) found in a study of Japanese households that
      the decision not to buy property induced by an increase in land prices was
      strong enough to turn a positive (land-) price elasticity of saving into a negative
      one.
47   If there is a bequest motive, one might expect that the savings rate declines
      less given the expectation that children will be affected negatively by higher
      housing prices either through higher rents or through higher purchasing prices.
      But it is not likely that this will fully compensate for the drop in savings
      induced by the wealth effect.
48   In Japan, the ratio of net wealth (including housing and land) to income rose
      from 5.0 in 1975 to 7.8 in 1987. The corresponding figures for the United
      States, Canada, and the United Kingdom stayed roughly between 4 and 5
      (Dean et al., 1990).
49   Assuming a time-separable utility function with non-increasing absolute risk
      aversion.
50   Whether or not this effect induces a decrease in saving depends on whether
      it offsets effects such as the generally observed increasing propensity to save
      at a higher income or a possible motive for joining the labor force which may
      have been to earn income for a housing purchase. It may be strengthened by
      higher purchases of durable goods or services, e.g. in connection with child
      care. Graham (1987) found evidence that increased labor-force participation of
      women lowers the saving rate.

REFERENCES

Ando, Albert, Guiso, Luigi, Terlizzese, Daniele, and Dorsainvil, Daniel 1991a:
    Saving, Demographic Structure and Productivity Growth: The Case of Japan.
    Paper presented at the conference on Saving behaviour: theory, international evid-
    ence and policy implications, held in Helsinki in May 1991.
Ando, Albert, Guiso, Luigi, and Terlizzese, Daniele 1991b: Savings as a Flexible
    Choice. Paper presented at the above conference.
Ando, Albert, and Modigliani, Franco 1963: The "Life Cycle" Hypothesis of Saving:
    Aggregate Implications and Test. *American Economic Review*, 53, No. 55–84.
Auerbach, Alan J., Cai, Jinyong, and Kotlikoff, Laurence J. 1990: US Demographics
    and Saving: Predictions of Three Saving Models. NBER Working Paper No.
    3404.
Auerbach, Alan J. and Kotlikoff, Laurence, J. 1991: The Impact of the Demographic
    Transition on Capital Formation. Paper presented at the above conference.
Barro, Robert J. 1974: Are Government Bonds Net Wealth? *Journal of Political
    Economy*, 82, No. 6, 1095–118.
Blades, Derek W. and Sturm, Peter H. 1982: The Concept and Measurement of
    Savings: The United States and Other Industrialized Countries. In Federal Reserve
    Bank of Boston, Saving and Government Policy, Conference Series No. 2, pp.
    1–30.

Boskin, Michael J. 1978: Taxation, Saving, and the Rate of Interest. *Journal of Political Economy*, 86, No. 2, S3–S27.

Bovenberg, Lans A., Andersson, Krister, Aramaki, Kenjii, and Chand, Sheetal 1989: Tax Incentives and International Capital Flows: The Case of the United States and Japan. IMF Working Paper No. WP/89/5.

Branson, William H. and Klevorick, Alvin K. 1969: Money Illusion and the Aggregate Consumption Function. *American Economic Review*, 59, No. 5, 832–49.

Byrne, William J. 1976: Fiscal Incentives for Household Saving. IMF Staff Papers, 23, No. 2, 455–89.

Bundesverfassungsgericht, 1989: Urteil des Zweiten Senats vom 27 Juni 1991 (2 BvR 1493/89), Karlsruhe.

Caballero, Ricardo J. 1990: Consumption Puzzles and Precautionary Savings. *Journal of Monetary Economics*, 25, 113–36.

Carroll, Chris and Summers, Lawrence H. 1987: Why Have Private Savings Rates in the United States and Canada Diverged? *Journal of Monetary Economics*, 20, 249–79.

Cutler, David M., Poterba, James M., Sheiner, Louise M., and Summers, Lawrence H. 1990: An Aging Society: Opportunity or Challenge? Brookings Papers on Economic Activity, No. 1.

David, Paul A. and Scadding, John L. 1974: Private Savings: Ultrarationality, Aggregation, and "Denison's Law." *Journal of Political Economy*, 82, 225–49.

Dean, Andrew, Durand, Martine, Fallon, John, and Hoeller, Peter 1990: Saving Trends and Behaviour in OECD Countries. OECD Economic Studies, No. 14.

Deaton, Angus 1977: Involuntary Saving through Unanticipated Inflation. *American Economic Review*, 67, No. 5, 899–910.

Deaton, Angus 1989: Saving and Liquidity Constraints. NBER Working Paper No. 3196.

Denison, Edward F. 1958: A Note on Private Saving. *Review of Economics and Statistics*, 40, 261–7.

Elmeskov, Jorgen, Shafer, Jeffrey, and Tease, Warren 1991: Savings Trends and Measurement Issues. OECD Working Paper No. 105.

Evans, Owen J. 1983: Tax Policy, the Interest Elasticity of Saving, and Capital Accumulation: Numerical Analysis of Theoretical Models. *American Economic Review*, 73, No. 3, 398–410.

Feldstein, Martin 1974: Social Security, Induced Retirement, and Aggregate Capital Accumulation. *Journal of Political Economy*, 82, No. 5, 905–26.

Feldstein, Martin 1980: International Differences in Social Security and Saving. *Journal of Public Economics*, 14, 225–44.

Feldstein, Martin 1982. Social Security and Private Saving: Reply. *Journal of Political Economy*, 90, 630–42.

Feldstein, Martin, and Bacchetta, Philippe 1989: National Saving and International Investment. Harvard Institute of Economic Research Discussion Paper No. 1463.

Feldstein, Martin and Horioka, Charles 1980: Domestic Saving and International Capital Flows. *The Economic Journal*, 90, 314–29.

Flavin, Marjorie A. 1981: The Adjustment of Consumption to Changing Expectations about Future Income. *Journal of Political Economy*, 89, No. 5, 974–1009.

Friedman, Milton 1957: *A Theory of the Consumption Function*, Princeton.

Graham, John W. 1987: International Differences in Saving Rates and the Life Cycle Hypothesis. *European Economic Review*, 31, 1509–29.

Green, Francis 1991: Institutional and Other Unconventional Theories of Saving. *Journal of Economic Issues*, 25, No. 1, 93–113.

Hayashi, Fumio 1989: Is Japan's Saving Rate High? Federal Reserve Bank of Minneapolis, *Quarterly Review*, pp. 3–9.

Hayashi, Fumio, Ito, Takatoshi, and Slemrod, Joel 1988: Housing Finance Imperfections, Taxation, and Private Saving: A Comparative Simulation Analysis of the United States and Japan. *Journal of the Japanese and International Economies*, 2, 215–38.

Horioka, Charles Yuji 1986: Why is Japan's Savings Rate So High? IMF Working Paper No. DM/86/44.

Kauffmann, Barbara 1990: Savings Behavior of Private Households in the United States and West Germany. *Jahrbücher für Nationalökonomie und Statistik*, 207, No. 2, 97–108.

Kimball, Miles, S. 1990a: Precautionary Saving and the Marginal Propensity to Consume. NBER Working Paper No. 3403.

Kimball, Miles S. 1990b: Precautionary Motives for Holding Assets. NBER Working Paper No. 3586.

Koskela, Erkki and Virén, Matti 1983: Social Security and Household Saving in an International Cross Section. *American Economic Review*, 73, No. 1, 212–17.

Koskela, Erkki and Virén, Matti 1984: Credit Rationing and Consumer Intertemporal Choice. *Oxford Economic Papers*, 36, 241–7.

Koskela, Erkki and Virén, Matti 1985: On the Role of Inflation in Consumption Function. *Weltwirtschaftliches Archiv*, 121, No. 2, 252–76.

Koskela, Erkki and Virén, Matti 1989: International Differences in Saving Rates and The Life Cycle Hypothesis – A Comment. *European Economic Review*, 33, 1489–98.

Kotlikoff, Laurence J. 1979: Testing the Theory of Social Security and Life Cycle Accumulation. *American Economic Review*, 69, 396–410.

Kotlikoff, Laurence J. 1984: Taxation and Savings: A Neoclassical Perspective. *Journal of Economic Literature*, 22, No. 4, 1576–629.

Kotlikoff, Laurence J. 1988: Intergenerational Transfers and Savings. *Journal of Economic Perspectives*, 2, No. 2, 41–58.

Lawrance, Emily C. 1991: Poverty and the Rate of Time Preference: Evidence from Panel Data. *Journal of Political Economy*, 99, No. 1, 54–77.

Maki, Atsushi 1989: Savings and Portfolio Behavior of Japanese Households. *Japan and the World Economy*, 1, 145–62.

Mankiw, Gregory N. and Zeldes, Stephen P. 1990: The Consumption of Stockholders and Non-Stockholders. *NBER Working Paper* No. 3402.

Mirer, Thad W. 1979: The Wealth-Age Relation among the Aged. *American Economic Review*, 69, No. 3, 435–43.

Modigliani, Franco 1990: Recent Declines in the Savings Rate: a Life Cycle Perspective. *Rivista di Politica Economica*, 80, No. 12, 5–41.

Ogawa, Kazuo 1990: Cyclical Variations in Liquidity-Constrained Consumers: Evidence from Macro Data in Japan. *Journal of the Japanese and International Economies*, 4, 173–93.

Poterba, James M. 1987: Tax Policy and Corporate Saving. *Brookings Papers on Economic Activity*, No. 2, 455–515.

Santillan, Javier 1991: The adequacy and allocation of world savings. In *Economic Papers of the Commission of the European Communities*. No. 88.

Shibuya, Hiroshi 1987: Japan's Household Savings Rate: An Application of the Life-Cycle Hypothesis. *IMF Working Paper* No. WP/87/15.

Sinn, Stefan 1990: Net external asset position of 145 countries. Estimation and Interpretation. *Kieler Studie* No. 234, Institut für Weltwirtschaft, Kiel.

Smith, Roger S. 1989: Factors Affecting Saving, Policy Tools, and Tax Reform: A Review. *IMF Working Paper* No. WP/89/47.

Stiglitz, Joseph E. and Weiss, Andrew 1981: Credit Rationing in Markets with Imperfect Information. *American Economic Review*, 71, No. 3, 393–410.

Sturm, Peter 1983: Determinants of Saving: Theory and Evidence. *OECD Economic Studies*.

Summers, Lawrence H. 1981: Capital Taxation and Accumulation in a Life Cycle Growth Model. *American Economic Review*, 71, No. 4, 533–44.

Summers, Lawrence H. and Carroll, Chris 1987: Why Is US National Saving So Low? *Brookings Papers on Economic Activity*, No. 2, 607–42.

Tabellini, Guido 1991: The Politics of Intergenerational Redistribution. *Journal of Political Economy*, 99, No. 2, 335–57.

Thaler, Richard H. 1990: Saving, Fungibility, and Mental Accounts. *Journal of Economic Perspectives*, 4, No. 1, 193–205.

Tullio, Giuseppe and Contesso, Francesco 1986: Do after tax interest rates affect private consumption and savings? Empirical evidence for 8 industrial countries: 1970–1983. *Economic Paper* No. 51 of the Commission of the European Communities.

Von Ungern-Sternberg, Thomas 1981: Inflation and Savings: International Evidence on Inflation-Induced Income Losses. *Economic Journal*, 91, 961–76.

Wilcox, David W. 1989: Social Security Benefits, Consumption Expenditure, and the Life Cycle Hypothesis. *Journal of Political Economy*, 97, No. 2, 288–304.

Wilcox, David W. 1991: Household Spending and Saving: Measurement, Trends, and Analysis. *Federal Reserve Bulletin*, 2–16.

US-Japan Working Group on the Structural Impediments Initiative (SII) 1991: First Annual Report: Tokyo.

Yoshikawa, Hiroshi, and Ohtake, Fumio 1989: An Analysis of Female Labor Supply, Housing Demand and the Saving Rate in Japan. *European Economic Review*, 33, 997–1030.

Zeldes, Stephen P. 1989: Consumption and Liquidity Constraints: An Empirical Investigation. *Journal of Political Economy*, 97, No. 2, 305–46.

2

Saving and Endogenous Growth: a Survey of Theory and Policy[*]

Willem H. Buiter

INTRODUCTION

The study of saving behavior has been a central theme of economics since the days when the subject was known as political economy. This chapter aims to provide a broad-ranging survey of some of the key issues involving the determinants of the savings rate and the consequences of different kinds of savings behavior for economic growth. It brings together and in minor ways extends results on overlapping generations (OLG) models and endogenous growth by Alogoskoufis and van der Ploeg (1990a,b, 1991), Saint-Paul (1990), Jones and Manuelli (1990) and Buiter and Kletzer (1991a,b,c).

Saving behavior, abstaining from current consumption, is one of two key determinants of economic growth. The other is the efficiency with which the resources that are saved are invested, that is, channeled into and allocated among alternative productive uses. This chapter will focus exclusively on the first issue: how much is saved. The view that saving is a key determinant of long-run potential output growth has not been popular since the early 1960s when the empirical study of aggregate production functions purported to show that the output elasticity of physical capital was low and that technological change, which was modeled as exogenous, accounted for a large fraction of the growth of output per worker (Solow, 1957).

A broader view of what constitutes investment, which encompasses R & D, additions to the stock of knowledge and human capital accumulation (formal

* The first draft of this chapter was written while I was a Visiting Scholar in the Research Department of the International Monetary Fund. The views expressed are those of the author and are not to be interpreted as necessarily indicating the position of the Executive Board of the International Monetary Fund. I would like to thank Xavier Sala-i-Martin for helpful comments on the first draft, and Ken Kletzer for many useful discussions on the general subject of overlapping generations models and endogenous growth.

and informal education, on the job training, etc.) has necessitated a broader view of what constitutes saving. Technical change has been endogenized and our view of the role of saving in the growth process has been correspondingly broadened. Where the old "exogenous growth" literature attributed to saving behavior at most a permanent effect on the *level* of per capita income but only a transitory effect on the *rate of growth* of per capita income, the new "endogenous growth" literature implies that differences in saving behavior will have permanent effects both on growth rates and levels of per capita income. (See e.g., Romer, 1986, 1990, Lucas, 1988, Barro, 1990, Barro and Sala-i-Martin, 1990, Sala-i-Martin, 1990a,b, Grossman and Helpman, 1991, and Helpman, 1991.)

The issue can be put very simply. The aggregate production function for the economy we are considering is linear in the aggregate capital stock, that is $Y = aK$, where Y is real output, K is the aggregate capital stock and a is some positive constant. Consider a closed economy without government. Capital depreciation is ignored. Let s denote the ratio of private saving to output. It follows that the growth rate of capital (and thus of output) is given by $\dot{K}/K = \dot{Y}/Y = s$a.

With constant returns to a factor (or to factors) that can be accumulated, anything that raises the savings rate s or the productivity of the accumulated factor(s) a will raise the growth rate of the economy. This chapter focuses on the determinants of s. The determinants of a are not considered.

Differences in savings behavior may be due to a variety of factors. One important set of determinants of saving are private preferences, that is private attitudes towards intertemporal choice. In standard neoclassical theory this is captured in such features of the preference ordering as the psychological or subjective pure rate of time preference, the intertemporal elasticity of substitution, attitudes towards intergenerational gifts and bequests and the parameters governing the precautionary demand for saving.[1] A second set of influences on private sector saving behavior is the nature of private sector anticipations concerning future asset returns and after-tax non-asset income. These can range all the way from Muth-rational expectations to myopic, adaptive or other behavioral hypotheses.

Demographic features constitute a third set of influences on private saving behavior. While the current age composition of the population must to a large extent be viewed as predetermined, that is, not subject to current public or private choice, its evolution over time will be influenced by private choices impinging on birth and death rates. Government policy too can influence the evolution of the demographic structure, both directly and by influencing private choices co-determining birth and death rates.

Finally, even for a given demographic structure, government policy can influence both the private and the total notional (private plus public) saving

rate. This can be done though policies involving redistribution among heterogeneous consumers (such as deficit financing and unfunded social security
retirement schemes) and through policies that alter the opportunity cost of
saving.

Endogenous growth theory has amplified the effects of changes in parameters
and exogenous variables.[2] Since the impact of policy on long-run growth has
slipped a derivative, special attention will be given in this chapter to the way in
which economic policy influences saving. Among the policy instruments that
will be considered are unfunded social security retirement schemes, deficit
finance, the taxation of wage and non-wage income, interest taxes and subsidies
and public consumption spending. The relationship between private and public
saving (the financial crowding out issue) has of course long been a central theme
of macroeconomics.

The linearity of the aggregate production function in the aggregate capital
stock represents a considerable simplification of the global dynamics of capital,
output and consumption, when compared to the neoclassical exogenous growth
model with constant returns to capital and the non-augmentable factor labor
jointly. As will become clear on pp. 79–93, by expressing stocks and flows as
ratios to the capital stock, the dynamic analysis involves one fewer state variable
than the corresponding exogenous growth model. The model is therefore a
useful didactic tool for a first introduction to growth theory.

Limitations of space restrict the scope of this chapter to the link between
saving and long-term growth. This means in particular that I omit consideration of the cyclical relationship between private and public saving behavior and
private investment, and of the role of fiscal and financial stabilization policy.
The separation of the saving decision from the investment decision in modern
capitalist economies with, to a first approximation, households doing the saving
(in the form of accumulation of financial assets) and firms making the capital
accumulation and R & D decisions, creates the possibility of intertemporal
coordination failure, where the ex-post balancing of saving and investment
occurs at a socially inefficient level. Asymmetric information between borrowers (investing firms) and lenders (saving households) may result in incompleteness
of the set of contingent forward markets. Financial intermediaries may emerge
that help overcome or at least mitigate the failure of market prices to convey all
information necessary for efficient saving and investment decisions. If this is
not privately rational, welfare-improving fiscal or regulatory interventions may
exist. The beginnings of rigorous analytical underpinnings to a formal theory of
financial market failure along these lines can be found in the work of Bernanke
and Gertler (1987).

The plan of the chapter is as follows. The first section develops the private
consumption side of the model. The following section restates the necessary
and sufficient conditions for absence of debt neutrality in the OLG model

under consideration, while the following section discusses the impact effect on saving of the social security retirement scheme first formalized by Saint-Paul (1990). The next section introduces a very simple model of the supply side that is consistent with endogenous growth in an OLG setting. The structure of property rights, together with the technology, permits new generations to participate in the market game with endowments whose value increases in line with the growth rate.[3]

In the final section I investigate the effects of changes in the parameters characterizing tastes (the time preference rate, the elasticity of intertemporal substitution), demography (the birth rate, the age-dependent labor power depreciation rate and the death rate), and fiscal policy (public debt, labor income taxes, the parameters describing the unfunded social security retirement scheme, the tax rates on capital rental income and on interest income, and exhaustive public consumption spending).

THE DEMAND SIDE OF THE MODEL

Private Consumption

Private consumption is given by the overlapping generations model of Blanchard (1985) and Weil (1990) as synthesized in Buiter (1988). At each instant t a consumer born at time $s \leq t$ solves the following optimum problem:

$$\max_{\{\bar{c}(s,v)\}} E_t \int_t^\infty \frac{1}{1-\gamma} \bar{c}(s,v)^{1-\gamma} \{\exp[-\rho(v-t)]\} dv \qquad \rho, \gamma > 0 \quad (2.1)[4]$$

$\bar{c}(s,v) \geq 0$ for all s and for all $v \geq s$.

Subject to the budget identity

$$\frac{d}{dt}\bar{a}(s,t) \equiv (r(t) + \lambda)\bar{a}(s,t) + \bar{x}(s,t) - \bar{\tau}(s,t) - \bar{c}(s,t) \qquad (2.2)$$

and the solvency constraint

$$\lim_{l \to \infty} \bar{a}(s,l) \exp\{-\int_t^l [r(u) + \lambda] du\} = 0. \qquad (2.3)$$

We also have

$$\bar{x}\{s,t\} = w(s,t)\bar{j}(s,t) \qquad (2.4a)$$

$$w(s,t) = w(t) \quad \text{for all } s \qquad (2.4b)$$

$$\bar{j}(s,t) = \bar{j}(t,t)\exp(-\tau(t-s)) \quad s \leq t \qquad (2.4c)$$

Exp$_t$ is the expectation operator, conditional on information at time t. γ is the elasticity of instantaneous marginal utility or the reciprocal of the intertemporal elasticity of substitution: a larger value of γ indicates a stronger desire to smooth consumption over time. ρ is the subjective rate of time preference, $\bar{c}(s,v)$ is consumption at time v by someone born at time s, $\bar{a}$ denotes financial wealth, $\bar{x}$ is the individual's labor income, w is the wage rate or the rental rate of human capital, $\bar{j}$ is the amount of labor power (in efficiency units) applied by the individual, $\bar{\tau}$ is the amount of lump-sum taxes net of transfers on labor income and r is the real interest rate. Each consumer faces a time- and age-independent instantaneous probability of death, $\lambda \geq 0$. Everyone currently alive will therefore, regardless of age, have the same life expectancy $1/\lambda$. This is of course very poor demography and it also means that the theory cannot expect to capture most of the life-cycle effects on saving. Human capital is homogeneous and its rental rate is the same for everyone currently alive (2.4b). Equation (2.4c) says that the human capital of a person born in period s equals that of a person born in period t times a factor $\exp(-\pi(t-s))$. This can be interpreted as ageing leading to the erosion, at the constant exponential rate π, of the raw labor endowment of an individual.

The term $\lambda\bar{a}$ on the right-hand side of equation (2.2) is due to the presence of efficient annuities markets. Consumers contract with annuities companies to receive a rate of return $\aleph$ on their financial wealth at each instant. When they die, their entire financial wealth goes to the annuity company. The annuities industry is competitive, risk neutral and has free entry. λ is both the instantaneous probability of death and the fraction of each (large) age cohort (and therefore of the total population) that dies at each instant. The zero expected profit condition implies that $\aleph = \lambda$.

I define human capital $\bar{h}(s,t)$ to be the present discounted value at time t (using the "risk-of-death-corrected" individual discount rate $r + \lambda$) of expected future *before-tax* labor income of someone born at time $s \leq t$.

$$\bar{h}(s,t) \equiv \int_t^\infty \bar{x}(s,v)\left(\exp\left\{-\int_t^v [r(u) + \lambda]\,du\right\}\right)dv \qquad (2.5a)$$

Similarly I define $\bar{\theta}(s,t)$ as the present discounted value, at time t, of the lifetime taxes expected to be paid by a household born in period s, that is

$$\bar{\theta}(s,t) \equiv \int_t^\infty \bar{\tau}(s,v)\exp\left\{-\int_t^v (r(u) + \lambda)\,du\right\}dv \qquad (2.5b)$$

Under rational expectations,[5] the solution to the consumer's problem is

$$\bar{c}(s,t) = \eta(t)[\bar{a}(s,t) + \bar{h}(s,t) - \bar{\theta}(s,t)] \qquad (2.6a)$$

$$\eta(t) = \left[\int_t^\infty \left\{\exp-\left[\left(\frac{\gamma-1}{\gamma}\right)\int_t^v r(u)\,du + (v-t)\left(\lambda + \frac{1}{\gamma}\rho\right)\right]\right\}dv\right]^{-1} \qquad (2.6b)$$

Note that this implies that

$$\frac{d}{dt}\bar{c}(s,t) = \gamma^{-1}(r - \rho)\bar{c}(s,t) \qquad (2.6c)^6$$

Aggregation

Without loss of generality I set $\mathfrak{N}(0)$, population at time zero, equal to 1, that is $\mathfrak{N}(0) = 1$. In addition to the constant death rate $\lambda \geq 0$ there is a constant birth rate $\beta > 0$. The rate of growth of population n is therefore constant and given by $n = \beta - \lambda$, that is $\mathfrak{N}(t) = \exp\{(\beta - \lambda)t\} = \exp\{nt\}$. Note that, when $\beta > 0$, total population at time t can be written as the sum of all survivors of previous generations, that is $\mathfrak{N}(t) = \beta \exp\{-\lambda t\}\int_{-\infty}^{t} \exp\{\beta s\}\,ds$. Raw labor power is assumed to decline with age at a constant proportional rate π. Let $l(s,t)$ be the raw labor power supplied at time t by the surviving members of generation s and $n(s,t)$ the number of members of generation s surviving at time t. It follows that $l(s,t) = n(s,t)\exp\{-\pi(t - s)\} = \beta \exp\{[(\beta + \pi)s-(\lambda + \pi)t]\}$. Summing over all past generations yields the aggregate supply of raw labor power, $L(t)$, given in equation (2.7).

$$L(t) = \frac{\beta}{\beta + \pi} \exp\{nt\}. \qquad (2.7)$$

Corresponding to any individual flow or stock variable $\bar{v}(s,t)$ I define the corresponding population aggregate $V(t)$ to be

$$V(t) = \beta \exp\{-\lambda t\}\int_{-\infty}^{t} v(s,t)\exp\{\beta s\}\,ds$$

if $\beta > 0$ and $V(t) = v(s,t)\exp\{-\lambda t\}$ if $\beta = 0$. The present discounted value, at time t, of the expected life-time taxes to be paid by all those currently alive $\Theta(t)$ deserves special mention; it is given by

$$\Theta(t) = \beta \exp\{-\lambda t\}\int_{-\infty}^{t} \bar{v}(s,t)\exp\{\beta s\}\,ds \qquad (2.8)$$

Lump-sum taxes (net of transfers) are assumed to vary with age in the following manner. Lump-sum taxes paid by a member of generation $s \leq t$, $\bar{\tau}(s,t)$, are the sum of an age-independent component, t_0, and an age-dependent component $t_1 \exp\{t_2(t - s)\}$ which grows exponentially with age, as shown in equation (2.9). In order to obtain dynamic systems with an interesting steady state, for the study of long-run effects of tax changes on pages 73–5, it is also assumed that individual taxes include a "scale component" $\varepsilon(t)$, which for the moment I only require to be positive:

$$\bar{\tau}(s,t) = [t_0 + t_1\exp\{t_2(t-s)\}]\varepsilon(t) \qquad (2.9)$$

Provided $\beta > t_2$, a necessary condition for total tax receipts to be bounded, total tax revenue at each instant t is given by:

$$T(t) \equiv \beta \, \exp\{-\lambda t\} \int_{-\infty}^{t} \bar{\tau}(s,t) \exp\{\beta s\} \, ds = \varepsilon(t) \left[t_0 + t_1 \left(\frac{\beta}{\beta - t_2} \right) \right] \exp\{nt\}$$

(2.10)

Since there are neither voluntary nor involuntary[7] bequests in our model, people are born without financial assets or liabilities, that is $\bar{a}(s,s) = 0$. It follows that aggregate consumption is given by:

$$C(t) = \eta(t)[A(t) + H(t) - \Theta(t)]$$ (2.11)

when η is defined in equation (2.6b) and

$$\dot{A}(t) = r(t)A(t) + X(t) - T(t) - C(t)$$ (2.12)

$$\dot{H}(t) = (r(t) + \beta + \pi)H(t) - X(t)$$ (2.13)

$$\dot{\Theta}(t) = (r(t) + \beta)\Theta(t) - T(t) - \Omega(t)$$ (2.14)

where

$$\Omega(t) \equiv \beta \, \exp\{nt\} \left[\frac{t_1 t_2}{\beta - t_2} \right] \int_{t}^{\infty} \varepsilon(z) \exp\left\{ -\int_{t}^{z} (r(q) + \lambda - t_2) \, dq \right\} dz$$ (2.15)

Integrating (2.13) forward, the aggregate human capital of those currently alive can be written as in equation (2.16a) and the aggregate tax burden faced by those currently alive as in equation (2.16b):

$$H(t) = \int_{t}^{\infty} X(v) \exp\left\{ -\int_{t}^{v} (r(u) + \beta + \pi) \, du \right\} dv$$ (2.16a)

$$\Theta(t) = \int_{t}^{\infty} [T(v) + \Omega(v)] \exp\left\{ -\int_{t}^{v} (r(u) + \beta) \, du \right\} dv$$ (2.16b)

The term π is present in the discount rate for human capital income in equation (2.16a) but not in the discount rate for future taxes in equation (2.16b) because the depreciation of raw labor power with age, at a constant rate π, only affects the before-tax component of labor income and not the tax bill. The term Ω on the right-hand side of equations (2.14) and (2.16b) is present if and only if there are age-dependent lump-sum taxes, that is if both t_1 and t_2 are non-zero and if the birth rate is positive. $\Omega(t)$ represents the contribution by those born at time t to the rate of change in the age-dependent component of the tax burden.

Ignoring Ω for the moment, we see that $H(t)$, the aggregate human capital of those currently alive, is the present discounted value of future after-tax wage income, where the discount rate is the real interest rate augmented by the birth rate β and the rate of labor power depreciation π. The presence of the birth rate signals that the future expected labor income of "new entrants" (those born after time t) is not owned by anyone currently alive. An operative intergenerational gift and bequest motive would cause the discount premium associated with β to disappear. So of course would a zero birth rate or a different structure of labor property rights, such as a society in which all labor is performed by people subject to hereditary slavery (see Buiter, 1989). In the Blanchard-Weil OLG model an "owner-occupier" system of labor property rights, taxation of labor income and a positive birth rate are necessary and sufficient for absence of debt neutrality. Uncertain lifetimes ($\lambda > 0$) do not belong to the set of necessary and sufficient conditions.

Equations (2.11) to (2.15) plus the definition of η in (2.6b) imply that the rate of change of aggregate consumption can be written as:

$$\dot{C} = [\gamma^{-1}(r - \rho) + n + \pi]C - \eta(\beta + \pi)A + \eta\Omega + \pi\eta\Theta \qquad (2.17)$$

The Government

At each instant t the government spends an amount $G(t) \geq 0$ on public consumption,[8] raises tax revenues $T(t)$ and finances any excess of current outlays over current revenues by issuing fixed real market value, variable interest rate bonds. Monetary financing is not considered. The stock of these bonds is denoted $B(t)$. The government budget identity is given in (2.18). Together with its solvency constraint, given in (2.19), it implies the government's intertemporal budget constraint given in (2.20); the current debt should equal the present discounted value of future primary (non-interest) surpluses:

$$\dot{B}(t) \equiv r(t)B(t) + G(t) - T(t) \qquad (2.18)$$

$$\lim_{l \to \infty} B(l)\exp\left[-\int_t^l r(u)du\right] = 0 \qquad (2.19)$$

$$B(t) = \int_t^\infty [T(v) - G(v)]\left\{\exp\left[-\int_t^v r(u)du\right]\right\}dv \qquad (2.20)$$

Equilibrium

Markets clear at each instant. In this closed economy real reproducible capital, K, and government debt are the only non-human stores of value. Financial market equilibrium therefore requires that (2.21) holds for all t:

$$A(t) = K(t) + B(t) \qquad (2.21)$$

Capital accumulation is governed by

$$\dot{K} = Y - \delta K - C - G \qquad (2.22)$$

where Y is gross real output and $\delta > 0$ the instantaneous rate of depreciation of capital.

DEBT NEUTRALITY

In this section I briefly review the necessary and sufficient condition for debt neutrality in our consumption model. None of the results of this section depend on the model of production.

I proceed as follows. In the aggregate consumption function given in equation (2.11) we substitute for A using equation (2.21), for H using equation (2.16a) and for Θ using equation (2.16b). Then add and subtract the term

$$\int_t^\infty G(v)\exp\left\{-\int_t^v [r(u) + \beta]\,du\right\}$$

and rearrange. This yields equation (2.23). When we replace this last step by the elimination of $B(t)$ from the aggregate private consumption function using the public sector intertemporal budget constraint (2.20), equation (2.24) results. For easy reference, the definition of η is reproduced as well.

$$C(t) = \eta(t)\left[K(t) + \int_t^\infty\left[X(v)\exp\left\{-\int_t^v (r(u) + \beta + \pi)\,du\right\}\right.\right. \tag{2.23}$$

$$\left.- G(v)\exp\left\{-\int_t^v (r(u) + \beta)\,du\right\}\right]dv\right]$$

$$+ \eta(t)\left[B(t) - \int_t^\infty\left[T(v) - G(v) + \beta\ \exp\{nv\}\left(\frac{t_1 t_2}{\beta - t_2}\right)\right.\right.$$

$$\left.\times \int_v^\infty \varepsilon(z)\exp\left\{-\int_v^z (r(q) + \lambda - t_2)\,dq\right\}dz\right]$$

$$\left.\times \exp\left\{-\int_t^v (r(u) + \beta)\,du\right\}dv\right]$$

$$C(t) = \eta(t)\left[K(t) + \int_t^\infty\left[X(v)\exp\left\{-\int_t^v (r(u) + \beta + \pi)\,du\right\}\right.\right. \tag{2.24}$$

$$\left.- G(v)\exp\left\{-\int_t^v r(u)\,du\right\}\right]dv\right]$$

$$+ \int_t^\infty \left\{ T(v) \left[\exp\{\beta(v-t)\} - 1 \right] - \beta \exp\{nv\} \left[\frac{t_1 t_2}{\beta - t_2} \right] \right.$$

$$\times \int_t^\infty \varepsilon(z) \exp\left\{ -\int_v^z (r(q) + \lambda - t_2) \, dq \right\} dz \right\}$$

$$\left. \times \exp\left\{ -\int_t^v (r(u) + \beta) \, du \right\} dv \right]$$

$$\eta(t) = \left[\int_t^\infty \left\{ \exp - \left[\left(\frac{\gamma - 1}{\gamma} \right) \int_t^v r(u) \, du + (v - t) \left(\lambda + \frac{1}{\gamma} \rho \right) \right] \right\} dv \right]^{-1}$$

From the government's intertemporal budget constraint given in equation (2.20) it is clear that the second term on the righthand-side of equation (2.23) is identically equal to zero if and only if the birth rate β equals zero. When that is the case, government debt and the intertemporal distribution of lump-sum taxes do not influence private consumption behavior. We are effectively (despite the possibility of a positive death rate) in a representative agent model. Debt neutrality breaks down if the intertemporal redistribution of lump-sum taxes associated with government borrowing redistributes life-time resources between agents that are heterogeneous with respect to their consumption behaviour (see Buiter, 1990). When $\beta = 0$ there are no new agents coming into the system. All those currently alive have the same life expectancy and the same marginal propensities to spend out of comprehensive wealth η.

The same conclusion is reached when $\beta = 0$ is set in equation (2.24). The third expression inside the big brackets on the right-hand-side of equation (2.24) disappears in that case. All that matters for aggregate consumption is the government's exhaustive spending program.

AN UNFUNDED SOCIAL SECURITY
RETIREMENT SCHEME

Following Saint-Paul (1990), I can analyze the consequences of the introduction (or an increase in the scale of) an unfunded social security retirement scheme by introducing balanced-budget redistribution from the young to the old. Again, the results do not depend on the model of production.

In this section, I evaluate the impact effect on aggregate consumption of changes in the parameters characterizing the social security retirement scheme, holding constant the initial stocks of capital, K, and government debt, B, and the expected future paths of interest rates, r, and wage income, X, and exhaustive public spending, G.[9] If aggregate consumption changes as a result of these parameter changes, there are likely to be consequences for the future behavior of such endogenous variables as output, the capital stock, the wage rate and the interest rate. On pp. 79–93 a simple dynamic general equilibrium growth model will be used to evaluate the dynamic responses of these and other endogenous variables.

Saint-Paul (1990) models an increase in the scale of an unfunded social security retirement scheme as follows.[10] Without loss of generality consider the case where the initial value of t_1 is positive. Consider an increase in t_1, the amount of tax paid by a newborn. This increase in taxes paid while young is accompanied by a change in the growth rate of the tax burden with age, t_2, which is just sufficient to keep total tax receipts at each point in time constant. From equation (2.10) this implies that

$$dt_2 = \left(\frac{t_2 - \beta}{t_1}\right) dt_1 \qquad (2.25)$$

Since $\beta > t_2$, an increase in t_1, with t_1 positive, requires a reduction in t_2 in order for total tax receipts to remain constant: pay more when young and less when old.

Note that, with the tax rule under consideration,

$$\bar{\theta}(s,t) \equiv \int_t^\infty \bar{\tau}(s,v) \exp\left\{-\int_t^v (r(u) + \lambda)\, du\right\} dv,$$

the present discounted value, at time t, of the life-time taxes expected to be paid by a household born in period s is given by:

$$\bar{\theta}(s,t) \equiv t_0 \int_t^\infty \varepsilon(v) \exp\left\{-\int_t^v (r(u) + \lambda)\, du\right\} dv + t_1 \exp\{t_2(t - s)\}$$

$$\times \int_t^\infty \varepsilon(v) \exp\left\{-\int_t^v (r(u) + \lambda - t_2)\, du\right\} dv$$

Therefore,

$$\Theta(t) \equiv \beta \, \exp\{-\lambda t\} \int_{-\infty}^t \bar{\theta}(s,t) \exp\{\beta s\}\, ds,$$

the present discounted value, at time t, of the expected life-time taxes to be paid by all those currently alive, is given by:

$$\Theta(t) = \exp\{nt\}\left[t_0 \int_t^\infty \varepsilon(v) \exp\left\{-\int_t^v (r(u) + \lambda)\, du\right\} dv \qquad (2.26)\right.$$

$$\left. + \left(\frac{t_1\beta}{\beta - t_2}\right) \int_t^\infty \varepsilon(v) \exp\left\{-\int_t^v (r(u) + \lambda - t_2)\, du\right\} dv\right]$$

It is easily checked that the effect on $\Theta(t)$ of an increase in t_1 with t_2 reduced so as to keep $T(t)$ constant is given by:

$$\left.\frac{d\Theta(t)}{dt_1}\right|_{dT(t)=0} = -\beta \exp\{nt\}\int_t^\infty (v-t)\varepsilon(v) \tag{2.27}$$

$$\times \exp\left\{-\int_t^v (r(u) + \lambda - t_2)\,du\right\}dv < 0$$

Balanced-budget redistribution from the young to the old therefore reduces the present discounted value of the total future taxes to be paid by those currently alive. Since all those currently alive have the same marginal propensities to spend out of comprehensive wealth, the result will be an increase in aggregate private consumption and a reduction in private saving. Since we are considering a balanced-budget operation, total private plus public saving also falls.

THE SUPPLY SIDE OF THE MODEL

To motivate the specification of the production side of the model it is necessary to remember that I am trying to construct the simplest possible competitive endogenous growth model with Yaari-Blanchard-Weil OLG demographics. I therefore want the aggregate production function to be linear in the aggregate capital stock, while the structure of property rights has to be such that in equilibrium new generations are born with endowments whose value rises at the endogenous rate of growth. We cannot achieve both objectives if the individual firm's production function were to be specified as linear in that firm's own capital stock, with no other essential scarce inputs such as labor, that are typically assumed to be owned by new-born households, even in the absence of private intergenerational gifts. We would be hard pushed to think of a plausible property rights structure that would give the new generations a claim to some share of the capital stock in existence when they are born. One way to ensure that the newborn can join fully in the endogenous growth game is to allow workers to appropriate the quasi-rents created by an economy-production externality. This is the approach adopted here.

The representative firm, i, produces a homogeneous output y_i with a production function, given in equation (2.28), which is positive for positive inputs, increasing, constant returns to scale in its two inputs, physical capital, K_i, and labor input in efficiency units $\mathcal{J}_i$, strictly concave and at least twice continuously differentiable. I define $k_i \equiv K_i/\mathcal{J}_i$:

$$y_i = F(K_i, \mathcal{J}_i) = \mathcal{J}_i f(K_i/\mathcal{J}_i) = \mathcal{J}_i f(k_i) \tag{2.28}$$

$\mathcal{J}_i$, which measures the ith firm labor input in efficiency units, is the product of L_i, the quantity of raw labor power hired by firm i and ε, the quality index of labor, which is the same for all firms.[11] I shall assume that, in the spirit of Sheshinski (1967), quality or efficiency is measured by the economy-wide capital-labor ratio.[12] The interpretation of "capital" should therefore probably be rather broader than plant, equipment and structures. Extreme simplicity is the main virtue of this model:

$$\mathcal{J}_i = \varepsilon L_i \tag{2.29a}$$

$$\varepsilon = K/L \tag{2.29b}$$

where $K \equiv \sum_{i=1}^{N} K_i$ and $L \equiv \sum_{i=1}^{N} L_i$

Firms hire workers and rent capital to maximize profits. They are price takers and also take ε to be independent of their own choices of K_i and L_i. This creates a positive externality in the private accumulation of capital and a negative externality in the use of labor.[13] Let $\tilde{w}$ be the wage of raw labor power (say the rental rate of one hour of labor time, where the hours per worker can vary with age, as determined by the parameter π). It follows that

$$\tilde{w} = \varepsilon [f(k_i) - k_i f'(k_i)]$$

The rental of a unit of efficiency labor, w, is of course given by:

$$w = \tilde{w}/\varepsilon = f(k_i) - k_i f'(k_i)$$

The private profit maximizing demand for capital is given by:

$$r = f'(k_i) - \delta$$

Here $\delta \geq 0$ is the constant exponential rate of depreciation of capital.

Letting $Y \equiv \sum_{i=1}^{N} y_i$, I aggregate across all firms to get

$$Y = \sum_{i=1}^{N} F\left(K_i, \frac{K}{L}L_i\right)$$

Using the fact that all firms are identical and the linear homogeneity of $F(\cdot, \cdot)$, the aggregate production function can be written as

$$Y = F(K,K) = Kf(1)$$

Defining $a = f(1) > 0$, I can write aggregate output as linear in K:

$$Y = aK \tag{2.30}$$

Note that the social return to an additional unit of physical capital is given by $a - \delta = f(1) - \delta$, while the private gross marginal product of capital, which I shall denote a', is given by $a' \equiv f'(1) < f(1) \equiv a$. Private capital accumulation does not allow for the non-appropriable benefit of raising the average quality of the labor force. In this model, the interest rate and the real wage are fixed by technology and constant:

$$r = f'(1) - \delta = a' - \delta \tag{2.31}$$

$$w = f(1) - f'(1) = a - a' \tag{2.32}$$

Since the economy is not viable if the net social marginal product of capital is negative, I assume:

$$a - \delta > 0$$

The net private marginal product of capital can either be positive or negative.

Note that this specification of the production technology would avoid a problem, signaled by Jones and Manuelli (1990), that can arise in finite-lifetime (Samuelson-Diamond) OLG models of endogenous growth. They consider a model where the one-sector technology of production in principle permits endogenous growth. The consumers' side of the model is the standard two-period Samuelson-Diamond OLG model without intergenerational gifts and bequests, in which the young have a positive endowment of labor that is constant from generation to generation. Growth peters out in the long run because the young generation does not have enough resources to purchase an ever increasing capital stock from the old. Our equations (2.28) and (2.29a,b) rule out this problem. The value of the labor endowment per worker, which is constant in physical units, is augmented one-for-one with the aggregate physical capital stock, which increases the efficiency of this physical quantity of labor.

In the Yaari-Blanchard-Weil OLG model of this chapter, there is of course no life-cycle pattern of saving. Since everyone, regardless of age, has the same remaining expected lifetime (which may be infinite), the young have the same marginal propensity to consume out of wealth, η, as the old. The Jones and Manuelli problem does show up in another form, however. Alogoskoufis and van der Ploeg (1990a,b, 1991) used the same aggregate production function, given in equation (2.30), as is used here. The individual firm's production function, however, was given by $y_i = F(K_i, K/N)$, $i = 1, \ldots, N$, with F linear homogeneous. There is an externality in the use of capital, because each individual firm takes the average capital stock (per firm) K/N as independent of its own choice of K_i. There is no labor input in the production function.

In the description of their model Alogoskoufis and van der Ploeg do not include labor among the productive inputs or endow new generations at birth with labor or with any other claims on resources that would give them a stake in the economy, let alone a stake that grows in value at the rate required to sustain endogenous growth. In terms of our model of consumption, $\bar{h}(t,t) = 0$, and the newborn cannot get into the game.[14] The model also cannot explain how those already in the game, who own the capital stock, ever got to own any capital if they started off at birth without any claim on valuable scarce resources.[15] The problem is one of property rights assignment. Fortunately, they then proceed as if workers are born endowed with claim on an equal per capita share of the marginal product of K/N. This makes their model effectively equivalent to the one of this chapter.

In Buiter and Kletzer (1991a,b), which develops an endogenous growth model with a Samuelson-Diamond (3-period) OLG demographic structure, the endowment of the young grows at a rate sufficient to sustain endogenous growth, but through a different mechanism. Equations (2.28) and (2.29a) are kept, but equation (2.29b) is replaced by something like

$$\frac{\dot{\varepsilon}}{\varepsilon} = \xi\left(\sum_j \frac{e_i}{\varepsilon}, \; ; \; \cdot\right) \qquad \xi_1 > 0$$

ε may be interpreted as the economy-wide stock of useful knowledge; e_j are the resources (education and training) spent by the jth household to augment its own knowledge and skills. There again is an externality because each household ignores the effect of its own education and training on ε, and thus on the productivity of other households currently alive or yet to be born (ε does not die when the households that contributed to it die: human capital may die but the stock of useful knowledge survives unscathed). This two-capital-goods structure permits endogenous growth.[16]

The Impossibility of Dynamic Inefficiency

From equation (2.22) we get

$$\frac{\dot{K}}{K} = a - \delta - \frac{C}{K} - \frac{G}{K}$$

The growth rate of capital is, since C and G are non-negative, never higher than the net social marginal product of capital. This economy, with its linear technology, is therefore never dynamically inefficient.[17] Clearly, a necessary condition for dynamic inefficiency is that the marginal product of capital be able to fall below the average product. With output linear in the capital stock, the social marginal and average products of capital are always equal to each other and constant.[18]

SAVING AND LONG-RUN GROWTH

To simplify the exposition, I shall start the analysis with the case of age-independent labor power ($\pi = 0$) and age-independent taxes ($t_1 = 0$ or $t_2 = 0$). Since capital is the natural "scale variable" of this economy, I shall consider the behavior over time of the growth rate of capital, of consumption per unit of capital, $C/K \equiv c$, and of public debt per unit of capital, $B/K \equiv b$. In order for the system to have steady states, I will treat government consumption per unit of capital, $G/K \equiv g$, and lump-sum taxes per unit of capital, $T/K \equiv \tau$, as the policy instruments.

Let $\mathcal{GK} \equiv \dot{K}/K$. From equations (2.17), (2.18), (2.21), (2.22), (2.30), (2.31) and (2.32), I obtain the following system of equations, familiar from the work of Alogoskoufis and van der Ploeg (1990a,b):

$$\mathcal{GK} = a - \delta - g - c \tag{2.33}$$

$$\dot{c} = -\eta\beta + [\gamma^{-1}(a' - \delta - \rho) + n - a + \delta + g]c - \eta\beta b + c^2 \tag{2.34}$$

$$\dot{b} = (a' - a + g)b + g - \tau + cb \tag{2.35}$$

Note that, since r is constant, η is also constant and given by

$$\eta = \left(\frac{\gamma - 1}{\gamma}\right)(a' - \delta) + \lambda + \frac{\rho}{\gamma} \tag{2.36}$$

I first consider the case where there is no public debt outstanding, $b = 0$, and the budget is balanced continuously through endogenous variations in the ratio of lump-sum, age-independent taxes to aggregate capital, τ.[19]

In this case the dynamics of the system is captured by a single quadratic differential equation in consumption per capita:

$$\dot{c} = -\eta\beta + [\gamma^{-1}(a' - \delta - \rho) + n - a + \delta + g]c + c^2 \tag{2.37}$$

Figure 2.1a shows the parabola representing equation (2.37) in $c-\dot{c}$ space, referred to henceforth as the *consumption parabola*. There are two stationary equilibria, one for a positive value of c (shown as c_1^*) and one for a negative value (shown as c_2^*).

$$c_{1,2}^* = 0.5\Big[-[\gamma^{-1}(a' - \delta - \rho) + n - a + \delta + g] \tag{2.38}$$

$$\pm \{[\gamma^{-1}(a' - \delta - \rho) + n - a + \delta + g]^2 + 4\eta\beta\}^{0.5}\Big]$$

Only the positive stationary equilibrium is economically meaningful. Note that c is a non-predetermined state variable and that c_1^* is an unstable equilibrium. Figure 2.1b graphs the inverse (with slope -1) linear relationship between

Figure 2.1

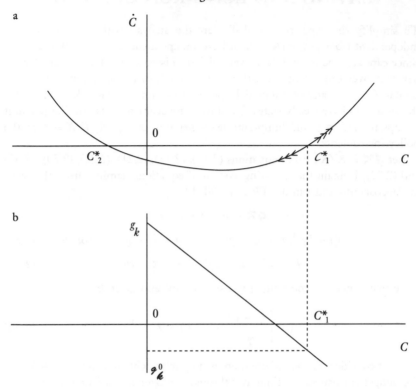

$\mathcal{GK}$ and c given in equation (2.33), referred to henceforth as the *capital growth line*. The minimum of the parabola need not be for positive value of c. Even if the economy is viable ($a > \delta$), the intercept of the line $\mathcal{GK} = a - \delta - g - c$ in figure 2.1b could be negative for a sufficiently large value of g. Even when the intercept is positive, the common steady-state growth rate of capital, output, and consumption can be negative, as shown in figure 2.1b.

A Balanced-Budget Increase in Public Consumption

When there is a balanced-budget increase in public consumption, the capital growth line shifts down vertically by the increase in g (as shown in figure 2.2a), and the consumption parabola shifts up and to the left, reducing the long-run equilibrium value of c. As shown in figure 2.2b, the effect on the long-run growth rate of capital is unambiguously negative: while the long-run consumption/capital ratio falls, it falls by less than the increase in the government consumption/capital ratio.

Figure 2.2

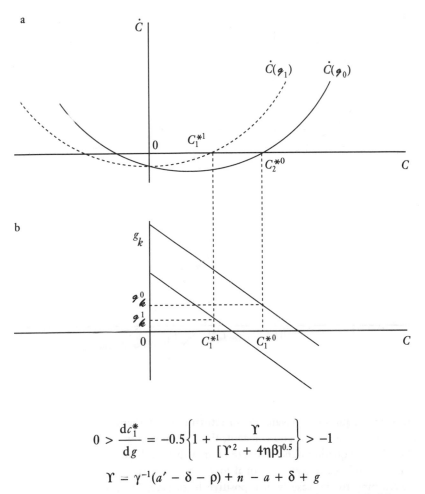

$$0 > \frac{\mathrm{d}c_1^*}{\mathrm{d}g} = -0.5\left\{1 + \frac{\Upsilon}{[\Upsilon^2 + 4\eta\beta]^{0.5}}\right\} > -1$$

$$\Upsilon = \gamma^{-1}(a' - \delta - \rho) + n - a + \delta + g$$

This result, that an increase in public consumption crowds out capital formation as well as private consumption is different from the result that would have been obtained in the representative agent version of the model (the special case where $\beta = 0$). When $\beta = 0$, government consumption only crowds out private consumption in the long run, leaving capital formation unchanged. More generally, in the representative agent model, any unanticipated, immediate permanent increase in public consumption causes an equal reduction in private consumption, in the short run as well as in the long run. Note from equation (2.37) that when $\beta = 0$, the $\dot{c}$ equation is homogeneous. There is a trivial stationary solution ($c_2^* = 0$) and a sensible stationary solution ($c_1^* = -[\gamma^{-1}(a' - \delta - \rho) + n - a + \delta + g]$ and $g^*x = \gamma^{-1}(a' - \delta - \rho) - \lambda$). Note that since the interest

Figure 2.3

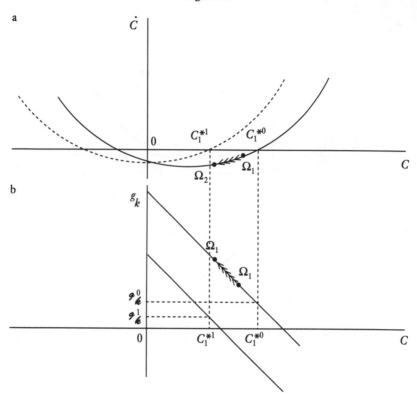

rate (which equals the private rate of return to capital) and the time preference rate both are exogenous and constant, they will not in general be equal to each other. From equation (2.6c) the rate of growth of individual consumption will, in and out of steady state, be equal to $\gamma^{-1}(a' - \delta - \rho)$.

Returning to the case with a positive birth rate, the transition to the new stationary equilibrium will be instantaneous if the increase in g is unanticipated and permanent. With K predetermined at the moment of the fiscal shock, the decline in c from c_1^{*0} to c_1^{*1} must be due to a fall in the level of consumption. Afterwards the rate of growth of aggregate consumption equals the new lower rate of growth of capital. If public spending is not intrinsically valued, this increase in public spending constitutes an unambiguous worsening of welfare.

If the announcement date of the increase in public consumption (t_0) precedes the implementation date (t_1), the behaviour over time of c and g_K is as shown in figure 2.3a,b. Starting from a stationary equilibrium at c_1^{*0} with a capital growth rate g^0_K, the level of consumption jumps to a lower level (a point such as Ω_1 in figure 2.3a) immediately (at t_0) when the unexpected news about the future

Figure 2.4

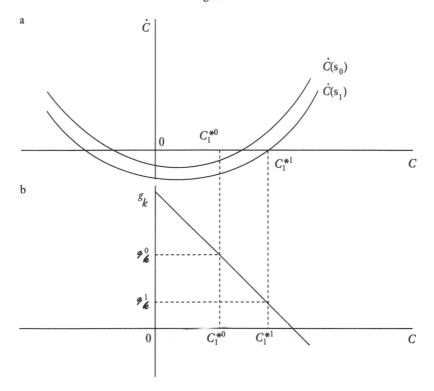

a

$\dot{C}$

$\dot{C}(s_0)$

$\dot{C}(s_1)$

0   C_1^{*0}

C_1^{*1} C

b

g_k

g_k^0

g_k^1

0   C_1^{*0} C_1^{*1} C

higher taxes associated with the future higher public spending arrives. Note that this initial decline in consumption is smaller than when the policy change is immediate ($t_0 = t_1$). Between the announcement date (t_0) and the implementation date (t_1) the level of consumption per unit of capital moves continuously from Ω_1 to Ω_2. At the implementation date t_1, the level of c is at its new steady state value and its rate of change jumps from the negative value at Ω_2 to zero. The rate of growth of the capital increases at the announcement date from $g^0\mathcal{K}$ to the value of $g\mathcal{K}$ at Ω_1 in figure 2.3a. Between the announcement date and the implementation date $g\mathcal{K}$ continues to rise. At t_1 the system has reached point Ω_2 and the rate of growth of the capital stock declines to its new, lower long-run equilibrium value.

An Increase in the Time Preference Rate

For reasons of space I henceforth only consider unanticipated announcements of immediate permanent shocks. As shown in figure 2.4a,b an increase in the pure rate of time preference leaves the capital growth line in figure 2.4b

Figure 2.5

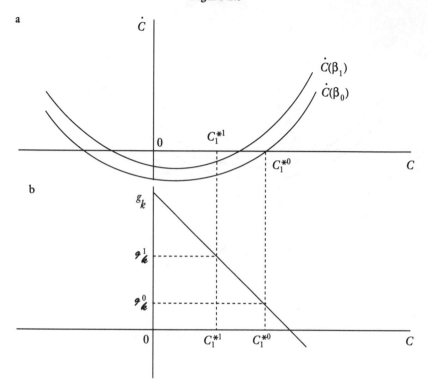

unaffected while the consumption parabola in figure 2.4a shifts down every-where. With the unanticipated permanent shock, the transition to the new higher steady-state level of consumption per unit of capital and lower steady-state growth rate of capital is immediate. Greater impatience results in more consumption in the short run but less growth and consumption in the long run.[20]

A Higher Birth Rate

As shown in figure 2.5a,b an increase in β leaves the capital growth line un-changed and shifts the consumption parabola up.[21] The new long-run equilib-rium has a higher growth rate and a lower consumption-capital ratio.[22] When the increase in the birth rate is unexpected, immediate, and permanent, the transition to the new steady state is immediate.[23]

A Reduction in Life Expectancy

Figure 2.4a,b can also serve (qualitatively) to illustrate the effects of an increase in λ, the instantaneous probability of death. As expected, shorter horizons boost the long-run consumption/capital ratio and reduce long-run growth.[24] The capital growth line does not shift and the consumption parabola shifts down.[25] If the reduction in life expectancy is unanticipated, immediate and permanent, the transition to the new steady state will be immediate.

Note that when the birth rate and the death rate increase by equal amounts, keeping the rate of growth of population constant, the model predicts a net reduction in the saving rate. Long-run consumption per unit of capital increases and the growth rate of the capital stock decreases:

$$\frac{\partial c_1^*}{\partial \beta} + \frac{\partial c_1^*}{\partial \lambda} = (\eta + \beta)\{[\gamma^{-1}(a' - \delta - \rho) + n - a + \delta + g]^2 + 4\eta\beta\}^{-0.5}$$

An Increase in the Intertemporal Elasticity of Substitution

It is obvious that the capital growth line is unaffected by the intertemporal elasticity of substitution $1/\gamma$. From equations (2.36) and (2.37) we obtain that:

$$\left. \frac{\partial \dot{c}}{\partial \frac{1}{\gamma}} \right|_{c \text{ given}} = (\beta + c)(a' - \delta + \rho)$$

The consumption parabola will shift up (down) if the private return to capital $a' - \delta = r$ exceeds (is below) the subjective time preference rate ρ. From equation (2.6c) we know that if $r > \rho$, individual consumption is low but rising. If less importance is attached to the smoothing of consumption over time ($1/\gamma$ increases), we should expect to move to an equilibrium with a lower level but a higher growth rate of consumption.[26] This is the case where the consumption parabola shifts up, as in figure 2.5a. If the change is unanticipated and permanent, the transition to the new steady state with its lower value of c and its higher value of $g\mathcal{K}$ will be instantaneous.

Capital Rental Taxes

A tax ζ_K on the rental income of capital (with the revenue returned as equal per capita lump-sum transfers) changes the arbitrage condition equating the returns on bonds to the returns from owning capital to:

$$r = f'(1) - \delta - \zeta_K$$

An increase in the capital income tax rate ζ_K is therefore equivalent in our model to a reduction in a' with a unchanged. The tax leaves the before-tax private marginal product of capital (and the social marginal product of capital) unchanged, and reduces the after-tax private rate of return to capital one-for-one. It is clear that an increase in ζ_K does not shift the capital growth line. Its effect on the consumption parabola is given by:

$$\left. \frac{\partial \dot{c}}{\partial \zeta_K} \right|_{c \text{ given}} = \left(1 - \frac{1}{\gamma}\right)\beta - \frac{1}{\gamma}c$$

In the frequently analyzed logarithmic utility case ($\gamma = 1$) the consumption parabola shifts down, as in figure 2.4a,b, raising long-run c and reducing long-run *gK*. For this result to be reversed and the consumption parabola to shift up, it must be true that $\gamma^{-1} < \frac{\beta}{\beta + c}$.[27] Note that in the representative agent special case of our model ($\beta = 0$), the (income-compensated) reduction in the rate of interest always unambiguously reduces saving. The consumption parabola shifts down, thus raising the long-run value of c and reducing the growth rate of capital.[28]

Considering taxes on interest income ζ_r does not add to the analysis, as the marginal private and social products of capital are unaffected. The before-tax interest rate would rise to offset the interest tax and leave the after-tax rate of interest unchanged.

An Unfunded Social Security Retirement Scheme

To study the long-run growth effects of the unfunded social security retirement scheme discussed on pp. 73–5, I set $\pi = g = 0$ and consider balanced budget schemes with $B \equiv 0$. I define:

$$\omega \equiv \Omega/K$$

From equations (2.15), (2.29b) and (2.31):

$$\omega(t) = \frac{\beta t_1 t_2}{\beta - t_2} \int_t^\infty \frac{K(v)}{K(t)} \exp\{-(a' - \delta + \beta - t_2)(v - t)\}\,dv \quad (2.39)$$

Note that the scale variable in the tax function, ε, is given by $\varepsilon = K/L$.

The equations of motion and the capital growth equation for this case are given in equations (2.40) through (2.42):

$$\dot{c} = -\eta\beta + [\gamma^{-1}(a' - \delta - \rho) + n - a + \delta]c + c^2 + \eta\omega \quad (2.40)$$

$$\dot{\omega} = (a' - a + \beta - t_2 + c)\omega - t_1 t_2 \left(\frac{\beta}{\beta - t_2}\right) \quad (2.41)$$

$$\mathcal{GK} = a - \delta - c \tag{2.42}$$

Note that the forward–looking integral in equation (2.39) exists only if $r + \beta - t_2$ exceeds the growth rate of capital $\mathcal{GK}$, in steady state. Also, ω cannot change sign for given t_1 and t_2. In what follows I only consider small changes in t_1 and t_2 that do not change the signs of these two tax parameters. For reasons of space, I shall look only at the case where both t_1 and t_2 are positive, which implies that ω is always positive.

The $\dot{\omega} = 0$ locus is given by

$$c = -[a' - a + \beta - t_2 - t_1 t_2 \left(\frac{\beta}{\beta - t_2} \right) \omega^{-1}] \qquad c \geq 0 \tag{2.43}$$

This is the truncated (for $c \geq 0$ and $\omega > 0$) rectangular hyperbola shown in figure 2.6. Its vertical asymptote is the vertical axis ($\omega = 0$) and its horizontal asymptote is $-(a' - a + \beta - t_2)$. For concreteness I assume in figure 2.6 that $-(a' - a + \beta - t_2) > 0$.

The $\dot{c} = 0$ locus is the "parabola on its side", shown in figure 2.6 given by

$$c^2 + [\gamma^{-1}(a' - \delta - \rho) + n - a + \delta]c + \eta(\omega - \beta) = 0. \tag{2.44}$$

Note that, on the $\dot{c} = 0$ locus, when $c = 0$, $\omega = \beta > 0$. In order for (2.44) to possess real non-negative solutions for c, we require

$$\omega \leq \beta + [\gamma^{-1}(a' - \delta - \rho) + n - a + \delta]^2 / 4\eta$$

and

$$- [\gamma^{-1}(a' - \delta - \rho) + n - a + \delta]$$
$$\pm \{[\gamma^{-1}(a' - \delta - \rho) + n - a + \delta]^2 - 4\eta(\omega - \beta)\}^{\frac{1}{2}} \geq 0.$$

Even when these conditions are satisfied, there need not be non-negative values of c and ω that solve both (2.43) and (2.44). In the rest of this subsection I only consider values of the parameters for which two stationary solutions with positive values for both ω and c do exist.

The long-run effect on c and w of an increase in t_1 with t_2 adjusting according to equation (2.25) so as to keep total tax receipts unchanged, yields:

$$\left. \frac{dc^*}{dt_1} \right|_{dT=0} = -\eta \left[\frac{\beta - t_2}{t_1} + \frac{\beta}{\omega^*} \right] \Delta^{-1} \tag{2.45a}$$

$$\left. \frac{d\omega^*}{dt_1} \right|_{dT=0} = (2c^* + [\gamma^{-1}(a' - \delta - \rho) + n - a + \delta]) \left[\frac{\beta - t_2}{t_1} + \frac{\beta}{\omega^*} \right] \Delta^{-1}$$

$$\tag{2.45b}$$

Figure 2.6

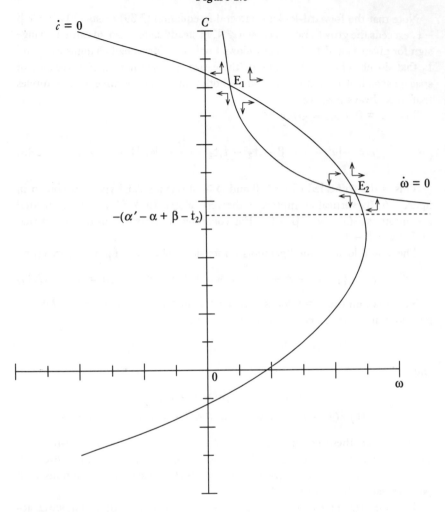

$$\Delta = \eta - (2c^* + [\gamma^{-1}(a' - \delta - \rho) + n - a + \delta]) \frac{t_1 t_2 \beta}{(\beta - t_2)(\omega^*)^2} \qquad (2.45c)$$

At a stationary equilibrium (c^*, w^*), the non-linear equations of motion can be approximated by the following system of linear differential equations with constant coefficients:

$$\begin{bmatrix} \dot{c} \\ \dot{\omega} \end{bmatrix} = \begin{bmatrix} 2c^* + [\gamma^{-1}(a' - \delta - \rho) + n - a + \delta] & \eta \\ \omega^* & \dfrac{t_1 t_2 \beta}{\omega^*(\beta - t_2)} \end{bmatrix} \begin{bmatrix} c - c^* \\ \omega - \omega^* \end{bmatrix} \qquad (2.46)$$

Figure 2.7

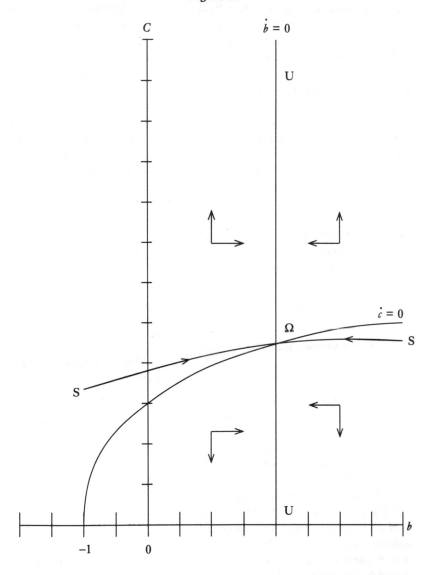

Since both state variables, c and ω, are non-predetermined, a stationary equilibrium which is locally unstable would guarantee a (locally) unique continuously convergent solution. Such a configuration is shown in figure 2.6 as E_1. Note that the determinant of the coefficient matrix on the right-hand side of equation (2.46), D, is given by $D = -\omega^* \Delta$. If the configuration of the stationary equilibrium is locally completely unstable, then D must be positive and Δ will be negative. Note that for this to be possible, it must be the case that $2c + > 0$. The second stationary equilibrium in figure 2.6, E_2, is a saddlepoint, and there is a (one-dimensional) local continuum of initial conditions from which the system will converge to that stationary equilibrium.

When Δ is negative (at a locally completely unstable stationary equilibrium such as E_1 in figure 2.6), one sees from equation (2.45a) that the stationary equilibrium value of c increases when t_1 is increased and t_2 reduced in a balanced-budget manner (when there is an increase in the scale of the unfunded social security retirement scheme). The long-run equilibrium value of ω declines. Graphically, the $\dot{\omega}$ locus shifts down when t_1 is increased and t_2 reduced with total taxes receipts constant.

When we take the locally completely unstable stationary equilibrium (E_1 in figure 2.6) as the one governing actual behavior, the transition to the new steady state following an unexpected, immediate and permanent increase in the scale of the unfunded social security retirement scheme will be instantaneous.

Finally, from the capital growth equation we again note that, as always except for the case where exhaustive public spending is raised, the decline in the growth rate of capital equals the increase in c.

Deficit Financing of a Tax Cut

The last case I consider will be the debt financing of a temporary cut in lump-sum taxes. For simplicity I again set $\pi = t_1 = t_r = 0$. The public spending/capital ratio g is also set equal to zero. There are now two state variables, c and b, whose behavior is governed by equations (2.47) and (2.48).

$$\dot{c} = -\eta\beta(1 + b) + [\gamma^{-1}(a' - \delta - \rho) + n - a + \delta]c + c^2 \qquad (2.47)$$

$$\dot{b} = (a' - a + c)b - \tau \qquad (2.48)$$

Note that, with τ exogenous, the possibility of unstable public debt dynamics is built into the model. Since $a' < a$, a larger value of the level of the public debt/capital ratio, b, will be associated with a larger negative rate of change of the public debt/capital ratio, $\dot{b}$, for small values of c (that is for large values of $\mathcal{GK}$). For large values of c (for low or negative values of $\mathcal{GK}$), however, larger values of b are associated with larger positive values of $\dot{b}$. Clearly, with τ exogenous, instability is in the air.[29]

For illustrative purposes I consider a tax function that always causes the public debt/capital ratio to converge to a unique stationary equilibrium value. It is given in equation (2.49).

$$\tau = \tau_0 + cb \qquad (2.49)$$

In addition to the exogenous component τ_0 (assumed constant), there is an endogenous component which exactly offsets the term cb in equation (2.48). With this tax function, the debt dynamics are now governed by:

$$\dot{b} = (a' - a)b - \tau_0 \qquad (2.50)$$

Since the constant private marginal product of capital a' is always less than the private (and public) average product of capital a, b always converges monotonically to its long-run equilibrium value b^* given by

$$b^* = (a' - a)^{-1}\tau_0 \qquad (2.51)$$

The $\dot{c} = 0$ locus is unaffected by the nature of the fiscal rule. It is given by the non-negative solutions to

$$c^2 + [\gamma^{-1}(a' - \delta - \rho) + n - a + \delta]c - \eta\beta(1 + b) = 0$$

In ω, c space, this is again a parabola "on its side." Economically the only interesting case is where $b \geq -1$. Since $K \geq 0$, $b = 1$ implies $B = -K \leq 0$. The total value of all productive resources in this economy is K. When $B = -K$, the government (as net lender to the private sector) effectively owns the entire stock of productive resources in the economy. The government clearly cannot lend more than that in this closed system, as there are no remaining private resources against which these loans can be secured. With $b \geq -1$, there is one positive stationary solution given by

$$c = \frac{1}{2}\Big[-[\gamma^{-1}(a' - \delta - \rho) + n - a + \delta] \qquad (2.52)$$

$$+ \{[\gamma^{-1}(a' - \delta - \rho) + n - a + \delta]^2 + 4\eta\beta(1 + b)\}^{\frac{1}{2}}\Big]$$

In $b-c$ space, the $\dot{c} = 0$ locus, shown in figure 2.7, starts at $b = -1$ and $c = 0$. For $b > -1$, c increases monotonically with b, but at a decreasing rate. In the limit as b goes to infinity, the slope of the locus goes to zero.

The $\dot{b} = 0$ locus is vertical in $b-c$ space. Since we only consider values of b greater than -1, it follows from equation (2.51) that we require

$$\tau_0 < a - a'$$

If this restriction is satisfied, there will be a unique stationary equilibrium, Ω, in figure 2.7. Locally, the system near Ω is a saddlepoint. Since there is one predetermined state variable b and one non-predetermined state variable c, this means that there will only be one continuously convergent solution. For a given value of τ_0, SS is the unique convergent saddlepath. The "most divergent" solution trajectory UU coincides with the $\dot{b} = 0$ curve. All solution trajectories other than SS will have an asymptote at UU (even though this may take them into the infeasible $c < 0$ region).

Figure 2.8a,b shows the response of c, b and $\mathcal{GK}$, the growth rate of the capital stock, to an unanticipated permanent reduction in τ_0. Since government exhaustive spending is unchanged, all this amounts to, as can be seen from the government intertemporal budget constraint given in equation (2.20), is a

Figure 2.8

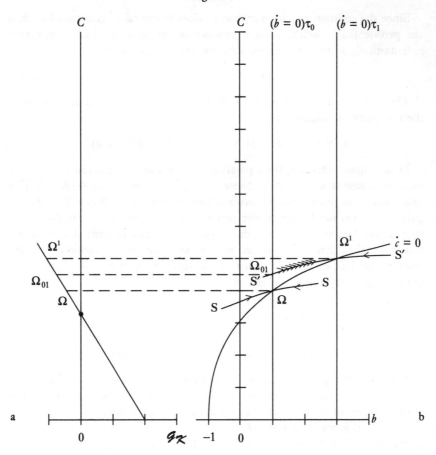

postponement of taxes that are constant in present discounted value (using the real interest rate r as the discount rate). Because the private sector effectively discounts at $r + \beta$ (since new tax-payers will be born who will share part of the burden of the postponed taxes), this intertemporal redistribution of taxation is also an intergenerational redistribution of taxation that leaves those currently alive better off.

Starting from an initial stationary equilibrium at Ω in figure 2.8b, the level of consumption immediately increases to Ω_{01}, the point on $S'S'$, the convergent saddlepath through the new long-run equilibrium Ω', that lies vertically above Ω in figure 2.8b. In figure 2.8a this corresponds to a discontinuous reduction in the growth rate of capital and output, from Ω to Ω_{01}. After the initial jump-increase in consumption, the consumption/capital ratio and the debt/capital ratio increase continuously along the convergent saddlepath $S'S'$ towards their new long-run equilibrium values at Ω'. The capital growth rate declines continuously from Ω_{01} in figure 2.8a to Ω'. This confirms the results obtained by Alogoskoufis and van der Ploeg (1990a,b).

As demonstrated in Saint-Paul (1990), alternative consumption trajectories supported by different intertemporal redistributions of taxation cannot be Pareto-ranked. Government borrowing, with debt serviced through lump-sum taxation (or balanced-budget redistribution schemes using lump-sum taxes and transfers such as the unfunded social security retirement scheme analyzed earlier) merely redistributes intergenerationally. Postponing taxation by borrowing will favor current over future generations, but there are no efficiency issues involved. This may seem surprising, since we are in a second-best world: the private return on capital $a' - \delta$ is below the social return $a - \delta$. This inefficiency, however, is not affected in any way by the intergenerational redistribution effected by the government through borrowing or through unfunded social security retirement schemes.

CONCLUSION

If the production technology of the economy (broadly defined) permits endogenous growth, one obvious lesson is that fiscal policy changes and changes in the parameters that govern private behavior can have long-run *growth-rate* effects as well as long-run *level* effects. The welfare implications of this "magnification" of the effects of exogenous shocks on the growth rate are not as straightforward as the positive implications. As was pointed out by Saint-Paul (1990), balanced-budget redistribution towards the old and deficit financing of tax cuts (even age-independent tax cuts) will reduce the long-run growth rates of capital, output and consumption. As long as the taxes involved are lump-sum, however, the trajectory with the lower growth rate will not be Pareto-dominated by that with the higher growth rate. There is intergenerational redistribution, from the future generations towards the present ones, but no free lunches are being served or taken away.

Against that, of course, it should be pointed out that the magnitude of the intergenerational redistribution associated with a given policy change is enhanced in endogenous growth models. Reasonable social welfare functions may suggest policies more favorable to a higher savings rate, if the returns to saving and accumulation are bounded away from zero sufficiently strongly to permit endogenous growth. In any case, even if the efficiency consequences of policy are not magnified, the distributional consequences will be. Policy is therefore likely to matter more in endogenous growth models than in exogenous growth models.

A second lesson emerges as a by-product of one of the less attractive features of the one-sector endogenous growth model used in this paper: the constancy of the real interest rate. In this model, as in the "Unpleasant Monetarist Arithmetic" model of Sargent and Wallace (1984), there is financial crowding out: government borrowing reduces total national saving and, in a closed economy, displaces private capital formation. So does an increase in the scale of the social security retirement scheme. Still, there is no movement of interest rates in response to the policy changes (or changes in private behavior) that cause the financial crowding out. In the world of our model, those who view financial crowding out as mediated necessarily through higher real interest rates would fail to identify the effect of government financing on private capital formation.

A third lesson is mainly for educators: the analysis of the response of economic growth to a variety of private or government shocks is considerably more straightforward when the economy is represented by the simplest endogenous growth model than when it is represented by the simplest exogenous growth model.

NOTES

1 In the standard expected utility framework with a time-separable utility function, the precautionary saving motive is governed by the third derivative of the instantaneous utility function.

2 Note, however, that the existence of permanent effects on the growth rates of capital, output and consumption does not automatically imply the existence of large efficiency effects. On pp. 79–93 we shall see examples where public policy permanently affects the growth rate, but the alternative growth paths cannot be Pareto-ranked. There will be large welfare effects, but these take the form of intergenerational redistributions of welfare.

3 In the finite-horizon OLG model of Samuelson and Diamond, this specification of technology and property rights means that the problem flagged by Jones and Manuelli (1990), that the value of the endowment of the young may not keep up with the value of the capital owned by the old (which the young are supposed to purchase from the old in equilibrium), will not occur. A richer specification of technology and property rights that achieves the same purpose was used by Buiter and Kletzer (1991a,b). In the age-independent time horizon OLG model of this chapter, the life-cycle issues emphasized by Jones and Manuelli are absent. The problem of ensuring that the new generations are endowed with scarce resources whose value can grow at an endogenously determined rate remains, however.

4 $\gamma = 1$ corresponds to the case of log utility.

5 The only uncertainty modeled explicitly is the uncertainty concerning the time of one's demise. Consumers born at time s are assumed to know that the probability of surviving till time $t \geq s$ is $\exp\{-\lambda(t - s)\}$. This term augments the subjective discount factor, which become $\exp\{-(\rho + \lambda)(v - t)\}$ for someone discounting, at time t, the utility of consuming at time $v \geq t$. The model can then be treated as a perfect foresight model.

6   Note that

$$\dot{\eta} = \eta \left\{ \eta - \left[\left(\frac{\gamma - 1}{\gamma} \right) r + \lambda + \frac{1}{\gamma} \rho \right] \right\}.$$

In steady state this gives a non-zero solution

$$\eta = \left(\frac{\gamma - 1}{\gamma} \right) r + \lambda + \frac{1}{\gamma} \rho.$$

In the logarithmic utility case ($\gamma = 1$) this reduces to $\eta = \rho + \lambda$, both in and out of steady state.

7   The absence of involuntary or unintended bequests is due to the assumption of perfect annuities markets.

8   Government capital formation is not considered. Public consumption either is intrinsically useless or, if useful, enters the private utility function in an additively separable manner.

9   We shall also consider the effects of changes in G and B.

10   Saint-Paul considers a "twisting" of the wage-age profile, that is a larger value of π combined with a higher value of the starting wage at age zero. What we do in this paper is equivalent in terms of its impact effect on the savings rate.

11   Note that ε is also the scale factor applied to the tax function given in equation (2.9). This permits a well-behaved steady state to exist in the model but has no other significance.

12   Sheshinski (1967) actually suggested using the economy-wide stock of physical capital as the index of labor efficiency, not the economy-wide capital labor ratio. Using this alternative specification would of course generate a model with unbounded static increasing returns to scale, something we do not wish to contemplate even at this level of abstraction. Romer (1986) and Lucas (1988) developed models with increasing static returns to scale in which the quality of labor is augmented not by the accumulation of physical capital but rather by accumulation of knowledge and skills.

13   The private marginal product of capital is $a' - \delta$ and the social marginal product of capital $a - \delta$. The private marginal product of labor is $a - a'$, its social marginal product is zero.

14   Unless the government transfers resources to them, by making $\overline{\theta}(t, t)$ positive.

15   One way to endow the newborn with capital at birth is for the government to make a capital transfer to them or for the government to commit itself credibly to a future sequence of current transfer payments.

16   An attractive feature of this model is that it does not imply a constant real interest rate.

17   Note, however, that it is not Pareto-efficient because of the capital stock (or labor) externality.

18   We owe this point to Olivier Blanchard. It is spelled out formally in Saint-Paul (1990).

19   Note that while the ratio of aggregate taxes on labor income to the aggregate capital

stock varies endogenously, each individual private agent takes the amount he pays in taxes on labor income to be independent of his individual accumulation of capital. The tax therefore remains a lump–sum tax on labor income and does not become a capital income tax.

20 $\dfrac{\partial c_1^*}{\partial \rho} = 0.5\gamma^{-1}\left\{1 - \dfrac{[\gamma^{-1}(a' - \delta - \rho) + n - a + \delta + g] - 2\beta}{\{[\gamma^{-1}(a' - \delta - \rho) + n - a + \delta + g]^2 + 4\eta\beta\}^{0.5}}\right\} > 0$ 21

21 From equation (2.37) we obtain that $\left.\dfrac{\partial c}{\partial \beta}\right|_{c\ \text{given}} = -\eta + c$. From the aggregate

consumption function we know that $C = \eta(A + H - \Theta)$. Since $A = K$ in our case we have $c = \eta(1 + (H - \Theta)/K)$. If human capital net of the present discounted value of taxes on human capital is non-negative, then $c > \eta$. We assume this condition to hold.

22 $\dfrac{\partial c_1^*}{\partial \beta} = 0.5\left\{-1 + \dfrac{[\gamma^{-1}(a' - \delta - \rho) + n - a + \delta + g] + 2\eta}{\{[\gamma^{-1}(a' - \delta - \rho) + n - a + \delta + g]^2 + 4\eta\beta\}^{0.5}}\right\}$

$(\eta - c)\{[\gamma^{-1}(a' - \delta - \rho) + n - a + \delta + g]^2 + 4\eta\beta\}^{-0.5} < 0$ provided human capital is positive.

23 An increase in the rate at which labor power decays with age, π, has exactly the same effect on c as an increase in the birth rate.

24 $\dfrac{\partial c_1^*}{\partial \lambda} = 0.5\left\{1 + \dfrac{-[\gamma^{-1}(a' - \delta - \rho) + n - a + \delta + g] + 2\beta}{\{[\gamma^{-1}(a' - \delta - \rho) + n - a + \delta + g]^2 + 4\eta\beta\}^{0.5}}\right\}$

$= (c + \beta)\{[\gamma^{-1}(a' - \delta - \rho) + n - a + \delta + g]^2 + 4\eta\beta\}^{-0.5} > 0.$

25 From equation (2.37) it follows that $\left.\dfrac{\partial \dot{c}}{\partial \lambda}\right|_{c\ \text{given}} \equiv -(\beta + c) < 0.$

26 $\dfrac{\partial c_1^*}{\partial \beta} = -(c + \beta)\,(a' - \delta - \rho)\,(2c + [\gamma^{-1}(a' - \delta - \rho) + n - a + \delta + g])^{-1}.$

27 Let the consumption/output ratio be 0.8 and the annual capital–output ratio 3.3. This means the $c = 0.24$. With $\beta = 0.01$, the intertemporal elasticity of substitution would have to be less than 0.04 for the consumption parabola to shift up instead of down as the capital income tax rate increases. Those who pretend to know about these things argue that this is too low a number. Halving or doubling the birth rate doesn't change that conclusion.

28 See Engel and Kletzer [1990] for the analysis of related issues in the context of an open economy OLG model with tariff revenues redistributed as a residence–based wealth subsidy.

29 Even with τ exogenous, the model is not necessarily badly behaved everywhere. There can, e.g., be a stationary equilibrium with a relatively small value of c and a negative value of b that constitutes, locally, a saddlepoint. The $b = 0$ locus in c–b space is a rectangular hyperbola with equation $c = a - a' + b^{-1}\tau$. Note that $c \geqslant 0$

Figure A

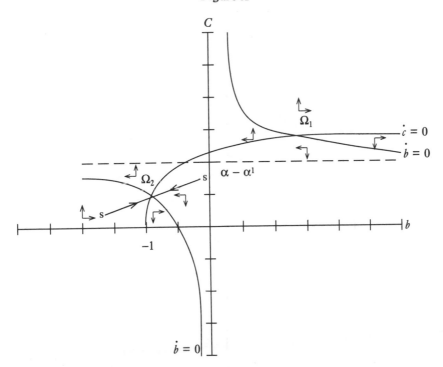

is equivalent to $\tau/b \geqslant a' - a < 0$. Negative values of b are therefore certainly not ruled out. In the following figures A and B some possible configurations are shown. Figure A is for a positive value of τ. There always is a high c stationary equilibrium, with a positive value of b, Ω_1, that is completely unstable. There may also be a low c equilibrium with a negative value of b, Ω_2, that is a saddlepoint. This will occur if $\tau/(a' - a) > -1$. A higher value of τ will raise the value of c (lower the value of $\dot{K}/K$) at the high c equilibrium (Ω_1) by shifting up the positive segment of the $\dot{b} = 0$ schedule. It will lower the value of c (raise $\dot{K}/K$) at the the low c equilibrium (Ω_2) by shifting down the negative segment of the $\dot{b} = 0$ schedule. In figure B, τ is negative. As shown in the figure, there may be no stationary equilibrium with a positive value of c. If there are two equilibria (not shown), they will both have the same sign for b. All this is sufficiently bizarre not to devote more time to it.

REFERENCES

Alogoskoufis, George S. and van der Ploeg, Frederick 1990a: Endogenous Growth and Overlapping Generation. Birkbeck College, University of London, Discussion Paper in Economics, November 26.

Figure B

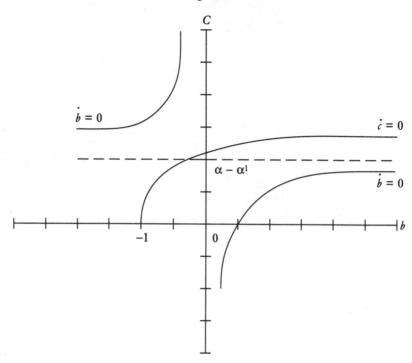

Alogoskoufis, George S. and van der Ploeg, Frederick 1990b: On budgetary policies and economic growth. Centre for Economic Research Discussion Paper, No. 496, December.

Alogoskoufis, George S. and van der Ploeg, Frederick 1991: On budgetary policies, growth and external deficits in an interdependent world. Paper presented at the NBER/CEPR/TCER Conference on Fiscal Policies in Open Macro Economies, January, Tokyo.

Barro, Robert J. 1990: Government Spending in a Simple Model of Endogenous Growth. *Journal of Political Economy*, 98, October.

Barro, Robert J. and Sala-i-Martin Xavier 1990: Public Finance in Models of Economic Growth, *NBER Working Paper* No. 3362, May.

Bernanke, B. and Gertler M. 1987: Banking and Macroeconomic Equilibrium. In W. A. Barnett and K. Singleton (eds.), *New Approaches to Monetary Economics*, Cambridge, Cambridge University Press: 89–111.

Blanchard, Olivier J. 1985: Debt, Deficits and Finite Horizons. *Journal of Political Economy*, 93, No. 2, April, 223–47.

Buiter, Willem H. 1988: Death, birth, productivity growth and debt neutrality. *Economic Journal*, 98, June, 279–93. Also in Willem H. Buiter, *Macroeconomic theory and stabilization policy*. Manchester: Manchester University Press (1989), 315–31.

Buiter, Willem H. 1989: Debt neutrality, Professor Vickrey and Henry George's "single tax" *Economics Letters*, 29, 43–7. Also in Willem H. Buiter, *Principles of Budgetary and Financial Policy*. MIT Press, 1990.

Buiter, Willem H. 1990: Debt neutrality, Redistribution and consumer heterogeneity. In W. H. Buiter, *Principles of Budgetary Financial Policy*, MIT Press, 1990. Also in *Essays in Honor of James Tobin*, W. C. Brainard et al. (eds). MIT Press, forthcoming.

Buiter, Willem H. and Kletzer, Kenneth M. 1991: Persistent differences in national productivity growth rates with a common technology and free capital mobility. *Journal of Japanese and International Economies*, 5, 325–53.

Buiter, Willem H. and Kletzer, Kenneth M. 1992a: Permanent Productivity Growth Differentials in an Integrated Global Economy. Yale University mimeo, June.

Buiter, Willem H. and Kletzer, Kenneth M. 1992b: Fiscal Policies and Productivity Growth in an Interdependent World Economy. Yale University mimeo, November.

Engel, Charles M. and Kletzer, Kenneth M. 1990: Tariffs and saving in a model with new generations. *Journal of International Economics*, February.

Grossman, Gene M. and Helpman, Elhanan 1991: *Innovation and Growth in the Global Economy*. Cambridge, MA: MIT Press.

Helpman, Elhanan 1991: Endogenous Macroeconomic Growth Theory. Mimeo, Tel Aviv University, August.

Jones, Larry E. and Manuelli, Rodolfo 1990: Finite Lifetimes and Growth. *NBER Working Paper* No. 3469.

Lucas, Robert E. Jr 1988: On the Mechanics of Economic Development. *Journal of Monetary Economics*, 22, 3–42.

Romer, Paul 1986: Increasing Returns and Long-Run Growth. *Journal of Political Economy*, 94, 1002–37.

Romer, Paul 1990: Endogenous Technological Change. *Journal of Political Economy*, 98, S71–S102.

Saint-Paul, Gilles 1990: Fiscal Policy in an Endogenous Growth Model. *CNRS-ENS-EHSS Document* No. 91–04.

Sala-i-Martin, Xavier 1990a: Lecture Notes on Economic Growth: Introduction to the Literature and Neoclassical Models, Volume I. *Economic Growth Center Discussion Paper* No. 621, December.

Sala-i-Martin, Xavier 1990b: Lecture Notes on Economic Growth: Five Prototype Models of Endogenous Growth, Volume II. *Economic Growth Center Discussion Paper* No. 622, December.

Sargent T. J. and Wallace, Neil 1984: Some Unpleasant Monetarist Arithmetic. In B. Griffith and G. E. Wood (eds), *Monetarism in the United Kingdom*. London: Macmillan, pp. 15–41.

Sheshinski, Eitan 1967: Optimal Accumulation with Learning by Doing. In Karl Shell (ed.), *Essays on the Theory of Optimal Economic Growth*. Cambridge, MA: MIT Press.

Solow, Robert M. 1957: Technical Change and the Aggregate Production Function. *Review of Economics and Statistics*, 39, 312–20.

Weil, P. 1990: Overlapping families of infinitely-lived agents. *Journal of Public Economics*, 38, 183–98.

3

Taxation and Savings

Jeffrey Owens[*]

INTRODUCTION

Policymakers and others in OECD countries perceive a shortfall of savings. During the 1970s and early 1980s, saving in the OECD area fell sharply, reaching a low point in 1983. For the OECD region as a whole, the ratio of gross national saving to GNP in the 1980s was, on average, three percentage points below the levels found in the 1960s and 1970s, although recently saving levels have increased (see figure 3.1).

The fall in the saving ratio has come at a time when there are increasing demands being placed upon savings in the OECD area, which is by far the largest supplier and user of world savings. Some of the factors which are expected to increase the demand on world saving include the need to replace public sector infrastructure; financing the cost of environmental programs; the cost of rebuilding the capital, stocks and military hardware of those countries affected by the Gulf crisis and the process of transforming central and Eastern European countries from planned to market economies.

All of these developments will, over the coming years, place a very heavy, although as yet unquantifiable, demands on world saving.

These developments explain why OECD governments have become increasingly concerned with both the level and composition of saving. This concern has led governments to examine ways in which the overall level of saving can be increased and measures can be found to improve the allocation of savings as between different assets. Much of this debate has centered on taxation and this is the focus of this chapter.

Coverage is limited to the impact of taxation on the level and composition of private, mainly household, saving. Other chapters deal with the questions of public sector saving and the effects of social security arrangements (contributions and benefits) on saving, so neither of these aspects is discussed in any depth. Similarly, little is said on the determinants of corporate saving, although tax

[*] The views expressed do not commit the OECD or its Member countries.

Figure 3.1 Saving as percentage of GNP, OECD area

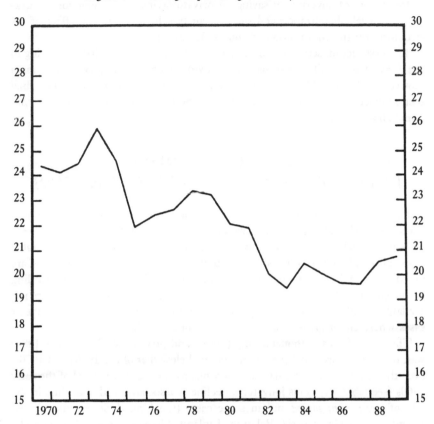

arrangements undoubtedly can have a major impact on saving in the corporate sector. Thus, the main focus of this chapter is on three issues:

How does taxation affect the level of private (i.e., business and household saving?
What impact does taxation have on the composition of household saving?
How do national tax regimes affect the international allocation of private savings between countries?

The perspective adopted is very much a structural rather than a macro-economic approach.

Although household saving decisions are taken on the basis of individual preferences and market conditions, they are also influenced by government policies which may give rise to distortions. Thus, governments are concerned about whether their own activities, both on the revenue and expenditure sides of their budgets, distort private saving decisions. The relevant questions relate to the impact of government saving on private saving, the interaction of taxation, financial liberalization and social security schemes, and the effect of tax structures on the composition of household saving.

The first section sets out some data on the level and composition of saving in the OECD area. The next sections provide a brief summary of the main motives for household saving, and examine the empirical evidence. The final section discusses the impact of taxation on the level, composition and international allocation of saving.

A STATISTICAL COMPARISON OF THE LEVEL OF SAVING IN OECD COUNTRIES

Table 3.1 provides an overview of trends in national saving and its component parts over the last 30 years. The source of the data is the OECD's *Annual National Accounts*, which attempts to provide data on an internationally comparable basis, although the data are still not fully comparable. Major differences are noted at the end of the table. The latest data are for 1989 or earlier, depending on the country. The starting period also varies so that data for the 1960s are not available for all countries. Other gaps represent incomplete sectoral coverage or cases where either gross or net figures are not available.

The ratio of gross national saving (public and private) to GNP in the 1980s was, on average, around 3 percentage points below that of the 1960s and 1970s, even though the recent rise has taken savings back towards the level of the early 1960s (see table 3.1). This long-term decline is associated with a decline in the rate of *government saving* and in some cases (the United States, the United Kingdom, Canada, Austria, Belgium, Finland, Greece, and the Netherlands) offset increases in private (household plus business) saving. The main factor behind the rise in saving ratios in recent years has been a reduction in the rate of government dissaving. Increased private saving ratios in this period were important only in Germany, Austria, Belgium, Finland, the Netherlands, Norway, and Australia. The increase in government sector saving is in part cyclical, so that there is a risk that it will not be sustained in the face of slower growth.

Private sector saving is by far the largest source of financing for national investment. Even though, as noted above, the contribution of government to national saving has been significant at certain times (notably in the 1960s) and in certain countries (Japan, Norway, and Switzerland), it is the private sector that generally has been the main provider of investment finance. Some of this saving has been intermediated, originating in the household sector, but much of it has been from internally-generated funds of business. In addition, as noted below, the foreign sector has become increasingly important in closing national saving/investment gaps (see table 3.2, pp. 114–15).

Table 3.1 Gross savings as a ratio of GNP

	1960s	1970s	1980s	1986	1987	1988	1989
United States							
National	19.7	19.4	16.3	14.7	14.5	15.3	15.4
Public	2.0	0.4	−2.0	−3.1	−2.1	−2.0	−1.6
Private	17.7	19.1	18.4	17.8	16.6	17.3	17.0
Japan							
National	34.5	35.3	31.7	31.9	32.4	33.7	34.0
Public	6.2	4.8	4.9	4.7	6.3	7.4	8.3
Private	28.3	30.5	26.9	27.2	26.1	26.2	25.6
Germany							
National	27.3	24.3	22.5	23.9	23.7	24.6	26.2
Public	6.2	3.9	2.0	2.4	1.8	1.3	3.7
Private	21.1	20.4	20.5	21.4	21.9	23.3	22.5
France							
National	26.2	25.8	20.4	20.2	19.9	20.7	21.3
Public	−	3.6	1.4	0.6	1.4	1.7	2.0
Private	−	22.2	19.0	19.5	18.5	19.0	19.3
Italy							
National	28.1	25.9	21.9	21.3	20.7	20.8	20.3
Public	2.1	−5.1	−6.5	−6.8	−6.3	−6.2	−5.7
Private	26.0	31.1	28.4	28.2	27.0	27.0	26.0
United Kingdom							
National	18.4	17.9	16.6	16.1	15.8	16.1	15.5
Public	3.6	2.6	0.5	0.0	0.8	2.9	3.2
Private	14.8	15.3	16.1	16.1	15.0	13.2	12.3
Canada							
National	21.9	22.9	20.7	18.7	19.5	20.9	20.6
Public	3.6	2.7	−1.5	−2.3	−1.3	−0.2	−0.7
Private	18.2	20.1	22.2	21.0	20.8	21.0	21.3
OECD							
Total	23.2	23.7	20.5	19.7	19.6	20.5	20.8
Austria							
National	27.7	28.0	24.3	23.6	23.8	25.2	26.2
Public	7.2	6.2	2.7	2.1	1.0	2.3	1.9
Private	20.5	21.8	21.7	21.5	22.8	23.2	24.3
Belgium							
National	22.4	23.1	16.8	17.3	17.8	19.6	21.1
Public	−	−1.6	−5.9	−6.5	−4.9	−4.2	−4.5
Private	−	22.4	22.7	23.8	22.7	23.8	25.6
Denmark							
National	23.3	20.9	15.5	16.8	16.7	17.3	18.1
Public	−	6.0	0.4	6.0	4.9	3.1	2.3
Private	−	14.9	15.1	10.8	11.8	14.2	15.8

Table 3.1 (Cont.)

	1960s	1970s	1980s	1986	1987	1988	1989
Finland							
National	25.4	26.9	24.4	22.6	22.4	24.8	26.2
Public	7.3	7.8	4.3	4.6	2.7	5.6	6.2
Private	18.0	19.1	20.1	18.0	19.7	19.1	20.0
Greece							
National	19.2	25.8	17.4	14.2	14.3	16.9	14.9
Public	3.9	2.3	−7.3	−7.5	−8.2	−11.4	−16.0
Private	15.3	23.5	24.7	21.7	22.4	28.3	30.8
Iceland							
National	25.4	24.8	18.7	18.4	16.5	16.5	17.3
Public	−	8.0	6.7	5.5	5.3	5.5	5.3
Private	−	16.9	12.0	12.9	11.2	10.9	12.0
Ireland							
National	18.4	21.3	18.6	17.9	20.0	20.7	22.6
Netherlands							
National	26.9	24.5	22.2	23.0	21.1	23.2	24.3
Public	4.6	3.3	−0.6	−0.7	−1.2	−0.7	−0.9
Private	22.1	21.1	22.7	23.7	22.3	23.8	25.2
Norway							
National	27.4	26.8	27.7	23.4	23.8	23.3	25.5
Public	8.1	7.9	8.6	9.0	8.3	6.4	5.1
Private	19.2	18.8	19.1	14.4	15.5	16.9	20.4
Portugal							
National	23.1	26.0	24.3	25.6	27.8	25.9	27.3
Spain							
National	25.1	25.2	20.9	21.8	21.7	22.9	22.3
Sweden							
National	24.0	20.9	17.2	17.9	18.1	18.7	19.1
Public	−	−	2.1	2.2	5.5	6.0	8.2
Private	−	−	15.1	15.8	12.6	12.6	10.9
Switzerland							
National	29.4	28.6	28.5	29.7	30.3	31.1	32.3
Public	4.5	3.9	3.6	4.3	4.3	4.2	3.9
Private	24.9	24.8	24.9	25.4	26.0	27.0	28.4
Turkey							
National	14.8	17.1	19.1	22.7	24.7	27.0	23.4
Australia							
National	24.7	24.0	20.7	20.0	21.7	23.8	22.5
Public	−	2.9	2.0	1.9	3.1	4.3	4.1
Private	−	21.2	18.7	18.1	18.6	19.5	18.4

Table 3.1   (Cont.)

	1960s	1970s	1980s	1986	1987	1988	1989
New Zealand							
National	21.2	22.0	19.3	21.0	18.3	17.7	18.4
Public	–	–	–	–	–	–	–
Private	–	–	–	–	–	–	–

a   Because of statistical discrepancies, the figures for private and public saving may not always total to national saving.
b   The household sector includes non-profit institutions; the corporate sector includes financial enterprises and quasi-corporate enterprises.
c   The difference between aggregate saving and investment is equal to the current-account balance only for countries which do not show capital transfers in their foreign accounts and no statistical discrepancy in the capital account of the nation. These two items are small in most countries, except for the *United Kingdom*, where the statistical discrepancy has become large in recent years.
d   In the cases of *Germany, Austria, Belgium* and the *Netherlands*, household saving is available only on a net basis and gross corporate saving includes depreciation of the housing stock.
e   Data for Italy are based on the old national accounts. The new accounts cover only the 1980s.
f   In some cases aggregate numbers are available for a longer period than sub-aggregates. The aggregate numbers usually include revisions, so that in this case sub-aggregates may not add to the total. In the case of the *United Kingdom*, these revisions are unusually large.

Source: OECD, *Annual National Accounts.*

The ratio of private-sector gross saving has been relatively stable over time. In many cases, the average gross private saving ratios in the 1980s were little different from the average for the 1960s. But there were some exceptions: private saving ratios were significantly higher in the 1980s in Canada, the United Kingdom, and Greece, and lower in Japan, France, and Australia. During the 1980s, private-sector saving ratios fell sharply in a number of countries. In most cases, these declines have been largely due to a fall in the household saving ratio, a development linked in most cases to financial market liberalization and wealth effects in the context of rising asset prices. Disinflation was important (for measurement and perhaps behavioral reasons) in reversing the inflation-induced bulge in measured saving during the 1970s.

THE MAIN MOTIVES FOR HOUSEHOLD SAVING

Before examining how taxation may influence the level and composition of household saving, it is necessary to analyze the reasons why households save.

Saving represents a decision not to consume current income and there are four major motives which may lead to such a decision:

1 Saving for retirement. Households build up their assets to finance consumption after retirement when current earned income is reduced or even becomes zero.
2 Precautionary saving. Saving is seen as a way of allowing for uncertainty about future developments. A household may wish to hold assets to meet possible emergencies, such as unemployment or sickness.
3 Saving for bequest. Households save to build up assets to bequeath to subsequent generations.
4 Purchasing "lumpy" assets. Some purchases (e.g., of a car) are "lumpy" and require households to accumulate the necessary funds in advance of the purchase.

Obviously, these motives are not mutually exclusive, and saving decisions will generally be influenced by more than one of them. Rational saving decisions will be based on some kind of optimizing behavior by which the levels and composition of saving are chosen so as to equalize the marginal benefits of alternative uses of income. In practice, there continues to be considerable uncertainty as to how to explain and to predict saving levels.

Retirement Saving

Saving for retirement forms the basis of life-cycle hypothesis (LCH) models of household consumption behavior. Models based on this approach generate the time-profile of consumption over the economic lifetime of the household, the underlying assumption being that the household maximizes its utility from the intertemporal consumption stream, subject to an available resource constraint. This requires that at any time the discounted present value of all future consumption equals the sum of present net wealth plus the discounted present value of all future earned income. The main features of the model are that a household accumulates wealth during the pre-retirement period by consuming less than its disposable income. Wealth reaches its maximum at retirement age, following which it is gradually decreased to finance current consumption. This implies that saving is positive during the pre-retirement phase of the household life-cycle and negative thereafter, averaging zero over the entire lifespan if net bequests made and received are zero. The time-profile of household consumption, and thereby saving, will depend on various factors, among which the market interest rate, the individual's rate of time preference and degree of risk-aversion, and the functioning of capital markets are considered to be the most important. The household saving ratio during the earning period of the life-cycle will also be strongly affected by the length of the retirement span relative to the income-earning period. Thus, both the expected lifetime and the retirement age should be important determinants of individual saving behavior.

The Bequest Motive

Households may accumulate wealth beyond the levels required to finance retirement consumption if they desire to pass on to future generations a part of their accumulated wealth. As is the case with most saving determinants, a bequest motive changes the size of the saving ratio only in an economy expanding due to population growth, productivity growth or both, otherwise the bequest motive would simply lead to the transfer of a constant level of assets from one generation to the next, with no effect on the overall saving ratio. In a growing economy, the bequest transferred between generations is increasing, requiring positive lifetime saving of each generation to guarantee heirs a constant ratio of inherited wealth to initial income. The quantitative impact of the bequest motive on the household saving ratio depends on the interest rate and the size of the bequest. While intergenerational gifts or bequests are indeed common, it is not clear whether they originate from the desire to leave bequests or from the fact that due to uncertainty about the date of death there may have been unspent retirement and precautionary savings. Also, it has been suggested by Horioka (1984) and Hayashi (1986), two Japanese economists, that bequest may be seen as a form of private annuity, under which the elderly receive care from their children in return for a bequest on death. This would be consistent with the life-cycle hypothesis of saving.

Precautionary Saving

Uncertainty pervades the decisions of households. They have no way of knowing their future income sources, date of death or trends in interest rates, all of which are assumed to be predictable in the life-cycle hypothesis. Households will be concerned to smooth out the effects of such unforeseen events as unemployment and illness. While there is little disagreement that uncertainty increases the demand for precautionary assets and thereby saving, it is difficult to quantify this relationship. There are no operational quantitative measures of uncertainty and objectively it is difficult to judge the extent to which precautionary saving contributes to the observed overall level of saving.

Purchase of Lumpy Consumer Items

The purchase of lumpy consumer items is often preceded by an accumulation of savings. While such saving is most common with respect to consumer durable purchases, it can, of course, also occur for current consumption expenditure, such as vacations. For the period in which the planned expenditure materializes, the household will reduce saving correspondingly. This type of saving is due to the imperfect matching of income receipts and consumption expenditure. An alternative way of acquiring consumer durables would be to buy the item first (for example, by accumulating net liabilities), making the necessary saving later in the form of gradual debt repayment.

EMPIRICAL EVIDENCE ON THE MAIN DETERMINANTS OF THE SAVING RATIO[1]

The life-cycle hypothesis for consumption, combined with the bequest motive, appears to provide the best explanation for the level of saving. According to this hypothesis, the rate of saving depends on (1) the rate of growth in per capita income, (2) the stock of wealth, (3) demographic characteristics and (4) the strength of the bequest motive. In a situation where there is no growth in income or population, the capital stock may simply be maintained, with the dissaving of those in retirement offset by the saving of those still working. If income and the population are growing, net saving is needed.

Income Flows and Wealth Holdings

Studies generally confirm a strong inverse relationship between wealth and saving. Bovenberg (1988) concluded that "empirical studies generally suggest that improvement in wealth positions due to the rising values of the stock market and housing have been a major factor behind the declining trend in private saving" (p. 2). Carroll and Summers (1987) also found the level of personal wealth as a fraction of disposable income helped explain the gap between United States and Canadian saving rates.

Several studies of saving in Japan have considered the effect of wealth on saving. Shinohara (1983) found that one of the factors affecting the Japanese saving rate was the "asset effect," or the low share of liquid assets in national income in Japan following World War II. Shibuya (1988), in his time-series analysis of Japan for the 1955–85 period, found that the ratio of household assets relative to expected lifetime income plays a significant negative role in explaining the rate of household saving in Japan. Oudet (1979) examined data for the United Kingdom and France, and concluded that the level of liquid assets relative to disposable income has a negative effect on the level of saving.

Investment incentives can also affect household saving. Increases in investment incentives lead to capital losses for owners of old capital. Since the elderly hold a large share of old capital, Auerbach and Kotlikoff (1982) have noted that "the intergenerational redistribution of resources away from the elderly, arising from investment incentives, leads to a major reduction in the economy's current consumption" (p. 40). Kotlikoff (1983) reports an implicit tax on holders of United States factory and equipment ranging from $230 to $290 billion resulting from the 1981 Tax Act.

A large proportion of household wealth is held in the form of government bonds. The likely effect of domestically held government debt on household saving is still unclear. Insofar as the current generation realizes that the wealth represented by the bonds is offset by the present value of tax payments required to redeem the government debt, household saving will increase so that a bequest can be passed on that is sufficient to cover the higher taxes. Growing evidence indicates, however, that households' consumption decisions do not fully take into account the effect of future taxes. Nicoletti (1988) found that in countries (Belgium and Italy) with "a long history of inflation and in which the sustainability of public debt and deficits has raised serious concerns" (p. 74), increased public debt may be offset by a rise in private saving; that in countries (Canada and the United States) where the concern is less but very real, government dissaving is partially offset by increased private saving; in other countries (France, Germany, Japan, and the United Kingdom), Nicoletti found little evidence that government deficits affect the private saving rate, a conclusion which is intuitively plausible.

The Bequest Motive

There is little agreement on the importance of the bequest motive for saving. One explanation for bequests is that they merely reflect an alternative way to prepare for retirement, and accordingly fit within the life-cycle model. This view is supported by some Japanese economists, who suggest that bequests in Japan are a form of private annuity, with the elderly receiving income and care from their children in return for a bequest (see Horioka, 1984 and Hayashi, 1986).

The relevance of the life-cycle model is less satisfactory in explaining some of the other evidence with respect to bequests. Indeed, Horioka (1990), in his recent literature survey on household saving in Japan, reports that "the collective evidence suggests . . . that saving for bequests is more important than saving for life cycle purposes" (p. 58) in Japan. Kotlikoff (1988) summarizes evidence that suggests that saving may occur for reasons other than to finance consumption during retirement. He mentions the propensity of the retired to hold on to their savings, the weakness of annuity markets, and the fact that substantial saving existed before retirement became commonplace. It has been estimated that the share of the wealth accounted for by intergenerational transfers in the United States is 80 percent (Modigliani, 1988), although other studies have reached much lower results (around 25 percent). Hurd (1990) recently observed that

Apparently parents transferred as much as (or possibly more than) they wanted to because they do not seem to alter their consumption behaviour with the aim of transferring more at death; that is, the bequest motive is inoperable. ... An implication of the tests of the bequest motive is that bequests appear to be largely accidental, the result of uncertainty about the date of death (p. 628).

Although the bequest motive may be important in saving decisions outside of, as well as within, a life-cycle model, we know little about how this motive affects the level of saving, and still less about how it affects the motive. The picture is further complicated by the fact that part or much of the bequest motive may be satisfied through inter vivos gifts rather than at time of death.

Demographic Variables

The following demographic variables can be expected to influence household saving:

Life expectancy   An increase in life expectancy will generally increase the household saving ratio because each person requires higher wealth accumulation to finance a constant consumption stream over a longer retirement span.

Retirement age   A decline in retirement age will increase the household saving ratio since each person requires a larger stock of wealth (relative to lifetime income) to finance consumption over the expanded retirement period.

Age distribution   The aggregate household saving ratio depends on the age distribution of households.

Family size   The size of the normal household will vary over the life cycle, which is likely to influence the time profile of consumption and thereby saving.

Labor market participation   The average age of entry into the job market of young people will influence the time profile of household consumption and the aggregate saving ratio. Similarly, the female participation ratio will determine the number of households with two income-earners. It has been argued that two-earner households are likely to have lower saving ratios (see Leff, 1969).

An analysis by Hagemann and Nicoletti (1989) led them to conclude that with an ageing population and other factors unchanged, "it can be expected that the private saving rate for a large proportion of the OECD area will decline over the very long run" (p. 27). Even in the very short term, Bovenberg and Evans (1990) found that changing demographics may contribute to a significant fall in the private saving rate within a country. They found that for the United States, the largest contributing factor to the decline in the personal saving rate from an average of 8 percent of disposable income in the 1970s to ... about 4 percent in the last three years is the change in the demographic structure – especially the rise in the share of the population over the age of 65. Demographic movements accounted for a decline in the saving rate of 2¹/₂ percentage points (p. 64).

Other studies have questioned the relationship between dependency ratios and private saving rates. For example, Bosworth (1990) found "some support for a demographic effect in five of the eleven countries for which data were available, but it had the wrong sign in two countries" (p. 380). Bentzell and Berg (1983) found that their "statistical analysis does not produce conclusive results concerning the effects of changes in the age distribution" (p. 177) on the savings rate in Sweden; and Graham, in his cross-country study, found that "the percent of population over 65 appears not to reduce the aggregate saving rate, as life cycle theory might suggest it should" (p. 1523).

Thus, ambiguity remains, and the extent to which the aged are dissavers will vary from country to country and even within a country over time.

Public and Private Pension Arrangements

Other chapters in this volume discuss the voluminous literature on the impact of pension arrangements on the propensity to save, so the present discussion can be brief. Insofar as saving for retirement is considered as a major motive for saving, the existence of public pension schemes could be expected to affect significantly the incentive to save in two ways:

First, their existence has a wealth effect as long as the anticipated benefits net of contribution have a positive present value. This should decrease private household saving.
Secondly, there is retirement effect. Households may retire earlier and may therefore save more when they are working.

The net outcome of these contradictory forces is a question for empirical research, as is the impact of the methods used to finance public pensions (in particular, pension schemes which are not fully funded may reduce national saving ratios). Yet the empirical studies on the effect of pension arrangements on household saving remain ambiguous.

In his recent survey of the literature, Smith concluded that it is difficult to be confident about how public pension programs affect private saving. Both the direction and magnitude of the effect remains debatable (Smith, 1990). This confirms the result of an earlier survey by OECD (Sturm, 1983).

There is rather more certainty on the effect of private pension schemes on household saving. Again, there are two effects:

The first is the retirement effect which would occur if private schemes enable early retirement and thereby encouraged household saving. This effect would be reinforced if households regarded pensions as less liquid than other forms of saving.

The second is that if employees regard their schemes as vested, then any income in private pension schemes could result in a one-to-one offset in other household saving.

Some authors (e.g., Burros) have also noted that pension schemes, by increasing the possibility of financial independence in old age, may motivate households to save more in other forms. Again, Smith concluded for his survey of the literature that private pension plans probably on balance increase household saving, although it was unclear how significant were these effects (Smith, 1990).

The Responsiveness of Private Saving to the Real Rate of Interest

The impact of interest rates on private saving is ambiguous, since a change in these interest rates has both an income and a substitution effect, which work in opposite directions. Therefore, the response of households to changes in interest rates is an empirical question. Unfortunately, the empirical work carried out to date is inconclusive. Studies in the United States in the 1970s and early 1980s suggested that interest rates have a significant positive effect on saving (see, for example, Boskin, 1978; Summers, 1981). Other studies (e.g., Weber, 1975; Howrey and Hymans, 1978) found little support for this conclusion. Thus, a recent survey concluded that "the general consensus in the literature is that positive elasticity estimates, either of consumption or saving, are fragile and fleeting" (Skinner and Feinberg, 1989). Consequently, there is little guidance that economists can provide on how saving is affected by changes in interest rates.

The International Dimension

This integration of financial markets should lead savings to flow across national borders to seek the highest expected risk-adjusted, after-tax rate of return. Capital flows tend to equalize the demand for and supply of saving and establish a common global real rate of return (adjusted for tax and risk). An *ex ante* increase in saving in one country could increase investment everywhere. Prior to the liberalization of financial markets, restrictions on international capital movements existed. National investment was constrained to some extent by national saving. Rates of return to capital differed. Under these conditions, there was a strong covariation of saving and investment within a country. As barriers to international financial and direct investment have been removed, this relationship seems to have been weakened.

During the 1960s and 1970s there was a broad balance between national saving and investment within OECD countries, for a few countries which remained habitual capital exporters (Switzerland and the Netherlands) or importers (Canada, Greece, Ireland, and some Nordic countries). Even when, as in the early 1970s, there was an oil price shock that effectively reduced the net saving of the industrialized countries and raised OPEC saving, saving/investment gaps were eradicated quickly.

Not only have national saving rates in the 1980s been lower than in the 1960s and 1970s, but gaps have persisted in a few countries where investment and saving over several years had previously been relatively well-balanced. The emergence of such divergences, which has been reflected in persisting current-account imbalances, has coincided with a period of greater international financial market liberalization and persistent exchange-rate misalignments.

Feldstein and Horioka (1980) tested the degree of capital mobility between countries by regressing domestic saving on domestic investment ratios, using cross-country data and average ratios over a period of several years. Results for the years 1960 to 1974, both for the entire period and for sub-periods, showed that domestic saving passed into domestic investment nearly one to one. A more explicit structural model which allowed for inter-country differences in saving behavior (e.g., differences in pension benefit/earnings replacement ratios or the age structure of the population) yielded the same results. These findings suggested that an increase in saving in one country added little to an internationally mobile pool of saving and investment. The result was generally confirmed by later studies, as indicated in table 3.2.

Nevertheless, the Feldstein-Horioka results are increasingly being questioned as barriers to capital flows are removed and as imbalances between national saving and investment levels develop. Some new research showed different results (Obstfeld, 1985, Turner, 1986). A repetition of Feldstein and Horioka's work – regressing five-year averages of saving on investment ratios – and extending the sample to 23 OECD countries and the time period to 1987 suggests a less important correlation of national saving and investment than previously. Foreign financing seems to have become more important and it has apparently become much easier to sustain saving/investment imbalances over longer periods. The rapid increase in international financial interdependence is also evident from the growth in foreign assets and liabilities.

Table 3.2 The relation between savings and investment ratios: a summary of earlier studies[a]

	Regression equation						R^2	Sample period[b]	Number of countries
Feldstein & Horioka (1980)	(I/Y)	=	0.035 (0.018)	+	0.89 (0.074)	(S/Y)	0.91	1960–74	16
	(I/Y)	=	0.029 (0.015)	+	0.91 (0.060)	(S/Y)	0.92	1960–4	16
	(I/Y)	=	0.039 (0.025)	+	0.87 (0.101)	(S/Y)	0.83	1965–9	16
	(I/Y)	=	0.039 (0.024)	+	0.87 (0.092)	(S/Y)	0.85	1970–4	16
Feldstein (1983)	(I/Y)	=	0.046 (0.042)	+	0.87 (0.185)	(S/Y)	0.57	1975–9	17
Sachs (1981)	Δ(CA/Y)	=	−0.30 (0.254)	−	0.59 (0.100)	Δ(I/Y)	0.73	1968–73 to 1974–9	15
Penati & Dooley (1984)	(I/Y)	=	0.030 (0.034)	+	0.88 (0.144)	(S/Y)	0.71	1971–81	19
	(CA/Y)	=	0.033 (0.028)	−	0.19 (0.114)	(I/Y)	0.11	1971–81	19
	Δ(CA/Y)	=	−0.015 (0.005)	+	0.05 (0.108)	Δ(I/Y)	0.01	1949–59 to 1971–81	19

Dolley, Frankel & Mathieson (1987)	(I/Y)	$=$	0.069 (0.026)	$+$	0.75 (0.104)	(S/Y)	0.79	1960–73	14
	(I/Y)	$=$	0.063 (0.039)	$+$	0.74 (0.173)	(S/Y)	0.57	1974–84	14
Turner (1986)	(I/Y)	$=$	0.033 (0.018)	$+$	0.83 (0.073)	(S/Y)	0.85	1960–74	23
	(I/Y)	$=$	0.073 (0.034)	$+$	0.72 (0.153)	(S/Y)	0.48	1975–83	23
	(I/Y)	$=$	0.102 (0.012)	$+$	0.58 (0.054)	(S/Y)	0.36	1975–83[c]	23

[a] I denotes domestic investment, S saving, Y gross national or domestic product and CA the current-account balance. Standard errors are shown below coefficients. The Δ indicates changes in average rates between periods.

[b] Investment and saving ratios are averages over the sample period.

[c] Nine-yearly observations pooled.

Other Factors

There are a number of other factors which could be expected to influence the level of household saving:

The personal distribution of income   If marginal saving ratios differ by income levels, then a redistribution of income will alter overall household saving ratios. Under the life-cycle approach, it can be expected that saving ratios do not change over the income distribution. A cross-country study by Kopitz and Gotur (1980) supported this conclusion.

The functional distribution of income   If saving ratios differ as between different types of income (e.g., wages, capital gains, dividends, etc.) then changes in this functional distribution could also be expected to alter household saving. A 1983 survey by the OECD found, however, no systematic relationship between saving ratios and different sources of income (Sturm, 1983).

Inflation   Inflation affects the rate of saving for at least three reasons. First, the real value of assets denoted in fixed terms, such as bonds, falls in times of unanticipated inflation. In the case of government bonds, the evidence suggests that reduced consumption due to this loss in wealth is unlikely to be fully offset by the fall in real tax revenues needed to redeem the debt in the future. Secondly, rapid changes in prices increase uncertainty in the economic environment, including increased uncertainty as to the real value of many assets. This increases saving for precautionary purposes. Third, if nominal interest expenses can be deducted for tax purposes in times of inflation, after-tax real interest rates may well be negative. This may provide a powerful incentive to consume. In spite of these potentially offsetting forces, the majority of evidence appears to support the hypothesis that the relation between the rate of inflation and the rate of saving is positive (Sturm, 1983).

Other factors that Horioka referred to in his comprehensive survey of factors affecting saving in Japan include: relative wealth of the elderly, availability of consumer credit, predominant forms of business units, work patterns, structure of total remuneration package, quantity of public services, and cultural factors (Horioka, 1990).

TAXATION AND THE LEVEL AND COMPOSITION OF PRIVATE SAVING

There are two main concerns which have encouraged countries to review the tax treatment of savings. First is the desire to provide a more neutral treatment of alternative saving instruments, what has come to be called the "provision of a level playing field." The second concern is the desire to shift part of the cost of retirement from the public to the private sector (part of the more general policy objective of reducing the size of the public sector) and to encourage households to shift their savings into productive forms (e.g., equities). These objectives conflict and require a tradeoff between neutrality and an interventionalist approach.

The Effects on the Level of Private Saving

The tax system may affect the level of private saving by reducing the taxation of income from capital and by providing tax benefits for current savers. Both of these measures work by increasing the after-tax rate of return on saving and therefore their effectiveness depends in part on the responsiveness of saving to the rate of return. Moreover, to increase national saving a tax incentive must increase private saving by more than it reduces government tax revenues.

Under the life-cycle approach to saving, tax variables appear in the household's budget constraint as drains on lifetime resources. The effects of a tax on wages and salaries and that of a consumption tax are equivalent from the household's point of view: they both effectively reduce the real purchasing power of lifetime resources, and thereby the level of the real consumption and saving streams. While this is true for the aggregate household sector, the substitution of a consumption tax for a progressive income tax is likely to have an important effect on after-tax income distribution across households. If the marginal propensity to save rises with income, such a tax change will tend to increase aggregate saving.

In addition, a tax on wages and salaries affects household saving through its impact on the work-leisure choice. An increase in the marginal tax rate on earned income will reduce work effort and income if the negative substitution effect from a lower after-tax marginal income is greater than the positive income effect. In this case, the level of saving will fall if there is no offsetting rise in the saving ratio. The direction of the change in the saving ratio cannot be determined *a priori* because a reduction in work effort could imply both fewer working hours before retirement and/or earlier retirement. The latter increases the need to save, while the effect of the former depends on whether leisure and consumption are substitutes or complements.

Capital taxes affect the tradeoff between present and future consumption by altering the net rate of return on saving. This applies to corporate profit taxes and income taxes on dividends and interest and capital taxes. Corporate profits taxes, insofar as they are not shifted into higher prices or compensated by lower wages, will ultimately reduce the rate of return to holders of financial assets. After-tax rates of return will be lower than before-tax rates under an income tax. Saving may be discouraged by discriminating against future relative to current consumption. Whether such a distortion is, in fact, important depends on the size of the tax wedge (the difference between before and after-tax rates of return) and the elasticity of saving with respect to the after-tax rate of return.

Because for a net saver the income and substitution effects are of opposing signs, the net effect of income taxation on saving is ambiguous. As noted earlier, empirical studies suggest that the responsiveness of saving to after-tax rate of return is still subject to debate.

In practice the quantification of these effects is difficult, given the existence of a large variety if assets, each associated with a different rate of return, risk, and effective tax rate.

Further complications arise from the interactions between taxation and inflation. Inflation premia built into interest payments are tax deductible at the firm level as a business expense, while they are treated as taxable income of the asset holder. The ultimate effect on the after-tax rate of return depends on a number of factors, such as the debt-equity ratio and the relative size of the marginal tax rate on household interest income, business profits (both retained and distributed), and capital gains. Furthermore, the equilibrium debt-equity ratio may be changed in response to inflation. Concerning equity, in most countries inflation tends to depress corporate profitability by raising the effective tax rate on corporate profits because the prevailing accounting rules for capital depreciation and inventory valuation are on a historical cost basis. However, there are offsetting effects from, for example, the reduction in the real value of debt and, for international investment, exchange rate movements. Reductions in the real value of debt, in turn, reduces the real net worth of households owning corporate bonds. Although scattered evidence suggests that the interplay of inflation and the tax system has adversely affected the after-tax return to savings – at least in the United States – the impact on saving itself depends on the size and the magnitude of the rate-of-return elasticity of saving.

A change in the tax on business profits may affect total private saving by changing the payout ratio of the firm. A tax system favoring retention leads to increasing business saving. The effect on total private saving depends on the household's reaction to this change. If, as seems likely, the household's marginal propensity to save out of capital gains is higher than that out of dividend income, the increase in business saving will be only partially offset by a reduction in household saving, leading to a rise in total private saving.

No current tax system tries to treat all forms of income in an equal manner (see table 3.5 pp. 126–9), and no existing tax system provides a total exemption of saving and capital income, from taxation as would be the case in a tax system with a pure expenditure tax. Research has increasingly indicated that current tax systems – which are a mix of income and expenditure systems – are in many cases likely to have a discouraging impact on saving, and that moves away from taxation of saving and capital income could provide substantial economic gains. For instance, simulations with dynamic general equilibrium models, such as those of Auerbach and Kotlikoff (1982), show that a shift away from capital taxation towards taxation of labor income, or a move towards a consumption tax, could increase capital formation and output substantially in the long run. In the former case, greater neutrality with respect to saving would come at the expense of a larger distortion of incentives to accept employment. It is also unlikely that the distributional consequences of such a shift would be politically acceptable, and it is unclear what would be the long-run revenue potential of a tax system with a less diversified tax base. Another argument against such a shift is that it could adversely affect human capital formation.

Many countries provide tax benefits for savers, especially those related to retirement pensions. A critical question arises as to whether such tax incentives increase aggregate household saving, or whether they only result in a transfer of saving into a preferentially-treated category. Carroll and Summers (1987) found strong evidence that the sharp divergence in Canadian and US saving rates since the end of the 1960s can partly be explained by the generous tax treatment of pension contributions in Canada, and Venti and Wise (1987) found some evidence that introduction of IRAs in the United States increased financial saving of households somewhat. For Japan, Shibuya (1987) found a small positive effect of generous tax exemption provisions for interest income on household saving.

The tax treatment of interest on loans may also influence saving levels. Insofar as interest is deductible for tax purposes, this could adversely affect the incentive to save. Most countries take the view that interest payments should be deductible from any income associated with it, but should not be deductible when there is no associated income. Thus, most countries allow deductibility of interest on borrowing for business purposes but do not allow deductibility of interest on borrowing for the purchase of consumer goods. A few countries (Denmark, the Netherlands, Norway, Sweden, and Switzerland), however, make no distinction between the various purposes for which the borrowing is made (see table 3.3). This is probably based on the principle that neutrality should prevail between deductibility of interest, irrespective of the purpose for which the loan is acquired. It is noteworthy that countries with the most generous treatment of interest deductibility (see table 3.3) also have some of the lowest saving ratios (see table 3.1).

If governments wish to encourage private sector saving, the studies surveyed in this chapter suggest that:

A shift from direct to indirect taxes may increase household saving ratios.
Given the higher propensity of corporations than households to save, shifting part of the tax burden from corporations to households may marginally increase overall private saving.
Limiting the deductibility of interest for consumer credit and housing may also increase household saving.

These are the three main policy options open to governments, but it should be stressed that the saving response to these changes is still largely unknown.

Table 3.3 The deductibility of interest payments, 1990

Country	Investment or business purposes	Interest on loans for: Home purchases or improvements — Principal residence	Interest on loans for: Home purchases or improvements — Secondary residence	Consumer purchases
Australia	TA(B)	ND	ND	ND
Austria	TA(O)	TA(C)	ND	TA(C)
Belgium	TA	TA(O)	TA(O)	ND
Canada	TA	ND	ND	ND
Denmark	TA	TA	TA	TA
Finland	TA	TA(C)	TA	TA(C)
France	TA(B)	TC(C)	ND	ND
Germany	TA	ND	ND	ND
Greece	TA	TA	TA(C)	ND
Iceland	TA(B)	TC(C)	ND	ND
Ireland	TA(B)	TA(C)	ND	ND
Italy	ND	TA(C)	TA(C)	ND
Japan	TA	ND[a]	ND[a]	ND
Luxembourg	TA	TA(C)	TA(C)	TA
Netherlands	TA	TA	TA	TA

New Zealand	TA	ND	ND	ND
Norway	TA	TA	TA	TA
Portugal	TA	TA(C)	TA(C)	ND
Spain	TA	TA(C)	TA(C)	ND
Sweden	TA	TA	TA	TA
Switzerland	TA	TA	TA	TA
Turkey	TA(B)	ND	ND	ND
United Kingdom	TA(B)	TA(C)/TC(C)[b]	ND	ND
United States	TA(O)	TA(C)	TA(C)	ND

TA   Tax allowance
TA(B) Tax allowance deductible for interest on loans for business purposes only
TC   Tax credit
ND   Not deductible (or creditable)
(C)   Subject to ceiling or maximum
(O)   Fully deductible but only against associated income

[a] In Japan there is a provision which allows a tax credit against income tax liability corresponding to 1% of outstanding loans related to home acquisition at the end of each year for a certain period.
[b] There is no relief for home improvement loans taken out after April 5, 1988.

The Effects on the Composition of Household Saving

There is broad agreement that taxation influences the composition of saving by changing the after-tax return on different types of assets. Tax provision can influence the composition of household saving in a variety of ways. First, income invested in certain assets may be deductible (e.g., contributions to pension plans). Secondly, the yield for an asset may be subject to a favorable tax treatment. Thirdly, the financial intermediary holding the funds may be tax exempt. The net tax incentive for any assets requires looking at each of these stages: the treatment at the time of purchase, during the holding period, at the time of disposal. Saving incentives can seriously distort the allocation of funds in national capital markets and these distortions may be much more significant than any tax-induced increase of the activity as a whole. They have also been criticized as eroding the tax base and altering arbitrarily the distribution of the tax burden. A further criticism is that many of these incentives encourage taxpayers to place their funds with institutional investments (pension funds, insurance companies, etc.). It is argued that this may discourage risk-taking, because such institutions are generally reluctant to provide venture capital to newly established small companies which have been considered as being in the forefront of technological developments and providing large employment opportunities. But it is questionable that the removal of these incentives will necessarily lead to a change in investment behavior of small savers, who may well be more concerned with the security of their investment than with making a big gain.

The most important areas where tax incentives are given are:

Home ownership generally receives favorable tax treatment (at least for principal residences). Table 3.3 summarizes the deductibility of interest on loans incurred in respect of house purchase, which for principal residences is partially or fully deductible in all countries except Australia, Canada, New Zealand, and Turkey. There are also other tax advantages provided to the housing sector under net wealth and capital gains taxation, as well as the absence of any tax on imputed income associated with home ownership in around half the OECD countries. In addition, in those countries where imputed income is taxed, the imputed income is usually well below the market value and/or taxed at very low rates.

Such favorable tax treatment is likely to make the after-tax return on housing attractive relative to other non-residential investments. This favorable treatment, especially when extended to more than one residence, may have a crowding-out effect on the availability of capital for productive investment and may distort consumption patterns. Consequently, a number of countries (Australia, Denmark, Ireland, Japan, New Zealand, the United Kingdom, and the United States) now provide less favorable treatment for home ownership than previously.[2]

Table 3.4 Pension and life insurance relief (1990)

Country	Pension contributions	Life assurance premiums
Australia	TA(C)	ND
Austria	ND	TA(C)
Belgium	TA	TA(C)
Canada	TC(C)	ND
Denmark	TA(C)	TA(C)
Finland	TA(C)	TA(C)
France	ND	TC(C)
Germany	TA(C)	TA(C)
Greece	ND	TA(C)
Iceland	ND	ND
Ireland	TA(C)	TA(C)
Italy	TA(C)	TA(C)
Japan	TA(C)	TA(C)
Netherlands	TA	TA(C)[a]
New Zealand	ND	ND
Norway	TA(C)	TC(C)
Portugal	TA(C)	TA(C)
Spain	TC(C)	TC(C)
Sweden	TA(C)	ND
Switzerland	TA(C)	TA(C)
Turkey	TA	TA(C)
United Kingdom	TA(C)	ND[b]
United States	TA(C)	ND

TA   Tax allowance
TA(C) Tax allowance, subject to a ceiling
TC   Tax credit
TC(C) Tax credit, subject to a ceiling
ND   not deductible or creditable

[a] In general, life assurance premiums are not deductible, but a deduction is possible for annuity premiums up to a ceiling.
[b] UK: relief for policies made before March 13, 1984.

Contributions to private pensions are deductible from income subject to tax in most countries (see table 3.4). A few governments have announced that they intend to shift the balance of pension provisions from the public to the private sector (e.g., Australia and the United Kingdom). In some cases, this policy has been implemented by providing a favorable tax treatment to the pension sector, either in the form of deductibility for contributions or a favorable treatment of the funds or the pension.

Contributions to life insurance are generally deductible up to a ceiling (table 3.4). However, a number of countries have recently abolished reliefs for insurance premiums (New Zealand, Sweden, and the United Kingdom).

Banks, national savings schemes, etc. Governments have also provided tax incentives for taxpayers saving through these various savings vehicles, and interest from such deposits is exempt from tax, subject to limits in Finland, Greece, New Zealand, and the United Kingdom. Incentives have, however, been recently tightened. In Japan, for example, the tax exemption for small savings was abolished (except for the aged and handicapped) from April 1988. The New Zealand exemption is to be abolished from 1991 and the Finnish interest tax relief has been made conditional on the rate of interest.

Equity holdings For equity holdings, a few countries (e.g., France and the United Kingdom) have tried to use the tax system to encourage households to invest in equities. Also, almost all countries provide a favorable tax treatment of income from capital gains and share participation schemes provided by employers to their employees.

Table 3.5 provides an overview of the treatment of different income sources under the personal income tax base in the late 1980s. It shows that there is an enormous variation in the income subject to tax in different countries. Table 3.6 provides an updated summary for the three sources of income which are of most relevance to this study: dividends, interest, and pensions. The conclusion suggested by these two tables is that no country provides a "level playing field" for different income sources. These tax differentials will change both the distribution of income and its functional distribution between different classes of income which, in turn, is likely to influence both the level and composition of saving.

Work undertaken by the Institute of Fiscal Studies in London attempted to measure the importance of these distortions (see Hill, 1984). The study estimates for a range of financial and non-financial assets the degree of fiscal privilege, defined as the percentage difference between the saver's marginal income tax rate and the real effective tax rate on each asset. The effective tax rate is in turn defined as the percentage difference between the pre-tax and post-tax real rate of return. The estimates presented in table 3.7 indicate great variation across assets in the degree of fiscal privilege, even for individuals facing the same marginal income tax rate. The effective tax rate for savers is much more dependent on the asset chosen than the marginal income tax rate faced, and in some cases the degree of fiscal privilege exceeds that implicit in exempting the asset's return from tax completely. The results are, however, particularly sensitive to the rate of inflation, an increase in which further widens the dispersion of fiscal privilege and also changes the relative position of different assets.

It is unclear how far saving behavior is affected by these incentives. The IFS study noted a correlation between the degree of fiscal privilege and movements in the composition of savings in the United Kingdom. There were, however, some notable exceptions to this, possibly reflecting the influence of other factors on savings behavior and the fact that the estimated tax advantages may not fully accrue to savers but may be partly captured by the favored institutions themselves. Nevertheless, to the extent that the features which characterize the taxation of savings in the United Kingdom also exist elsewhere, the effects produced may by of sufficient concern to warrant further investigation.

Taxation and the International Allocation of Saving

Financial market liberalization and the removal of non-tax barriers on international capital flows have increased the potential impact of differences in national taxation regimes on the international allocation of saving. If capital markets are completely integrated and if countries achieve capital import neutrality in their tax regimes (i.e., the effective tax rates on an investor in a country are the same, irrespective of whether the investor is a resident or a non-resident), then after-tax rates of return will be equalized between countries and there will be an optimum world-wide allocation of saving.

This, of course, assumes that savings are responsive to after-tax rates of return which in the recent past may have been rather unrealistic. Financial liberalization, however, may have increased this responsiveness by making it easier for savers to diversify their portfolios. Under these new conditions, tax differentials may influence where a saver places his investments. The discussion which follows focuses on interest-bearing assets since these are likely, in practice, to be the type of asset most influenced by tax differentials.

Many OECD countries provide a *de facto* more favorable treatment of interest received by non-residents than resident investors. The effects of these tax provisions can be measured by looking at the tax wedge between the market interest rate and the return of the saver. In the case of bank deposits and government bonds, the relevant tax provisions are (1) any withholding taxes at source, (2) and the relevant marginal tax rate of the holder of these assets, at least insofar as interest income is aggregated with other sources of income, (3) and the relevant capital gains tax rate insofar as bonds are concerned.

These tax provisions are given in table 3.8. The *personal tax rates* given in table 3.8 reflect the highest statutory tax rate on interest receipts, and where data are available, the *average* marginal tax rate on interest payments are also given. Several countries have provisions whereby personal taxes on interest are lower than the statutory rate. For example, Belgium charges only a 10 percent tax rate on interest. A withholding tax on interest for resident individuals is levied in 14 countries (Austria, Belgium, Finland, France, Greece, Ireland,

Table 3.5 Summary of income subject to tax in OECD countries

Income source	Australia (1987/88)	Austria (1982)	Belgium (1987)	Canada (1986)	Denmark (1987)	Finland (1985)	France (1987)	Germany (1987)	Greece (1987)	Iceland (1989)
1. Employment income	I	I	I	I	I	I	I	I	I	I
2. Fringe benefits*										
2.1 Employers' contributions to sickness schemes	I	N	N	N	N	N	N	N	N	N
2.2 Employers' contributions to private pension schemes	N	N	N	N	N	N	P	P	N	N
2.3 Other benefits	I	I	I	I	I	I	I	I	I	I
3. Net business income	I	I	I	I	I	I	I	I	I	I
4. Interest income										
4.1 Government bonds	I	N	P***	I	I	N	I	I	N	N
4.2 Certain savings accounts	I	I	P***	I	I	N	I	I	N	N
4.3 Pension savings accounts**	I	I	P***	I	I	I	I	I	I	N
4.4 Other bank accounts*	I	I	P*****	I	N	N	I	I	N	N
4.5 Others	I	I	P***	I	I	I	I	I	N	N
5. Dividend income	I	I	P***	I	I	I	I	I	I	I
6. Other investment income	N.A.	N.A.	N.A.	N.A.	N.A.	N.A.	N.A.	N.A.	N.A.	N.A.
7. Rent income	I	I	P	I	I	I	I	I	I	I
8. Imputed rent*	N	N	P	N	I	I	N	N	I	N
9. Public pensions	I	I	I	I	I	I	I	I	I	I

10. Private pensions, annuities and
life assurance

10.1 Private pensions	I	I	I	I	I	I	I	I
10.2 Annuities	P	P	I	I	I	I	I	I
10.3 Life assurance-periodical	I	N	I	N	N	N	N	I
10.4 Life assurance-lump sum	N	N	I	N	N	N	N	N
11. Social transfers								
11.1 Unemployment	I	N	I	I	I	I	N	I
11.2 Sickness	I	N	I	I	I	I	N	I
11.3 Invalidity or injury	P	P	I	I	P	N	P	I
11.4 Strike pay	I	I	N	I	I	I	I	I
11.5 Family allowance	N	N	N	N	N	N	N	N
11.6 Dwelling allowance	N	N	N	N	N	N	N	N
11.7 Others	N	P	N	N.A.	N	P	N	N.A.
12. Alimony an maintenance receipts	N	N	I	I	I	I	I	N
13. Capital gains*								
13.1 Short-term	P	I	P	P	P	P	P	P
13.2 Long-term	P	P	P	P	P	N	P	P
14. Others								
14.1 Foreign earnings	I	I	I	I	I	I	P	I
14.2 Foreign pensions	I	I	I	I	I	I	P	I

Table 3.5 (Cont.)

Income source	Ireland (1985/86)	Italy (1985)	Japan (1990)	Netherlands (1988)	Norway (1987)	Spain (1987)	Sweden (1987)	Turkey (1990)	United Kingdom (1986/87)	United States (1988)
1. Employment income	I	I	I	I	I	I	I	I	I	I
2. Fringe benefits*										
2.1 Employer's contributions to sickness schemes	N	N	N	I	I	N	N	N	N	N
2.2 Employers' contributions to private pension schemes	N	N	N	N	N	N	N	N	N	N
2.3 Other benefits	I	I	P	P	P	I	P	P	P	P
3. Net business income	I	I	I	I	I	I	I	I	I	I
4. Interest income										
4.1 Government bonds	I	N***	I	I	I	I	I	I	I	I
4.2 Certain savings accounts	I	I	I	I	I	I	I	I	I	I
4.3 Pension savings accounts**	I	I	I	I	I	P	I	I	I	I
4.4 Other bank accounts	I	I	I	I	I	I	I	I	I	I
4.5 Others	I	I	I	I	I	I	I	I	I	I
5. Dividend income	N.A.	N.A.	N.A.	N.A.	N.A.	I	I	N	I	N.A.
6. Other investment income	I	I	N.A.	I	I	I	N.A.	N.A.	N.A.	N.A.
7. Rent income	I	I	I	I	I	I	I	I	I	I
8. Imputed rent*	N	I	N	I	I	I	I	N	N	I
9. Public pensions	I	I	I	I	I	I	I	N	N	N

10. Private pensions, annuities and life assurance

Income source									
10.1 Private pensions	N	I	I	I	I	I	I	I	P
10.2 Annuities	I	I	I	I	P	I	I	I	P
10.3 Life assurance-periodical	N	N	I	N	I	N	I	N	P
10.4 Life assurance-lump sum	N	N	I	N	N	N	N	N	P
11. Social transfers									
11.1 Unemployment	N	I	N	I	I	I	I	I	I
11.2 Sickness	N	I	N	I	I	I	I	N	P
11.3 Invalidity or injury	P	N	N	I	P	N	N	N	P
11.4 Strike pay	N	N.A.	I	N	I	I	I	N	P
11.5 Family allowance	N	N	N	I	N	N.A.	N	N	P
11.6 Dwelling allowance	N	I	I	I	N	N.A.	N	P	P
11.7 Others	P	P	N.A.	P	N	N.A.	N	P	P
12. Alimony and maintenance receipts	I	N	N	I	I	I	P	N	I
13. Capital gains*									
13.1 Short-term	I	N	I	I	P	I	P	P	I
13.2 Long-term	I	N	I	P	P	P	P	P	I
14. Others									
14.1 Foreign earnings	I	P	I	I	I	I	I	I	P
14.2 Foreign pensions	I	P	I	I	I	I	P	P	I

* Income source dealt with in more detail in *The Personal Income Tax Base* (OECD, 1990)
** Refers to personal accounts only, i.e., accrued interest in pension funds is excluded
*** Or I at the choice of the taxpayer
**** Interest from future issues is taxable
I Income source subject to tax
P Some components of income source subject to tax, others not
N Income source not subject to tax
N.A. Information not applicable
[ ] The situation as of January 1, 1989

Source: *The Personal Income Tax Base: a comparative study* (OECD, 1990)

Table 3.6 Reliefs for specific sources of income, 1990

Country	Dividends	Interest	Pensions and Retirement income
Australia			Tax credit given in respect of certain social security pension
Austria	Subject to tax at half the statutory rate which would be applicable on entire taxable income		Tax credit of fixed amount for pensions
Belgium		Interest from certain savings accounts exempt up to a limit	Tax credit for retirement pensions
Denmark			Higher personal reliefs for pensioners
Finland		Fixed tax allowance	Tax allowance
France	Fixed tax allowance	Interest on first savings account with postal services exempt	Proportionate deduction from pensions subject to a ceiling
Germany		Certain interest payments exempt, e.g., on government bonds	Tax allowance related to income
Greece	Fixed tax allowance for dividends of stocks registered in stock market	Interest in bank accounts and on certain government bonds excluded from income subject to tax	

	Dividends	Interest	
Iceland	Subject to a ceiling, dividend income up to 15% of total value of share is exempt	Interest generally exempt	
Ireland	Subject to certain conditions, 50% of dividend income from manufacturing companies is exempt	Exemption for certain government interest	
Japan		Exemption for interest on a small deposits and government bonds received by certain persons, e.g. qualified aged persons.	Fixed allowance
Luxembourg	Fixed tax allowance for certain dividend income	Fixed tax allowance for saving deposit or government bond interest	
Netherlands	First Gld 1,000 of dividend income exempt. For married couples the exemption is Gld 2,000.	First Gld 1,000 of interest income exempt. For married couples the exemption is Gld 2,000	

Table 3.6 (Cont.)

Country	Dividends	Interest	Pensions and Retirement income
New Zealand	First NZ$ 100 of interest and dividend income exempt in 1990 (this relief to be abolished from 1991)		
Norway	Tax allowance for dividends and interest subject to a ceiling		
Portugal	Distributions from domestic portfolio investment funds are exempt		Tax allowance
Turkey	Dividend derived by resident taxpayers are not taxable.		
United Kingdom	Income from investment in a Personal Equity Plan exempt	Minor reliefs for certain savings bank and other government interest	Public pensions generally exempt from tax

Table 3.7 The degree of fiscal privilege for basic rate taxpayers in the United Kingdom[a]

Asset type	1958–9 to 1962–3	1963–4 to 1967–8	1968–9 to 1972–3	1973–4 to 1977–8	1978–9 to 1982–3
Five-year insurance contract	156	161	139	120	132
House with 50 percent mortgage	12	50	100	192	104
Pension contributions (10 years)	65	71	71	63	56
Pension contributions (25 years)	46	51	51	41	37
Consumer durables (50 percent loan)	109	130	96	70	31
National savings accounts	40	40	40	33	31
Ten-year insurance contract	64	64	40	9	28
House owned outright	–7	0	2	5	0
Twenty-year insurance contract	13	11	–13	–48	–27
Shares (3 percent dividend)	–6	–13	–31	–43	–42
Gifts (3 percent coupon)	–8	–21	–34	–80	–47
Shares (5½ percent dividend)	–39	–39	–55	–66	–60
Building society accounts	–7	–26	–66	–133	–78
Unit Trusts	–50	–42	–60	–101	–81

[a] Fiscal privilege is calculated as the difference between the asset owner's marginal income tax rate and the effective tax rate on the asset's real return. It is assumed that the pre-tax real rate of return on all assets is equal to 3 percent per annum. No account is taken of the effects of corporate taxation.

Source: Hill (1984), table 2.5, p. 53.

Table 3.8 Tax rates applied to interest payments (January 1991)

Country	Tax rate on interest under the personal income tax		Withholding tax on domestic interest rates	Top rate of capital gains tax
	Top rate	Average marginal rate		
Australia	48.3	39	–	48.3
Austria	50	39.7	10	50
Belgium	10	10	10	0
Canada	49.1	39.5	–	36.8
Denmark	57.8	51.1	–	57.8
Finland	0	0	10	0
France	18.1	5.6	18.1	18.1
Germany	53	39.1	–	0
Greece	0	0	25–40	0
Iceland	0	0	–	39.8
Ireland	53	38.4	30	50.0
Italy	12.5	12.5	12.5–30	20
Japan	20	20	20	20
Luxembourg	51.25	25.6	–	0
Netherlands	60	42	–	0
New Zealand	33	n.a.	30	0
Norway	40.5	n.a.	–	40.0
Portugal	25	25	25	10
Spain	56	31.5	25	56.0
Sweden	30	30	30	30
Switzerland	43.5	30.8	35	0
Turkey	10	10	10	50.0
United Kingdom	40	24	–	40.0
United States	36	28	–	36.0

Source: Taxing Profits in a Global Economy (OECD, 1991).

Italy, Japan, New Zealand, Portugal, Spain, Sweden, Switzerland, and Turkey) ranging between 12.5 percent and 40 percent (see table 3.8). In Germany a 10 percent withholding tax on interest was abolished as of July 1, 1989. In Belgium, France, and Portugal, the receiver of interest can choose the withholding tax as the final tax paid.

In most countries, double taxation treaties reduce the rate of withholding on interest payments to non-residents, sometimes completely abolishing such taxes. Thus, most of the interest flows to OECD treaty partners from France, Germany, Iceland, Ireland, Luxembourg, Netherlands, Norway, Sweden,

Switzerland, United Kingdom, and United States are not subject to a withholding tax.

Also, it is important to note that interest income on euro–deposits and euro–bonds are generally not taxed by the countries that host the market. Even where cross-border flows are subject to a withholding tax, the residence country (at least within the OECD area) will provide a credit for the tax paid in the source country. Thus, the relevant tax rate becomes the marginal tax rate of the source country, at least insofar as the investor is not in the position of having excess credits. Thus, either no taxation or residence taxation tends to be the rule for cross-border interest flows, at least insofar as investors either choose or are forced (because of exchange of information provisions) to declare their interest income to the tax authorities of their home country.

All of this suggests that taxation is probably more or less neutral with respect to interest flows arising for international portfolio debt investment traded in euro–markets. Taxation does, however, appear to discriminate in favor of non-resident portfolio investment (i.e., capital import neutrality is not achieved.[3] Although it is unclear how far this will produce a misallocation of saving (this will depend on the view taken on the efficiency of international capital markets), it will result in a redistribution of the tax base between countries, with resulting revenue losses and gains for countries.

It is of interest to speculate what will be the impact of current tax reforms on the level and composition of saving. In most OECD countries, reforms involve three main characteristics:

marginal schedule rates of tax are reduced;
the tax base is widened as tax incentives are removed and new sources of income taxed;
there is a shift from income to consumption taxes.[4]

A number of countries (e.g., Denmark, the United States) have also shifted part of the tax burden from households to corporations. For the most part, these reforms have been revenue-neutral.

These reforms will tend to increase somewhat the level of saving since the income effect of tax cuts is insignificant because they are revenue neutral, whereas the substitution effect is probably positive (although weak) since an intertemporal substitution of saving for consumption should be encouraged by a lowering of marginal tax rates and a shift from income to consumption taxes. Another potential positive impact will come about where the reforms reduced tax incentives for borrowing, as was the case in Denmark, Norway, and Sweden. It has been estimated in Denmark that household saving increased by 1.5 percent as a result of recent tax reforms and, in particular, the limits placed on the deductibility of interest (see Skatterministeriat, 1989, Okonnisk, Oversigt).

The shift of the tax burden from households to firms may, however, depress saving, as may the wealth-increasing effect of the elimination of investment incentives.

The effect on the composition of saving is more difficult to predict since it depends upon the nature of the tax changes. Insofar as reforms provide a more equal treatment of different saving instruments (which is *not* the case in most countries), then tax-induced distortions in saving patterns will become less important.

NOTES

1   This section draws upon a summary prepared by Roger Smith of the University of Alberta and is part of a larger study undertaken by the OECD on taxation and saving.
2   For a more extensive discussion, see *Tax Policies and Urban Housing Markets* (OECD, 1986).
3   For further explanation, see *Taxing Profits in a Global Economy* (OECD, 1991).
4   For details, see Annex I in *Role of Tax Reform in Central and Eastern European Economies* (OECD, 1991).

REFERENCES

Auerbach, Alan J. and Kotlikoff, Laurence J. 1982: Investment versus Savings Incentives: The Size of the Bang for the Buck and the Potential for Self-Financing Business Tax Cuts. *NBER Working Paper* 1027 (Cambridge, Mass.: National Bureau of Economic Research, November).

Bentzell, Ragnar and Berg, Lennart 1983: The Role of Demographic Factors as a Determinant of Savings in Sweden. In Franco Modigliani and Richard Hemming (eds.), *The Determinants of National Saving and Wealth*. London: Macmillan.

Boskin, Michael J. 1978: Taxation, Saving, and the Rate of Interest. *Journal of Political Economy*, 86 (April).

Bosworth, Barry P. 1990: International Differences in Saving. *American Economic Review* 80, 2 (May).

Bovenberg, A. Lans 1988: Private Saving: Measurement and Analysis of Recent Trends. Unpublished; Washington, D.C.: International Monetary Fund.

Bovenberg, A. Lans and Evans, Owen 1990: National and Personal Saving in the United States: Measurement and Analysis of Recent Trends. *Staff Papers* 37, 3, International Monetary Fund. Washington, September.

Carroll, Chris and Summers, Lawrence H. 1987: Why Have Private Saving Rates in the United States and Canada Diverged? *Journal of Monetary Economics*, Vol. 20 (September).

Hagemann, Robert P. and Nicoletti, Giuseppe 1989: Ageing Populations: Economic

Effects and Implications for Public Finance. *Working Paper* No. 61, Department of Economics and Statistics. Paris: OECD.

Hayashi, Fumio 1986: Why is Japan's Saving Rate So Apparently High? In *NBER Macroeconomics Annual 1986*, Stanley Fischer (ed.). Cambridge, Mass.: MIT Press.

Heller, Peter 1989: Ageing, Savings, Pensions in the Group of Seven Countries: 1980–2025. *Journal of Public Policy* 9, 2 (April–June).

Hill, J. 1984: Saving and Fiscal Privilega. Institute for Fiscal Studies. London.

Horioka, Charles Yuji 1984: The Applicability of the Life-Cycle Hypothesis of Saving to Japan. *The Kyoto University Economic Review*, 54 (October).

Feldstein, M. and Horioka, Charles Yuji 1980: Domestic Saving and International Capital Flows. *Economic Journal*, 90 (June).

Horioka, Charles Yuji 1990: Why is Japan's Household Saving Rate so High? A Literature Survey. *Journal of Japanese and International Economies* 4, 1 (March).

Howrey, E. Philip and Hymans, Saul H. 1978: The Measurement and Determination of Loanable Funds. *Brookings Papers on Economic Activity*, 3. Washington, D.C.: The Brookings Institution.

Hurd, Michael D. 1990: Research on the Elderly: Economic Status, Retirement, and Consumption and Saving. *Journal of Economic Literature*, 28 (June).

Kopitz, George and Gotur, Padma 1980: The Influence of Social Security on Household Savings: A Cross-Country Investigation. *Staff Papers* 27, 1. Washington: International Monetary Fund, March.

Kotlikoff, Laurence J. 1983: National Savings and Economic Policy: The Efficacy of Investment and Savings Incentives. *American Econonic Review*, 73 (May).

Kotlikoff, Laurence J. 1988: Intergenerational Transfers and Savings. *Journal of Economic Perspectives*, 2 (Spring).

Leff, N. 1969: Dependency Rates and Saving Rates. *American Economic Review* (9th December).

Modigliani, Franco 1988: The Role of Intergenerational Transfers and Life Cycle Saving in the Accumulation of Wealth. *Journal of Economic Perspectives*, 2 (Spring).

Nicoletti, Giuseppe 1988: A Cross-Country Analysis of Private Consumption, Inflation and the Debt Neutrality Hypothesis. *OECD Econonic Studies*, 11 (Autumn).

Oudet, Bruno A. 1979: Data and Studies on Saving in France: A Survey. In *Social Security versus Private Saving*, George M. von Furstenberg (ed.). Cambridge, Mass.: Ballinger.

Obstfeld, M. 1985: Capital Mobility in a World Economy *NBER Working Paper* No. 1962.

Shibuya, Hiroshi 1987: Japan's Household Savings Rate: An Application of the Life-Cycle Hypothesis. *IMF Working Paper* WP/87/15. Washington, D.C.: International Monetary Fund.

Shibuya, Hiroshi 1988: Japan's Household Savings: A Life-Cycle Model with Implicit Annuity Contract and Rational Expectations. Unpublished; Washington, D.C.: International Monetary Fund.

Shinohara, Miyohei 1983: The Determinants of Post-War Savings Behavior in Japan. In *The Determinants of National Saving and Wealth*, Franco Modigliani and Richard Hemming (eds). New York: St Martin's Press.

Skinner, Jonathan and Feinberg, Daniel 1989: The Impact of the 1986 Tax Reform on Personal Saving. *Working Paper* No. 90–3, The Office of Tax Policy Research. Ann Arbor: School of Business Administration, University of Michigan, December.

Smith, Roger S. 1990: Factors Affecting Saving, Policy Tools, and Tax Reform: A Review. *Staff Papers* 37, 1. International Monetary Fund: Washington, D.C., March.

Sturm, Peter H. 1983: Determinants of Saving: Theory and Evidence. *OECD Economic Studies*, 1 (Autumn).

Summers, Lawrence H. 1981: Capital Taxation and Accumulation in a Life Cycle Growth Model. *American Economic Review*, 71 (September).

Turner, P. 1986: Savings Investment and the Current Account. *Bank of Japan Monetary and Economic Studies* (October).

Venti, Steven F. and Wise David A. 1987: IRAs and Saving. In *The Effects of Taxation on Capital Accumulation*, Martin S. Feldstein (ed.). Chicago: University of Chicago Press.

Weber, Warren E. 1975: Interest Rates, Inflation, and Consumer Expenditures. *American Economic Review*, 65 (December).

Part II

Empirical Evidence

4

US Saving Behavior in
the Post-War Period*

Lawrence J. Lau

INTRODUCTION

The post-war US saving rate, as conventionally measured, is well known to be low by international standards. It is worthwhile examining the trends in the actual consumption and saving data of the United States. Figure 4.1 presents the aggregate personal consumption expenditures for the US economy from 1948 to 1980 in constant 1972 prices. Aggregate consumption expenditure has grown steadily during this period, with an apparent acceleration in the rate of growth beginning in the early 1960s. The average annual rate of growth in real consumption rose from 2.9 percent in the period 1950–62 to 3.3 percent in the period 1963–80, an increase of 13 percent. Had consumption continued growing at its slower early post-war pace, annual real consumption would have been at least 6 percent less by 1980 than in fact occurred. The growth in consumption per household, however, was much slower in the 1963–80 period than in the 1950–62 period (see the discussion on pp. 165–70 below).

Figure 4.2 presents the ratio of personal consumption of GNP. From the 1950s to the early 1960s, consumption was relatively constant as a share of GNP. Beginning in the early 1960s, it fell for several years, and then fluctuated in a narrow band around 0.62 through the end of the 1970s.

Figure 4.3 looks at the flip side of consumption, namely saving. It presents the actual personal saving (as measured in the National Income and Product Accounts (NIPA)) to GNP ratio. From a very low rate in the immediate post-war period, personal saving as a ratio of GNP rose rapidly in the late 1940s, was fairly stable around 5 percent throughout the 1950s, rose to a little over 6

* This chapter is based, in part, on joint research done by Dr Michael Boskin, Dr Mah-Lih Chen, and the author. The author wishes to thank both Michael Boskin and Mah-Lih Chen for helpful discussions. Responsibility for any error is solely the author's.

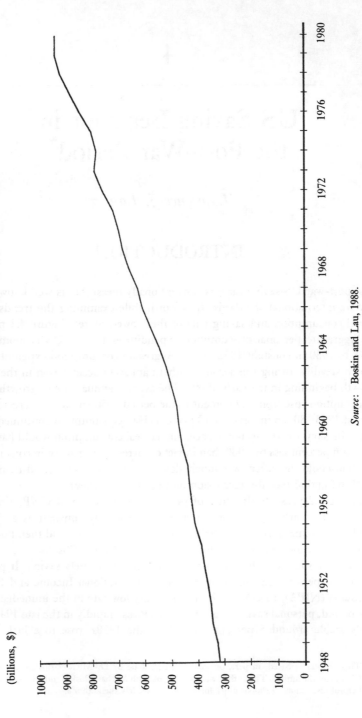

Figure 4.1 Aggregate personal consumption expenditures (billion, 1972$)

Source: Boskin and Lau, 1988.

Figure 4.2 Comsumption/GNP

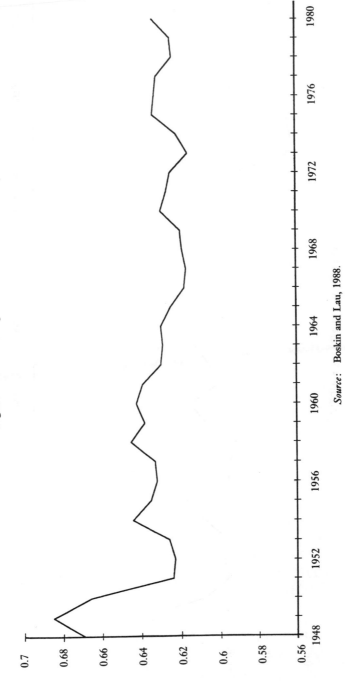

Source: Boskin and Lau, 1988.

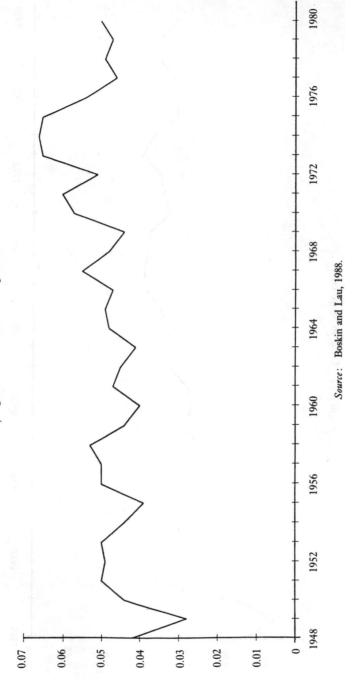

Figure 4.3 Personal saving/GNP

Source: Boskin and Lau, 1988.

percent in the early 1970s, and has been on a somewhat downward trend from the mid-1970s to 1980 (a trend which has continued into the 1980s).

To put the decline in the personal saving rate in the proper context, figure 4.4 presents the business saving to GNP ratio and the private saving to GNP ratio from 1947 through 1987. It is apparent that the decline in the private saving rate, which began in the mid-1970s, was primarily due to a decline in the personal saving rate and not in the business saving rate. In fact, the business saving rate has actually been rising since the early 1970s.

What were the proximate causes of these changes in the consumption and saving behavior of the United States? To what extent do changes in relative prices (e.g., real after-tax rates of return to saving) and demographics (as reflected by the shares of wealth held by households headed by persons of different ages and vintages) affect aggregate consumption? The objective of this chapter is to assess the importance of various factors affecting aggregate consumption and saving in the post-war period and to account for the growth of aggregate consumption on the basis of these factors, drawing on some recent research of Boskin and Lau and their associates.

THE MODEL OF AGGREGATE
CONSUMPTION OF BOSKIN AND LAU (1988)

A new empirical analysis of aggregate United States consumption and saving for the period 1947–80 is developed and presented by Boskin and Lau (1988).[1] The Boskin and Lau (1988) model recognizes explicitly that households with different characteristics, e.g., age, may be heterogeneous in their behavior and that the aggregate consumption and saving behavior may therefore depend on the changing composition of households by characteristics and may not be adequately portrayed by a single representative consumer. The model integrates longitudinal and cross-sectional microeconomic data on household characteristics, such as age cross-tabulated by income (or wealth), with the traditional aggregate time-series data, such as consumption, income, wealth, prices, wage rates, and interest rates, using the theory of exact aggregation.[2]

One important theoretical underpinning of the Boskin and Lau (1988) model is the life-cycle consumption hypothesis of Modigliani and Brumberg (1954), which attaches special importance to the lifetime wealth constraint and age for current consumption at the individual household level, and demographics and the distribution of wealth at the aggregate level. However, Boskin and Lau (1988) make no explicit optimizing assumption on the part of the individual households in their model.

An alternative to the life-cycle hypothesis is the Ricardian equivalence hypothesis, the modern restatement of which is due to Barro (1974). This hypothesis,

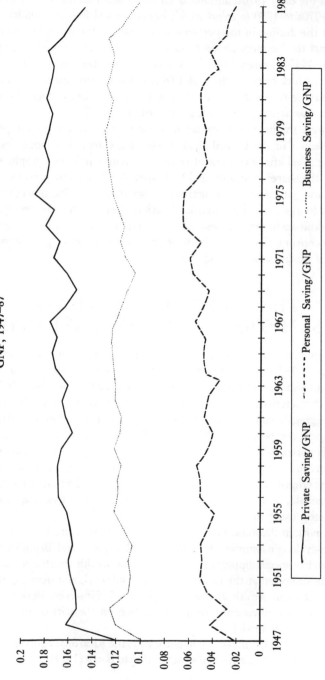

Figure 4.4   Personal saving/GNP, business saving/GNP, and private saving/
GNP, 1947–87

——— Private Saving/GNP   – – – – – Personal Saving/GNP   .... Business Saving/GNP

Source: Boskin and Lau, 1988.

also known as the intergenerational altruism model, has the striking time-series implication that changes in the age distribution of resources should not affect aggregate consumption, conditional on aggregate resources, because transfers among cohorts will result in exactly offsetting consumption and saving behavior so as to maintain aggregate consumption constant. Numerous time-series consumption function studies of this phenomenon and attempted tests of the Ricardian equivalence hypothesis are surveyed and criticized in Barth, Iden, and Russek (1984–5) and Bernheim (1987). While the results of these studies are not uniform, and are subject to some methodological criticisms (see especially the discussion in Bernheim, 1987), the bulk of the research results tends to reject a strict interpretation of the Ricardian equivalence hypothesis. However, most studies also reject complete Keynesian myopia and estimate that future taxes are at least partially anticipated. Perhaps a quasi-consensus estimate is that a one-dollar debt for tax substitution would increase consumption about 30 to 40 cents (see Boskin, 1988).

A more direct test, less susceptible to some of the criticisms of the traditional time-series consumption functions, is performed by Boskin and Kotlikoff (1985). They build a finite approximation of an intergenerationally altruistic infinitely-lived optimal consumption program and test whether the age distribution of resources affects consumption. They reject the independence of aggregate consumption from the age distribution.

The Boskin and Lau (1988) model does not adopt either the life-cycle hypothesis or the Ricardian equivalence hypothesis. It uses a flexible functional form which can be consistent with either hypothesis. Boskin and Lau (1988) impose minimal assumptions on household behavior. They impose the wealth constraint and the restriction of "no money illusion," but not necessarily utility maximization, on the individual household demand functions.[3] The rationale for maintaining the hypothesis of summability is simply that each individual household can make its lifetime consumption, leisure, and bequest choices only within its wealth constraint. The rationale for maintaining the hypothesis of zero degree homogeneity is simply that each individual household should not change its lifetime consumption, leisure and bequest choices if the set of possible choices (represented by all available choices within the wealth constraint) is unchanged. Note that the two hypotheses do not imply utility maximization of the individual household. The decision-making process within each household can be arbitrary as long as it is stationary over time.

Specification of the Aggregate Expenditure Functions

The aggregate consumption and leisure expenditure functions used by Boskin and Lau (1988) are obtained by adding up the individual consumption and leisure expenditure functions across all households:

$$\sum_i p_t C_{it} = [(\alpha_c + \beta_{cc}\ell np_t + \beta_{cz}\ell nw_{0t} + \beta_{cr}\ell n(1+r_t))\sum_i W_{it} \tag{4.1}$$

$$- (\beta_{cc} + \beta_{cz})\sum_i W_{it}\ell nW_{it} + \sum_j \sum_i \alpha_{cj} D_{it}^j W_{it}]/$$

$$[1 + \beta_c(\ell np_t - \ell nw_{0t}) + \beta_r \ell n(1+r_t)]$$

$$\sum_i w_{it} Z_{it} = [(\alpha_z + \beta_{zc}\ell np_t + \beta_{zz}\ell nw_{0t} + \beta_{zr}\ell n(1+r_t))\sum_i W_{it} \tag{4.2}$$

$$- (\beta_{zc} + \beta_{zz})\sum_i W_{it}\ell nW_{it} + \sum_j \sum_i \alpha_{zj} D_{it}^j W_{it}]/$$

$$[1 + \beta_c(\ell np_t - \ell nw_{0t}) + \beta_r \ell n(1+r_t)]$$

where C_{it} is the quantity of consumption, Z_{it} is the quantity of leisure,[4] W_{it} is the value of total wealth, and w_{it} is the wage rate of the head, of the ith household in the tth period, respectively; p_t, w_{0t}, and r_t are the price of current consumption, the standard wage rate, and the real after-tax rate of interest, of the tth period, respectively; and D_{it}^j is a dummy variable which takes the value one if the ith household is of the jth type in the tth period and zero otherwise; and $(\sum_i W_{it}\ell nW_{it}) / \sum_i W_{it}$ can be interpreted as "entropy," a measure of the variability or the degree of inequality of the distribution of wealth over individual households and $(\sum_i D_{it}^j W_{it})/\sum_i W_{it}$ can be identified as the share of aggregate wealth held by households of the jth type in the tth period.

The dependent variables of equations (4.1) and (4.2), aggregate nominal consumption and leisure expenditures, are likely to show sustained increases over time because of both the increase in the number of households and inflation. In order to mitigate the possibility of heteroscedasticity of the stochastic disturbance terms, both sides of equations (4.1) and (4.2) are divided by aggregate wealth in the tth period, obtaining the aggregate consumption expenditure to wealth and leisure expenditure to wealth ratios:

$$\frac{\sum_i p_t C_{it}}{\sum_i W_{it}} = [(\alpha_c + \beta_{cc}\ell np_t + \beta_{cz}\ell nw_{0t} + \beta_{cr}\ell n(1+r_t)) \tag{4.3}$$

$$- (\beta_{cc} + \beta_{cz})\sum_i W_{it}\ell nW_{it}/\sum_i W_{it} + \sum_j \sum_i \alpha_{cj} D_{it}^j W_{it}/$$

$$\sum_i W_{it}]/[1 + \beta_c(\ell np_t - \ell nw_{0t}) + \beta_r \ell n(1+r_t)]$$

$$\frac{\sum_i w_{it} Z_{it}}{\sum_i W_{it}} = [(\alpha_z + \beta_{zc}\ell np_t + \beta_{zz}\ell nw_{0t} + \beta_{zr}\ell n(1+r_t)) \tag{4.4}$$

$$- (\beta_{zc} + \beta_{zz}) \sum_i W_{it} \ell n W_{it} / \sum_i W_{it} + \sum_j \sum_i \alpha_{zj} D_{it}^j W_{it} /$$

$$\sum_i W_{it}] / [1 + \beta_c(\ell n p_t - \ell n w_{0t}) + \beta_r \ell n (1 + r_t)]$$

The age-cohorts explicitly distinguished in the Boskin and Lau (1988) model are 14–24, 25–34, 35–44, 55–64 and over 65. Because of the presence of the constants α_c and α_z in equations (4.3) and (4.4), it is not necessary to have a dummy variable for households headed by persons in the age-cohort of 45–54 years. Boskin and Lau (1988) also introduce dummy variables distinguishing households headed by persons who were born prior to 1939 (the Depression vintage) from those born after 1939 (the post-Depression vintage). This Depression-vintage dummy variable is further decomposed into two separate dummy variables, one for households headed by persons aged 35 and above, and one for households headed by persons aged 34 and below. In addition, Boskin and Lau (1988) introduce one non-household specific independent variable which is believed to influence current consumption and leisure decisions, and unemployment rate, represented by the natural logarithm of the prime age white male unemployment rate (UE), in percent, and a time trend. The distributional variables as well as the unemployment rate move quite independently of one another and of the pure time trend.

Finally, Boskin and Lau (1988) add stochastic disturbance terms to both the consumption and leisure expenditure share equations. The stochastic disturbance terms are assumed to have a constant variance-covariance matrix over time and are possibly correlated across equations but not across time periods. Boskin and Lau (1988) use annual data from 1947 through 1980 for the estimation. The method of estimation used is nonlinear instrumental variables (see, for example, Gallant and Jorgenson (1979)). The set of instrumental variables used includes various demographic variables such as cohort population shares, proportions of female-headed, single and non-white households, lagged dependent variables, prices, wages, interest rates and cohort-wealth shares, oil prices and military expenditures, life expectancy, the ratio of non-white to total population, and the female labor force participation rate. The final specification of the aggregate consumption and leisure expenditure share functions take the form:

$$\sum_i p_t C_{it} / \sum_i W_{it} \tag{4.5}$$

$$= \left[(\alpha_c + \beta_{cc} \ell n p_t + \beta_{cz} \ell n w_{0t} + \beta_{cr} \ell n (1 + r_t)) \right.$$

$$\left. - (\beta_{cc} + \beta_{cz}) \left(\sum_i W_{it} \ell n W_{it} / \sum_i W_{it} \right) \right.$$

$$+ \alpha_{c14}\left(\sum_i D_{it}^{14}W_{it}/\sum_i W_{it}\right) + \alpha_{c25}\left(\sum_i D_{it}^{25}W_{it}/\sum_i W_{it}\right)$$

$$+ \alpha_{c35}\left(\sum_i D_{it}^{35}W_{it}/\sum_i W_{it}\right) + \alpha_{c55}\left(\sum_i D_{it}^{55}W_{it}/\sum_i W_{it}\right)$$

$$+ \alpha_{c65}\left(\sum_i D_{it}^{65}W_{it}\right) + \gamma_{cT} + TIME + \gamma_{CU}UE$$

$$+ \gamma_{cv.34}\left(\sum_i D_{it}^{39.34-}W_{it}/\sum_i W_{it}\right)$$

$$+ \gamma_{cv.35}\left(\sum_i D_{it}^{39.35+}W_{it}/\sum_i W_{it}\right)\Bigg] /$$

$$[1 + \beta_c(\ell np_t - \ell nw_{0t}) + \beta_r \ell n(1 + r_t)] + \varepsilon_{ct}$$

$$\sum_i w_{it}Z_{it}/\sum_i W_{it} \tag{4.6}$$

$$= \Bigg[(\alpha_z + \beta_{zc}\ell np_t + \beta_{zz}\ell nw_{0t} + \beta_{zr}\ell n(1 + r_t))$$

$$- (\beta_{zc} + \beta_{zz})\left(\sum_i W_{it}\ell nW_{it}/\sum_i W_{it}\right)$$

$$+ \alpha_{z14}\left(\sum_i D_{it}^{14}W_{it}/\sum_i W_{it}\right) + \alpha_{z25}\left(\sum_i D_{it}^{25}W_{it}/\sum_i W_{it}\right)$$

$$+ \alpha_{z35}\left(\sum_i D_{it}^{35}W_{it}/\sum_i W_{it}\right) + \alpha_{z55}\left(\sum_i D_{it}^{55}W_{it}/\sum_i W_{it}\right)$$

$$+ \alpha_{z65}\left(\sum_i D_{it}^{65}W_{it}/\sum_i W_{it}\right)$$

$$+ \gamma_{zT} + TIME + \gamma_{zu}UE$$

$$+ \gamma_{zv.34}\left(\sum_i D_{it}^{39.34-}W_{it}/\sum_i W_{it}\right)$$

$$+ \gamma_{zv.35}\left(\sum_i D_{it}^{39.35+}W_{it}/\sum_i W_{it}\right)\Big] /$$

$$[1 + \beta_c(\ell np_t - \ell nw_{0t}) + \beta_r\ell n(1 + r_t)] + \varepsilon_{zt}$$

In the final specification there is only one vintage dummy variable for the consumption expenditure equation, that is, there is a uniform vintage effect for all ages.[5]

It is important to note that the Boskin and Lau (1988) model focuses entirely on the household side – the demands for current and future consumption and leisure. The households are assumed to behave as price-takers, that is, as if their individual actions do not affect the (possibly subjective) joint distribution for current and future prices. The model leaves unexplained the current and future prices, wealth and its distribution. Thus, it is a partial equilibrium model.

The Empirical Results

The aggregate data are taken from standard sources. The methods for deriving expected inflation and the expected present value of human and non-human wealth are briefly described in the Appendix of Boskin and Lau (1988). For human wealth, Boskin and Lau (1988) estimate an age-wage profile[6] and discount expected future earnings of each age cohort by the sum of the real after-tax discount rate and mortality probability. They also take into account, in the estimation of the human wealth and the leisure endowment of the household, the changes in the size and composition of the average household. For non-human wealth, Boskin and Lau (1988) blow up, for each category of property income, the sum across all age cohorts so that it conforms to the corresponding NIPA aggregate totals, and then capitalize total property income for each age cohort. The details of the data construction are discussed in the Appendix of Boskin and Lau (1988).

In the aggregate, the Boskin and Lau (1988) model fits the data quite well by the usual statistical criteria. The first hypothesis tested by Boskin and Lau (1988) is whether the specification of the age-profile effects used is better than a flat age profile (that is, no age effects). The hypothesis of a flat age profile is rejected. A number of additional hypotheses commonly found in the literature on consumption behavior are also tested in Boskin and Lau (1988). They are:

Unitary wealth elasticity Individual household consumption (and leisure) expenditure is proportional to individual household wealth.

Permanent income hypothesis This hypothesis is often identified with Friedman (1957).[7] It implies that consumption (and leisure) expenditure is proportional to wealth, and, in addition, that the factors of proportionality depend only on the rate of interest but not the prices, given wealth.

Absence of interest rate effects   This hypothesis implies that both consumption and leisure expenditures are, *given wealth*, independent of the real after-tax rate of interest. However, it does not preclude a change in the real rate of interest from affecting consumption expenditure indirectly through its effect on the revaluation of wealth (the so-called "Summers' effect").

Complete price independence   This hypothesis implies that the consumption and leisure expenditures are fixed independently of current and expected future prices, given wealth.

All of these hypotheses are rejected by Boskin and Lau (1988).

The actual estimation results themselves are striking. The most important finding is the substantial estimated difference in the shares of wealth consumed between households headed by persons born prior to and those born after 1939, *at the same age*, other things being equal. We shall identify the former group of households as Depression vintage households and latter group as post-Depression vintage households on the grounds that the first group experienced first-hand the hardships of the Great Depression. The share of wealth held by Depression vintage households has a statistically significant and large negative effect on aggregate real consumption. For every one percentage point increase in the share of wealth held by this group of households, the aggregate consumption-wealth ratio declines by 1.40 percentage points. In other words, if wealth were to be held entirely by this group, or if all other groups behaved similarly to this group, the consumption-wealth ratio would have been lower by 1.4 percentage points, a very significant amount![8]

Bifurcating the population into households headed by persons born before and after 1939 may seem extreme, but the Great Depression was a cataclysmic event for a whole generation of people which altered indelibly the attitude and behavior of those who experienced it. The non-existence of the vintage effect is strongly rejected. In addition, the vintage effects are found to be statistically significant even in the presence of a time trend variable, which in principle would reflect a uniform decline (or rise) in the share of wealth consumed over time.

Holding vintage constant, substantial age effects on consumption and leisure are also found. Thus, policies which shift resources among age groups are likely to affect aggregate consumption and saving. Strong evidence is also found of relative price effects, including those of real after-tax rate of interest. The time trend variable has a statistically significant positive effect. The estimated coefficient for the unemployment rate has the expected negative sign and is statistically significant. A change in the size distribution of wealth is found to have a negative effect on aggregate consumption, so that an increase in the degree of inequality of the size distribution of wealth, holding average real wealth constant, is expected to decrease aggregate consumption.

The real after-tax rate of interest is found to have a statistically significant effect: an increase in the real rate of interest, holding human and non-human wealth and hence, total wealth, constant, increases the consumption expenditure. Such a change in the real after-tax rate of interest lowers the forward prices of future consumption, under our assumptions, relative to the spot price of current consumption. The effect on current consumption is, however, theoretically ambiguous. Here it is found to be positive, which suggests that current and future consumption are more complements than substitutes. Correspondingly, its effect on saving (as defined in the National Income and Product Accounts) is negative.

COMPARATIVE STATICS OF CONSUMPTION AND SAVING

One important set of questions pertaining to consumption and saving has to do with the magnitudes and directions of the comparative static effects. Boskin and Lau (1988) provide estimates of the comparative static effects of changes in the current price of consumption, after-tax wage rate, wealth, and the real after-tax rate of interest on the consumption and saving, as defined in the National Income and Product Accounts (NIPA), of individual households. According to the NIPA definition, current saving is the difference between current income and current consumption and excludes any net change in wealth due to revaluations.

The saving of the ith household in the tth period, S_{it}, may be defined as the difference between current full income and current expenditure on consumption and leisure:

$$S_{it} = w_{it}\overline{Z}_{it} + (r_t + \pi_t)NHW_{it} - p_t C_{it} - w_{it}Z_{it} \qquad (4.7)$$

where $\overline{Z}_{it}$ is the maximum quantity of leisure and NHW_{it} is the value of non-human wealth of the ith household, and π_t is the rate of inflation, in the tth period.[9] It is assumed that $\partial \ell n \pi_t / \partial \ell n p_t = 0$. Current saving, S_{it}, may take negative values. If S_{it} is negative, $\dfrac{\partial \ell n S_{it}}{\partial \ell n p_t}$ is taken to be $\dfrac{1}{S_{it}} \dfrac{\partial S_{it}}{\partial \ell n p_t}$. The same applies to the other saving elasticities. In particular, the elasticities of saving with respect to wealth, the rate of interest and the wage rate may be computed as follows:

$$\frac{\partial \ell n S_{it}}{\partial \ell n W_{it}} = \left[-\frac{E_{it}}{S_{it}} \frac{\partial \ell n E_{it}}{\partial \ell n W_{it}} + \frac{(r_t + \pi_t)NHW_{it}}{S_{it}} \right]; {}^{.10} \qquad (4.8)$$

$$\frac{\partial \ell n S_{it}}{\partial \ell n HW_{it}} = \left[-\frac{E_{it}}{S_{it}} \frac{\partial \ell n E_{it}}{\partial \ell n W_{it}} + \frac{HW_{it}}{W_{it}} \right]; {}^{.11} \qquad (4.9)$$

$$\frac{\partial \ell n S_{it}}{\partial \ell n NHW_{it}} = \left[-\frac{E_{it}}{S_{it}} \frac{\partial \ell n E_{it}}{\partial \ell n W_{it}} \frac{NHW_{it}}{W_{it}} + (r + \pi_t) \frac{NHW_{it}}{W_{it}} \right], \qquad (4.10)$$

$$\frac{\partial \ell n S_{it}}{\partial \ell n r_t} = \left[-\frac{E_{it}}{S_{it}} \frac{\partial \ell n E_{it}}{\partial \ell n r_t} + r_t \frac{NHW_{it}}{S_{it}} \right]$$

where E_{it} is total expenditure, that is, the sum of consumption and leisure expenditures, and HW_{it} is the value of human wealth, of the ith household in the tth period.

Boskin and Lau (1988) also compute the elasticities of consumption and saving with respect to the after-tax wage rate and the real after-tax rate of interest under the assumption of full revaluation of human wealth of the household. Non-human wealth of the household is assumed to consist entirely of floating rate assets and liabilities and hence to remain unchanged with respect to changes in the real after-tax rate of interest. They make use of the fact that $(\partial \ell n HW_{it})/(\partial \ell n w_{it}) = 1$ under the assumptions on expectations. The values of $\frac{HW_{it}}{W_{it}}$ and $\frac{\partial \ell n HW_{it}}{\partial \ell n r_t}$ are calculated numerically for each age–cohort based on its current expected future wage rates and real rates of interest. In particular,

$$\frac{d \ell n S_{it}}{d \ell n w_{it}} = \frac{\partial \ell n S_{it}}{\partial \ell n w_{it}} + \frac{\partial \ell n S_{it}}{\partial \ell n HW_{it}} \qquad (4.11)$$

$$\frac{d \ell n S_{it}}{d \ell n r_t} = \frac{\partial \ell n S_{it}}{\partial \ell n r_t} + \frac{\partial \ell n S_{it}}{\partial \ell n HW_{it}} \cdot \frac{\partial \ell n HW_{it}}{\partial \ell n r_t} \qquad (4.12)$$

With positive saving, both $\dfrac{\partial \ell n S_{it}}{\partial \ell n HW_{it}}$ and $\dfrac{\partial n HW_{it}}{\partial \ell n r_t}$ are expected to be negative.

Thus, $\dfrac{d \ell n S_{it}}{d \ell n r_t} \geq \dfrac{\partial \ell n S_{it}}{\partial \ell n r_t}$, that is, the elasticity of saving with respect to the real after-tax rate of interest with human wealth evaluation is expected to be greater than that without human wealth revaluation. With negative saving, the opposite is true. These same formulae are also used in the calculation of the aggregate elasticities.

Table 4.1 Estimated Elasticities of Consumption and Saving with respect to Wealth, Interest Rate, Wage Rate, and Price
(Calculated for households headed by persons in the age-cohort 45–54 with the independent variables evaluated at their 1972 values)

WITHOUT HUMAN WEALTH REVALUATION

Elasticity with respect to	CONSUMPTION		SAVING	
	Pre-1939	*Post-1939*	*Pre-1939*	*Post-1939*
Total wealth	0.643	0.727	−10.810	7.747
	(10.350)	(15.336)	(−13.009)	(15.069)
Human wealth	0.550	0.622	−9.249	6.629
	(10.350)	(15.336)	(−13.009)	(15.069)
Non-human wealth	0.093	0.105	0.322	−0.046
	(10.350)	(15.336)	(2.684)	(−0.623)
Real interest rate	0.190	0.165	−2.679	1.745
	(1.729)	(8.147)	(−6.443)	(7.440)
Wage rate	−0.027	−0.020	10.617	−6.567
	(−0.264)	(−0.232)	(9.192)	(−8.812)
Price of consumption	−0.616	−0.707	−4.040	2.500
	(−9.831)	(−10.782)	(−4.593)	(4.098)

WITH HUMAN WEALTH REVALUATION

Elasticity with respect to	CONSUMPTION		SAVING	
	Pre-1939	*Post-1939*	*Pre-1939*	*Post-1939*
Real interest rate	0.075	0.035	−0.748	0.361
	(4.212)	(2.630)	(−2.715)	(2.424)
Wate rate	0.523	0.602	1.369	0.059
	(7.927)	(8.946)	(1.560)	(0.098)

Numbers in parentheses are asymptotic t-ratios.
Source: Boskin and Lau (1988).

In table 4.1, the Boskin and Lau (1988) estimates of the elasticities of consumption and saving of a representative household headed by a person in the 45–54 age cohort in 1972 with respect to total, human, and non-human wealth, the real after-tax rate of interest, the wage rate, and the price of consumption are presented for both the Depression and post-Depression vintages of households.[12] The first set of estimates in table 4.1 is labelled "without human wealth revaluation," that is, they measure the effects of changes in the independent variables on consumption and saving of the household, *holding both human and non-human wealth* of the household constant. However, in reality, when the real after-tax rate of interest changes, wealth can be expected to remain constant only if it is held entirely in the form of floating-rate assets and liabilities. In general, if the stream of future incomes of an asset remains the same, the value of the asset is expected to decrease with an increase in the real after-tax rate of interest. Under the assumption that non–human wealth is held entirely in the form of floating-rate assets (and liabilities), so that it would be insensitive to changes in the real rate of interest, only human wealth would be revalued in response to a change in the real after-tax rate of interest. The second set of estimates in table 4.1 measures the effects of changes in the independent variables on consumption and saving of the household, *taking into account its effect on the valuation of the human wealth* of the household. It is therefore labelled *"with human wealth revaluation."* The same consideration applies to the effects of changes in the wage rate, which can also be expected to affect the valuation of the human wealth of the household directly.

The estimated consumption and saving in 1972 prices for the Depression vintage household are $13,760 and $1,629 respectively. The corresponding estimates for the post-Depression vintage household are $18,060 and –$2,633.[13] Thus, saving turns out to be negative for the post-Depression vintage household headed by a person in the 45–54 age cohort in 1972! The elasticities of saving for the post-Depression vintage household must therefore be interpreted with the negative sign in mind. The separate estimated consumption and saving for the Depression and post-Depression vintage households also serve to illustrate the magnitude of the difference in the consumption and saving behavior between them.[14]

With only a few exceptions, to be noted below, the estimated elasticities of consumption and saving presented in table 4.1 are all statistically significant. The elasticities of consumption with respect to total wealth fall between the narrow range of 0.64 and 0.73 for all – Depression as well as post-Depression vintage – households. The effect of total wealth on saving is negative and statistically significant for households of both vintages. The elasticity of saving with respect to total wealth is –10.8 for the Depression vintage household and 7.75 for the post-Depression vintage household.[15] The elasticities of consumption with respect to human wealth are somewhat smaller in value than the corresponding elasticities with respect to total wealth – ranging between 0.55 and 0.63. The effect of human wealth on saving is, like total wealth, also negative and statistically significant, but somewhat smaller in absolute value than the effect of total wealth. The elasticities of consumption with respect to non–human wealth are approximately equal to 0.1 and statistically significant. Translated to the more customary marginal propensities to consume out of non–human wealth, the estimates are about 0.032, quite similar to the usual time-series estimates. The effect of non–human wealth on saving is positive but statistically significant only for the Depression vintage household. The elasticity of consumption with respect to the price of consumption is negative, as expected, and statistically significant – ranging between −0.61 and −0.71. The effect of the price of current consumption on saving is negative and statistically significant. The elasticity of saving with respect to the price of consumption is approximately −0.4 for the Depression vintage household and 2.5 for the post-Depression vintage household.

Holding both human and non-human, and hence total, wealth constant, the elasticity of consumption with respect to the real after-tax rate of interest is found to be statistically significant for the post-Depression vintage household but not for the Depression vintage household. The magnitude of the estimated elasticity is not large – less than 0.2. The effect of a change in the real rate of interest on saving is negative and statistically significant for households of both vintages. For the Depression vintage households, the elasticity of saving with respect to the real rate of interest is −2.7. For the post-Depression vintage households, saving is negative, and the elasticity of saving is therefore a positive 1.7. This finding of a large negative effect of the real rate of interest on saving may seem surprising but may be dependent on the NIPA definition of saving as well as the assumption that wealth is held constant. The elasticities of consumption with respect to the wage rate are small and negative but not statistically significant, although it is suggestive of possible complementarity between current consumption and current leisure. The effect of the wage rate on saving is positive, large and statistically significant.

With full human wealth revaluation, however, the comparative static effects of changes in the real after-tax rate of interest and the wage rate change considerably. The elasticities of consumption with respect to the real after-tax rate of interest become much smaller in magnitude but are statistically significant. Similarly, the elasticities of saving with respect to the real after-tax rate of interest are reduced in absolute value by a factor of between 3 and 5. The elasticities of consumption with respect to the wage rate become statistically significant and range between 0.52 and 0.61. The effects of the wage rate on saving become statistically insignificant.

The finding that with full human wealth revaluation, the effect of the real after-tax rate of interest on saving is negative and statistically significant may also seem surprising in view of the results of some other aggregate time-series consumption function studies, e.g., Boskin (1978) and Summers (1982, 1984), and warrants further investigation. This "backward bending" household supply curve of saving is, however, suggestive of a target-saving (wealth) hypothesis.

It is also apparent from table 4.1 that the estimated comparative static effects differ quite systematically between the Depression and post-Depression vintages of households. One broad generalization appears to be that the elasticities of consumption for the Depression vintage households are all smaller in absolute value than the corresponding ones for the post-Depression vintage households. Thus, the consumption of the Depression vintage households is less sensitive (or elastic) to changes in the economic environment. By contrast, the elasticities of saving for the Depression vintage households are all larger in absolute value than the corresponding ones for the post-Depression vintage households. Thus, the saving of the Depression vintage households is more sensitive (or elastic) to changes in the economic environment.

In addition to varying between the Depression and post-Depression vintage households, the comparative static effects also vary significantly across age cohorts and households with different ratios of non-human to total wealth. This is illustrated in figures 4.5 and 4.6. Figure 4.5 shows how the effects on saving, with full human wealth revaluation, of a one percent change in the real after-tax rate of interest in 1972, differ between Depression and post-Depression vintages and across age cohorts. Figure 4.6 shows how the effects on saving, with full human wealth revaluation, of a one percent change in the real interest rate in 1972, differ across households headed by persons in the 45–54 age cohort with different ratios of non-human to total wealth. Note, in particular, that the effects turn from negative to positive as the ratio of non-human to total wealth exceeds approximately 25 percent.

It is of some interest to calculate the interest elasticity of *aggregate* personal saving, taking into account the joint distribution of households by wealth, Depression and post-Depression vintage, age cohort; and the ratio of non-human to total wealth. This parameter measures the percentage change in *aggregate* personal saving in response to a one-percent change in the real after-tax rate of interest. This elasticity may be calculated to be −0.87 (with human wealth revaluation) in 1972 and −0.02 in 1980. Thus, it is apparent that in the aggregate, assuming *full human wealth revaluation*, the interest elasticity of saving is negative but in any event quite small within the prevailing ranges of values of the independent variables.

The value of the interest elasticity of saving has been a subject of tremendous controversy (see, for example, Howrey and Hymans, 1980) because of its implication for fiscal policy, structural tax policy, and the social rate of discount, to name but a few. The results reported here are somewhat different from the results of Boskin (1978) and Summers (1981, 1982, 1984) concerning the effects of the real after-tax rate of return on aggregate saving. As discussed earlier, revaluing human wealth always increases the interest elasticity of saving for a household with positive saving and decreases it for a household with negative saving. With some households saving and others dissaving, the aggregate effect, being a weighted average, is in general indeterminate.

LIFETIME CONSUMPTION AND SAVING

Since the Boskin and Lau (1988) model of aggregate consumption is derived by summing up the consumption of individual households, it is possible to identify,

Figure 4.5 Change in saving for a 1% change in the real interest rate, by age cohort[a] (1972 values)

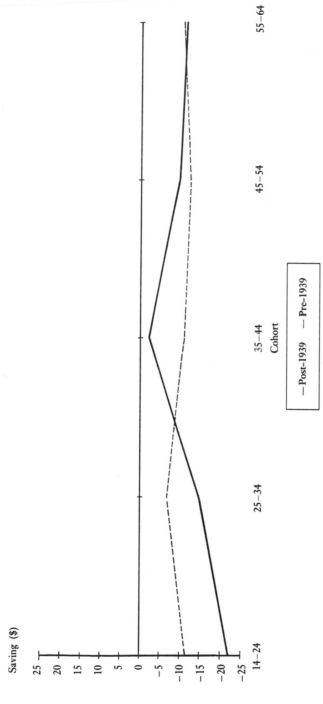

[a] Evaluated at mean level of NHW for each cohort. Real interest rate in 1972 was 3.56%.

Source: Boskin and Lau, 1988.

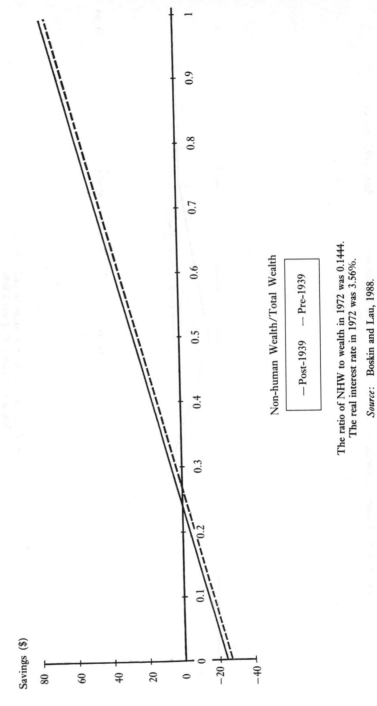

Figure 4.6 Change in saving for a 1% change in real interest rate, for the 45–54 age cohort[a] (1972 values)

Non-human Wealth/Total Wealth

—Post-1939 ---Pre-1939

The ratio of NHW to wealth in 1972 was 0.1444.
The real interest rate in 1972 was 3.56%.

Source: Boskin and Lau, 1988.

from their estimated aggregate consumption expenditure function, the parameters of the individual household consumption functions by age-cohort and by Depression or post-Depression vintage. Once these age-cohort and vintage-specific consumption functions are identified, it is possible to follow a household, distinguished by vintage, through its entire lifetime, beginning with an assumed level of initial non-human wealth and keeping track of its wealth accumulation and decumulation. This exercise has been carried out by Boskin, Chen, and Lau (1991), who simulate the consumption and saving behavior separately for the Depression and post-Depression vintage households over their entire lifetimes. For the simulation, price levels such as the average wage rate[16] and the prices of consumption are set at their 1972 levels. Initial non-human wealth (at age 25) is set at $15,000 in 1972 prices. The real after-tax rate of interest is set at 2 percent per annum. Under these assumptions, the lifetime total income, consumption and saving profiles for a household are generated through simulations beginning at age 25.

The results of the Boskin, Chen, and Lau (1991) simulations are presented in figures 4.7 , 4.8 and 4.9. Figure 4.7 presents the lifetime total income profile for the Depression and post-Depression vintage households. The income of the post-Depression vintage household is higher than that of the Depression vintage household at every age until after 65, the hypothetical retirement age. Two humps are recognizable from the total income profiles of both the Depression and post-Depression vintage households. They may be explained by changes in the labor participation rate of the members within the household in the middle ages as well as by the changes in the levels of non-labor income which relate directly to the levels of non-human wealth. Figure 4.8 presents the lifetime consumption profile for both vintages of households. There are, again two recognizable humps, although the second hump is less pronounced for the post-Depression vintage of households. The first hump may reflect the increased size of the household during the child-rearing years. Finally, figure 4.9 presents the lifetime saving profiles, which are the differences between the respective total income and consumption profiles. It appears that a young household saves a considerable proportion of its current income, possibly as a potential down payment on the purchase of a residence. The child-rearing mid-life years are years of significant dissaving (from the point of view of the household). In the older ages, after the children are grown, there is again an increase in saving in anticipation of retirement. These simulated age profiles of consumption and saving do appear to follow a pattern that is consistent with a weak form of the life-cycle hypothesis of Modigliani and Brumberg (1954) that the propensities to consume and save vary with age.

The differences in total income, consumption, and saving between the two vintages of households, at the same age, are quite pronounced. It is worth noting that the post-Depression vintage household not only have higher total

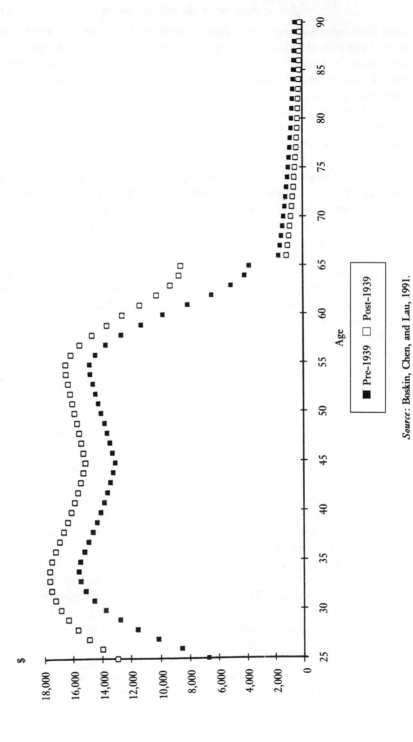

Figure 4.7 Total income in constant 1972 dollar

Age

■ Pre-1939 □ Post-1939

Source: Boskin, Chen, and Lau, 1991.

Figure 4.8 Consumption expenditure in constant 1972 dollars

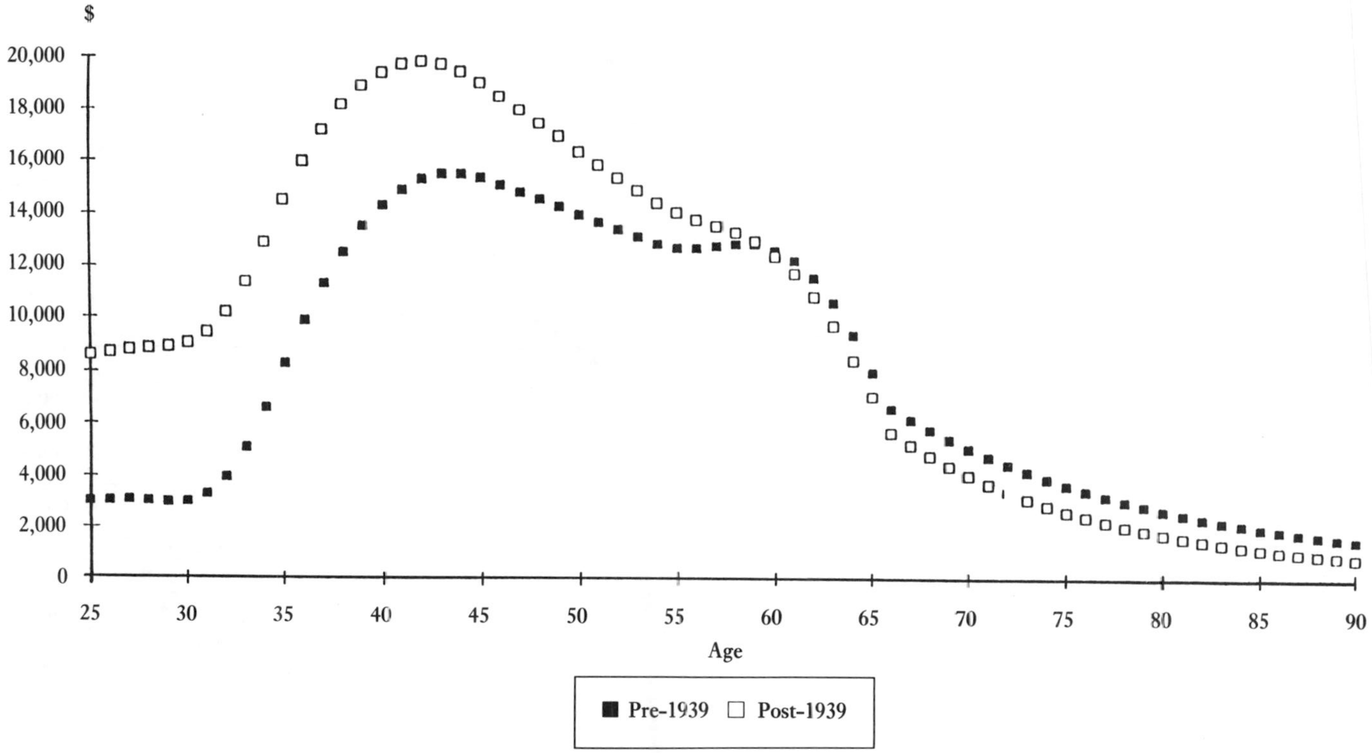

Pre-1939 ☐ Post-1939

Source: Boskin, Chen, and Lau, 1991.

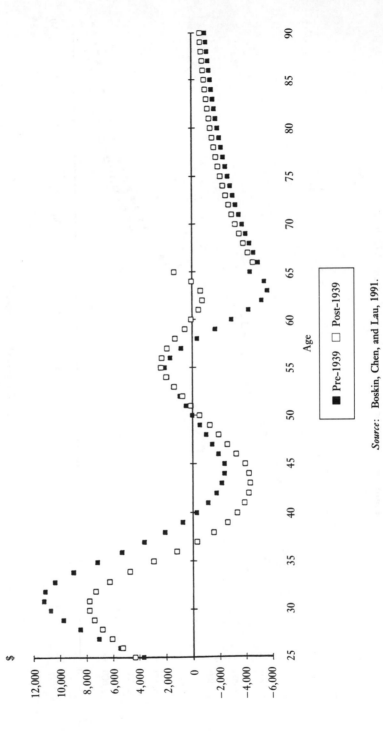

Figure 4.9 Savings (real interest rate = 2%) in constant 1972 dollars

■ Pre-1939 □ Post-1939

Source: Boskin, Chen, and Lau, 1991.

incomes but also consume significantly more than the Depression vintage households when both are at comparable young ages. However, the difference in consumption (but not in total income) diminishes as they both grow older. As retirement approaches, and after retirement, the post-Depression vintage households consume less than the Depression vintage households at the same age. The opposite is true of saving. The post-Depression vintage households save considerably less than the Depression vintage households when both are at young ages. The difference diminishes as they grow older. As retirement approaches, the post-Depression vintage households begin to save more than the Depression vintage households at the same age. After retirement, the post-Depression vintage households dissave less than the Depression vintage households, which may reflect the lower levels of accumulated wealth.

These simulations demonstrate first, that consumption and saving at the level of the individual household depend very significantly on the age of the head of household, and second, that there are very large differences in the consumption and saving behavior between the Depression and the post-Depression vintages of households. Thus both the age composition and the vintage composition of households are likely to be important factors in the explanation of consumption and saving behavior over time at the aggregate level.

SOURCES OF GROWTH OF AGGREGATE CONSUMPTION, 1950–80

A more direct assessment of the importance of the age composition and vintage composition effects, as well as those of other independent variables, on aggregate consumption (and hence aggregate personal saving) has been undertaken by Boskin and Lau (1988). They decompose the rate of growth in aggregate real consumption in the United States for the period 1950–80 into components corresponding to the various factors affecting the growth of consumption, such as the growth of population and number of households, and changes in the average real wealth per household, the size and age distribution of wealth, real after-tax wage rate, real after-tax rate of interest, the unemployment rate, the share of wealth held by Depression vintage households, the time trend, etc. In other words, they attribute the rate of growth in aggregate real consumption to changes in each of the relevant factors.

The 30-year period between 1950 and 1980 is divided into two sub-periods: 1950–62 and 1963–80. (Recall from figure 4.1 that the growth of aggregate consumption expenditure accelerated around 1962–3.) The annual percentage change in aggregate real consumption was 2.89 percent in the 1950–62 period but accelerated to 3.27 percent in 1963–80 period.[17]

The rate of change of aggregate real consumption may first be decomposed

Table 4.2 Decomposition of average annual growth rate of aggregate real consumption (1950–62) (with human wealth revaluation)

Average annual percentage change in aggregate real consumption	2.87
Change due to growth in the number of households	1.30
Net annual percentage change in real consumption per household	1.59

Variable *(average annual change over sample)*	*Percent. pt. change in growth of real cons. due to:*	*Percent. of total growth of real cons. due to:*
Average real non-human wealth		
(−1.49%)	−0.12	−7.5
Real wage rate (1.46%)	0.53	33.3
Real interest rate		
(3.23 percentage points)	0.19	11.9
Size distribution of real wealth	−0.12	−7.5
Age distribution of real wealth	0.20	12.6
Depression vintage		
(−0.50 percentage point)	0.22	13.8
Time trend	0.60	37.7
Log of prime age white male		
unemployment rate		
(−0.73 percentage point)	0.06	3.8
Other	0.03	1.9

Source: Boskin and Lau (1988).

into the sum of the rates of change of real consumption per household and the rate of change of the number of households. This is accomplished in the first three lines of tables 4.2 and 4.3. It appears that a large fraction of the acceleration in the average annual rate of growth of aggregate real consumption in the United States in the mid to late 1960s and 1970s was due to an increased rate of household formation. There was still an increase in the average real consumption per household; but the substantial increase in the number of households, due partly to population growth, changing living patterns and lifestyles, and rising life expectancies, accounts for almost 45 percent of the rate of growth in aggregate real consumption in the period 1950–62, and almost 68 percent in the period 1963–80. Moreover, it is apparent that there is a sharp decline in the rate of growth of real consumption *per household*, from 1.6 percent per annum to 1.05 percent per annum, between the two sub-periods.

The rate of change of real consumption *per household* may be further decomposed into the sum of the effects of its proximate determinants such as the

Table 4.3 Decomposition of average annual growth rate of aggregate real consumption (1963–80) (with human wealth revaluation)

Average annual percentage change in aggregate real consumption	3.27
Change due to growth in the number of households	2.22
Net annual percentage change in real consumption per household	1.05

Variable *(average annual change over sample)*	*Percent. pt. change in* *growth of real cons.* *due to:*	*Percent. of total* *growth of real cons.* *due to:*
Average real non-human wealth		
(−0.29%)	−0.02	−1.9
Real wage rate (0.69%)	0.30	28.6
Real interest rate		
(−2.85 percentage points)	−0.26	−24.8
Size distribution of real wealth	−0.05	−4.8
Age distribution of real wealth	−0.64	−61.0
Depression vintage		
(−3.12 percentage points)	1.23	117.1
Time trend	0.55	52.4
Log of prime age white male		
unemployment rate		
(1.70 percentage points)	−0.13	−12.4
Other	0.07	6.7

Source: Boskin and Lau (1988).

changes in real wealth per household, the real wage rate, the real after-tax rate of interest, the distribution of real wealth by size, age cohort and vintage, the time trend, and the unemployment rate. There are two alternative ways to treat the human wealth variable: one can take the rate of change of real human wealth per household as either independently determined or derivative, determined primarily by the rates of change of the real wage rate and the real after-tax rate of interest. In this chapter, only the results for the second alternative, which attributes to the real wage rate and the real after-tax rate of interest not only their direct effects but also their indirect effects through the revaluation of human wealth, are presented.

The effect of the change in the distribution of wealth by age cohort is obtained by adding up all the effects of changes in the shares of wealth held by each age-cohort. This effect can be further decomposed into a pure age composition effect (which holds the average relative wealth per household of each age cohort constant) and a pure change in *relative* wealth effect (which holds the age composition of households constant). It turns out that the two components tended to work in opposite directions. For both sub-periods, the effects of changes in the age composition of households are responsible for the bulk of the effect of changes in the age distribution of wealth.[18]

The results of the decomposition exercise are presented in the remainders of tables 4.2 and 4.3. For the first period, the most important source of growth of real consumption per household is the time trend, reflecting possibly a secular change in taste, which accounts for 38 percent of the rate of growth in real consumption per household; followed by the real wage rate, which accounts for one-third of the rate of growth in real consumption per household; which is in turn followed by the share of wealth held by the Depression vintage households (accounting for 14 percent) and then by the age distribution of real wealth (accounting for 13 percent). Thus, age and vintage distribution of wealth combined account for more than a quarter of the rate of growth in real consumption per household. The real rate of interest, despite its increase by more than three percentage points during this first period, only accounts for less than 12 percent of the rate of growth in real consumption per household. The remaining variables neither individually nor collectively account for a significant percentage of the rate of growth in real consumption per household.

The role of the time trend in this "growth accounting" exercise is not unlike that of technical progress in the traditional analysis of the sources of growth in aggregate real output. It is in effect a measure of our ignorance. However, it is noteworthy that the distribution of wealth by vintage is still economically and statistically significant even in the presence of the time trend variable. Moreover, the time trend variable has been found by Boskin and Lau (1988) to perform much better in terms of goodness of fit than many other trend-like variables such as the female labor force participation rate, the proportion of non-white to total population (households), the share of wealth held by households headed by non-white persons, life expectancy at birth and at age 20, social security coverage and social security wealth, average weekly work hours, etc. And whenever the time trend variable is present in the estimating equation, the other variable(s) become statistically insignificant. Why the time trend has this large effect deserves further research.

For the second period, the most important source of growth of real consumption per household is the decline in the share of wealth held by the Depression vintage households, which accounts for 117 percent of the rate of growth in real consumption per household; followed by the age distribution of wealth, which accounts for −61 percent of the rate of growth in real consumption per household; which is in turn followed by the time trend (accounting for 52.4 percent) and then by the real wage rate (accounting for almost 29 percent). Age and vintage distribution of wealth, whose effects are in opposite directions, combined account for more than 56 percent of the rate of growth in real consumption per household, still the single most important source of growth. The real rate of interest, which decreased by almost 3 percentage points during this second period, accounts for almost a quarter of the rate of growth in real consumption per household. The remaining variables neither individually nor collectively account for a significant percentage of the rate of growth in real consumption per household.

The share of wealth held by the Depression vintage households is much more important in terms of explaining the rate of growth of real consumption per household in the second sub-period because it declined very slowly, by only 0.50 percentage point, during the first sub-period but feel by 3.12 percentage points during the second sub-period. Correspondingly, the share of wealth held by households headed by persons born after 1939 grew slowly during the first sub-period but accelerated during the second sub-period as the baby boomers came of age.

What emerges from this "growth accounting" exercise is that the overwhelmingly important factors for explaining the rate of growth in aggregate real consumption between 1950 and 1980 are demographic in nature: changes in the rate of household formation and in the distributions of wealth by age and vintage of households. In addition to the demographic factors, the time trend variable, possibly reflecting a secular change in taste, is also very important, accounting for 38 percent of the rate of growth in real consumption per household in the first sub-period and 52 percent in the second sub-period. Moreover, the changes in the percentage points attributable to the time trend variable in the two periods are very similar – 0.06 between 1950 and 1962 and 0.55 between 1963 and 1980.

The relative prices – real wage rates and real interest rates – can be important when their effects are in the same direction. During the first sub-period, the two relative prices combined account for 45 percent of the rate of growth in real consumption per household. During the second sub-period, however, the real wage rate continued to rise, albeit at a reduced rate, but the real rate of interest fell significantly. Their effects canceled each other out and together they account for less than 4 percent of the rate of growth in real consumption per household.

The average real non-human wealth per household and the size distribution of wealth variables do not appear to be important determinants of the growth of real consumption per household.[19] Finally, the business cycle effect, proxied by the logarithm of the prime age white male unemployment rate, is found to have very little impact on the rate of growth of real consumption per household, despite its secular trend over the sub-periods.

These results suggest that the dramatic changes in the age distribution of income and wealth in the United States in the post-war period (documented more fully for the 1968–84 period by Boskin, Kotlikoff and Knetter, 1985) had substantial *net* impacts on the growth of aggregate consumption and saving. Indeed, the rapid shift of wealth toward post-Depression vintage households kept consumption growing rapidly despite increases in life expectancy and the growth of income and wealth in the hands of retired persons (who by definition were born prior to 1939 in the period under study). In other words, the post-Depression generation's greater propensities to consume at young ages offset the movement of the Depression generation into ages with greater propensities to save. Had the post-1939 birth cohorts shown similar consumption and saving patterns to the pre-1939 birth cohort, aggregate consumption would have increased substantially less and aggregate personal saving would have been quite a bit higher than in fact occurred.

CONCLUDING REMARKS

The most important conclusion of this brief overview of the results of the studies of Boskin and Lau (1988) and Boskin, Chen, and Lau (1991) is the critical dependence of US aggregate consumption and saving on the age and vintage distribution of resources. Boskin and Lau (1988) find strong evidence of a systematic variation in aggregate consumption and saving with changes in the age and vintage distribution of household wealth in the economy. Especially significant is the substantial estimated difference in the shares of wealth consumed between households headed by persons born before and after 1939, the Depression and post-Depression vintage households, respectively.

In figure 4.10, the results of a hypothetical calculation done by Boskin and Lau (1988) of what total personal saving would have been if the post-1939 generation had the same saving propensities, conditional on age and the other variables in our consumption expenditure function, as the pre-1939 generation. This vintage effect is so large that if the age-specific conditional saving rates of the post-Depression vintage households were as large as those of the Depression vintage households, the private saving rate would have more than doubled its actual value in 1980.

In essence, the aggregate personal saving rate may be considered as a weighted average of those of two vintages of households, Depression and post-Depression, each with its own specific age-saving profile (see pp. 158–65), with the later vintage's profile lying below that of the earlier vintage and young and middle ages, across different age cohorts. Since the share of aggregate income received and hence total wealth held by those in the post-Depression vintage has been growing through time, further erosion of the aggregate personal saving rate is to be expected, *ceteris paribus*, as in fact occurred in the 1980s. Thus, the vintage effect is one important explanation for the decline in the aggregate personal saving rate from the average of 6.3 percent in the early 1970s to the average of 4.0 percent in the 1980s.[20]

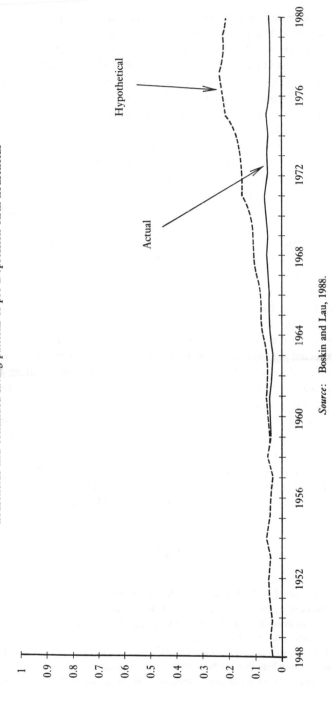

Figure 4.10 Increase in aggregate personal saving/GNP if post-Depression birth households had continued saving patterns of pre-Depression birth households

Source: Boskin and Lau, 1988.

There does not seem to be a satisfactory non-tautological explanation as to why there is such large apparent difference in the *age-specific* consumption and saving rates between Depression and post-Depression birth cohorts. But is this large vintage effect plausible? It is often mentioned anecdotally that persons who lived through the Depression are reluctant to borrow, whereas, again anecdotally, but buttressed by aggregate credit statistics, the growth of credit and borrowing for a wide range of purposes has become a part of life for persons born since the Depression. However, one might conjecture that part of this is due to the tax laws allowing deductibility of consumer interest payments with rising marginal income tax rates in the period under study for the bulk of the population. Additional research is needed to shed light on this issue.

A somewhat surprising conclusion is the relative insensitivity of aggregate saving to changes in the real after-tax rate of interest, assuming that households fully revalue their human wealth. Boskin and Lau (1988) demonstrate how the elasticity varies with the ratio of non-human to total wealth of the individual household. Their result suggests that the elasticity is likely to be low or negative for households with few assets.

The one ray of hope for the personal saving rate, in the absence of a major change in the consumption and saving behavior of the post-Depression vintage households (or another Depression), is that the share of wealth held by the Depression vintage households has already declined significantly. It is therefore not expected to continue to contribute substantially to the decline in the aggregate personal saving rate. Moreover, the Post-Depression vintage households will soon begin to plan for their retirement and increase their saving rate. The demographics are such that the younger age–cohorts, which typically save less, will be relatively smaller for the next decade or two. Perhaps the aggregate personal saving rate in the United States will reverse its downward trend in the 1990s. If this were to materialize, and assuming that net US government saving does not fall significantly (for example, by running a larger real government budget deficit), the United States may even become once more a net source of saving to the rest of the world in the early decades of next century.

NOTES

1 Boskin and Lau (1988) also include leisure, which is generally omitted from most studies of aggregate consumption, in their study.
2 For a discussion of the theory of exact aggregation, see Lau (1982), and Jorgenson, Lau, and Stoker (1980, 1982).
3 However, the specification used by Boskin and Lau (1988) is consistent with utility-maximizing behavior without necessarily imposing it.
4 Leisure per person per year is measured as the difference between the maximum of

hours available, defined to be 4,400 hours per year, and the actual number of hours worked. Alternative assumptions on the maximum number of hours available had little effect on the results.

5 However, two vintage dummy variables, one for households headed by persons aged 35 and above and one for households headed by persons aged 34 and below are required for the leisure expenditure share function.

6 Male age-earnings profiles, controlling for education, race, etc., are quite stable over time in the US, and surprisingly similar across countries (see, for example, Smith and Welch, 1986 and Psacharopoulos, 1981).

7 See also Blanchard's (1985) derivation and discussion.

8 Note that Boskin and Lau (1988) allow the age cohort and vintage effects to interact; however, they find a uniform average vintage effect for the consumption expenditure function.

9 Note that the net change in the value of wealth, including capital gains or losses and transfers, is not included in this NIPA definition of saving. Of course, transfers net to zero for the economy as a whole (except for net unilateral transfers to foreigners).

10 It is assumed that the change in wealth results from equal proportional changes in both human and non-human wealth.

11 We note that this effect is expected to be negative for positive saving because the NIPA definition of saving does not include the net change in wealth due to revaluation.

12 Of course, no-one in the post-Depression (post-1939) vintage would actually have been in the age cohort 45–54 in 1972. The estimated elasticities for the post-Depression vintage are therefore hypothetical – they measure how these households would have behaved in 1972 if all the independent variables (including age) except vintage were the same.

13 These figures are taken from Boskin and Lau (1988).

14 It is worth noting, however, that the Depression vintage household also enjoys more leisure than the post-Depression vintage household. Thus, the post-Depression vintage household both consumes more and works harder (the labor force participation rate of the post-Depression vintage households is considerably higher).

15 Bear in mind that current saving is negative for the post-Depression vintage household head by a person in the 45–54 age cohort at the 1972 values of the other independent variables.

16 The real wage rates faced by the heads of the individual households depend on their ages in accordance with an estimated wage-age profile.

17 The Boskin and Lau (1988) analysis is confined to the period 1950–80 because of unusual swings in consumption and saving rates during the first few years after World War II.

18 For complete details, see Boskin and Lau (1988).

19 The average *total* real wealth per household declined very slightly in the first sub-period and resulted in a net decrease in real consumption per household of approximately one-tenth of a percentage point, whereas in the latter sub-period, average total real wealth per household increased substantially and accounted for more than one-half percentage point of the rate of growth in real consumption per household.

20 Between 1980 and 1987.

REFERENCES

Ando, A. and Modigliani, F. 1963: The Life Cycle Hypothesis of Saving: Aggregate Implications and Tests. *American Economic Review*, 53, 55–84.

Aschauer, D. 1985: Fiscal Policy and Aggregate Demand. *American Economic Review*, 75, 117–27.

Attanasio, O. P. 1991: A Cohort Analysis of Saving Behavior by US Households: Why Were Saving Rates So Low in the US During the 1980s. Mimeo.

Attanasio, O. P. and Browning, M. 1991: Consumption Over Life Cycle and Consumption Over the Business Cycle. Mimeo.

Auerbach, A. J. and Kotlikoff, L.J. 1983: An Examination of Empirical Tests of Social Security and Savings. In E. Helpman et al. (eds), *Social Policy Evaluation: An Economic Perspective*. New York: Academic Press, pp. 161–79.

Auerbach, A. J. and Kotlikoff, L. J. 1990: Demographics, Fiscal Policy and US Saving in the 1980s and Beyond. In L. H. Summers (ed.), *Tax Policy and the Economy*. Cambridge, MA: MIT Press.

Barro, R. J. 1974: Are Government Bonds Net Wealth? *Journal of Political Economy*, 82, 1095–118.

Barro, R. J. 1978: *The Impact of Social Security on Private Saving: Evidence from US Time Series*. Washington, DC: American Enterprise Institute.

Barro, R. J. and Sahasakul, C. 1983: Measuring the Average Marginal Tax Rate from the Individual Income Tax. *Journal of Business*, 56, 419–52.

Barth, J. R., Iden, G. and Russek, F. S. 1984–5: Do Federal Deficits Really Matter? *Contemporary Policy Issues*, 3, 79–95.

Bernanke, B. S. 1984: Permanent Income, Liquidity, and Expenditure on Automobiles: Evidence from Panel Data. *Quarterly Journal of Economics*, 99, 587–614.

Bernheim, D. 1984: Dis-saving After Retirement. *National Bureau of Economic Research Working Paper* No. 1409.

Bernheim, D. 1987: Ricardian Equivalence: An Evaluation of Theory and Evidence. *National Bureau of Economic Research Macroeconomics Annual* 263–304.

Blanchard, O. 1985: Debt, Deficits, and Finite Horizons. *Journal of Political Economy*, 93, 223–47.

Blinder, A. and Deaton, A. 1985: The Time-Series Consumption Function Revisited. *Brookings Papers on Economic Activity*, 2, 465–511.

Boskin, M. J. 1978: Taxation, Saving and the Rate of Interest. *Journal of Political Economy*, 86, 3–27.

Boskin, M. J. 1987: Concepts and Measures of Federal Deficits and Debt and Their Impact on Economic Activity. *National Bureau of Economic Research Working Paper* No. 2332.

Boskin, M. J. 1988: Consumption, Saving and Fiscal Policy. *American Economic Review*, 78, 401–7.

Boskin, M. J., Chen, M.-L. and Lau, L. J. 1991: Life-Time Consumption and Saving of Individual US Households: A Simulation Study. Mimeo.

Boskin, M. J. and Hurd, M. 1984: The Effect of Social Security on Retirement in the Early 1970s. *Quarterly Journal of Economics*, 99, 767–90.

Boskin, M. J. and Kotlikoff, L. J. 1985: Public Debt and US Saving: A New Test of the Neutrality Hypotheses. *Carnegie-Rochester Conference Series*, 55–86.

Boskin, M. J., Kotlikoff, L. J. and Knetter, M. 1985: Changes in the Age Distribution of Income in the United States, 1968–1984. *National Bureau of Economic Research Working Paper* No. 1766.

Boskin, M. J. and Lau, L. J. 1978: Taxation and Aggregate Factor Supply: Preliminary Estimates. In Department of the Treasury, *1978 Compendium of Tax Research*, 3–15.

Boskin, M. J. and Lau, L. J. 1988: An Analysis of Post-war US Consumption and Saving. *National Bureau of Economic Research Working Papers* No. 2605 and 2606.

Boskin, M. J., Robinson, M., and Huber, A. 1988: Government Saving, Capital Formation and Wealth in the United States, 1947–1985. In R. Lipsey and H. S. Tice (eds), *The Measurement of Saving, Investment, and Wealth*. Chicago: Univ. of Chicago Press, 1992.

Christensen, L. R. and Jorgenson, D. W. 1973: US Income, Saving, and Wealth: 1929–1969. *The Review of Income and Wealth*, 19, 329–62.

Danziger, S., van der Gaag, J., Smolensky, E. and Taussig, M. 1982: The Life Cycle Hypothesis and Consumption Behaviour of the Elderly. *Journal of Post-Keynesian Economics*, 5, 208–27.

Darby, M. R. 1979: *The Effects of Social Security on Income and the Capital Stock*. Washington, DC: American Enterprise Institute.

David, M. and Menchik, P. L. 1981: The Effect of Social Security on Lifetime Wealth Accumulation and Bequests. *Institute for Research on Poverty Discussion Paper* No. 671.

David, P. A. and Scadding, J. L. 1974: Private Savings: Ultrarationality, Aggregate Saving, and Denison's Law. *Journal of Political Economy*, 82, 225–49.

Deaton, A. 1986: Life Cycle Models of Consumption: Is the Evidence Consistent with the Theory? *National Bureau of Economic Research Working Paper* No. 1910.

Diamond, P. and Hausman, J. A. 1984: Individual Retirement and Savings Behaviour. *Journal of Public Economics*, 23, 81–114.

Feldstein, M. S. 1974: Social Security, Induced Retirement, and Aggregate Capital Accumulation. *Journal of Political Economy*, 82, 905–26.

Feldstein, M. 1978: Reply. In R. J. Barro, (ed.), *The Impact of Social Security on Private Savings: Evidence from US Time Series*. Washington, DC: American Enterprise Institute.

Feldstein, M. 1982: Government Deficits and Aggregate Demand. *Journal of Monetary Economics*, 9, 1–20.

Flavin, M. R. 1981: The Adjustment of Consumption to Changing Expectations About Future Income. *Journal of Political Economy*, 89, 974–1009.

Friedman, M. 1957: *A Theory of the Consumption Function*. Princeton: Princeton University Press.

Fuchs, V. 1971: Differences in Hourly Earnings Between Men and Women. *Monthly Labor Review*, 94, 9–15.

Gallant, A. R. and Jorgenson, D. W. 1979: Statistical Inference for a System of Simultaneous, Nonlinear, Implicit Equations in the Context of Instrumental Variables Estimation. *Journal of Econometrics*, 113, 272–302.

Gorman, W. M. 1953: Community Preference Field. *Econometrica*, 21, 63–80.

Hall, R. E. 1978: Stochastic Implications of the Life Cycle-Permanent Income Hypotheses: Theory and Evidence. *Journal of Political Economy*, 86, 971–87.

Hall, R. E. 1985: Real Interest and Consumption. *National Bureau of Economic Research Working Paper* No. 1694.

Hall, R. E. 1986: The Role of Consumption in Economic Fluctuations. In R. J. Gordon (ed.), *The American Business Cycle: Continuity and Change.* Chicago: University of Chicago Press, pp. 237–66.

Hall, R. E. and Mishkin, F. S. 1982: The Sensitivity of Consumption to Transitory Income: Estimates from Panel Data on Households. *Econometrica*, 50, 461–81.

Hansen, L. P. and Singleton, K. J. 1983: Stochastic Consumption, Risk Aversion, and the Temporal Behaviour of Asset Returns. *Journal of Political Economy*, 91, 249–65.

Harrod, R. F. 1948: *Towards a Dynamic Economics.* New York: Macmillan.

Hayashi, F. 1982: The Permanent Income Hypotheses: Estimation and Testing by Instrumental Variables. *Journal of Political Economy*, 90, 895–918.

Hayashi, F. 1985: Tests for Liquidity Constraints: A Critical Survey. *National Bureau of Economic Research Working Paper* No. 1720.

Howrey, E. P. and Hymans, S. H. 1980: The Measurement and Determination of Loanable-Funds Saving. In J. A. Pechman (ed.), *What Should Be Taxed: Income or Expenditure?* Washington, DC: The Brookings Institution, 1–31.

Hubbard, C. and Judd, K. 1987: Finite Lifetimes, Borrowing Constraints, and Short-Run Fiscal Policy. Mimeo.

Hurd, M. 1987: Savings and Bequests. *American Economic Review*, 77, 298–312.

Jorgenson, D. W., Lau, L. J. and Stoker, T. M. 1980: Welfare Comparison Under Exact Aggregation. *American Economic Review*, 70, 268–72.

Jorgenson, D. W., Lau, L. J. and Stoker, T. M. 1982: The Transcendental Logarithmic Model of Aggregate Consumer Behavior. *Advances in Econometrics*, 1, 97–238.

Kormendi, R. C. 1983: Government Debt, Government Spending, and Private Sector Behaviour. *American Economic Review*, 73, 994–1010.

Kotlikoff, L. J. and Summers, L. H. 1981. The Role of Intergenerational Transfers in Aggregate Capital Accumulation. *Journal of Political Economy*, 89, 706–32.

Kurz, M. 1984: Capital Accumulation and Characteristics of Private Intergenerational Transfers. *Economica*, 51, 1–22.

Lau, L. J. 1982: A Note on the Fundamental Theorem of Exact Aggregation. *Economics Letters*, 9, 119–26.

Lau, L. J. 1992: *Exact Aggregation.* Amsterdam: North-Holland Publishing Company, forthcoming.

Leimer, D. and Lesnoy, S. 1982: Social Security and Private Saving: New Time Series Evidence. *Journal of Political Economy*, 90, 606–29.

Mirer, T. W. 1979: The Wealth-Age Relation Among the Aged. *American Economic Review*, 69, 435–43.

Modigliani, F. and Brumberg, R. 1954: Utility Analysis and the Consumption Function: An Interpretation of Cross-Section Data. In K. K. Kurihara (ed.), *Post-Keynesian Economics.* New Brunswick, NJ: Rutgers University Press, 388–436.

Psacharopoulos, G. 1981: Returns to Education: An Updated International Comparison. *Comparative Education*, 17, 321–41.

Sargent, T. J. 1978: Rational Expectations Econometric Exogeneity, and Consumption. *Journal of Political Economy*, 86, 673–700.

Shorrocks, A. F. 1975: The Age-Wealth Relationship: A Cross-Section and Cohort Analysis. *Review of Economics and Statistics*, 57, 155–63.

Skinner, J. 1988: Risky Income, Life Cycle Consumption and Precautionary Savings. *Journal of Monetary Economics*, 22, 237–55.

Smith, J. P. and Welch, F. 1986: Closing the Gap: Forty Years of Economic Progress for Blacks. *Rand Corporation Report* R-330-DOL.

Summers, L. H. 1981: Taxation and Capital Accumulation in a Life Cycle Growth Model. *American Economic Review*, 71, 533–44.

Summers, L. H. 1982: Tax Policy, the Rate of Return and Savings. *National Bureau of Economic Research Working Paper* No. 995.

Summers, L. H. 1984: The After Tax Return Does Affect Private Savings. *American Economic Review*, 74, 249–53.

Summers, L. H. and Carroll, C. 1989: Why Is US Saving So Low? *Brookings Papers on Economic Activity*, 1.

Venti, S. F. and Wise, D. A. 1990: Have IRA's Increased US Saving? Evidence from Consumer Expenditure Surveys. *Quarterly Journal of Economics*.

5

Saving in Western Europe

Jean-Paul Fitoussi and Jacques Le Cacheux

INTRODUCTION

In the last couple of years, there has been a growing concern amongst economists and economic policy-makers about the likelihood of worldwide insufficiency
of saving. From an European perspective, such a diagnosis would, at first sight,
seem paradoxical, at least from the standpoint of conventional Keynesian wisdom: indeed, measured unemployment is currently at very high levels in Western
Europe, and it has been so, with slight fluctuations, for over a decade, while real
growth has been, on average, quite sluggish. A traditional Keynesian reading of
the current European situation would interpret such signs of an apparent slack
as evidence of an *ex ante* excess saving.

Two major lines of reasoning appear to be motivating this renewed concern
about the level of saving: first, the sense that, with the systematic and structural
transformation of Eastern Europe and the Soviet Union, together with the continuing backwardness in most developing countries, world investment needs
have increased, while the saving potential has not, which may cause serious
tensions on the financing of investment in industrialized countries and may
thus hinder growth in the OECD; second, the awareness that the current level
of saving in these countries is inadequate to provide for a sufficient amount of
pensions and benefits for future retirees, given rapidly ageing populations in all
industrialized countries. While recent developments in the East have tended to
reinforce the case for worldwide insufficient saving, a number of observations
seem to suggest that this phenomenon may, to a large extent, be traced back to
the previous decade. Indeed, a broad characterization of world economic developments in the 1980s reveals some of the major symptoms usually associated
in economic analysis with a situation of insufficient saving: real interest rates
have been persistently higher in the 1980s than in previous decades, albeit with
some fluctuations and sometimes large differentials between Europe, the US

and Japan; measured domestic saving ratios appear lower than in the past; and real economic growth has been relatively sluggish, on average, though with occasional accelerations – in the US from 1983 till 1985, in Europe from 1987 till 1990.

In order to be able to pass judgment on this thesis and bring empirical evidence to bear on it, one needs to analyze observed trends in both saving and investment. The purpose of this chapter is to try and answer the following questions: How are European developments in the 1980s and early 1990s fitting into the general picture? Have they been different? If so, how can the specificities of the Western European situation be explained? To this end, we first review some of the available empirical evidence on Western European saving and investment, both in the aggregate and through the various components of domestic saving. Some important measurement difficulties are addressed after this review of empirical evidence. The third section is dedicated to a discussion of some major determinants of private saving and its allocation, insofar as they seem to have a direct bearing on the observed situation in Western Europe. The following section offers an account of how saving and investment in Europe have been affected by developments in the rest of the world, mostly in the US. We then discuss some important persisting factors in the current saving trends. The last section brings together some major conclusions and discusses the prospects from a Western European perspective.

TRENDS IN NATIONAL SAVING AND INVESTMENT IN WESTERN EUROPE

Europe is presently experiencing higher real rates of interest and higher unemployment than other major OECD countries; it has practically zero current account balance, in the aggregate. Yet its growth rate is relatively low and economic activity may further deteriorate with the current slowdown of the German economy. How have patterns of saving and investment evolved in recent years? Are there common features amongst European countries, or is the EC an heterogeneous group in that respect?

Global Trends in Saving, Investment and Current Accounts in Western Europe

As is well known from flow national accounting identities, net national – or domestic – saving is identically equal to the current account balance.[1] For our analytical purpose, it may be usefully decomposed into three major components: private saving (Sp), private investment (Ip), net public saving (Sg):

$$CA = S - I$$
$$CA = (Sp - Ip) + Sg$$

with $$Sg = T - G = T - (Cg + Ig + Pg)$$

Figures 5.1a and b show the evolutions of the gross national saving ratios and of the gross domestic investment ratios in the European part of the OECD and in the EC over the past two decades. Though not exactly identical, due to a slight difference in geographical coverage, they display similar patterns: a sharp downfall of both saving and investment in the aftermath of the first oil price shock, followed by a modest recovery; the decline is more protacted in the 1980s, the trough being reached in 1982–3, but the recovery is even slower and only slighty accelerated over the last two years of the decade.[2] For ten years (1974–83), gross investment has consistently exceeded gross saving – except in 1978 – so that the current accounts of both areas have been in deficit (figure 5.2). After four successive years of surpluses, aggregate current accounts have again plunged into the red in 1988–9, with the investment recovery at the end of the decade. Although the downfall in national saving and investment ratios appears quite dramatic compared with the early 1970s – and with the 1960s – current levels are not without historical precedents. In fact, from a longer-term perspective, the ratios observed everywhere in the 1960s and early 1970s looked exceptionally high (Maddison, 1991). But real growth rates and employment rates were also high. In all these respects, the European experience is not markedly different from that of the rest of the OECD (Bosworth, 1990).

Developments in Individual Components of Saving in Selected European Countries

In spite of these clearly common trends in gross national saving and investment ratios, there are nonetheless country-specific developments. Within Western Europe, the national saving rates display different levels[3] and varying profiles (figure 5.3). In some countries – Italy and the United Kingdom, for instance – the downward trend in the gross national saving rate persists through the end of the 1980s; in others – most notably Germany[4] and, to some extent, the Netherlands – a clear reversal has taken place in the early 1980s, and national saving ratios are almost back to their pre-oil-shock levels. Finally in countries like France, there are signs of an improvement from the mid-1980s, but the level is still far below that of the 1960s.

Such idiosyncracies are the outcomes of the interplay of various kinds of country-specific factors – structure of the financial sector, tax structure, policy reactions external and internal shocks ⊨ – some of which will be developed below.

Figure 5.1   Gross national saving and gross domestic investment, 1970–89
a OECD-Europe

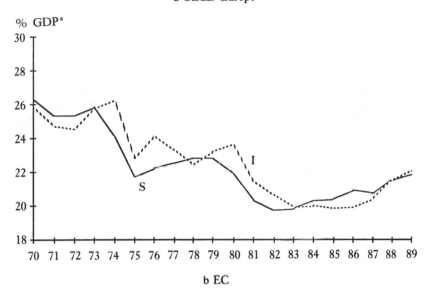

b EC

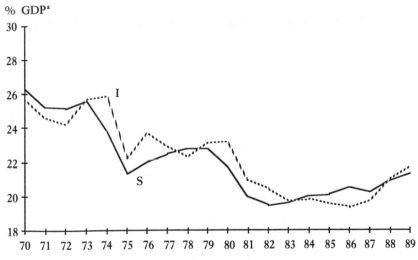

^a   At current prices and PPA.
Source: OECD, National Accounts

Figure 5.2 Current account balance: OECD–Europe and EC, 1970–89

% GDP^a

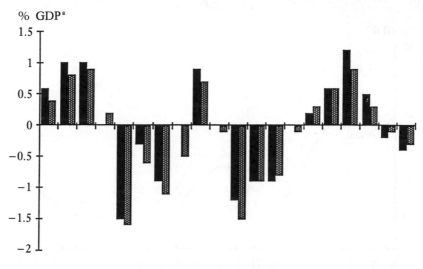

^a   At current prices and PPA.
Source: OECD, Nation Account

Figure 5.3 National saving rates: France, Germany, Italy, the Netherlands, the United Kingdom, 1970–89

% GDP

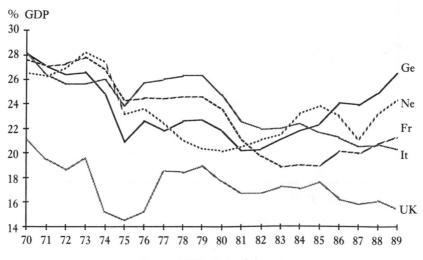

Source: OECD, National Accounts

One major feature of the decline in gross national saving that is common to almost all Western European countries is the severe reduction in gross public saving in the immediate aftermath of each of the two oil-price shocks (figures 5.4a and b). Gross saving by general government has been fluctuating since 1975, but in most countries it has never recovered pre-shock levels and has been especially low during the first half of the 1980s.

The time profiles of private saving rates in the various countries are much less marked. But within the private sector, the contributions of each category of agents have varied substantially. Private saving may be split into household saving (Sh) and corporate saving (Sf):

$$Sp = Sh + Sf$$

Figures 5.5a and 5.5b show the evolutions of household[5] and corporate saving ratios in two major European countries. In Germany, where firms rely relatively less on external sources of financing, corporate saving is consistently higher than household saving and is responsible for most of the fluctuations, especially the recovery in the late 1980s. In France, corporate saving used to represent a much smaller share of total gross private saving, but it has been growing from its minimum in 1982, while household saving has gone on declining with only a slight improvement at the end of the decade.

Composition of Investment

Along with the drastic reduction in domestic investment ratios in Europe, already noted, there have been quite significant changes in the composition of domestic investment in all countries. With the rise in capital consumption, the gap between gross and net investment has tended to widen, on average, both in the public and in the private sectors.[6] Within private investment, it may be useful to distinguish household investment in housing (Ih) and productive investment by firms (If):

$$Ip = Ih + If$$

Except for Italy, where it is traditionally lower than in other major European countries, the share of residential investment in total fixed capital formation by the private sector has declined in the 1980s (figure 5.6). Just like the bulge observed in the first years of the past decade, this downward trend mostly mirrors the fluctuations in productive capital formation by the private sector, which accelerated after 1987.

Finally, it should be noted that the sharp reduction in gross public saving has been accompanied, in most countries, by an equally severe cut in public investment, albeit with significant country-specific elements. Thus, for instance, the need for infrastructure in East Germany has recently led to a marked increase

Figure 5.4 Private and public shares in national saving
a Germany, 1970–89

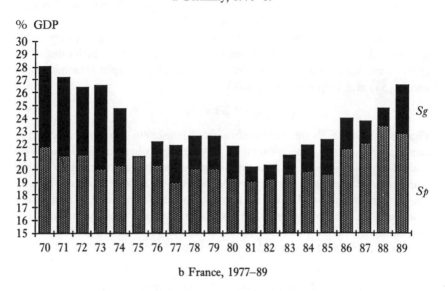

b France, 1977–89

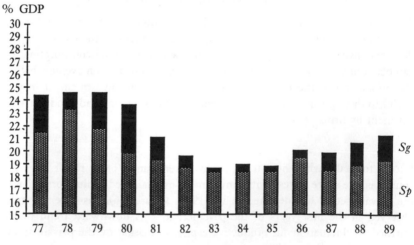

Source: OECD, National Accounts

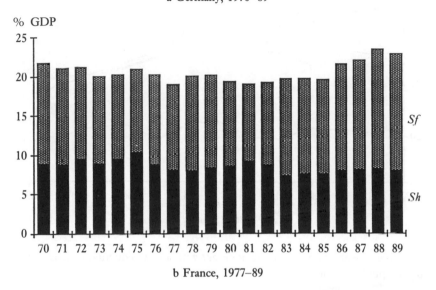

Figure 5.5 Components of private saving
a Germany, 1970–89

b France, 1977–89

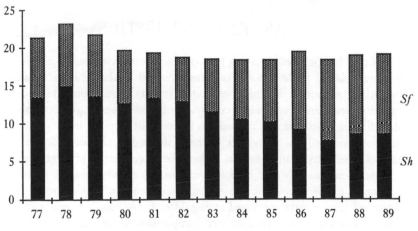

Source: OECD, National Accounts

Figure 5.6   Share of residential investment in fixed capital formation: France,
Germany, Italy, the United Kingdom, 1977–89

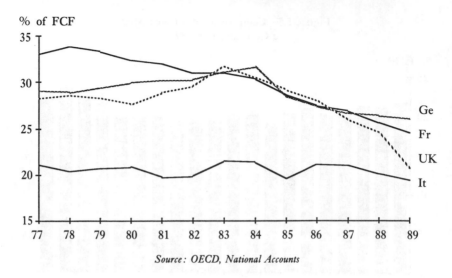

Source: OECD, National Accounts

in public investment in Germany, together with a new reduction in gross saving
by the public sector.

MEASUREMENT ISSUES

International comparisons of saving behavior by sectors give rise to a number of
difficulties relating to definitional and measurement issues. The discrepancies
between the economic definition of saving and its translation into national
accounting practices in individual countries introduce some significant biases,
which, for the most part, are unlikely to be constant through time.

In economic analysis, an agent's saving is defined as the increment over a
period of time in its wealth position, either gross – relating to gross saving – or
net of depreciation. However, national accountants usually measure saving by
the fraction of disposable income not spent on current consumption. This
practice is likely to make measured saving differ from "true" economic saving,
especially when it comes to the sectoral composition of national saving. In the
case of households, whose saving behavior is usually regarded as central to the
analysis, national accounting conventions introduce three major categories of
biases: those arising from the composition of the household sector – mainly
whether it includes individual entrepreneurs or not; those relating to country-
specific, institutional arrangements – most notably the financing of pensions;
finally, biases due to differences between "economic" and accounting definitions

of current consumption and current income (Galibert and Le Dem, 1989). While the first two categories should lead to caution when comparing saving levels internationally, they are unlikely to be highly variable in time. The third type, however, makes measured saving differ more or less from true economic saving according to fluctuations in the general economic context, and many developments observed during the past two decades may well have increased the gap.

Institutional differences in the way various benefits are provided and financed may generate substantial variations in the sectoral composition of measured saving. The single most important factor in this respect relates to retirement provisions. If, as is likely, a fraction, at least, of national saving is motivated by the desire to secure resources for retirement years (see below), then the institutional arrangements concerning pensions matter a lot, not only in the determination of saving behaviors of the various sectors, but also in measurement. From this point of view, Western Europe is quite a heterogeneous collection of countries, with varying degrees of involvement of the public sector in pension provisions. With compulsory public pension schemes, households' disposable income is diminished by the amount of social contributions, so that their saving rate in terms of disposable income appears smaller. In pay-as-you-go systems, such as the French one, the public funds' accounts arc usually approximately balanced on a yearly basis, so that it does not interfere much with measured saving: both contributions and benefits being included in households' disposable income, the net aggregate outcome is barely affected. On the contrary, in those countries where capitalization is important – either private, whether left with households or taken care of by firms as in Germany, or through a system of public funds accumulating and investing reserves – while total measured saving tends to be higher, its sectoral composition depends on the precise financing scheme.

Similar corrections probably ought to be made in order to take account of other types of benefits which, in some countries, are provided by the public sector on the basis of social contributions or general taxes, whereas they have to be privately financed in others, where they appear in households current consumption. The foremost examples of such benefits are health care and education: with public provision and/or financing, households disposable income is less, due to compulsory contributions, but their current consumption is also less, so that the measured saving rate tends to be larger. In a similar vein, the higher the fraction of consumption-based taxes in total tax revenues, the larger is households' disposable income, but the smaller is the measured share of saving in disposable income.

All these institutional factors help explain part of the differences in measured national saving and its composition. Their influence is, however, relatively less on saving ratios – as a percentage of GDP – than on saving rates – as a percentage of disposable income. Moreover, apart from episodes of institutional changes, they are not likely to vary widely in time and cannot therefore explain large fluctuations over a decade or two.

The "economic" corrections that one may want to introduce are potentially more important in this respect. The first one concerns consumer durables: in national accounts, purchases of such items are counted as current consumption, even though economic logic would have only the flow of services from durables included in consumption, with the purchase being treated as an investment and its financing as saving. Correcting for this misrepresentation tends to increase measured household saving rates in all countries, but to varying extents (Galibert and Le Dem, 1989). Moreover, insofar as durables account for an ever increasing fraction of households' consumption, the gap between measured and "true" saving tends to widen in time, with possible fluctuations linked to waves of acquisitions.

The second important source of distortion in national accounts is inflation. In economic analysis, an agent's saving is supposed to be the increment in his real wealth, that is net of any capital losses incurred through inflation. National accounts thus tend to overstate saving whenever there is inflation – the more so the higher the inflation rate – insofar as a fraction of measured saving is only meant to compensate for the erosion of the real value of accumulated wealth. In general, taking account of this nominal bias tends to lower measured saving ratios in the 1970s and more so in the early 1980s (Modigliani, 1990), especially in the most inflationary countries. It would also make the saving ratios of the mid-1980s – when inflation was at its lowest – look more like those of the late 1980s.

Finally, variations in the relative prices of the various assets held by households affect their real wealth through real capital gains and losses that should also be included in any meaningful measure of saving. These capital gains and losses are incurred primarily on financial assets, pension rights and housing. For the most part, they have been negative in real terms in the 1970s, which would lead to revising measured saving downward. On the contrary, most assets held by households have benefitted from large relative price increases during the 1980s. Although this general trend has had some country-specific variants and some fluctuations in time – the stock market crashes of 1987 and 1990, movements in bond price, waves of speculation and collapse in real estate in various cities or regions – its overall effect has probably been to raise "true" saving above measured saving in the 1980s.

ON SOME DETERMINANTS OF PRIVATE SAVING AND ITS ALLOCATION

In most current analyses of aggregate saving determination, the behavior of households is assumed to be the core determinant. The dominant models picture the individual as a rational "consumption-smoothing machine," using his/her saving to transfer purchasing power and provide for future consumption. Saving decisions and the allocation of wealth are thus guided by private expectations concerning future consumption wants, future incomes and future rates of return on various assets. In such a world, the real interest rate has the double function of being a synthetic indicator for expected real rates of return, insofar as financial markets are efficient, and of being the discount factor used to calculate the present values of future variables – income streams, levels of satisfaction, etc. Because individual consumers hold perfect expectations, there are able to see through the "corporate veil," as well as through the "government veil." Their perfect awareness makes them act so as to counter any undesirable development in public or corporate saving.

The basic building-block in most modern theories of saving determination is the life-cycle hypothesis.[7] In its simplest version, it states that consumers smooth their consumption profiles: saving thus acts as a buffer in the presence of income fluctuations and is essentially motivated by the desire to provide for consumption during retirement. In such a framework, bequests may be rationalized either through an externality in consumption – individuals care for the welfare of their heirs – or through fundamental uncertainty regarding the date of one's death, in which case they would be mostly involuntary.[8] At one extreme, if individual households value the future well-being of their offspring as much as their own, they behave as if they had infinite lifetimes. The model may also accommodate imperfections in the economic environment, such as liquidity constraints, which alter the time profile of saving and help explain the observation of accumulation for the purpose of down-payments, quite frequent in the case of consumer durables and housing.

Households' Wealth

The major implications of models incorporating the life-cycle hypothesis into an overlapping-generations setting[9] are unambiguous as far as aggregate saving is concerned. The first one is that aggregate household saving rate is positively correlated with the real rate of growth of the economy.[10] This conclusion conforms with the general observation of the reduction in saving – and investment – ratios as being broadly in line with that of real growth rates in most countries.[11]

The second major conclusion is that the ratio of household aggregate wealth over aggregate income is constant in a steady growth environment (Modigliani, 1986). It is, however, negatively related to the (constant) growth rate of the economy, so that adjustments to a lower growth path – whatever the causes of the slowdown – should entail a rising wealth/income ratio. Indeed given the saving motives underlying the life-cycle hypothesis, households ought to have a target wealth/income ratio depending on their expectations of future returns and future economic conditions. On this point, too, there is ample evidence: although reliable and comprehensive household wealth accounts are not available over long time periods for all European countries, all indicators reflect a marked increase in household wealth/income ratios everywhere. As already noted, such a rise is, to a large extent, attributable to real capital gains on assets held in households' portfolios. In particular, real share prices have been increasing substantially in all countries throughout the 1980s (figures 5.7a–c), whereas they had declined during the 1970s. Similarly, households have, in the aggregate, benefitted from large real capital gains on housing and real estate, which the recent downturn in property values in most countries have only slightly dented.

Although it has been accompanied by wide variations in relative asset prices, the sharp increase in real interest rates at the begining of the 1980s and the persistance of high levels since then (see figures 5.8a–c) point to a general and sustained increment in asset real rates of return. The effect of a rise of real interest rates on household saving is notoriously difficult to ascertain, both theoretically and empirically. Economic theory identifies various channels through which interest rates influence saving decisions in opposite directions: the discount-rate effect implies that people value present satisfaction more than future consumption; the income and wealth effects tend to favor saving. Empirical studies have usually failed to reach unambiguous results, but evidence from the past two decades would seem to suggest that, during the adjustment to a new regime, characterized by higher real rates of return and a higher wealth/income ratio, the negative effects of higher interest rates on saving might dominate.

Alongside with sweeping changes in the financial regulatory environment – various deregulations in domestic financial markets and banking, liberalization of international capital movements – as well as mushrooming financial innovations, these changes in relative asset prices and real rates of return have induced a considerable reshuffling of household total and financial portfolios. While data on total household portfolios are not readily available on a comparable basis, it is possible to compare the evolutions of the structure of households' financial asset holdings in a few countries over the past 20 years, putting them into perspective with similar data on the US personal sector (figures 5.9a–d). In spite of striking differences, mostly due to country-specific regulations, traditional organizations of financial and banking sectors, as well as tax treatments of the various types of assets (Gubian and Le Cacheux, 1987), the dramatic growth in household financial portfolios has been accompanied by reallocations that have some common features in all countries: the share of money and liquid assets has shrunk, though it remains significant in continental Europe; in those countries where households traditionally hold corporate shares – most, with the major exception for Germany, the fraction they represent in total portfolios has increased, reflecting mostly capital gains; mutual funds have also expanded, while

Figure 5.7 Share prices (1985 = 100)
a USA and Japan

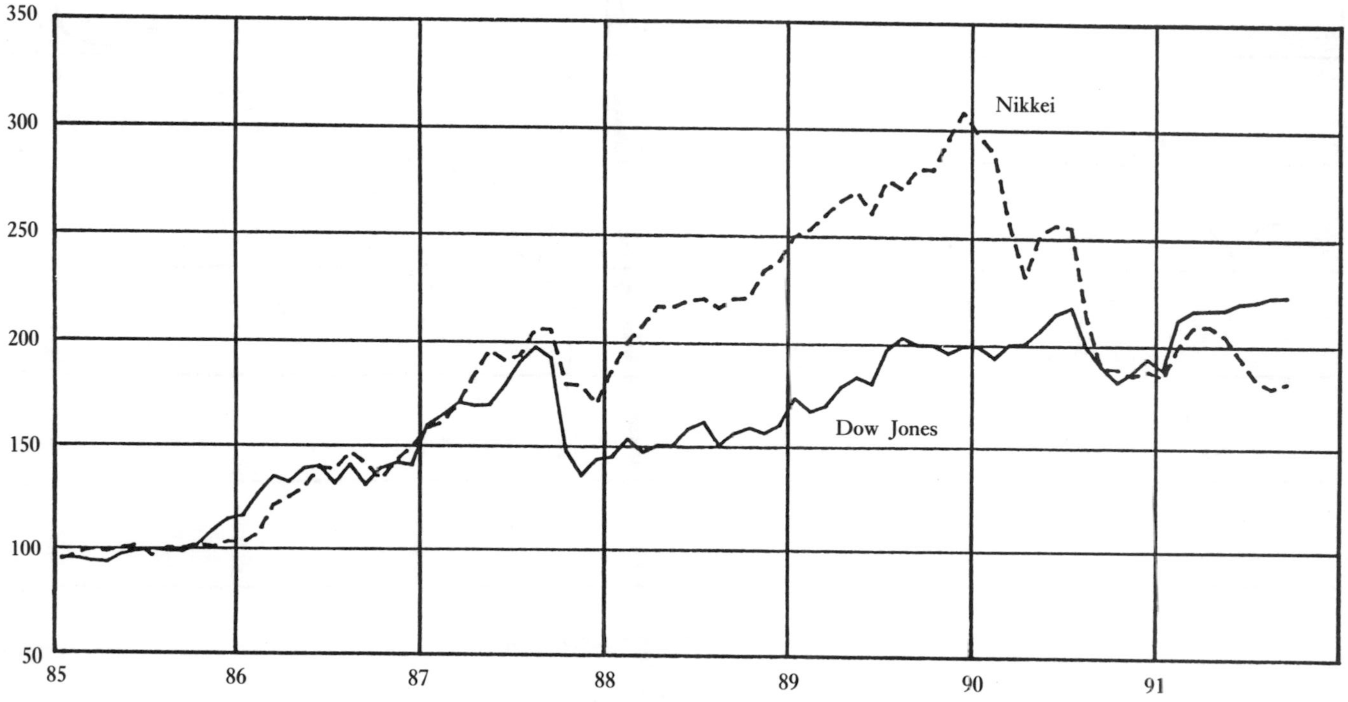

Figure 5.7 (Cont.)

b Germany and United Kingdom

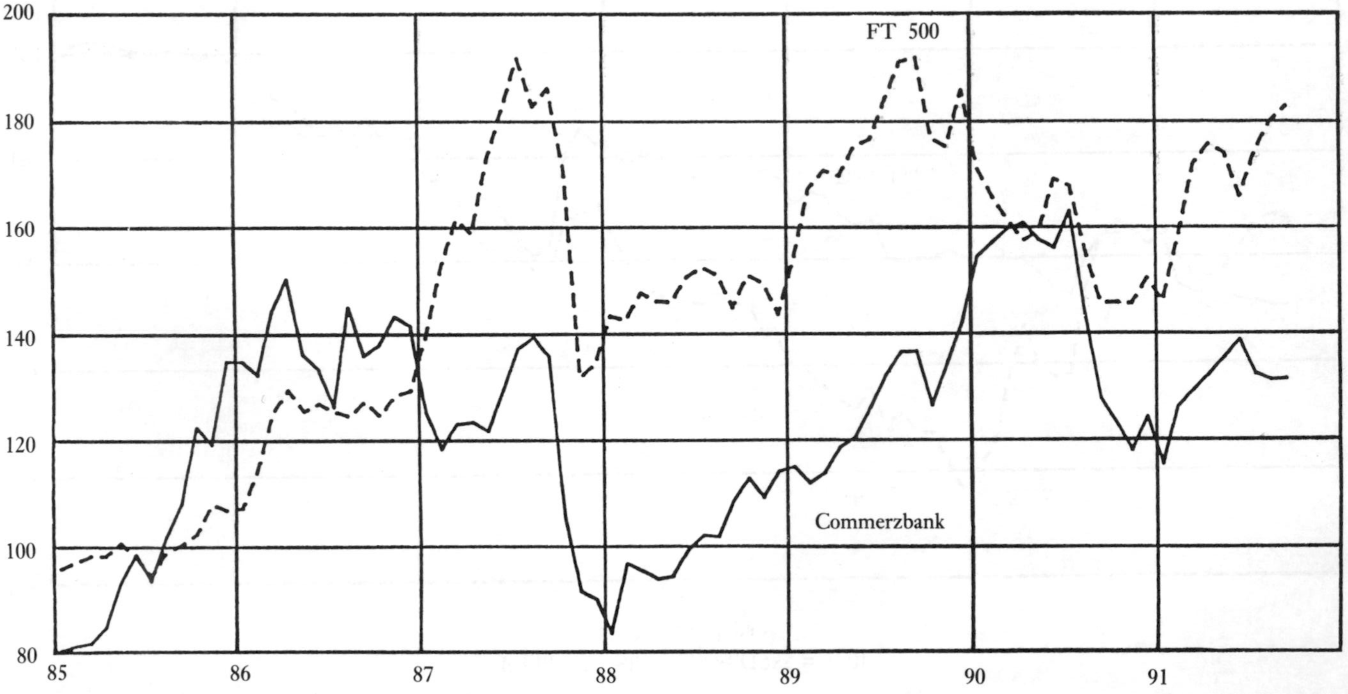

c France

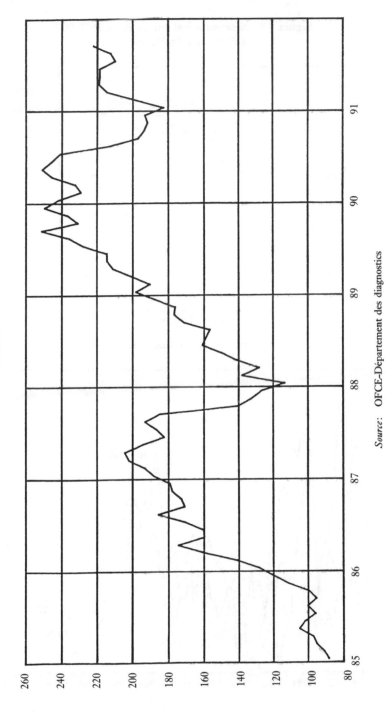

Source: OFCE–Département des diagnostics

Figure 5.8   Short-term real interest rates, 1971–90
a EMS, OECD, Europe

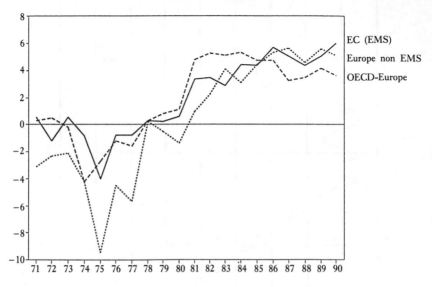

b Belgium, the Netherlands, Germany

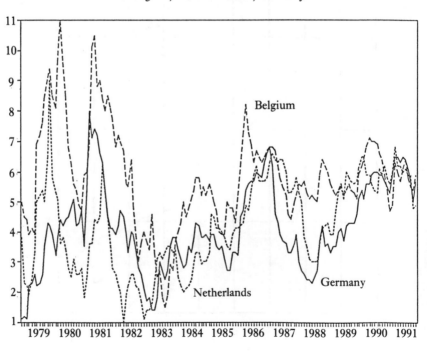

c Italy, France, Spain, United Kingdom

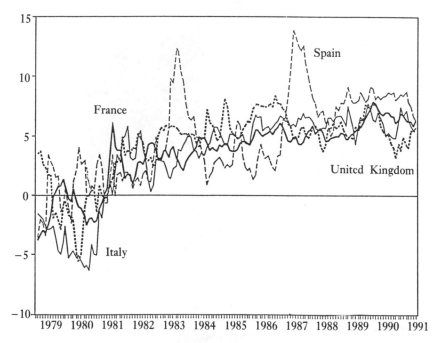

Source: OFCE-Département des diagnostics

the relative share of bonds varies from one country to the other, according to firms' propensity to use this source of financing and to the size of the public debt outstanding. Germany, the country with the least financial deregulation, the smallest increase in real interest rates and the most stable private saving ratio, has also experienced the least change in the structure of household financial portfolios.

Demographic Changes

The life-cycle, overlapping-generations models of saving also imply that the demographic structure of a country's population ought to play a major part in the determination of its private saving ratio. This effect essentially derives from the simple aggregation of individual savings of people at different stages in their life-cycles, hence with different accumulation behavior according to the life-cycle hypothesis. Schematically, such models suggest that the younger the population, the lower the aggregate private saving ratio; the more rapidly the national population is ageing, the higher the saving ratio ought to be. This

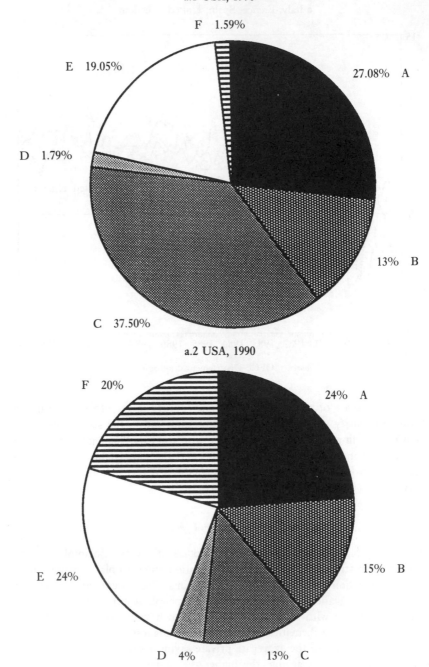

Figure 5.9 Structure of households' financial porfolios
a.1 USA, 1970

F 1.59%

E 19.05%

27.08% A

D 1.79%

13% B

C 37.50%

a.2 USA, 1990

F 20%

24% A

E 24%

15% B

D 4%

13% C

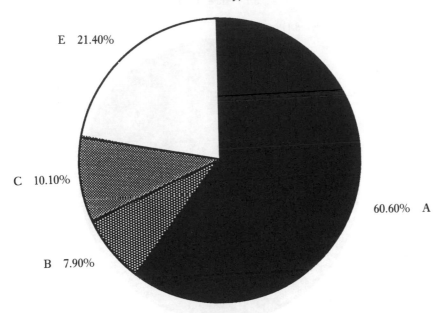

b.1 Germany, 1970

E 21.40%

C 10.10%

B 7.90%

60.60% A

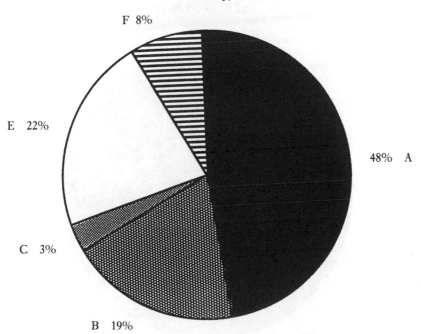

b.2 Germany, 1990

F 8%

E 22%

C 3%

B 19%

48% A

Figure 5.9 (Cont.)

c.1 France, 1970

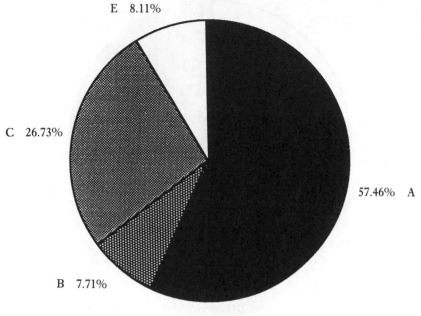

E   8.11%

C   26.73%

57.46%   A

B   7.71%

c.2 France, 1990

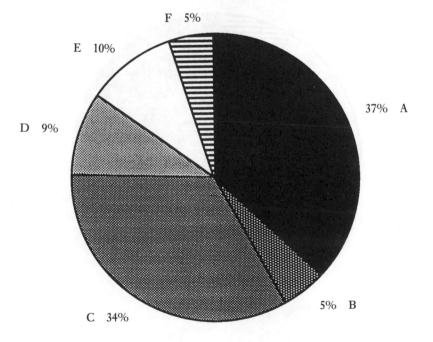

F   5%

E   10%

D   9%

37%   A

5%   B

C   34%

d UK, 1990

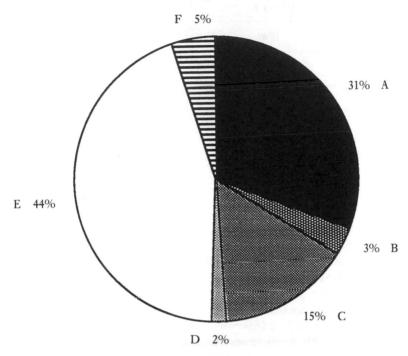

F   5%

31%   A

3%   B

15%   C

D   2%

E   44%

A = Money and liquid assets
B = Bonds
C = Shares
D = Mutual funds
E = Pension funds and life insurance
F = Others
Source: 1970: Gubian and Le Cacheux, 1987; 1990: Artus, 1991.

prediction appears to be broadly consistent with available evidence on private saving in the various countries. At the very least, the ranking of countries according to their private saving level is in conformity with that derived from their ageing prospects, as shown in table 5.1 for a selection of large industrialized countries.

Such trends in national demographic structures would tend to suggest that private saving ratios – or at least personal saving ratios – should be increasing in the near future. And, according to the life–cycle hypothesis, this improvement in saving ratios ought to happen spontaneously, as people, in the aggregate, start saving more to provide for their consumption during retirement.

Table 5.1   Ratio of population over 65 over working-age (15–64) population in major countries, 1990–2030 (in %)

	1990	2000	2010	2020	2030
USA	18.7	18.3	18.5	25.0	31.7
Japan	16.6	22.4	27.4	33.7	31.8
Germany (West)	22.5	25.1	30.3	33.2	43.4
France	21.0	23.5	24.0	30.5	35.9
UK	23.1	22.3	22.1	25.6	31.3

Source: OECD.

Severe Shortcomings in Current Models of Aggregate Private Saving

In spite of their elegance and strong intellectual appeal, models built upon the life-cycle hypothesis do not seem to perform very well in empirical applications. In particular, they appear ill-suited for the analysis of short- and medium-term fluctuations in aggregate personal saving rates: thus, for instance, many such models predicted a marked increase in private saving ratios during the 1980s, which scarcely materialized (Auerbach and Kotlikoff, 1991).

Part of the trouble seems to arise from the life-cycle hypothesis itself. Evidence from surveys of personal consumption and personal finance indicates that individual households do not appear to behave according to the pattern predicted by the hypothesis (Bosworth, 1990), even when due account is taken of such amendments to the basic assumptions as bequests, liquidity constraints, etc.

The major objections that can be raised against these assumptions are well known. Indeed, they were already cited by such prominent figures of economic analysis as Keynes, Ramsey, Pigou and economists working on externalities (Baumol, Scitovsky, for example).[12] First, the representative-agent framework, even when generations overlap – so that one dimension of agents' heterogeneity, namely age, is taken into account, fails to recognize the diversity of individual situations which may entail aggregate consequences of developments having distributional effects: thus, for instance, an increase in real interest rates redistributes income and wealth from debtors to creditors and may induce different reactions in each category.

More fundamentally perhaps, current models of aggregate saving behavior rest on a number of strong assumptions regarding financial market efficiency and private expectations and far-sightedness, which appear rather extreme. The existence of financial intermediaries and wide differences across countries in corporate financial structures and financing pratices – due to different traditions and regulations – render the "corporate veil" quite opaque for individual savers-investors who have to rely on their current perception of prospective returns to make their saving and portfolio investment decisions. There may thus be times in which commonly shared views about future real rates of return are mistaken,[13] leading to fluctuations in private saving unjustified in a perfect-knowledge, perfect-foresight world. The same may also happen with regard to future incomes or future prices of consumption goods, etc.

In particular, while life-cycle, overlapping-generations models suppose that individuals are able to foresee their future tax liabilities over their entire lifespan, available evidence does not seem to support the assumption that private agents can accurately see through the "government veil," with regard either to public debt or to public pension schemes. In these models, provided that consumers care more about their own well-being than about that of their heirs, the government is effectively in a position to redistribute wealth amongst generations through the issuance of public debt, to be serviced and repaid by taxes levied on incomes of future generations. If, however, households care as much for their prospective heirs as they do for themselves, they can undo, through their saving, accumulation, and bequest decisions, what governments do to intergenerational wealth distribution. This conclusion, known as the "Ricardian equivalence theorem" (Barro, 1974),[14] implies the existence of a unitary negative correlation between household saving and public sector saving. Although there is some evidence that some offsetting of public dissaving through increased private saving has taken place in countries where public debt has been growing fast in the last decade and is currently at very high levels – such as Italy or Belgium (Nicoletti, 1991) – the hypothesis of strong link between public and private saving does not seem to fare well when confronted with available evidence in Western European countries over the past two decades.

INTERNATIONAL TRANSMISSION OF SHOCKS AND MACROECONOMIC ADJUSTMENT IN EUROPE: A TALE OF TWO CONTINENTS

This brief review of some determinants of household saving apparently points to movements in real interest rates and relative asset prices as having played a major part in the aggregate developments observed over the past decade in Europe: the dramatic increase in household non-human wealth that has taken place through real asset price changes, along with portfolio reallocations, may have induced a downward revision in households' desired saving in the process of adjustment to a higher wealth/income ratio. However plausible, such an explanation begs the question of why real interest rates and real asset prices have risen so much in the early 1980s and how subsequent macroeconomic developments can be reconciled with their variations over the past decade.

The simple traditional theory of real interest rate determination pictures it as the outcome of the confrontation of the aggregate supply of saving with the aggregate demand of financing for investment purposes. From this perspective, it is therefore often alleged that the initial drop in aggregate saving has caused the increase in real interest rates, which in turn triggered the sharp downward adjustment in domestic investment. Although such a simple explanation may help to understand medium- and long-run developments in saving and investment in the world economy, it is not appropriate to account for observed variations in Western Europe, for at least two reasons: first, real interest rates appear to be heavily influenced by monetary policies, at least in the short run; second, Europe is not a closed economy. Indeed it is not an open economy either, but rather a collection of interdependent, small open economies, and this characteristic seems to matter much when it comes to macroeconomic policy decisions. Aggregate developments in European countries may therefore be better understood in terms of reactions and adjustments to external shocks originating in their environment, and more specifically in the US economy.[15]

Together with the second oil-price shock, European countries have been hit, during the first years of the 1980s, by an external financial shock originating in the US, still by far the largest economy in the world and thus in a position significantly to influence developments in the rest of the world. This major external shock mainly took the form of a sharp rise in real interest rates abroad, which, through financial market interdependence, induced both a similar rise in domestic real rates in Europe and a sustained, real appreciation of the dollar in terms of European currencies. Whatever the factors that kept real interest rates high in the US after 1983, it is quite clear that the initial impulse is to be found in the particular policy mix pursued in the 1979–82 period by government and monetary authorities in the US: the combination of a very tight monetary policy with progressively looser fiscal policy at federal level is likely to have been a prime mover in real interest rate and real exchange rate developments during those years.

In Germany, the leading European country in the European Monetary System, (EMS) monetary authorities tried to fight the "imported" inflationary consequences of both the oil-price shock and the dollar appreciation, as well as the negative effects on that country's current account, so that monetary conditions were tightened, and the real interest rates somewhat increased.[16] Other European countries, which had pegged their currencies to the DM in March 1979, had to pursue even tighter macroeconomic policies in order to keep their intra-European exchange rate from falling, while also fighting the inflationary consequences of the external shocks. Both the asymmetric functioning of the EMS exhange-rate mechanism and the fact that European countries have to face individual external constraints – tighter macroeconomic policies in one country causing a degradation of the current account balances in the neighboring, commercially interdependent countries – implied that macroeconomic policy reactions had to be more severe in Germany's partner countries, to avoid suffering a devaluation of their currencies within the EMS exchange-rate mechanism (Le Cacheux and Lecointe, 1987).[17]

Within each European country, the reactions of the private sector to this altered economic environment may be schematically described by considering successively what happens in the corporate sector, then the major adjustments in household saving behavior. The rise in real interest rates first dictates an upward adjustment in the real rate of return on productive capital. This, according to standard neoclassical growth theory, can only be achieved through a reduction of the capital output ratio, which will be permanent if interest rates stay at their higher level. Adjustment of the capital stock cannot be instantaneous and will therefore involve a phase of sharply reduced investment expenditures by domestic firms, as well as a stepping up of capital consumption through economic obsolescence and capital scrapping. Hence, during that period, one ought to observe a reduced gross domestic investment ratio, and an even more reduced net domestic investment ratio, all the more so as these adjustments and macroeconomic policy reactions are likely to generate a slow-down in real growth, thus more adjustment in the capital stock.

The rise in the required real rate of return on capital will usually imply a downward pressure on production costs and a corresponding upward movement in gross profit margins, i.e., mark-ups over unit costs. This is so in the neoclassical world of pure competition; in an imperfectly competitive market environment, which would appear to be a more appropriate characterization of actual goods markets, the increase in desired mark-ups is likely to be even more pronounced, as both the higher real rates of interest and the real depreciation of European currencies combine to push gross profit margins up (Fitoussi and Phelps, 1988; Fitoussi and Le Cacheux, 1989). In the aggregate, such pressures tend to deteriorate the inflation/output tradeoff and are thus likely to induce restrictive macroeconomic policy reactions, insofar as domestic disinflation, current account balance and fixed intra-EMS exchange rates are top priority objectives of the various national governments in Europe. As these factors tend to push real growth below potential, unemployment will rise, unless real wages are perfectly flexible downwards, which is clearly not the case in Western Europe. In other words, the overall adjustment in corporate profitability requires a change in primary income distribution – a rise in the gross profit share in national income and corresponding fall in wage share – which can only be achieved gradually and via an increase in unemployment, due to real wage stickiness.

In the household sector, higher real interest rates may induce capital losses in the initial adjustment phase, but the rising real return on capital should soon be reflected in rising real asset prices, which is in broad agreement with available evidence. Both the reduced rate of growth of real incomes and the higher wealth/income ratio are then likely to trigger a downward adjustment in household saving ratios. Parallel to this movement, the progressive increase in the gross corporate profit share and the gradual adjustment of corporate indebtedness level to the new environment of higher real interest rates will be translated into rising corporate saving ratios.

Judging from the empirical evidence analyzed in the foregoing, these various adjustments must have taken some time and were probably completed by the mid-1980s in Western Europe. In subsequent years, the combination of the real depreciation of the dollar, falling prices of oil and other primary commodities and progressively falling real rates of interest have contributed to ease inflationary pressures in Europe, allowing for less restrictive macroeconomic policies. Most of the adjustment in the capital stock, in relative factor shares in national income and in the private wealth/income ratio having been achieved by then, the more favorable economic environment has permitted a recovery, with falling unemployment rates and rising investment and saving ratios.

FACTORS OF PERSISTENCE IN PUBLIC SECTOR SAVING

While the major features of observed developments in Western European countries over the past decade seem broadly to fit this general outline, the evolution of public sector saving ratios requires additional scrutiny, since it appears to have been hovering around very low levels in the second half of the 1980s and to be deteriorating again rapidly over the past couple of years. With stocks of outstanding public debt already representing a substantial share of national annual income in the various European countries at the beginning of the past decade, the sharp rise in real interest rates and the reduction in real growth rates have combined to induce a potentially explosive increase in debt/GDP ratios, merely due to the marked increment in the share of public debt servicing in government expenditures. This evolution could only be curbed by pursuing more restrictive fiscal policies, in an attempt to increase public saving. In such circumstances, national fiscal policies have tended to become procyclical, since any slow-down in economic activity entails reduced tax revenue which is bound to prompt spending cuts aimed at preventing a further accumulation of public debt, that has become so costly in terms public interest payments to private creditors. At the same time, tight monetary policies barred any monetary financing of public deficits, whereas disinflation also meant reduced revenue from seigniorage in those countries – mostly Southern European states – that had traditionally been relying on such an additional source of financing to complement poorly performing national tax systems.

While the rise in public indebtedness has had major consequences on overall national saving in the various European countries, to the extent that it has not been offset by a compensating increase in private – household – saving, it also had major redistributive effects, insofar as interest payments to the state's creditors have tended to benefit those households who already had the highest incomes and wealth.

Finally, a number of changes in national tax systems have contributed to make the low level of public saving more persistent than it otherwise would have been. First, the various income-tax rate cuts and tax reforms carried out in many European countries – as well as in the US – have resulted in national tax systems being much less progressive than in the past. Together with the marked reduction of inflation, this reduced progressiveness of tax systems is reflected in smaller elasticity of government revenue with respect to national nominal income. Moreover, insofar as tax rates on capital incomes have everywhere been drastically reduced in response to higher international capital mobility and enhanced competition to attract foreign investors, the alteration of primary income distribution in favor of non-labor incomes has further reduced national tax receipts and prevented in some countries – France and Italy, in particular – any significant cut in marginal tax rates on labor incomes.[18]

CONCLUDING REMARKS

If our account of past evolutions in saving in European countries contains some elements of truth, current developments in Western Europe would not seem to feed optimism. Indeed, prospects for the balance of saving and investment are not bright, at least in the short to medium run. Due to the various persistent factors that have been identified above, public saving ratios are unlikely to pick up, while that of the general government of reunited Germany has deteriorated sharply. Whereas household saving ratios have shown signs of recovery in recent years, corporate saving has apparently been shrinking again in many countries.

The recent dramatic changes in Eastern Europe – German reunification, transition of Eastern European countries and the former Soviet Union to market economies – has greatly enhanced financing needs. For Western European countries, such an external shock has consequences that are broadly comparable to those of the US-originating shock of the early 1980s: higher real rates of interest and higher required real rate of return on domestic investment, together with a lower capital/output ratio (Fitoussi and Phelps, 1990).[19] It is therefore not surprising that European economies appear to be going through a repetition of the process of adjustment observed in the early 1980s, with slow growth – except in Germany, for which the shock is partly internal – and rising unemployment rates.

Once again, the functioning of the EMS has tended to put extra pressure on national governments in Germany's partner countries to adjust; in particular, tighter external constraints in the form of deteriorating current accounts have forced more restrictive macroeconomic policy stances, while revived inflationary pressures in Germany is triggering a more restrictive turn in Germany too. It may only be hoped that a major move toward a monetary union in Europe might alleviate some of these constraints and allow for a smoother adjustment; but this will, in any case, not happen in the short run.

NOTES

1   Note, however, that the statistical discrepancy between net national saving and the current account balance is currently quite substantial in most OECD countries, and has been growing over the last decade.

2   The drop in saving and investment ratios is even more pronounced in terms of net flows, insofar as capital consumption has increased everywhere as a share of GDP.

3   Country differences in levels are to some extent due to differences in institutions – such as social security – and in national accounting conventions. For international comparison purposes, it is usually better to harmonize, which brings the various national rates to much more comparable levels (Galibert and Le Dem, 1989). See below.

4   All the data in this chapter refer to pre-unification West Germany.

5   Here the term "households" refers to the non-corporate private sector. It therefore includes individual enterprises. Saving ratios are expressed as a percentage of GDP, not of disposable income.

6   Difficulties arising from the measurement of capital consumption will not be developed here, but should be kept in mind when interpreting the data.

7   This hypothesis was put forward by Modigliani and Brumberg in 1954. For a recent survey of later developments, with bibliographical references, see Modigliani, 1986.

8   For this to happen, one has to assume away the possibility of buying insurance contracts that would cover such risk.

9   For a detailed exposition of this kink of model, see Auerbach and Kotlikof, 1987.

10   In such general equilibrium frameworks, both rates are endogeneous so that causality runs both ways.

11   In financially integrated, open economies, saving and investment may be expected to diverge. The observation that they are in fact highly correlated (see pp. 186–8) has been interpreted by some authors as evidence of a low degree of capital

mobility (Feldstein and Horioka, 1980), but might also reflect policy reactions (see below).

12 For a synthetic account of these debates, see Phelps, 1965.

13 The recent literature of "rational bubbles" has established the possibility of such developments even when individuals act rationally.

14 Ricardo cited this possibility, but only to discard it as irrelevant. Many authors also evoked but dismissed this assumption well before its revival by Barro. See the discussion in Phelps, 1965.

15 The reasoning in this section is based on mechanisms that have been described and formalized in Fitoussi and Phelps, 1988; Fitoussi and Le Cacheux, 1989.

16 The jump in real interest rates between the 1970s and the early 1980s appears much smaller in Germany, where they had been relatively high during the 1970s, than elsewhere (see figures 5.8a–c).

17 Exchange-rate realignments have, in fact, been quite frequent during the first years (1979–83) of the EMS.

18 Average tax rates on labor incomes have even actually increased in these countries, due to the need to finance increased spending on pensions and unemployment benefits, leading to rising rates of social contributions.

19 Note, however, that real interest rates are currently much lower in the US than in Europe, while there has been a marked real depreciation of the dollar in terms of European currencies over the past few years.

REFERENCES

Artus, Patrick 1991: Epargner, investir et croître. Rapport du groupe "Allocation internationale de l'épargne." Paris, Commissariat général du Plan, juin.

Auerbach, Alan J. and Kotlikoff, Laurence J. 1987: *Dynamic Fiscal Policy*. Cambridge, MA: MIT Press.

Auerbach, Alan J. and Kotlikoff, Laurence J. 1991: The Impact of Demographic Transition on Capital Formation. Paper presented at the Conference on Saving Behaviour: Theory, International Evidence and Political Implications. Helsinki, Finland, May.

Barro, Robert J. 1974: Are Government Bonds Net Wealth? *Journal of Political Economy*, 82, no. 6, November, 1095–117.

Bosworth, Barry P. 1990: The Global Decline in Saving: Some International Comparisons. Paper presented at the Conference on Saving, Policy and Growth, Canberra, Australia, July 12–13.

Feldstein, Martin S. 1980: International Differences in Social Security and Saving. *Journal of Public Economics*, 14, no. 2; 225–44.

Feldstein, Martin S. and Horioka, Charles 1980: Domestic Saving and International Capital Flows. *Economic Journal*, 90, June, 314–29.

Fitoussi, Jean-Paul and Le Cacheux, Jacques, 1989: Une théorie des années quatre-vingt. *Revue del l'OFCE*, 29, October, 117–60.

Fitoussi, Jean-Paul and Phelps, Edmund S. 1988: *The Slump in Europe*. Oxford: Basil Blackwell.

Fitoussi, Jean-Paul and Phelps, Edmund S. 1990: Global Effects of Eastern European Rebuilding and the Adequacy of Western Saving. *OFCE Working Paper*, July.

Galibert, Alain and Le Dem, Jean 1989: Epargne des ménages américains: les enseignements d'une comparaison internationale. *Economie prospective internationale*, first quarter, 61–90.

Gubian, Alain and Le Cacheux, Jacques 1987: Fiscalité des placements liquides et financiers des ménages en France, en RFA et aux Etats-Unis. *Revue de l'OFCE*, 18, January, 175–213.

Kotlikoff, Lawrence J. 1989: *What Determines Savings?* Cambridge, MA: MIT Press.

Le Cacheux, Jacques and Lecointe, François 1987: Les contradictions du Système monétaire européen. *Lettre de l'OFCE*, 50, December.

Maddison, Angus 1991: A Long Run Perspective on Saving. Paper presented at the Conference On Saving Behaviour: Theory, International Evidence and Policy Implications, held in Helsinki, May.

Modigliani, Franco 1986: Life Cycle, Individual Saving and the Wealth of Nations. Nobel Lecture, *American Economic Review*, 76, no. 3, June, 297–313.

Modigliani, Franco 1990: Recent Declines in the Saving Rate. *Rivista di Politica Economica*, December.

Nicoletti, Giuseppe 1991: Consommation privée et endettement public en Italie et en Belgique. *Revue de l'OFCE*, 37, July, 79–119.

OECD 1989: Saving Trends and Behaviour in OECD Countries. *OECD Working Papers*, 67.

Phelps, Edmund S. 1965: A Critique of Neutralism. In *Fiscal Neutrality toward Economic Growth*, London: McGraw-Hill; reprinted in A. Sen (ed.), *Growth Economics*, Penguin Modern Economics Readings.

Summers, Lawrence S. and Carroll, G. 1987: Why is US National Saving so Low? *Brookings Papers on Economic Activity*, 2, 607–35.

6

Saving in Eastern Europe and the former Soviet Union[*]

Barry W. Ickes

INTRODUCTION

What determines saving in socialist economies? By their nature, socialist economies substitute centrally-planned decisions about capital accumulation for those that would be made by private businesses and households, as is the case in a market economy. This suggests that an examination of saving behavior in socialist economies will look at different factors than would be the case in a market economy. In a market economy decisions about saving and investment depend on attitudes towards thrift and the opportunities available to transform current consumption into future consumption. Indeed, as Robert Solow notes:

> Almost any important question we wish to ask about the saving-investment process has an unambiguous if perhaps approximate answer in terms of rates of return. . . . I don't see how a nation can have a rational investment policy until it has found approximate answers to such questions as these: what is the social rate of return to saving? Is there a substantial gap between the private and social returns to saving and investment? What are the long run consequences of thrift? (Solow, 1963, pp. 16–34).

If one accepts Solow's argument, which is indeed a hard one to dispute, then it is apparent that investment policies in the Soviet Union and Eastern European economies were highly irrational. For nowhere in the discussions of saving and investment in these countries is there an attempt to answer these fundamental

* The bulk of this paper was written while I was visiting the Economics Department of the University of Michigan, whose hospitality is greatly appreciated. I would also like to thank Annette Brown for excellent research assistance, and Heidi Applegate for comments on a previous draft of this paper. All remaining errors are my own responsibility.

questions about rates of return. Any understanding of the "long run consequences of thrift" are missing. Of course this could be a fault of the literature
rather than the decision-making process itself. But the actual record supports
the view that this process was highly irrational. Indeed, one motivation for
economic reform in these countries was the recognition that high rates of
investment were not producing adequate results in terms of economic growth.

The purpose of this chapter is to examine the saving process in the economies of the Soviet Union and Eastern Europe. Given the changes that are
currently taking place in these economies it is important to distinguish the
period before 1989 and the present. As the institutions of socialism are disman-
tled the saving-investment process changes dramatically. This process is well-
enough understood for the pre-reform period. The implications of economic
reform for saving behavior are less understood, but may play a critical role in
the near-term success of reforms.

When examining saving in the classical Soviet-type economy (STE) it is
important to distinguish between public and private saving. In an STE personal
private saving plays a distinctly minor role in aggregate capital accumulation.
The resources held by the public in savings accounts are negligible compared
with aggregate savings.[1] This is only natural given the share of GNP that
remains in the public sector in STEs, and, in particular, the fact that almost
all productive capital is in the public sector. The decision over how much of
society's output should be devoted to future production is one of the most
important decisions made by central planners. The resources are gathered
from the state sector and allocated to investment projects, for the most part,
via the government's budget. Of course the public is still sacrificing current
consumption. But the decision over the size of this sacrifice is made at the
center.

This sharp dichotomy between private saving and capital accumulation breaks
down with economic reform. With reform, it is no longer the case that all resources flow through the government's budget. Private agents make decisions
over how much to save and invest. This is made more important by the
availability of finance that accompanies reform. Although government policy
can still have an effect on aggregate saving in a market economy, the impact is
much less than in an STE. Hence it is important to ask what will happen to
aggregate saving with reform. How will the transition to a non-planned saving-
investment policy proceed?

The rest of the chapter proceeds as follows. First saving behavior in the
classical socialist system is examined. The distinction between aggregate saving
and household saving is highlighted. Then the chapter focuses on the effects of
transition on the saving process. It is useful to divide this into the impact effects
of the transition on saving and the institutional changes brought about by the
move towards markets.

Table 6.1   Investment Ratios (percent)

	1976–81	1984	1985	1986	1987
Bulgaria	35.4	33.2	35.5	36.3	37.2
Czechoslovakia	33.7	30.6	31.4	31.0	31.5
GDR	30.6	26.3	25.9	26.1	26.9
Hungary	37.2	29.2	28.8	30.4	30.9
Poland	30.7	25.2	25.8	25.8	26.8
Romania	41.3	35.9	34.5	32.5	31.3
Soviet Union	30.3	29.9	29.8	31.0	31.7

Source: United Nations, *Economic Survey of Europe*, 1987 and 1988, table 3.4.2.

SAVING IN THE CLASSICAL SOCIALIST SYSTEM

The Saving Decision Under Classical Socialism

The saving decision in a market economy is typically viewed as the choice between present and future consumption. Households are seen as balancing the desire for present consumption against the reward that comes from sacrificing current for future consumption. The level of saving in a society is thus determined by the opportunities available for transforming present into future consumption, and the preferences of agents over different time patterns of consumption. Of course many factors may enter into this balance, such as the age distribution of the population, the rate of growth of the economy, and agents' expectations about the time-path of government fiscal policy. What is crucial, however, is that aggregate saving is determined by the individual decisions of households, firms, and the government.

Saving in a classical Soviet-type economy (STE) is determined in a different fashion. Of course the same factors come into play, but the decision over the time-path of consumption is essentially a political one. Indeed the terminology used by analysts of STEs illustrates the difference. The very term *saving* is reserved for references to household saving, even though this makes up a small portion of aggregate saving. One is hard-pressed to even find a reference to aggregate saving. Of course there are discussions of capital formation or investment. But analysts have simply refrained even from discussing this in terms of aggregate saving.

In practice the desire for rapid economic growth in STEs has led to very high rates of investment by international standards, This is evident in table 6.1 which gives the ratio of investment to net material product[2] for selected years

Table 6.2   Gross investment as a percentage of GNP

Bulgaria	28
Czechoslovakia	25
GDR	24
Hungary	29
Poland	27
Romania	38
Soviet Union	30
West Germany	23
Japan	31
United Kingdom	17
Canada	25
France	21
United States	19

Source: Gregory and Stuart, 1989, pp. 402–3.

(prior to the systemic changes since 1989). For each of the countries, this ratio is quite high, varying from around 25 percent in Poland to 37.2 percent for Bulgaria in 1987.

Some perspective on these ratios can be gained from table 6.2 which presents a comparison with some western countries. Note that the data in table 6.2 is the share of investment in *GNP* (rather than NMP) for 1982. It is clear from table 6.2 that only Japan invests a share of GNP comparable to that of the former socialist bloc. Indeed the inability to stem the deterioration in the growth rate of GNP via high rates of investment was a major factor in the realization that fundamental reform was needed in these economies. But what these numbers do indicate, however, is the capacity of the STE to post high saving rates for sustained periods.

Despite the high saving rates maintained by the various STEs, aggregate economic performance has steadily declined. This has been manifested in declining rates of growth in output and consumption.[3] Without engaging in a debate about the causes of the slowdown,[4] it is important to note that as investment levels have remained high, this is strong evidence of a decline in the rate of return to investment.

How then is the saving decision made in an STE? As a first step, it is useful to conceive of the planners solving an intertemporal utility maximization problem, as that of maximizing (6.1) subject to equations (6.2) to (6.3):

$$\sum_{t=0}^{\infty} \beta^t U(c_t) \qquad\qquad (6.1)$$

subject to:

$$k_{t+1} - k_t = F(k_t, n_t) - c_t - \delta k_t \qquad (6.2)$$

and:

$$0 \leq n_t \leq 1 \qquad (6.3)$$

where c_t is consumption per worker in period t, k is capital per worker, $F(\cdot)$ is a production function (with all the normal assumptions about its shape), δ is the rate of depreciation, β is the planners' discount factor, and n_t is per capita labor supply, which we initially assume is equal to one.[5]

The solution to the planners' problem (6.1–3) gives an optimal time-path for consumption and the capital stock, and hence from (6.2) for investment.[6] Define total supply of goods per worker (including undepreciated capital) to be $f'(k_t) = F(k, 1) + (1 - \delta)k$. The optimal solution will allocate c_t so that:

$$\partial U(c_{t-1}) = \beta \partial U(c_t) f'(k_t) \qquad (6.4)$$

Equation (6.4) states that the marginal rate of substitution – evaluated by the planners – is equal to the product of the gross return to investment, $f'(k_t)$, and the discount factor, β. Hence if $\beta f'(k_t) > 1$ – i.e., the planners are relatively more patient (are willing to sacrifice present for future consumption) – then

$$\frac{\partial U(c_{t-1})}{\partial U(c_t)} > 1$$

which in turn implies that $c_t < c_{t+1}$ – in other words, that consumption will grow over time. One might characterize the Stalinist period then as one where β is close to unity and $f'(k_t)$ was *perceived* to be high.

This simple model characterizes a frequently held view about saving in STEs: that the savings rate is determined exclusively by the planners.[7] In this view the composition of output between consumption and investment is treated as a planners' decision, in respect to which the public is passive. Emphasis is placed on the planners' attitudes towards maximizing the rate of economic growth, which leads them to choose high rates of saving and investment.

The importance of the planners in determining the savings rate cannot be denied; nonetheless, this characterization is too simple. It ignores the fact that agents in STEs are not passive. They respond to incentives, and must be induced to sacrifice consumption. The intertemporal consumption path chosen by the planners must be consistent with household preferences, otherwise agents will not supply the labor effort needed to produce planned output.[8] Although it is true that the planners determine the supply of consumption goods and the money incomes of the population at any point in time, this choice is not a free variable; households respond to this choice in determining their labor supply decisions. Consequently the planners must give due consideration to the willingness of households to supply labor (Ickes, 1990a).[9]

Suppose, for example, that the planners set c_t^* too low relative to household money incomes. Then with fixed prices there will be an excess demand for goods. If there were no second economy, then shortages would occur, and households would supply less labor since they find themselves constrained in the goods market. This would then lead to a fall in output.

In the presence of a second economy[10] the excess demand on the official markets will be translated into increased demand in the second economy. Prices will rise in the latter to clear the market. But as the return to working in the second economy rises, workers will tend to "steal" more hours from the official economy, again resulting in a fall in output.[11] In either case the population is not passive in the face of excess demand. The supply of labor is thus not simply fixed in an STE. Hence the planners cannot treat the composition of output as a free variable.

One simple away around this is to assume that planners and consumers have the same preferences over consumption paths. But this is to ignore the incentives problem that is at the heart of the problems of the STE. A more satisfactory treatment may be reached by considering the savings problem as if it were analogous to a taxation problem. The planners wish to devote a portion of national income to a given purpose, but the share of income they can extract will depend on the willingness of individuals to pay. If the "tax rate" is set too high, then agents will evade the tax and revenues will decrease. Indeed, as is discussed on pp. 218–20, a very large proportion of aggregate saving in STEs is collected via taxation. In this framework the planners' choice over the time-path of consumption is constrained by the preferences of households. If too much consumption is deferred, then current output may be affected.

In this expanded framework, planners choose the time-path of consumption taking into account the effect of the supply of consumer goods on the supply of labor.[12] The time preference of households does have an effect on the savings rate via the feedback from consumer goods supply to labor supply. If the planners attempt to defer too much consumption, households respond by reducing labor effort. The saving decision is still actually carried out by the planners when they set targets for aggregate consumption and investment. But these decisions are conditioned by the behavior of households.

The important point to emphasize is that the determination of the time-path of aggregate consumption is essentially a different decision from that of how much households will save out of their *money incomes*. Although the planners must take into consideration household preferences when deciding current consumption, they also determine aggregate money income. The amount that households save *out of their money incomes* is therefore a different decision from that of aggregate savings.[13] Given the solution for consumption, c_t^*, the planners set prices and money income accordingly. Whether or not the money income of the population is set to clear the goods market, at given prices, is a somewhat controversial question (which we discuss below). But this is really a different problem from that of the nature of the aggregate saving decision. For the latter, the critical issue is how aggregate output is divided between consumption and accumulation.

If the planners do determine consumption and saving along the lines of the preceding model, then one would expect that consumption in these economies would be less volatile than income and investment. That is, if the planners determine saving based on intertemporal optimization, then they ought to engage in (some) consumption smoothing. This stands in obvious contrast to the dominant view in the literature that consumption in STEs is treated as a buffer for fluctuations in output (e.g., Bauer, 1978). In this view investment priorities are primary, and consumption is used as a cushion to soak up shocks to output.

The predictions of the *consumption-smoothing-planner hypothesis* and the *consumption-as-buffer hypothesis* are very different. When the economy experiences an adverse shock, a consumption-smoothing planner would dampen the decline in consumption and shift more of it to investment.[14] If, on the other hand, consumption is really a buffer, then consumption ought to be more variable than output. Is there any evidence that would allow one to distinguish between these two views?

As a first pass one might simply look at the variance in consumption and investment, and then compare that to the variance in income. If one actually measures the variance of the growth rates of these variables in STEs, it is immediately apparent that the variance of investment is indeed greater than that for output, which is in turn greater than that of consumption. This is not, however, a proper test of either the consumption-as-buffer hypothesis, or the hypothesis that planners smooth consumption. The reason is that if planners smooth consumption they should respond to changes in permanent income (which we may think of as the equilibrium growth path) not actual income itself.

Angus Deaton (1987) (also Campbell and Deaton, 1989) has suggested that the proper comparison is not between the variance of consumption and income, but rather between the variance of consumption and the variance of the innovation in the income process. This is because consumption decisions made by forward-looking agents (as in the model of equations 16.1–3, above) would reflect information about future income that is forecastable. Hence it is only the *innovation* to the income process – the new information – that should affect consumption. Of course, in STEs it is not households but rather the planners who decide on the level of consumption. But if planners are forward-looking, it may still be revealing to see how smooth consumption is relative to innovations to output.

Table 6.3 Measures of smoothness in consumption and investment

Country	variance of the income process[a]	variance of consumption[b]	variance of investment[c]
Bulgaria	.00023	.00029	.00482
Czechoslovakia	.00044	.00049	.00295
GDR	.00006	.00029	.00192
Hungary	.00075	.00039	.00533
Poland	.00149	.00221	.01274
Soviet Union	.00024	.00027	.00067

[a] Sample variance of the innovations ε from autoregressions of the first differences of the log of output (y_t):

$$y_t = C + \rho y_{t-1} + \varepsilon_t$$

except in the case of the Soviet Union where the estimated model is AR(3), and Hungary where output is a random walk (hence we used the variance of y_t itself).
[b] Variance of the first differences of consumption.
[c] Variance of the first differences of investment.

Source: Ickes, 1990b.

Table 6.3 reports the variances in the innovation process to output in the various STEs, as well as the variances of consumption and investment. The latter is included for information, and also to see if planners smooth investment. The innovations in the income process are the deviations of the actual series from the estimated ARMA processes for output.

The results in table 6.3 indicate that the variance in consumption is smaller than that for investment in all the cases. Interestingly, the innovation process in income is less variable than the variance in consumption for all of the cases, save Hungary (which is not surprising given that Hungarian output follows a random walk!), although for several cases the variances are quite close. This suggests, perhaps, that planners in STEs adjust consumption to innovations in output itself, as opposed to the permanent changes only in the latter. But the difference in the variances is not that great. Some consumption smoothing clearly is taking place. That it is not complete is not at all surprising, given the lack of financial markets in STEs, the relative reluctance of planners to borrow externally for consumption purposes, and the focus on short-run balancing that seems to typify central planning.

An alternative way to analyze how planners determine consumption is to see if consumption and output are co-integrated. Note again that this would be a test of planners' behavior rather than that of households. If planners adjust consumption to changes in permanent income, that is if there is an equilibrium relationship between consumption and income, then we would expect the two

Table 6.4 Co-integration tests[a,b]

Country	C and Y	I and Y
Bulgaria	−2.11	−1.58
Czechoslovakia	−3.06	−2.47
GDR	−2.07	−0.56
Hungary	−3.13	−1.05
Poland	−1.50	−2.15
Soviet Union	−2.88	−2.72

[a] Values reported in the table are the t-statistics of the coefficient ρ_1 in the second stage regression (ii):

$$\text{(i)} \quad x_{j,t} = \beta_0 + \beta_1 y_t + \varepsilon_{j,t}$$
$$\text{(ii)} \quad \Delta\varepsilon_{j,t} = \rho_1 \varepsilon_{j,t-1} + \rho_2 \Delta\varepsilon_{j,t-1} + \mu_t$$

where j = consumption and investment respectively, and y is output.
[b] None of the t-statistics are significant at the 10 percent level.

Source: Ickes 1990b.

variables to be linearly related, i.e., they should be co-integrated. Some might indeed argue that it is investment and output that are co-integrated in STEs, given the planners' focus on growth.

Table 6.4 reports the results of tests for co-integration between consumption and income (and investment and income). Notice that this is a very strong test. Suppose that consumption and output are determined jointly, but that due to policy changes – such as reforms, etc. – the consumption–income ratio is altered (a one-time change) during the sample. Then an econometrician will most likely reject the co-integration hypothesis, even though by assumption the two variables are jointly determined.

The results in table 6.4 are quite consistent across countries. In none of the cases can we reject the hypothesis that the variables are *not* co-integrated. This is, of course, consistent with the results in table 6.3. As we noted above, those results seem consistent with the view that planners adjust consumption in response to innovations in current, rather than permanent, income. In that case one would not expect consumption and income to be co-integrated. Notice that we also fail to reject the null hypothesis with respect to investment and output.

These results should not be surprising. Once it is recognized that consumption is not entirely a planners' decision alone, then it is open to question whether a "planners' permanent income hypothesis" makes any sense. Notice that it is only the planners – with access to international financial markets – that have the capability to engage in full consumption smoothing. Internal financial markets are quite underdeveloped (nonexistent) in the STEs. Households are consequently likely to encounter liquidity constraints. As is discussed in the next section, consumer credit markets were non-existent in the classical STEs. Hence it is hardly surprising to find consumption responding to innovations in actual income.[15]

The empirical results seem to provide evidence against both the consumption-as-buffer hypothesis *and* the planners' permanent income hypothesis. It is interesting to note that both of these hypotheses take the saving decision to be the sole province of the central planners. The difference between the two views is how the decision is made, not who makes it. In the consumption-as-buffer view the planners determine saving based on their preferences about growth, and use consumption as a reserve against which investment plans can be preserved. In the planners' permanent income hypothesis, the planners smooth consumption to maximize their utility. The difference between these views is in how consumption will fare in the face of a shock to, for example, output. In the former view consumption will fall. In the latter, investment will take the brunt of the effects. As we have seen, the evidence for both theories is weak, though it is perhaps a bit stronger against the consumption-as-buffer view.

There is, of course, an alternative hypothesis about consumption in STEs, which suggests that in making the saving decision planners had to take household preferences as a constraint. This is not to suggest that the saving rate reflected a social rate of return equal to the discount rates of households in STEs. This is clearly not the case. But it does suggest that the planners consider the feedback from consumer goods availability to labor supply when making the saving decision. Notice that this view goes against the consumption-as-buffer hypothesis. If planners worry about the output effects from a shortfall of consumer goods they will be less likely to shift a fall in output on to consumption.

To date, relatively little work has been done on the nature of the saving decision in the STE. Some further evidence about saving may be gleaned from discussions of household saving and the "chronic shortage" hypothesis, discussed below, pp. 220–5. The discussion turns now, however, to the mobilization of saving in STEs.

Mobilization of Saving in the Classical STE

How is saving mobilized under classical socialism? In a market economy households channel their saving to firms through financial intermediaries, such as banks, savings and loans, and securities markets. In the STE a very different channel is utilized. STEs typically had both commercial and savings banks. But their purpose was not financial intermediation.[16] Indeed, in an STE the primary channel for transforming saving into investment is the government budget.[17]

It is crucial to recognize that in the pre-reform system the state budget combined two functions that are distinct in market economies: (1) the provision of goods and services typically provided by governments, and (2) the savings-investment process that is performed by a financial system in a market economy.[18] Public and private finance are intertwined in the pre-reform system.[19] Investment is financed not through a financial system that intermediates between businesses and households,[20] but rather by the government as the owner of the capital stock. Since enterprises are owned by the state rather than by the private sector, profits stay within the public sector. There is no need for intermediation, since household income is net of the return to capital. Profits are then divided between retained earnings and remittances to the central budget (which can be thought of as dividends paid to the "true owners").

The two primary sources of investment in a planned economy are retained earnings by enterprises and grants from the government budget. Consequently, resources that would typically flow through a financial system in a market economy flow through the government budget in a planned economy. Centrally financed investment, for example, is a component of government expenditure.[21] Hence the public budget is partly used as a saving-mobilization device. Economic reform will change this, and in order to make the public finances consistent with a market economy, a severing of the private financial functions from the public finances is required.

Since the state owns essentially all the reproducible capital in an STE, the difference between the retail price of a good and its cost of production (including depreciation but excluding the return to capital) can be thought of as the profits of the socialist sector. It then does not really matter if these are collected as retained earnings by the state-owned enterprises, or accrue to the central budget via enterprise remittances or turnover taxes. These are just alternative means for the state to collect the "return" to its assets.

The center uses its revenue from "operating the production sector" to finance both public consumption and investment. Centrally financed investment is quite large in STEs, though its share in total investment has varied over time and place.[22] In addition to grants from the state, retained earnings and the amortization fund also provide resources for investment.

Aside from the remittances of enterprises ("dividends"), the turnover tax is a central source of budget revenue in STEs. It is the difference between the retail price and the wholesale price. Notice that it is a specific duty. That is, it does not depend on the value of the commodity in question. If one views the state sector in STEs as one large enterprise, then the revenue from the turnover tax can be thought of as one component of profits.

The Soviets have often claimed in fact, that the turnover tax is not a tax at all, but rather the "surplus product" created in industry (Nove, 1986, p. 249). There is an important sense in which this view is correct. Since the turnover tax is the difference between a centrally-determined wholesale price and a centrally-determined retail price, the amount of retained profits and turnover tax revenue is arbitrary. If, for example, the wholesale price of a good is raised with the retail price unchanged, the turnover taxes have fallen but profits have risen. The "tax" burden on the population is left unchanged.[23]

Of course not all budget revenue in an STE goes to investment. The center also provides public consumption and defense. The key point, however, is that a major portion of investment in STEs does flow through the government's budget. This is not surprising given the nature of the system; it is, after all, a centrally-planned economy. Moreover, taxation is a rather effective means of mobilizing resources. Since saving stays essentially within the production sector of the STE, there is no need for financial institutions to channel saving from the ultimate savers, households, to the eventual users of the funds, enterprises. In this way the planners can direct the allocation of investment to its various uses. Of course, the effectiveness with which this allocation has been conducted is one of the most serious problems in the STE.[24]

The Household Saving Decision under Classical Socialism

What determines the household's decision to save under socialism? Do the institutions of the socialist system alter the motivations to save? It has been frequently argued (most notably by Igor Birman) that households have little motive for saving in the classical socialist system.[25] One might argue, however, that households in STEs would have similar motives for saving as in market economies, although the force of the various motives may differ. This question is important even if household saving comprises only a small part of national saving in these economies. The reason is that the notion of forced saving (or the associated notion of the monetary overhang) has very sharp implications for price liberalization and economic reform.

When economists study the saving decisions of households in market economies the primary determinants of saving are the desire to smooth income over the life-cycle, the desire to leave bequests, and as a precautionary reserve against uncertainty. The same approach can be used to study saving in STEs.[26] In the STE, however, these motives are, in each case, attenuated. The need to save for retirement is reduced by the near-universal coverage of the state's pension system.[27] Households in STEs also leave bequests, but the universal provision of education lessens the need for this. And there is also a smaller need for precautionary saving, since in the classical STE cyclical fluctuations in output rarely manifested themselves in fluctuations in employment.

One of the most important differences between STEs and market economies is that in the former there is an absence of any significant life-cycle variation in income (Ofer and Pickersgill, 1980, p. 123). This occurs primarily because wage differentials are reduced in STEs compared to market economies. Furthermore, the effect of seniority on wages is also less in STEs than in market economies.[28] Since wages are the major share of income for households in STEs, smooth wage profiles implies that the need to save in order to smooth life-cycle variation in income will be reduced.

The hump in earnings is also reduced by the pension system in STEs which tend to replace a higher portion of pre-retirement earnings than is the case in the United States.[29] Although pensions are still quite low, it is the difference between pre- and post-retirement income that is a major determinant of the hump in earnings, and consequently of life-cycle saving.

The lack of a significant hump in earnings profiles results in less life-cycle saving in STEs than in market economies like the US. Although there is little available evidence, it seems that the same can be said for intergenerational transfers. Since the state owns most of the housing stock, this component – which is the major portion of intergenerational transfers in the US – of bequests is likewise absent in STEs.[30] Hence two of the major forces that lead to saving in market economies are absent or attenuated in STEs.

What then are the major motives for household saving in STEs? One of the most important is to finance the purchase of consumer durables, such as automobiles. Given the absence of a consumer loan market, such big-ticket items must be purchased with cash. Hence households must build up large stocks of saving in order to finance these purchases. The official price of an automobile in the Soviet Union, for example, was about $3\frac{1}{2}$ to 5 years' income at the average official wage.

Another important component of saving is as a precaution against emergency. Although the state offers free health service in STEs, in practice citizens need to make side payments in order to secure adequate and timely care. Indeed, most services in the STE require the purchaser to offer a little extra on the side (*na levo*, on the "left" in the Soviet Union). Hence households save in order to be able to make such payments. This motive is clearly stronger in STEs than in most market economies. Nonetheless, household income – as opposed to national income – is considerably less variable in STEs than in market economies.[31] Consequently there is less of a need to save as a precaution against fluctuation in incomes.

There is, however, a precautionary demand for savings that is more prevalent in STEs than market economies. This is as a precaution against the availability of goods.[32] As the availability of goods is uncertain in an STE, households tend to save so that if they get "lucky" and find the goods available they will have the means with which to buy them. Saving is thus an option on the chance that goods show up in the stores. While this effect is clearly present in STEs, and completely absent in market economies, the empirical importance of this motive is difficult to assess.

Thus for various reasons households in STEs have less reason to engage in consumption smoothing compared with identical households in market economies. Households are also faced with fewer opportunities to save. The range of assets in which households can place their wealth is severely limited. Savings deposits, in the classical period, paid fixed nominal interest rates of around 2–3 percent. Given the hidden inflation that these economies experienced, especially in the 1980s, this amounted to a negative real return. Given that the capital stock was socially owned, there was little outlet into productive investment. Hence the return to postponing consumption was greatly reduced by the lack of financial assets. This reduces the level of household saving in these countries below what it otherwise may be.

Although most of the institutional differences between STEs and market economies seem to suggest that saving rates will be lower in the former, there is a strong current in the literature suggesting that households in STEs *save too much* (e.g., Birman, 1980). The argument is that because of repressed inflation households in STEs are forced to save. The "forced-saving" hypothesis has had wide currency among specialists in the field, and has also led to some interesting debates.[33] Since the presences of a "savings overhang" has important implications for the transition in STEs it is worth examining this position in some detail.

The basic postulate of the savings overhang position is that households in STEs have little motive to save, hence evidence that growing savings held by the population must be forced savings, and is direct support for the hypothesis. Adherents of this view essentially consider the consumption decision to be like that of the simple model on pp. 211–18, where the planners determine the aggregate level of consumption and money income. With fixed prices and money incomes set exogenously, an excess demand for goods is translated into forced savings, which is manifested in the growth of cash balances and savings deposits. This view is sometimes referred to as the *chronic excess demand hypothesis*.[34]

Advocates of the savings overhang view typically point to the growth of savings deposits relative to retail trade – figure 6.1 plots this for the Soviet Union – as evidence of the overhang. As is clear in the figure, this ratio has been growing steadily over time. Since saving is a stock and retail trade a flow, however, this is hardly surprising. To obtain some idea about "forced saving" it is more illuminating to look at the *change* in savings deposits – which is essentially savings, given the limited range of investments that Soviet households can make – relative to retail trade, as in figure 6.2. This ratio is much more volatile than the savings deposits-retail trade ratio. Moreover, it appears that three distinct periods can be identified in the figure. From the early 1950s until the mid-1960s this ratio seemed fairly steady in the 1–3 percent range. Then in the mid-1960s the ratio jumps to a higher rate, centered around 5 percent.

Figure 6.1   Soviet Union: household savings, 1950–90

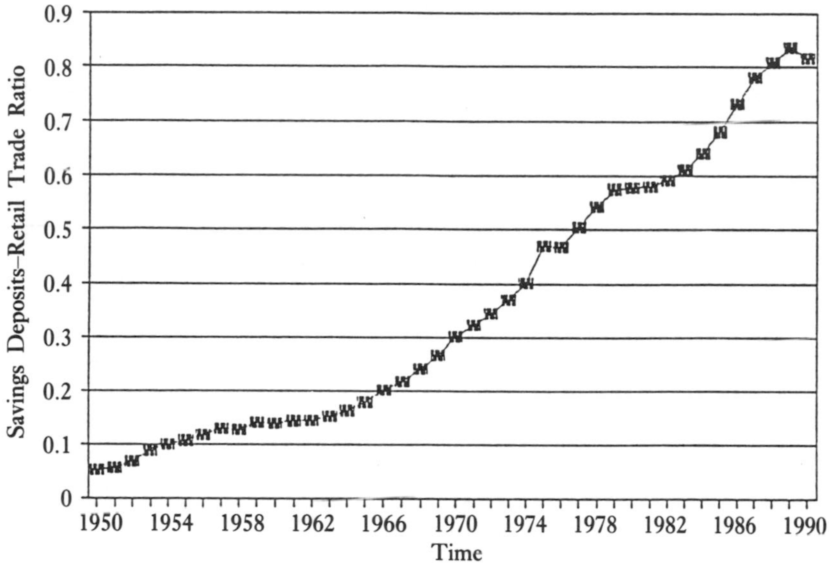

Source: Roberts, 1992.

Then in the early 1980s another break is apparent; one observes steady growth in the savings – retail trade ratio during this period.[35]

An alternative way to look at saving is as a proportion of income. In figure 6.3 the average (APS) and marginal (MPS) propensities to save out of personal disposable income are displayed. Looking at the APS ("the savings rate") it is evident that from the mid-1960s to the late 1980s there is an upward trend, although the saving rate dipped in the early 1980s.[36] But it is also clear that the saving rate is rather stable, and that it is not very high by international standards.

Figure 6.3 also plots the marginal propensity to save, and it is clear that this is much more volatile than the savings rate itself. Since income is relatively stable in the Soviet Union, the variation in the MPS is coming from changes in saving from year to year.[37] This can be taken as lending support to the *chronic excess demand hypothesis*. If personal income is rather stable but additions to savings are not, then it is not unreasonable to conclude that fluctuations in the availability of retail goods are the prime determinant of annual changes in saving.

The chronic excess demand hypothesis has been forcefully criticized by Richard Portes and his associates in various papers over the years. Portes's basic point is that the planners ought to be able to get the aggregate level of money

Figure 6.2 Soviet Union: savings rate, 1951–90

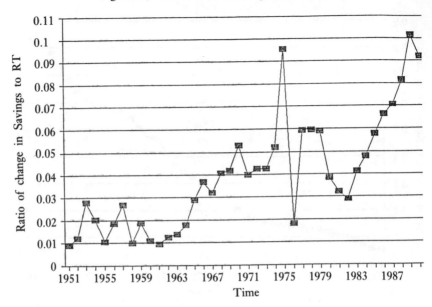

Source: Roberts, 1991.

income correct – it is the problem of relative prices that is most vexing. In Portes's approach the supply of consumer goods is adjusted to the state of the market. There may be mistakes, but there is no reason to expect that these mistakes would be biased in favor of aggregate excess demand. Hence one may expect excess demand to appear in some periods, excess supply in others.

An example of this approach is Portes, Quandt, Winter, and Yeo (1987). They assume that the planners have a long-run plan for consumption growth (given perhaps by a model like that of pp. 211–18) and that they adjust the supply of consumer goods depending on their observations of the state of the market in a given period. Thus they assume that the planners choose the supply of consumer goods to minimize a quadratic loss function defined over the deviations of actual and planned consumption. They use this to derive an equation for the consumption plan that is a linear function of the previous period's actual consumption, planned consumption, and excess demand, well as excess demand in the period being planned. The model is empirically implemented for Poland over the period 1955 to 1980, and the data seems to support the hypothesis that "planners do appear to try to adjust announced plans and actual supply in order to reduce excess demand" (Portes et al., 1988, p. 36).

The basic argument of Portes and his colleagues is that planners adjust the

Figure 6.3   Average and marginal propensities to save, 1966–87

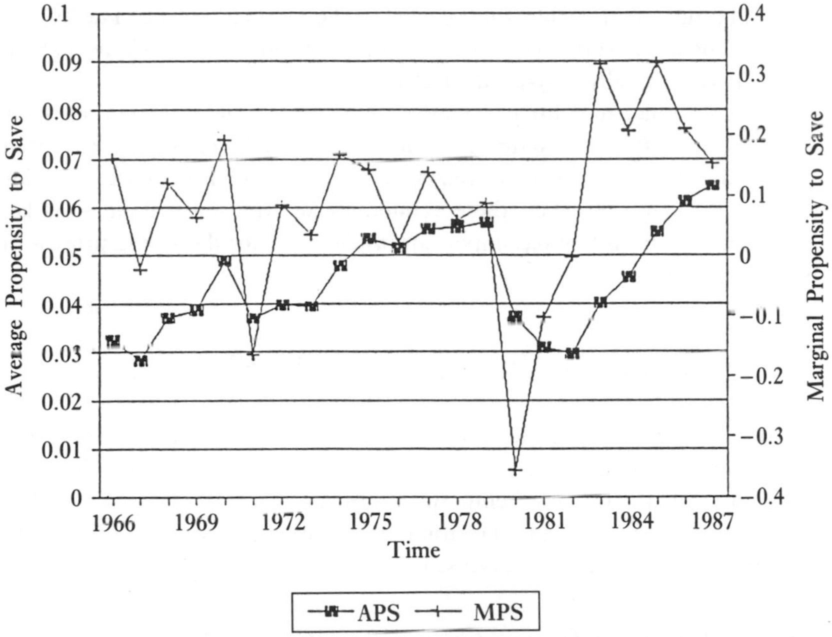

Source: CIA, 1989.

supply of consumer goods to prevent the emergence of chronic shortage. Another argument against the saving overhang view focuses on the second economy. In each of the STEs under consideration, an economically significant parallel economy developed alongside the official one. In these parallel economies prices are flexible. Several important implications follow. First, in comparisons of savings rates (as in figures 6.1 and 6.2) the base to which saving is compared is understated since value added in the parallel economy should be counted as part of national income. Second, since prices in the second economy are the true shadow prices, one should deflate by these prices rather than by official indexes which greatly understate inflation. Both of these effects operate to reduce the measured saving rate, and cast doubt on the chronic shortage hypothesis.

Summary

The institutional features of the classical STE leads to high aggregate savings, a relatively low proportion of which is done by the household. Compared with

market economies several features are striking. First, relatively little of aggregate saving goes through the financial system. Pension funds play a very small
role. And little of household wealth is held in the form of housing. The bulk of
saving is mobilized via the center's provision of consumer goods relative to total
output. It is essentially a by-product of the tax system.

STEs are similar to many developing countries in that they have relatively
underdeveloped financial systems.[38] The effect of this on saving has been
attenuated in STEs by the use of the tax system as a mobilization device. This
will change, however, when these economies are transformed into market
economies. The transition has important implications for the saving process in
the former STEs.

SAVING AND THE TRANSITION

The transition from a regime of central planning to a market economy has
dramatic effects on the saving process. These effects are of two types. First, the
transition itself implies new (temporary) burdens that will affect the level of
aggregate saving. Second, the transition affects the very nature of the saving-
investment process itself. We discuss each in turn.

Impact Effects of the Transition of Saving

The impact effects on saving of the transition to a market economy are several.
One of the most important is the effect of price liberalization on household
saving.[39] Many analysts argue that households in STEs are involuntary savers
due to the shortages that are endemic in a regime with price controls. If
households are indeed holding excess savings, then price liberalization may
cause a dramatic rundown of household assets, with dramatic consequences for
the price level. The force of this argument, however, depends on the assumption
that households can be forced to save involuntarily.

Given the existence of a black market, consumers always face an operational
decision (they are not at a corner): they can purchase goods on the black market.
Hence, their savings cannot reflect just a piling up of useless balances. If they
in fact do save an abnormally high amount, this must reflect a judgment that
the marginal utility of deferred purchases is higher than the marginal utility
of purchases on today's black market. Given the existence of a black market,
consumers must be on the appropriate saving demand curve. Thus, to evaluate
the "saving overhang" story, the standard theory of saving can be applied.
Saving is determined by expectations of future income relative to current income,
and the relative rates of return on savings accounts versus holding durable
goods and cash. One must, of course, take some care in using correct shadow or

black market prices to infer those rates of return. In that case, however, theory of saving does not predict anything like the saving overhang scenario.

Before turning to the theory, it is important to note that the empirical evidence adduced to support the notion of a saving overhang is usually interpreted in a misleading way. Estimates of the saving overhang are typically made by comparing the growth in savings deposits to the growth in income.[40] A comparison of savings deposits and income is presented, as in figures 6.1 or 6.2. But the calculation of high holdings of savings, relative to income, values the latter at official prices rather than transaction prices.[41] Since this understates the value of nominal income relative to savings, it overstates the saving rate.[42]

It is also hard to believe in a saving overhang on theoretical grounds. The only reason for a large volume of saving is that consumers must think they will get a better deal waiting to spend tomorrow, rather than spending today. They must believe that black market goods will cost less tomorrow, so that the effective real interest rate is very high. Alternatively, they could believe that rationed goods will become more available with no significant price increases in the future, so that the value of their savings will be higher. Neither belief sounds very plausible.

Even if it is supposed that a large amount of saving exists, what kind of events would cause a rush out of savings into consumer goods? Again, saving is a forward-looking decision: it is not determined by whether today is a good time to buy relative to the past, as implied by the saving overhang story. It is determined by whether today is a good time to buy relative to the future. Thus, to generate the rush out of saving and into consumer goods described by the saving overhang story, consumers must expect goods to be more available during the transition than afterward. They must believe that goods will become harder to acquire in the future, so that it is better to buy today rather than keep money in the bank and buy tomorrow.[43]

This expectation is unlikely: the whole point of a price liberalization is that goods should become more, not less available. The one possible channel that could cause a run out of deposits is that if there is a price-level increase during the liberalization, and bank interest rates are frozen, then consumers would decrease savings in order to hoard goods. This represents, in effect, a change in the composition of assets held as wealth.

One exception to the analysis so far is consumers who are liquidity constrained and hence must accumulate large savings balances to purchase "big ticket" items like automobiles. As was noted above, this is an important motive for saving in STEs. When prices are freed, and if credit markets are present, these individuals will indeed carry lower savings. One would expect this effect to be small, especially since the development of consumer credit markets will take time.

So far, the analysis has focused on rates of return (correctly measured, i.e., using the shadow value or black-market value of money rather than posted prices of rationed goods) as determinants of saving. The other determinant of saving is, of course, income: consumers raise their stock of savings if they think income in the future will decrease, and vice versa. One can make a case that this channel produces some of the effect predicted by the saving overhang. Before the liberalization, it is a reasonable expectation that things are only going to get worse, so consumers will want to save. As long as real interest rates (again, measured relative to black-market goods) on saving accounts are slightly positive, they will hold such accounts rather than hoard durable goods. After a liberalization, consumers may expect that incomes will rise, and thus decrease their stock of savings.

This channel is limited, however, by two considerations. First, the liberalization would have to be completely unexpected. If consumers expect a liberalization and subsequent rise in incomes, they will not have a large stock of savings to begin with. Second, consumers will not unload their entire stock of savings on getting news that future incomes will be higher. They will follow the usual permanent income rule and spend a constant fraction of their entire wealth, including savings and the present value of labor income, in each period. The change in expectations of future income means that a larger fraction of the initial stock of saving will be spent each period, say from 5 to 10 percent, but the theory of saving does not predict that consumers will suddenly dump their entire stock in favor of consumer goods.

There is an important force that suggests that households will actually increase their savings during the transition. The features of the STE induced households to hold rather low ratios of wealth to national income compared with market economies. Given the sudden transition to a market regime one might expect that households will to build up their stocks of wealth.[44] Since uncertainty about income will be rising, and as the state will no longer be providing the wide range of services as it did in the STE, one would expect that households will alter their saving behavior. To take one example, in the STE the state acts as insurer for a wide variety of risks, especially business risks. As these economies become market economies this insurance will become privatized and households will save by purchasing insurance contracts.

Michael Alexeev (1991a) has recently proposed a novel reason why savings may rise in the transition, and may in fact be higher in the new steady state. He points out that in the classical STE an important source of retirement income of the elderly is their ability to queue and then resell goods in the second economy. As the elderly are endowed with free time, they can convert this to income through queuing in official markets. But this source of income is eliminated in the transition to a free-price economy. Hence workers will need to save to provide for retirement. Alexeev shows, in the context of an overlapping generations model, that this effect may be important. Of course it is difficult to assess the empirical significance of this factor.

Figure 6.4 Investment ratios

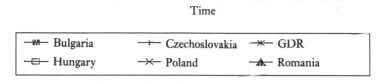

Source: World Bank.

Of course some of the increased saving by households will be offset by a decline in public-sector saving. As the state role in the economy recedes, so will its role in the saving mobilization process. The income from production will accrue to a new set of owners. Hence some of the increase in private saving is just a transfer that results from a change in the nature of ownership. One suspects, however, that the household's need to improve its balance sheet will, for the near term, more than offset the increase in income from production, since the transition seems likely to lower income from the state sector.

An important consequence of the weakening of central control in many STEs during the 1980s has been a decline in capital accumulation. This is evident in figure 6.4 which plots the ratio of gross domestic investment to gross domestic output for each of the East European STEs in this decade. This pattern, with the sole exception of Bulgaria, is quite striking. In each case this ratio has declined in what appears to be a secular shift in this ratio.

Notice that the decline in the savings ratio exhibited in figure 6.4 occurs *before* 1989. This suggests that this shift has more to do with the deterioration in performance of the STEs than in the effects of the transition. This "structural shift" has been little noted in the literature. What might explain it?

Figure 6.5   Hungary: composition of output

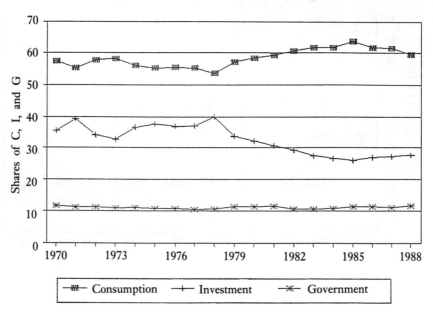

Source: Heston and Summers, 1991.

The decline in the investment share of national income is most likely the reverse of an offsetting increase in the consumption share. This is clearly the case for Hungary (see figure 6.5) where good data is now available. A similar scenario would almost certainly hold for the other East European countries (save, obviously, Bulgaria). One could argue that this is the response to the birth of Solidarity in 1980 and the attendant consequences for the strength of Communist regimes in its aftermath. But it is difficult to see why this should be true for all East European countries. Alternatively one could argue that growing contacts with the West increased the demand for current consumption on the part of households in these countries, and consequently raised the cost, in terms of current production, to the planners of postponing consumption. Or, one could attribute this shift in the composition of output to a recognition that the investment share was too high given the return, and that the way to better performance required this shift.

In any event this decline in capital accumulation is likely to be accentuated in the early period of reform. The reason is that economies in transition will likely incur transitory expenditures, and, at the same time, some components of government revenue may be reduced. Examples of the former would include expenditures for shutting down some state enterprises, retraining of workers, and restructuring in general. The decline in revenues is likely given the need to revamp the public finances. Hence one might expect the government budget to worsen temporarily, further reducing aggregate saving.[45]

Saving in the New Regime

How will the saving process be altered by the regime change? That is, what permanent changes will be brought about by the change in institutions as these economies become market economies? A facile answer is that they will be just like market economies. A more useful question looks at the near term, and asks how the elimination of socialist institutions will alter the saving process, and what implications this might have for the transition.

The effects on the saving process brought about by the change in regime are dramatic. Many goods and services that used to be provided by society will now be provided by individuals. Insurance, as noted on pp. 226–31 above, is one example. Home ownership, already growing in the late 1980s, is another. As households tend to hold more of their wealth in their homes, the supply of savings available for investment in industry may decline.[46]

The move to a market economy will bring with it many institutional changes that will raise saving. Thus, for example, one would expect an increase in the variance of economic fluctuations, especially unemployment. Not only is income likely to be more variable with the transition to markets, but profit income, which is more variable than wage income in capitalist countries, will now become a more important source of household income. This increased income uncertainty should lead to a rise in saving, as households attempt to smooth consumption. This is the result we would expect to observe from risk-averse households that must cope with greater income uncertainty – a rise in precautionary saving. At the same time, the transition to a market economy ought to increase wage differentiation over time (i.e., steeper wage profiles), and hence should provide a greater motive for life-cycle saving.

In the transition these effects should be even more important than in the long run. First, the very uncertainty of transition ought to make households cautious. More importantly, however, the underdeveloped state of financial markets means that households will still not have access to market institutions to smooth income in the near term. Hence risk-averse households are likely to self-insure to smooth in the transition. Moreover, with underdeveloped credit markets those households that may wish to borrow against future income will find this very difficult. So dissaving will be lower until these institutions mature.

If these conjectures are correct, one suspects that the RSTEs will be major importers of capital in the near term. Transition is a process that will improve the long-run performance of these economies. But there will likely be a short-run cost. To traverse this pass successfully, foreign investment will be most helpful. For the near term this region will almost certainly be a net importer of foreign capital, *if the RSTEs can avoid triggering capital flight*. This is always a potential problem in countries where the financial markets are insufficiently developed, or where they are overly regulated.

The immaturity of financial markets in the transition will be one of the most important roadblocks in the transition. It will make privatization more difficult because it will make it harder for newly privatized firms to obtain capital.[47] One suspects, however, that it is precisely in this area that institutional innovation will be greatest. This is necessary as the capital market is a *tabula rasa* in formerly socialist economies. The only prediction that can be made with confidence is that the saving process in the RSTEs will change dramatically, and the importance of removing impediments towards saving and investment cannot be overstated.

NOTES

1   Household savings in Hungary, for example, did not exceed one percent of GDP through 1990 (Abel and Bonin, 1991, p. 13).
2   Net material product is the measure of aggregate output used in STEs. The major difference between NMP and GNP is the exclusion of services ("unproductive" activities) from the former. Consequently a country's NMP is always smaller than its GNP or GDP. Where available, comparisons will be made using GDP (recalculated in the west from official statistics). But for some purposes only GDP is available.
3   For evidence on the Soviet case see Ickes, 1991a.
4   On the causes of the slowdown in growth in the Soviet case see, for example, Weitzman, 1983 or Desai, 1987.
5   In the absence of foreign borrowing, we would add the constraint that c_t be less than or equal to aggregate output. There may also be a lower bound to consumption that derives from political constraints.
6   Which is, of course, the same thing as saving in the model.
7   Although the view that the planners set the saving rate is widespread, it is rarely expressed in the form of the solution to a planners' problem. For a good discussion of this view, and the alternative as well, see von Brabant (1990).
8   Technically, the problem is that in the simple model of equations (6.1–3) it is implicitly assumed that there is full employment, and that labor is supplied perfectly inelastically, i.e., that $n = 1$.
9   The notion that households can vary the amount of labor offered in response to the effective real wage was, at one time, a rather controversial proposition, since the length of the workweek in state enterprises was uniform. Recent scholarship (e.g., Gaddy, 1991) documents the importance of the second economy in introducing flexibility through, for example, the phenomenon of "stolen hours."
10   On the role of the second economy in the Soviet Union, see Grossman, 1977.
11   "Stolen hours" refers to that portion of the work week for which workers are paid but do not actually work. As discussed by Gaddy (1991), stolen hours are a part of the wage bundle over which employees in the state sector are choosing. When the

real wage in the second economy rises, state-sector enterprises must increase wages to maintain their labor force. Since nominal wages are under strict controls, enterprise managers often respond by increasing the amount of stolen hours offered.

12 In STEs households have relatively little freedom to alter the hours of labor offered. They can, however, alter the amount of effort put forward, and the amount of labor hours "stolen from the job."

13 This suggests that the major difference between socialist and capitalist economies is in the *place* where saving is accumulated. In the former, saving is accumulated primarily in the production sector and the tax system – the role of households is attenuated by the institutional structure of the system. In capitalist economies, a greater portion of national income is distributed to households (i.e., capital's share), hence more of aggregate saving is accumulated in the household sector.

14 An agent that engages in consumption smoothing would borrow in the face of an adverse shock. Although this option is also open to a planner in an STE, this channel for smoothing was relatively infrequently utilized. This was due, in some measure, to the restrictions put on foreign investment by central planning, in terms of pricing, profit repatriation, and supply availability. It also reflects the unwillingness of planners to rely excessively on foreign capital for political reasons, though this reluctance waned greatly in the last half of the 1970s and the first half of the 1980s.

15 It should be noted that failure to reject the null hypothesis does not necessarily mean that planners do not smooth consumption. It may just mean that the relationship between output and consumption has changed over the sample period. It is perhaps too much to suppose that planners would behave in a manner that resembles the permanent income hypothesis (even if one can derive such behavior from an optimal planning problem). This is especially the case given that an important feature of planners' behavior in centrally-planned economies (CPEs): planning from the achieved level. To the extent that planners behave in this manner, aggregate consumption will depart from the strict predictions of the permanent income hypothesis. Instead consumption will depend, to a large extent, on last period's income (or consumption). It will be important, in future research to develop tests that discriminate more carefully among the competing hypotheses.

16 The primary purpose of banks in the STE is as a monitoring device. Enterprises cleared accounts through the state bank. This avoided the use of cash, and hence made for better control of the enterprise sector. Savings banks, which paid a small nominal interest rate (around 2 percent), were a channel for saving. But the magnitudes were very small compared with aggregate saving.

17 To be more specific one must note the role of retained earnings. But when one considers the economic "equivalent" of intermediation in an STE, the relevant institution is the government budget. Moreover, as is emphasized below, the dividing line between retained earnings and remitted profits is essentially arbitrary.

18 The major expenditure item in the USSR State Budget, for example, is "Allocations to the National Economy," of which investment and subsidies make up the major components.

19 The implications of economic reform on the private financial system are discussed in Ickes, 1991a.

20   Households typically engaged in some saving but this was a rather small component of aggregate saving. Deposits in state savings banks typically afforded negative real interest rates (typically about 2 percent nominal rates).

21   This suggests that comparisons of budget deficits in the STEs and market economies are a bit misleading. In advanced industrial countries a large portion of corporate investment is financed by issuing debt. In STEs the equivalent transaction occurs when the central government issues debt. But this debt will be included in the government's budget figures (unlike corporate debt). There is one important difference, however. In the market economy the debt issue does not lead to an increase in the country's monetary base!

22   Centrally-financed investment (that is through the state budget; this is different from centralized investment, see Nove, 1986, p. 249) probably reached its zenith in the Soviet Union of the 1930s. In the post-war period there has been an increasing reliance on self-financing of investment, and away from the turnover tax.

23   One should also note that subsidies for retail goods are essentially negative turnover taxes. Hence the burden on households should be calculated based on net turnover taxes. In the Soviet Union, for example, subsidies have grown rapidly since the mid 1970s so that by the late 1980s they were about equal to the gross revenue from turnover taxes (Ofer, 1990, p. 311).

24   On the problems of investment allocation in STEs see, for example, Berliner, 1976 and Desai, 1987.

25   See for example, Birman, 1980 or Birman and Clarke, 1985.

26   Ofer and Pickersgil 1980, and Alexeev, 1991b, are about the only papers that attempt to explain saving in an STE using the standard theory of saving behavior.

27   This does not mean that the payments are necessarily adequate. Estimates for the Soviet Union place a very large share of the retired population in poverty.

28   See Chapman, 1977, and the IMF-World Bank-OECD-EBRD study (1991), 2, 150, for details on the Soviet case. The wage differential between wage workers and salary workers fell quite markedly from 1956 to 1986 as wage compression intensified (1991, table IV. 6.8).

29   The *Study* (vol. 1) reports data on the replacement ratio of pensions in the Soviet Union. The ratio is about 50 percent of pre-retirement income for most wage earners (more for very low income workers).

30   It would, perhaps, be more accurate to say that this component of intergenerational transfers is made by the *state*.

31   This is primarily due to two factors. First, in STEs households do not receive profit income, which is considerably more variable than national income as a whole. Second, planners in STEs smooth wage income, presumably for political reasons. Of course, this refers to official incomes, excluding income from second-economy activity.

32   For a model of this effect see Acharya and Spagat, 1990.

33   See von Brabant, 1990 for a recent survey of one component of this debate, that between Kornai – who argues that there is chronic shortage in STEs – and Portes. Kornai's argument, forcefully put forward in a number of articles, is that excess demand in STEs leads to *forced substitution* into less preferred goods. This leads to an understatement of excess demand, because it is manifested in consumption.

34   Ellis and Naughton, 1990, provide a model of household saving in the presence of rationing. They point out that it is not always true that a tightening of rations leads to an increase in saving.

35   The downturn in this ratio in 1990 probably reflects fears of a monetary confiscation, which would fall disproportionately on savings deposits. As it happened, of course, cash holdings were the most vulnerable.

36   Since the growth rate of income was declining in the mid 1980s one can speculate as to the cause of the rise in the APS. It could be due to stable saving behavior in the face of what is expected to be a transitory decline in the growth rate of income. The problem with this explanation is that if households viewed the slowing of growth as temporary, they ought to have dipped into savings, rather than the reverse. Of course the underdevelopment of consumer credit mitigates against this force.

37   The coefficient of variation of the change in saving is more than ten times higher than the coefficient of variation of the change in income.

38   Blejer and Cheasty (1989) discuss the role of fiscal policy in mobilizing saving in developing countries. They suggest that public sector surpluses be used as a means of augmenting private saving in developing countries with underdeveloped financial systems. STEs essentially used this strategy as well. It is not at all clear, however, that this strategy will be available in the transition, given the pressure on government budgets resulting from enterprise shutdowns and lost revenues.

39   The analysis in this section draws heavily on Cochrane and Ickes, 1991.

40   The annual growth rate of savings deposits in the Soviet Union has been over 10 percent, and as high as 14 percent, since 1986 (see *PlanEcon Report*, VI, November 23, 1990).

41   See, for example, the calculations and discussion of excess savings in the Soviet Union, in "Stabilization, Liberalization, and Devolution: An Assessment of the Economic Situation and Reform Process in the Soviet Union," *European Economy*, 45 (December 1990), and the study by the IMF, World Bank, OECD, and the EBRD, *A Study of the Soviet Economy*, vol. 1, February 1991.

42   There are two effects to consider. First, using official prices understates nominal income, since effective transaction prices are higher. If one purchases meat in a free market at eight times the official price, eight times the rubles must be expended. Second, ignoring the second economy means ignoring a large component of personal income. The numerator, on the other hand, is comprised of cash and savings deposits, so it is not biased downward in this way.

43   The concern that liberalization may lead to a rush to buy goods would seem more appropriate to a policy of *delayed* liberalization. If the government announces that prices will be liberalized after some interim period, then hoarding would be a rational response in order to beat the price increases.

44   Alexeev (1991b) argues that this process has already begun in the former Soviet Union.

45   A related problem is that of pensions. New democracies, especially in the Baltic Republics, have already called for a lowering of the retirement age. This will clearly lower saving in the transition to the new steady state, as those "early retirees" will increase their consumption.

46 This effect is noted by Blanchard, Dornbusch, Krugman, Layard, and Summers, 1991, p. 76.
47 On the problems of the capital market in the transition, see Ickes, 1991b, and Ickes and Ryterman, 1991.

REFERENCES

Abel, Istvan, and Bonin, John 1991: Two Entrance Ramps along the Road to Market: Hungary and Poland as Contrasting Approaches to the Transformation. Paper presented to the Conference on the East European Transformation, Princeton, New Jersey, May.

Acharya, A. and Spagat, M. 1990: Individual Savings and Monetary Overhang: A Model with Empty Shelves and a Second Economy. Unpublished, Brown University.

Alexeev, Michael, 1991a: Savings and Retail Price Reform in a Queue-Rationed Economy. Paper presented to the Conference on the East European Transformation, Princeton, New Jersey, May.

Alexeev, Michael 1991b: Saving Behavior and Soviet Reform. Paper presented to the Western Economics Association, Seattle, July.

Bauer T. 1978: Investment Cycles in Planned Economies. *Acta Oeconomica*, 21, no. 3, 243–60.

Berliner, Joseph 1976: *The Innovation Decision in Soviet Industry*. Cambridge: MIT Press.

Birman, Igor 1980: A Reply to Professor Pickersgill. *Soviet Studies*, XXXII, 4, October, 586–91.

Birman, Igor, and Clarke, Roger 1985: Inflation and the Money Supply in the Soviet Economy. *Soviet Studies*, XXXVII, 4, October, 494–504.

Blanchard, Oliver, Dornbusch, Rudiger, Krugman, Paul, Layard, Richard and Summers, Lawrence, 1991: *Reform in Eastern Europe*. Cambridge: MIT Press.

Blejer, Mario I. and Cheasty, Adrienne 1989: Fiscal Policy and Mobilization of Savings for Growth. In M. I. Blejer and K. Chu (eds), *Fiscal Policy, Stabilization, and Growth*. IMF, pp. 33–49.

Campbell, John and Deaton, Angus 1989: Why is Consumption so Smooth? *Review of Economic Studies*, 56, 3, June, 357–74.

Chapman, Janet 1977: Recent Trends in the Soviet Industrial Wage Structure. Kennan Institute for Advanced Russian Studies, Washington, DC.

CIA 1989: USSR: *Estimates of Personal Incomes and Savings*. Sov 89–10035 (April).

Cochrane, John H. and Ickes, Barry W. 1991: Inflation Stabilization in Reforming Socialist Economies: The Myth of the Monetary Overhang. *Comparative Economic Studies*, XXXIII, 2, Summer, 97–122.

Deaton, Angus 1987: Life-cycle Models of Consumption: Is the Evidence consistent with the Theory? In Truman Bewley (ed.), *Advances in Econometrics*. Cambridge: Cambridge University Press, 121–48.

Desai, Padma 1987: *The Soviet Economy*. London: Basil Blackwell.

Ellis, Christopher, and Naughton, Barry 1990: On the Theory of Household Saving in the Presence of Rationing. *Journal of Comparative Economics*, 14, 2, June, 269–85.

Gaddy, Clifford G. 1991: The Labor Market and the Second Economy in the Soviet Union. *Berkeley-Duke Occasional Papers on the Second Economy in the USSR*, #24.

Gregory, Paul and Stuart, Robert 1989: *Comparative Economic Systems*. 3rd edition, Boston: Houghton Mifflin.

Grossman, Gregory 1977: The "Second Economy" of the USSR. *Problems of Communism*, 26, 5, September–October, 25–40.

Heston, Alan and Summers, Robert 1991 The Penn World Tables (Mark 5): An Expanded Set of International Comparisons, 1950 – 88. *Quarterly Journal of Economics*, CVI, 2, May, 327–68.

Ickes, Barry W. 1990a: A Macroeconomic Model for Centrally-Planned Economies. *Journal of Macroeconomics*, 12, 1, Winter, 23 – 45.

Ickes, Barry W. 1990b: Consumption, Investment, and Output in the Cyclical Fluctuations of Centrally-Planned Economies. Working Paper, The Pennsylvania State University, October.

Ickes, Barry W. 1991a: Soviet Macroeconomic Policy and Performance: Implications for Perestroika. Working Paper, The Pennsylvania State University.

Ickes, Barry W. 1991b: What To Do Before the Capital Markets Arrive. Paper presented to the Conference on the East European Transformation, Princeton, New Jersey, May.

Ickes, Barry W. and Ryterman, Randi 1991: The Role of Capital Markets in the Transition. Working Paper, The Pennsylvania State University, September.

Ickes, Barry W. and Slemrod, Joel 1991: Tax Implementation Issues in the Transition from a Planned Economy. International Institute of Public Finance, 47th Congress, Leningrad, August.

International Monetary Fund, The World Bank, OECD, and European Bank for Reconstruction and Development 1991: A *Study of the Soviet Economy*. Washington, DC, February.

Nove, Alec 1986: *The Soviet Economic System*. 3rd edition, London: Allen and Unwin.

Ofer, Gur 1990: Macroeconomic Issues of Soviet Reforms. *NBER Macroeconomics Annual*, 5, 297–334.

Ofer, Gur and Pickersgill, Joyce 1980: Soviet Household Saving: A Cross Section Study of Soviet Emigrant Families. *Quarterly Journal of Economics*, XCV, 1, August, 121– 44.

Pickersgill, Joyce 1983: Household Saving in the USSR. In F. Modigliani and R. Hemming (eds), *The Determinants of National Saving and Wealth*. London: Macmillan, 272–85.

Portes, Richard, Quandt, Richard E., Winter, David and Yeo, Stephen 1987: Macroeconomic Planning and Disequilibrium: Estimates for Poland, 1955–1980. *Econometrica*, 55, 1, January, 19–41.

Roberts, Bryan 1991: Repressed Inflation and the Soviet Growth Slowdown. Unpublished, MIT.

Solow, Robert 1963: *Capital Theory and the Rate of Return*. Chicago: Rand McNally.

von Brabant, Jozef M. 1990: Socialist Economics: The Disequilibrium School and the Shortage Economy. *Journal of Economic Perspectives*, 4, 2, Spring 157–75.

Weitzman, Martin 1983: Industrial Production. In A. Bergson and H. Levine (eds), *The Soviet Economy: Towards the Year 2000*. London: Allen and Unwin, 178–90.

7

Saving in Japan

*Charles Yuji Horioka**

INTRODUCTION

The shortage of capital (saving) in the Middle East, unified Germany, Eastern Europe, the Soviet Union, the United States, the developing countries, and indeed throughout the world has recently drawn an increasing amount of attention and has spurred a revival of interest in Japanese saving behavior for two reasons. First, Japan is one of the few countries in the world with a surplus of saving, and second, there are those who believe that the Japanese experience may be able to provide some lessons for countries trying to raise their own saving rates.

The goal of this chapter is to provide some basic facts about saving in Japan and to survey selectively the literature on the subject.[1] The chapter is organized as follows: first I present a variety of data on Japanese saving and attempt to determine whether Japan's saving rate is high by international standards even after conceptual differences and deficiencies have been eliminated; then, I survey the literature on Japanese saving behavior with emphasis on the issue of whether the life–cycle model or the dynasty model has greater applicability in the case of Japan; and finally, I summarize and conclude.

To preview my main findings, I find that Japan's saving rate remains high even after conceptual differences and deficiencies have been eliminated but that the gap relative to other countries is not as wide as the official figures suggest, and that Japan's saving rate has shown a downward trend since at least 1976 (with the exception of the national saving rate during the 1983–8/9 period). In addition, I find that the life–cycle model is far more applicable in Japan than the dynasty model. Bequests are relatively prevalent in Japan, but they appear to be primarily unintended or accidental bequests arising from risk aversion in the face of uncertainly about future medical expenses, the timing of death, etc., or intended bequests motivated by implicit annuity contracts between aged parents

* The author is grateful to David Campbell, Franco Modigliani, and Fumio Ohtake for helpful comments and discussions.

and their children or by a strategic bequest motive, all of which are fully consistent with the life-cycle model.

SAVING DATA AND CONCEPTUAL ISSUES

In this section, I present a variety of data on Japanese saving and attempt to determine whether Japan's saving rate is high by international standards even after conceptual differences and deficiencies have been eliminated. I first present unadjusted data from the National Income Accounts (Kokumin Keizai Keisan) of Japan, compiled by the Economic Planning Agency (Keizai Kikaku-chō), and then make (or at least discuss) a number of adjustments to the data.

All of the data presented are based on the United Nations' new System of National Accounts (SNA), are net of depreciation (the consumption of fixed capital), are on a calendar year basis, and incorporate the October 1990 benchmark revision (based on 1985 prices), the detailed data from which were published in March 1991 (refer to the Appendix, p. 278, for details).

Unadjusted Data

Table 7.1 presents data on the saving of the various sectors of the economy as a ratio of national disposable income. Data for the following sectors are shown:

1 The household sector narrowly defined (households and private unincorporated non-financial enterprises)
2 Private non-profit institutions serving households
3 The household sector broadly defined ((1) and (2))
4 The business sector (non-financial incorporated enterprises and financial institutions)
5 The private sector ((3) and (4))
6 The government sector
7 The economy as a whole ((5) and (6)).

Table 7.2 presents data on the composition of saving by sector using the same sectoral breakdown, and table 7.3 presents data on the following saving rates:

1 SHR = the household saving rate narrowly defined, defined as SH/YDH
2 SHNR = the household saving rate broadly defined, defined as SHN/YDHN
3 SPR = the private saving rate, defined as SP/YP
4 SNR = the national saving rate, defined as SN/NDI,
where SH = the saving of the household sector narrowly defined (households and private unincorporated non-financial enterprises)

Table 7.1 Trends in saving in Japan (ratios to national disposable income)

Year	Household sector narrowly defined	Private non-profit institutions serving households	Household sector broadly defined	Business sector	Private sector	Government sector	Economy as a whole
1955	9.8	0.4	10.2	1.3	11.5	3.7	15.2
1956	10.5	0.4	10.9	1.5	12.4	5.0	17.4
1957	9.9	0.3	10.2	4.1	14.3	6.0	20.3
1958	9.9	0.5	10.4	2.9	13.3	4.7	18.1
1959	10.9	0.4	11.4	3.7	15.0	5.3	20.4
1960	11.0	0.3	11.3	7.1	18.3	6.5	24.8
1961	12.0	0.2	12.2	7.2	19.4	7.5	26.9
1962	11.9	0.1	12.1	5.4	17.4	7.4	24.8
1963	11.6	0.0	11.6	5.2	16.8	6.8	23.6
1964	12.0	0.2	12.1	5.0	17.1	6.6	23.7
1965	12.5	0.1	12.6	3.6	16.2	6.1	22.3
1966	11.7	0.0	11.7	5.8	17.5	5.6	23.2
1967	10.6	0.0	10.6	8.7	19.3	6.4	25.6
1968	12.7	0.0	12.7	8.7	21.3	6.6	27.9
1969	12.6	-0.0	12.6	9.7	22.3	6.9	29.2
1970	12.8	-0.0	12.7	10.7	23.4	7.6	31.1
1971	13.3	0.1	13.5	7.1	20.6	7.9	28.5
1972	13.7	0.2	13.9	7.3	21.2	6.9	28.2
1973	15.5	0.3	15.8	5.8	21.5	7.8	29.3
1974	18.7	0.2	18.9	0.5	19.4	7.3	26.7
1975	19.3	0.3	19.6	-0.8	18.8	3.7	22.4
1976	19.7	0.2	19.9	0.8	20.8	2.3	23.0

1977	18.2	0.2	18.4	1.5	19.9	2.6	22.5
1978	17.1	0.4	17.5	3.8	21.3	1.6	22.9
1979	14.7	0.3	15.0	4.0	19.1	2.7	21.8
1980	14.6	0.3	14.8	3.3	18.1	3.0	21.1
1981	15.0	0.3	15.3	2.4	17.6	3.5	21.2
1982	13.6	0.3	13.9	2.8	16.6	3.2	19.9
1983	13.2	0.2	13.4	2.7	16.1	2.7	18.8
1984	12.8	0.2	12.9	3.3	16.2	3.7	19.9
1985	12.4	0.1	12.5	3.5	16.0	4.9	20.9
1986	12.8	0.1	12.9	3.4	16.3	4.7	21.1
1987	11.5	0.1	11.6	3.2	14.9	6.6	21.4
1988	11.0	0.1	11.1	3.8	14.9	7.9	22.8
1989	10.9	0.2	11.1	2.6	13.8	9.0	22.7
1955–69	11.3	0.2	11.5	5.3	16.8	6.1	22.9
1970–89	14.5	0.2	14.7	3.6	18.3	5.0	23.3
1955–89	13.1	0.2	13.4	4.3	17.7	5.4	23.1

The figures are in percentage terms, refer to saving net of historical cost depreciation, and are on a calendar year basis. Totals may not add due to rounding error.
See text for definitions.

Source: National Income Accounts of Japan. See Appendix for details.

Table 7.2 Trends in Japan's saving rate

Year	Household saving rate narrowly defined	Household saving rate broadly defined	Private saving rate	National saving rate
1955	11.9	12.2	13.6	15.2
1956	12.9	13.1	14.6	17.4
1957	12.6	12.7	17.0	20.3
1958	12.3	12.7	15.7	18.1
1959	13.7	14.0	17.7	20.4
1960	14.5	14.6	21.7	24.8
1961	15.9	15.9	23.1	26.9
1962	15.6	15.5	20.9	24.8
1963	14.9	14.8	20.0	23.6
1964	15.4	15.3	20.3	23.7
1965	15.8	15.6	19.2	22.3
1966	15.0	14.8	20.6	23.2
1967	14.1	13.9	22.7	25.6
1968	16.9	16.6	25.2	27.9
1969	17.1	16.8	26.4	29.2
1970	17.7	17.4	28.0	31.1
1971	17.8	17.8	24.8	28.5
1972	18.2	18.2	25.4	28.2
1973	20.4	20.5	26.0	29.3
1974	23.2	23.2	23.6	26.7
1975	22.8	22.9	22.2	22.4
1976	23.2	23.3	24.0	23.0
1977	21.8	21.8	23.1	22.5
1978	20.8	21.0	24.4	22.9
1979	18.2	18.3	22.1	21.8
1980	17.9	18.0	21.1	21.1
1981	18.4	18.5	20.8	21.2
1982	16.7	16.8	19.5	19.9
1983	16.1	16.1	18.7	18.8
1984	15.8	15.8	19.1	19.9
1985	15.6	15.6	19.1	20.9
1986	16.1	16.0	19.4	21.1
1987	14.7	14.7	18.0	21.4
1988	14.3	14.3	18.3	22.8
1989	14.2	14.3	17.1	22.7
1955–69	14.6	14.6	19.9	22.9
1970–89	18.2	18.2	21.7	23.3
1955–89	16.6	16.6	21.0	23.1

The figures are in percentage terms, refer to saving net of historical cost depreciation, and are on a calendar year basis.
See text for definitions.

Source: National Income Accounts of Japan. See Appendix for details.

YDH = the disposable income of the household sector narrowly defined, defined as CH + SH

CH = the final consumption expenditure of the household sector narrowly defined

SHN = the saving of the household sector broadly defined, defined as SH + SNP

SNP = the saving of private non-profit institutions serving households

YDHN = the disposable income of the household sector broadly defined, defined as YDH + CNP + SNP

CNP = the final consumption expenditure of private non-profit institutions serving households.

SP = private saving, defined as SHN + SB

SB = the saving of the business sector (non-financial incorporated enterprises and financial institutions)

YP = private national income, defined as YDHN + SB

SN = national saving, defined as SP + SG

SG = the saving of the government sector

NDI = national disposable income, defined as YP + CG + SG[2]

CG = the final consumption expenditure of the government sector

As table 7.3 shows, the household saving rate narrowly defined (broadly defined) fluctuated in the 11.9 to 23.2 percent (12.2 to 23.3 percent) range during the 1955–89 period, while the private and national saving rates fluctuated in the 13.6 to 28.0 percent and 15.2 to 31.1 percent ranges, respectively, during the same period. The period-wide averages of the four saving rates were 16.6, 16.6, 21.0, and 23.1 percent, respectively. Thus, all four saving rates have fluctuated over a broad range but have been relatively high on average.

Turning to the sectoral composition of saving (see table 7.2), the share of the household sector narrowly defined ranged from 41.1 to 86.0 percent and averaged 57.7 percent during the 1955–89 period, while the shares of private non-profit institutions serving households, the business sector, and the government sector ranged from −0.1 to 2.7 percent, −3.6 to 34.5 percent, and 7.1 to 39.4 percent, and averaged 1.0, 17.9, and 23.4 percent, respectively, during the same period. Thus, the household sector narrowly defined has accounted for the largest share of national saving throughout the post-war period, and the high level of the household saving rate narrowly defined appears to be the main cause of the high level of Japan's overall saving rate. However, the saving of the business and government sectors have also been important during certain periods, with the share of the business sector exceeding 30 percent during the 1967–70 period and the share of the government sector exceeding 30 percent during the 1987–9 period.[3]

Table 7.3 Trends in the composition of saving in Japan

Year	Household sector narrowly defined	Private non-profit institutions serving households	Household sector broadly defined	Business sector	Private sector	Government sector
1955	64.2	2.7	66.8	8.8	75.6	24.4
1956	60.2	2.1	62.4	8.7	71.1	28.9
1957	48.6	1.7	50.3	20.3	70.6	29.4
1958	54.9	2.7	57.6	16.2	73.8	26.2
1959	53.7	2.1	55.8	18.0	73.8	26.2
1960	44.3	1.3	45.5	28.4	74.0	26.0
1961	44.6	0.8	45.4	26.7	72.1	27.9
1962	48.1	0.5	48.7	21.6	70.3	29.7
1963	49.1	0.2	49.3	22.0	71.3	28.7
1964	50.4	0.7	51.1	20.9	73.0	28.0
1965	55.9	0.5	56.3	16.3	72.6	27.4
1966	50.4	0.1	50.6	25.1	75.6	24.4
1967	41.2	0.1	41.3	33.9	75.2	24.8
1968	45.4	0.0	45.4	31.1	76.5	23.5
1969	43.2	-0.1	43.1	33.2	76.3	23.7
1970	41.1	-0.1	41.1	34.5	75.5	24.5
1971	46.9	0.5	47.4	24.9	72.3	27.7
1972	48.6	0.8	49.4	26.0	75.4	24.6
1973	52.9	0.9	53.8	19.7	73.5	26.5
1974	70.1	0.9	71.0	1.8	72.8	27.2
1975	86.0	1.4	87.3	-3.6	83.7	16.3
1976	85.5	1.0	86.5	3.7	90.2	9.8

1977	80.9	0.9	81.8	6.6	88.4	11.6
1978	74.7	1.8	76.4	16.5	92.9	7.1
1979	67.5	1.5	69.1	18.4	87.4	12.6
1980	69.1	1.2	70.3	15.5	85.9	14.1
1981	70.8	1.3	72.1	11.2	83.3	16.7
1982	68.3	1.5	69.8	13.9	83.7	16.3
1983	70.3	1.1	71.4	14.3	85.7	14.3
1984	64.0	0.8	64.8	16.5	81.3	18.7
1985	59.3	0.6	59.9	16.6	76.5	23.5
1986	60.8	0.7	61.4	16.0	77.5	22.5
1987	53.7	0.6	54.3	15.1	69.4	30.6
1988	48.3	0.5	48.8	16.6	65.4	34.6
1989	48.0	0.9	48.9	11.7	60.6	39.4
1955–69	50.3	1.0	51.3	22.1	73.4	26.6
1970–89	63.3	0.9	64.3	14.8	79.1	20.9
1955–89	57.7	1.0	58.7	17.9	76.6	23.4

The figures represent percent of national saving, refer to saving net of historical cost depreciation, and are on a calendar year basis. Totals may not add due to rounding error.

See text for definitions.

Source: National Income Accounts of Japan. See Appendix for details.

Depreciation Adjustment

As noted earlier, the National Income Accounts of Japan conform in general to the United Nations' new SNA, but there is at least one important difference – namely that depreciation (the consumption of fixed capital) is valued at historical cost rather than replacement cost.[4] If capital goods prices are increasing, historical cost depreciation will be less than replacement cost depreciation, and since net saving is calculated by subtracting depreciation from gross saving, net saving based on historical cost depreciation will be greater than net saving based on replacement cost depreciation. In other words, the fact that depreciation is valued at historical cost in Japan, whereas it is valued at replacement cost in most other countries, will lead to an upward bias in the saving-rate gap between Japan and other countries.

Fortunately, it is possible to obtain estimates of replacement cost depreciation from the stock and other accounts of the National Income Accounts of Japan using the method developed by Hayashi (1986, 1989a, 1989b) and to use these figures to obtain estimates of net saving based on replacement cost depreciation. Table 7.4 presents saving rate data based on replacement cost depreciation for the 1970–89 period (the data needed to calculate replacement cost depreciation were not available for earlier years), and as this table shows, saving rates based on replacement cost depreciation are far lower than those based on historical cost depreciation. The difference range from 0.7 to 2.8 (0.8 to 2.7) percentage points and averages 1.9 (1.9) percentage points in the case of the household saving rate narrowly defined (broadly defined) and range from 0.2 to 5.9 (1.1 to 7.3) percentage points and averages 3.8 (4.9) percentage points in the case of the private (national) saving rate. In other words, adjusting depreciation to a replacement cost basis causes the average household saving rate narrowly defined (broadly defined) to fall from 18.2 to 16.3 (18.2 to 16.4) percent and the average private (national) saving rate to fall from 21.7 to 17.9 (23.3 to 18.4) percent. Thus, differences in the valuation of depreciation can account for a substantial proportion of the saving rate gap between Japan and other countries.

Treatment of Capital Transfers

Another conceptual issue concerns capital transfers. Capital transfers are *not* included in saving in the National Income Accounts of Japan or in the United Nations' new SNA but *are* included in saving in the National Income and Product Accounts of the United States. Thus, the differing treatment of capital transfers will create a bias in the saving rate gap between the United States and other countries (Hayashi, 1986, p. 152).

In my opinion, it is preferable to include capital transfers in saving, as is done in the National Income and Product Accounts of the United States. In the case

Table 7.4   Trends in Japan's depreciation-adjusted saving rate

Year	Household saving rate narrowly defined	Household saving rate broadly defined	Private saving rate	National saving rate
1970	17.0	16.6	27.6	29.8
1971	16.9	16.8	24.1	26.9
1972	17.2	17.2	25.2	27.0
1973	18.7	18.7	24.6	26.9
1974	20.8	20.8	18.2	20.8
1975	21.1	21.2	17.3	16.9
1976	21.4	21.4	19.0	17.0
1977	19.9	19.9	18.3	16.8
1978	18.9	19.1	19.8	17.1
1979	15.8	16.0	17.0	15.6
1980	15.2	15.3	15.2	13.8
1981	16.0	16.1	15.7	14.9
1982	14.3	14.5	14.5	13.5
1983	13.8	14.0	13.9	12.6
1984	13.6	13.7	14.4	14.0
1985	13.4	13.5	14.8	15.6
1986	14.2	14.3	15.6	16.2
1987	12.7	12.9	14.3	16.7
1988	12.5	12.7	14.6	18.2
1989	12.3	12.6	13.7	18.4
1970–89	16.3	16.4	17.9	18.4

The figures are in percentage terms, refer to saving net of replacement cost depreciation, and are on a calendar year basis.
See text for definitions and calculation method.

Source: National Income Accounts of Japan. See Appendix for details.

of the household sector, capital transfers consist primarily of inheritance and gift taxes paid to the government and hence are negative. It seems preferable to exclude such taxes from household saving and from household disposable income because their disposition is not at the discretion of households and because they do not result in an increase in the net worth of the household sector. In the case of the business sector, capital transfers consist primarily of capital subsidies from the government (for example, subsidies paid to private railway companies for the purpose of decaying the cost of constructing a new railway line) and hence are positive. It seems preferable to include such subsidies in the saving of the business sector because they are, in effect, negative taxes that increase the after-tax profits of the firm and because the firm is required to retain them within the firm for the purpose of financing investment. Finally, in the case of the government sector, inheritance and gift taxes received from households increase the government surplus, while capital subsidies paid to firms reduce it, and thus it seems preferable to include both types of capital transfers in government saving (the former as a plus item and the latter as a minus item).

Tables 7.5 and 7.6 show saving rate data that include capital transfers in saving (saving is based on historical cost depreciation in table 7.5 and on replacement cost depreciation in table 7.6), and as these tables show, including capital transfers in saving lowers the household saving rate narrowly defined (broadly defined) by at most one percentage point (0.8 percentage points). By contrast, it raises the private saving rate (by at most 0.5 percentage points) in most years because the increase in business saving more than offsets the decline in household saving. Finally, it lowers the national saving rate (by at most 0.3 percentage points) because the decline in government saving more than offsets the increase in private saving.

Thus, the impact of including capital transfers in saving is minimal, raising or lowering the various saving rates by at most one percentage point. However, since capital transfers are already included in saving in the National Income and Product Accounts of the United States, this factor can explain up to one percentage point of the US-Japan gap in the household and national saving rates (though not in the private saving rate).

Trends over Time

Japan's saving rate shows similar trends over time regardless of what income concept is used in the denominator, regardless of how depreciation is valued, and regardless of whether or not capital transfers are included in saving. The household saving rate (whether narrowly or broadly defined) showed an upward trend until 1976 and downward trend thereafter, while the private and national saving rates showed an upward trend until 1970 and a downward trend thereafter (except that the national saving rate showed a renewed upturn from 1983 until 1988 or 1989). Thus, the various saving rates have shown the same humped pattern over time, with the only difference being that the peak occurred six years later in the case of the household saving rate.

Note, moreover, that the fluctuations over time in Japan's saving rate have been very wide. For example, if we focus on the unadjusted figures (those that value depreciation at historical cost and exclude capital transfers), the household saving rate narrowly defined (broadly defined) increased 1.94-fold (1.91-fold) during the 1955–76 period and declined by 38.8 percent (38.6 percent) during the 1976–89 period, falling to pre-1960 levels by 1989. Similarly, the private saving rate increased 2.06-fold during the 1955–70 period and declined

Table 7.5 Trends in Japan's saving rate (inclusive of capital transfers)

Year	Household saving rate narrowly defined	Household saving rate broadly defined	Private saving rate	National saving rate
1955	11.8	12.1	14.0	15.2
1956	12.8	13.0	15.0	17.3
1957	12.4	12.6	17.3	20.1
1958	12.2	12.5	16.0	17.8
1959	13.6	13.8	17.9	20.2
1960	14.3	14.4	21.9	24.7
1961	15.8	15.8	23.3	26.7
1962	15.4	15.3	21.2	24.7
1963	14.8	14.6	20.3	23.5
1964	15.3	15.1	20.7	23.7
1965	15.6	15.4	19.6	22.2
1966	14.8	14.6	20.9	23.1
1967	13.9	13.7	23.0	25.5
1968	16.7	16.4	25.5	27.8
1969	16.9	16.6	26.7	29.2
1970	17.1	17.1	28.3	31.0
1971	17.1	17.4	25.1	28.4
1972	17.4	17.7	25.6	28.1
1973	19.6	20.1	26.3	29.3
1974	22.6	22.9	24.0	26.7
1975	22.2	22.6	22.5	22.4
1976	22.7	23.0	24.3	23.0
1977	21.2	21.5	23.4	22.5
1978	20.3	20.7	24.8	22.9
1979	17.6	18.0	22.5	21.8
1980	17.3	17.7	21.6	21.0
1981	17.9	18.2	21.2	21.1
1982	16.1	16.4	19.7	19.8
1983	15.4	15.7	18.9	18.7
1984	15.2	15.4	19.1	19.9
1985	14.9	15.1	19.2	20.9
1986	15.3	15.5	19.4	21.0
1987	13.8	14.0	17.9	21.4
1988	13.3	13.5	18.0	22.7
1989	13.3	13.6	17.0	22.7
1955–69	14.4	14.4	20.2	22.8
1970–89	17.5	17.8	21.9	23.3
1955–89	16.2	16.3	21.2	23.1

The figures are in percentage terms, refer to saving net of historical cost depreciation and inclusive of capital transfers, and are on a calendar year basis.
See text for definitions.

Source: National Income Accounts of Japan. See Appendix for details.

Table 7.6 Trends in Japan's depreciation-adjusted saving rate (inclusive of capital transfers)

Year	Household saving rate narrowly defined	Household saving rate broadly defined	Private saving rate	National saving rate
1970	16.3	16.3	27.9	29.8
1971	16.2	16.4	24.4	26.8
1972	16.4	16.7	25.3	27.0
1973	17.8	18.3	24.9	26.8
1974	20.2	20.5	18.6	20.7
1975	20.4	20.9	17.7	16.8
1976	20.8	21.2	19.3	17.0
1977	19.3	19.6	18.6	16.8
1978	18.4	18.8	20.2	17.1
1979	15.2	15.7	17.5	15.5
1980	14.6	15.0	15.7	13.8
1981	15.4	15.8	16.2	14.9
1982	13.7	14.1	14.8	13.5
1983	13.1	13.5	14.1	12.5
1984	12.9	13.3	14.4	14.0
1985	12.7	13.1	14.9	15.5
1986	13.4	13.8	15.6	16.1
1987	11.8	12.2	14.2	16.7
1988	11.5	11.9	14.4	18.2
1989	11.4	11.9	13.5	18.3
1970–89	15.6	15.9	18.1	18.4

The figures are in percentage terms, refer to saving net of replacement cost depreciation and inclusive of capital transfers, and are on a calendar year basis.
See text for definitions and calculation method.

Source: National Income Accounts of Japan. See Appendix for details.

by 38.9 percent during the 1970–89 period, falling to pre-1959 levels by 1989, while the national saving rate increased 2.04-fold during the 1955–70 period, declined by 39.6 percent during the 1970–83 period, falling to pre-1957 levels by 1983, and increased by 21.4 percent during the 1983–8 period. Moreover, the fluctuations over time have been even wider in the case of the figures based on replacement cost depreciation. For example, the decline in Japan's household saving rate narrowly defined (broadly defined) during the 1976–89 period was 42.4 percent (41.1 percent), while the decline in the private saving rate during the 1970–89 period was 50.6 percent. Finally, the decline in the national saving rate during the 1970–83 period was 57.8 percent, while the increase during the 1983–9 period was 46.3 percent. Thus, it is certainly not true that Japan's saving rate has maintained a uniformly high level throughout the post-war period.

Other Conceptual Issues

I have discussed two conceptual issues above – namely, (1) the measurement of depreciation and (2) the treatment of capital transfers – but there are numerous other conceptual issues relating to the definition and measurement of saving. What follows is only a partial listing of some of these other issues.

The treatment of consumer durables   As noted by Blades (1983, 1988), Blades and Sturm (1982), Shafer, Elmeskov, and Tease (1991), and others, purchases of consumer durables are included in consumption in the national income accounts of all countries, but it is theoretically preferable to include purchases of consumer durables (net of depreciation) in saving and the flow of services therefrom in consumption. Boskin and Roberts (1988) and Hayashi (1986, p. 155) show that doing so causes the US-Japan gap in the personal saving rate to narrow considerably.[5]

The treatment of the government sector   In the National Income Accounts of Japan and in the United Nations' new SNA, government investment is properly classified as investment (saving), whereas in the National Income and Product Accounts of the United States, all government spending, including government investment, is classified as consumption (Boskin and Roberts, 1988, and Hayashi, 1986, pp. 151–2; 1989a; 1989b). Moreover, another difficulty is that the Japanese figures on the depreciation of the government sector cover only buildings and hence are substantially downward biased (Hayashi, 1986, p. 151).[6] The first problem will cause Japanese saving rate figures to be upward biased relative to those of the US, whereas the second problem will cause Japanese saving rate figures to be upward biased relative to those of most other countries.

The treatment of capital gains and losses   Capital gains and losses on equities, land, and other assets are typically not included in saving, but it could be argued that they should be inasmuch as they lead to a change in net worth. Dekle and Summers (1991) and Hayashi (1986, p. 160) show that capital gains (especially those on land) have been considerable in the case of Japan and that including them in saving causes the US-Japan saving rate gap to widen even further.[7]

It is not clear what the net impact would be of adjusting the saving rate figures of Japan and other countries to take account of the conceptual differences and deficiencies noted above. Accounting properly for consumer durables and eliminating differences in the treatment of the government sector would cause the saving rate gap between Japan and other countries to narrow, but including capital gains and losses in saving would cause this gap to widen. Moreover, there are other conceptual issues as well such as the proper treatment of expenditures on education and those on research and development, and to the best of my knowledge, their impact on saving has not been analyzed in detail (see, for example, Blades, 1983, Blades and Sturm, 1982, and Shafer, Elmeskov, and Tease, 1991). Thus, it is premature to make a definitive statement above the exact size of the saving rate gap between Japan and other countries, but it is probably safe to conclude that Japan's saving rate is higher than those of most other countries though not by as much as the official figures suggest. It should be added, however, that Japan's saving rate (however, defined) has shown a downward trend since at least 1976 (with the exception of the national saving rate during the 1983–8/9 period).

A SELECTIVE SURVEY OF THE LITERATURE ON JAPANESE SAVING BEHAVIOR

In this section, I survey the literature on Japanese saving behavior with emphasis on the issue of whether the life-cycle model or the dynasty model has greater applicability in the case of Japan. This is an issue of crucial importance for the following reasons.

First, there is an ongoing controversy in the United States and other countries about whether the life-cycle model or the dynasty model has greater applicability, and additional evidence (albeit on a different country) will help to resolve this controversy.

Second, it would be interesting to know which model has greater applicability in a non-Western society in which the family unit is alleged to be close-knit and in which individuals are alleged to care about the continuity and prosperity of the families to which they belong.

Third, the degree of applicability of life-cycle and dynasty models will determine whether such factors as the age structure of the population, life expectancy, the retirement age, the labor force participation rate of the aged, the rate of productivity growth, the level of social security (public old-age pension) benefits, the level of the government debt and of government budget deficits, and bequest taxes will affect the saving rate. Many life-cycle-related factors (for example, the young age structure of the population, the long life expectancy, the early retirement age, the rapid rate of productivity growth, and the low level of social security benefits) have been cited as possible causes of the high level of Japan's saving rate, and thus the present analysis will shed light on which of the various explanations that have been advanced to explain the high level of Japan's saving rate are valid. Moreover, the present analysis also has important policy implications inasmuch as the government may wish to influence the level of the saving rate and/or may be concerned about the adverse impact of various government programs and policies on the saving rate.

Fourth, Japan's population is ageing at an unprecedented rate, and the impact of this rapid ageing of the population on future trends in Japan's saving rate is currently being hotly debated. Information on the degree of applicability of the life-cycle model to Japan will help resolve this debate and make it possible to project more accurately future trends in Japan's saving rate.

There are a number of types of evidence that shed light on whether the life-cycle model or the dynasty model is more applicable:

1 Evidence on the extent to which the aged dissave (decumulate wealth).
2 Evidence on the impact of life-cycle-related factors on saving and on the labor supply of the aged.
3 Evidence on the shares of life-cycle wealth and transfer wealth (wealth deriving from intergenerational transfers).
4 Evidence from public opinion surveys on people's attitudes towards saving, bequests, etc.
5 Empirical evidence on the nature of the bequest motive.

I examine each of these types of evidence in turn.

Evidence on the Saving Behavior of the Aged

Many authors have analyzed the saving behavior of the aged in Japan, but all of the studies to date have beset by one or more of the following problems:

Sample selection bias   In most household surveys, direct data are available only for the so-called "independent aged" (the aged who are heads of households, where head of household is defined as the household member with the highest income), and as noted by Ando (1985), Ando, Yamashita, and Murayama, (1986), Ando and Kennickell (1987), Hayashi (1986, p. 179), Hayashi, Ando, and Ferris (1988), and Horioka (1984), one cannot make inferences about all the aged based on the independent aged alone, because they are unlikely to be representative of all the aged. The independent aged consist of the aged living apart from their children and the aged who live with, but have higher incomes than, their children. In either case, the independent aged are likely to be wealthier than the dependent aged and more likely to be working. Moreover, there is an additional problem in the case of the independent aged who live with their children but have higher incomes than their children – namely that only data for the household as a whole (inclusive of cohabiting children) are available.

Thus, a finding that the independent aged save does not necessarily mean that all the aged save.

Ando (1985), Ando, Yamashita, and Murayama (1986), Ando and Kennickell (1987), Hayashi (1986), and Hayashi, Ando, and Ferris (1988) attempt to circumvent these problems by indirectly estimating the consumption, saving, income, and wealth of the dependent aged (the aged who live with their children). The method they use is to subtract figures on nuclear families from figures on extended families for each aged group, and to attribute the difference to cohabiting parents. As ingenious as this method is, however, it requires the assumption that nuclear and extended families are identical except for the presence or absence of cohabiting parents, and this assumption is unlikely to be satisfied. For one thing, the aged parents of nuclear families are far more likely to be deceased than those of extended families for obvious reasons, and thus nuclear families are far more likely to have received a bequest in the past. Moreover, their probability of having received a bequest in the past will increase with age. Bequests received in the past will, of course, be included in the household's wealth (see *The role of intergenerational transfers*, below), and thus calculating the wealth of the dependent aged by subtracting the wealth of nuclear families from that of extended families will lead to a downward bias, and moreover, the magnitude of the bias will increase with age. A finding that the wealth of the dependent aged declines with age may merely reflect this bias and does not necessarily imply that the dependent aged are dissaving (see Hayashi, 1986, p. 184).

Note, however, that the saving (flow) data obtained using the method of Ando and his collaborators will not be similarly biased, and moreover, that an alternative method employed by Hayashi, Ando, and Ferris (1988) – that of seeing how the wealth of extended families varies with the age of the older generation when the age of the younger generation is held constant – will also be free of this bias.

Turning finally to the aged who live with their children but have higher incomes than their children, Hayashi, Ando, and Ferris (1988) circumvent the problem noted above by including them with the dependent aged and calculating their consumption, income, saving, and wealth in the save way as described above.

Self-selection bias Inferences based on wealth data on the independent aged by age may be spurious due to what Hayashi, Ando, and Ferris (1988, p. 466) call self-selection bias. Since the poorer aged are more likely to die, join their children's households, or (if they are already living with their children) to be displaced by their children as the household head, the sample of the independent aged will become more and more biased toward the relatively wealthy aged with increases in age. Thus, for example, a finding that the wealth of the independent aged increases with age may merely reflect self-selection bias rather than the absence of dissaving.

The treatment of capital gains Stock data are generally valued at current market value and hence measures of the flow of saving that are calculated from stock data will include capital gains on land, equities, and other assets, even though saving in the form of capital gains does not necessitate any out-of-pocket saving and is omitted from conventional measures of saving. Thus, a finding that wealth (at market value) fails to decline with age may merely reflect the presence of capital gains and does not necessarily imply an absence of dissaving.

The cohort effect The saving behavior of the aged can be inferred only from longitudinal aged-wealth profiles, and thus if only data on cross-sectional age-wealth profiles are available, they must be adjusted for the so-called "cohort effect." The cohort effect states that, in the presence of productivity growth, older cohorts will have lower lifetime incomes and hence lower wealth holdings at any given age than younger cohorts. The wealth of older cohorts must therefore be adjusted upward by the amount of productivity growth in order to obtain longitudinal age-wealth profiles (see Hayashi, 1989b, and Hayashi, Ando, and Ferris, 1988). A declining cross-sectional age-wealth profile does not necessarily imply that the aged are dissaving: it might merely reflect the fact that older cohorts could not save as much as younger cohorts because of their lower lifetime incomes. In order to conclude that the aged are dissaving, the rate of decumulation must exceed the rate of productivity growth.

The role of intergenerational transfers The wealth of younger households may include bequests and other intergenerational transfers in addition to their own saving, and conversely, the wealth of older households may decline not only as a result of dissaving for the purpose of financing their living expenses but also as a result of *inter vivos* transfers to their children. Thus, a finding of a declining age-wealth profile for the aged does not necessarily imply life-cycle-related dissaving (see Hayashi, Ando, and Ferris, 1988).

Coverage of assets In many cases, the coverage of assets is incomplete. For example, data on land, housing, consumer durables, and/or other real assets are often unavailable, and in some cases, the data on financial assets and liabilities are also incomplete. In theory, intangible wealth such as human wealth and social security wealth should also be included, but data thereon are even less available.

Studies of the saving behavior of the aged can be classified by whether they make use of stock data or flow data. Of the six problems enumerated above, all six apply in the case of stock data but only the first, second, and sixth in the case of flow data. Thus, studies based on flow data are in general more reliable.

Studies based on flow data   Looking first at studies based on flow data, these studies can be further broken down into those that look at the independent aged and those that look at the dependent aged. Of the studies that look at the independent aged, Ishikawa (1987, 1988a, 1988b) finds that their total saving is positive but that the financial saving of the independent aged who are self-employed or unemployed is slightly negative. Ando (1985) and Ando, Yamashita, and Murayama (1986) find that most categories of the independent aged dissave after a certain age: they find that the saving of multiple-person salaried worker households, single-person salaried worker households, and single-person self-employed or unemployed households, becomes negative after the age of 70, 65, and 61, respectively; the saving of multiple-person self-employed or unem-ployed households remains positive throughout but becomes negligible in amount. Hayashi, Ando, and Ferris (1988) find that the saving rate of the independent aged declines with age and becomes negative starting with the 80–4 aged group (the 60–4 aged group in the case of the single aged), while Ohtake (1991b) also finds that the saving rate of the independent aged declines with age, becoming negative beginning with the 80–4 age group in the case of those without living children and beginning with the 85–9 age group in the case of those who have living children but live apart from them.[8] Finally, Takayama (forthcoming) and Takayama et al. (1989) find that a substantial proportion of the non-working aged dissave if the saving rate is adjusted for the depreciation of housing and consumer durables.

Of the studies that look at the dependent aged, Ishikawa (1988b) finds that the presence of aged parents slightly lowers the total saving of merged house-holds but that the effect is significant only if housing tenure is controlled for, while Hayashi, Ando, and Ferris (1988) find that the saving rate of the depend-ent aged declines with age and becomes negative for those living in households in which the younger generation is 65–9 and the older generation is 87.[9]

Thus, the evidence is somewhat mixed, but on balance, it suggests that both the independent and dependent aged dissave, at least after they reach their eighties.

Studies based on stock data   Turning to studies based on stock data and looking first at studies that look at the independent aged, Hayashi, Ando, and Ferris (1988) find that their wealth (inclusive of housing, residential land, and consumer durables) peaks in the 60–4 age group and declines thereafter in the case of the unadjusted data and peaks in the 80–4 age group and declines slightly there-after in the case of data adjusted for the cohort effect. In addition, they find that the wealth of the single aged declines with age except in the 80–4 age group in the case of the unadjusted data and peaks in the 80–4 age group and declines thereafter in the case of data adjusted for the cohort effect. Ando (1985) and Ando, Yamashita, and Murayama (1986) find that the wealth of multiple-person households peaks in the 56–60 age group (the 51–5 age group in one case) and generally declines thereafter, while the wealth of single-person households peaks later (in the 56–60, 61–5, or 71–5 age groups, depending on the year and occupation) and generally declines thereafter (if cells in which the number of observations is too small for the results to be reliable are disregarded). Ohtake (1991a) finds that the wealth of the independent aged and the aged who live with their children but maintain separate budgets declines with age, while Takayama et al. (1989, pp. 13–15) find that the financial assets and financial net worth of the independent aged peak in the 60–4 age group and decline thereafter, while their real assets and total net worth peak in the 65–9 age group and decline only slightly thereafter. However, Ando, Yamashita, and Murayama, and Takayama et al., apparently do not make any adjustments for the cohort effect.[10]

Looking next at studies of the dependent aged, Hayashi, Ando, and Ferris (1988) find that their wealth (inclusive of housing, residential land, and consumer durables) peaks for those living in households in which the younger generation is 25–9 and the older generation is 57, and declines thereafter (except in the case of those living in households in which the younger generation is 60–4 or 70–4 and the older generation is 85 or 88) in the case of the unadjusted data, and that their wealth peaks for those living in households in which the younger generation is 60–4 and the older generation is 85 and declines thereafter in the case of data adjusted for the cohort effect.[11,12]

Moreover, Hayashi, Ando, and Ferris (1988) also find that the wealth of extended families shows some tendency to decline as the age of the older generation increases, holding constant the age of the younger generation. This suggests that the dependent aged dissave, but the results are not completely clear cut, and moreover, the results would be even less conclusive if an adjustment were made for the cohort effect.

Finally, Dekle (1988, 1990) analyzes data for a sample containing both dependent and independent aged and finds that their financial wealth declines slightly with age but that their real estate wealth and total wealth increase significantly with age.[13]

Thus, the studies based on stock data are generally consistent not only with one other but also with the studies based on flow data, showing a tendency for wealth to peak in the early eighties and to decline thereafter if the data are adjusted for the cohort effect. Dekle (1988, 1990) fails to find evidence of decumulation by the aged, but he finds that it is only housing assets that continue to increase with age; the increase in housing assets with age may be due to capital gains thereon and does not necessarily imply positive out-of-pocket saving. Moreover, his findings may be due in part to self-selection bias arising from the tendency of the wealthy to live longer, as Dekle himself notes. Thus, his findings are not necessarily inconsistent with those of the other studies.

Nonetheless, our conclusion must be regarded as tentative because all of the studies surveyed – especially those based on stock data – are beset by one or more of the six problems enumerated above. Moreover, the various problems create biases in offsetting directions (for example, the cohort effect) and the role of intergenerational transfer, and the problem relating to the methodology of Ando and his collaborators (see the discussion of sample selection bias, above) create a biases in favor of a finding of decumulation, while sample selection bias, self-selection bias, and the treatment of capital gains create a bias in the opposite direction), and thus not even the direction of the overall bias can be determined a priori. A more definitive verdict will have to await the appearance of better data and/or better research methodologies.

Evidence on the Impact of Life-Cycle-Related Factors on Saving and on the Labor Supply of the Aged

In this subsection, I survey the evidence on the impact of selected life-cycle-related factors on saving and on the labor supply of the aged.

The impact of income (productivity) growth on saving   Most studies find that income (productivity) growth has a positive and significant impact on saving, as predicted by the life-cycle model (see Horioka, 1990c, pp. 76–80, for a survey of the relevant literature). Moreover, Modigliani and Sterling (1983) find, using cross-country data, that Japan's rapid rate of income growth was by far the most important cause of the high level of her private saving rate during the high growth period of the 1960s.

The impact of the age structure of the population on saving   Most studies using cross-country data find that the impact of the age structure of the population on the saving rate is as predicted by the life-cycle model, with the proportion both of minors and of the aged (relative to the working-age population or to the total population) having a significant negative impact thereon (see, for example, Horioka, 1989, and Modigliani and Sterling, 1983). Moreover, Horioka (1991a) obtains similar results using time series data for Japan.

The impact of social security on saving   Ando (1985), Ando, Yamashita, and Murayama (1986), Aso and Noguchi (1988), Dekle (1988, 1990), Homma et al. (1987), Noguchi (1982, 1983), Ogawa (1991a), Sasaki and Tachibanaki (1985), Takayama (forthcoming), Takayama et al. (1990b), Yamada (1987, 1990),

Yamada, Yamada, and Liu (1990), and Yoshikawa (1982) have analyzed the impact of social security (public old-age pensions) on private saving in Japan, and virtually all of them find that the former has a significant negative impact on the latter, as predicted by the extended life-cycle model (Feldstein, 1974). The only exceptions are Ando, Ando, Yamashita, and Murayama, Homma et al., and Yoshikawa, who obtain mixed results, and Dekle, who obtains insignificant results.

The impact of social security on the labor supply of the aged   Virtually all analyses of the impact of public pensions on the labor supply of aged males find that the former has a significant negative impact on the latter (see Takayama (forthcoming) and Takayama et al. (1990) for a careful analysis as well as a useful literature survey). This relationship, which Feldstein (1974) refers to as the "induced retirement effect," is fully consistent with the extended life-cycle model.

Thus, the evidence on the impact of life-cycle-related factors on saving and on the labor supply of the aged strongly supports the life-cycle model.

Evidence on the Shares of Life-Cycle and Transfer Wealth

A number of studies have applied the methodology of Kotlikoff and Summers (1981) to the case of Japan in order to estimate the shares of life-cycle and transfer wealth (wealth deriving from intergenerational transfers). Kotlikoff and Summers employ two alternative approaches, and both approaches have been tried in the case of Japan.

One approach is the "cumulation of life-cycle saving" approach. Under this approach, life-cycle wealth is obtained by cumulating the past life-cycle saving of those currently alive, where life-cycle saving in a given year is calculated as the difference between disposable income and consumption in that year, and transfer wealth is then obtained by subtracting life-cycle wealth from total wealth.

The other approach is the "flow of bequests" approach. Under this approach, the annual flow of bequests is estimated from data on inheritance taxes, etc., and a blow-up factor is used to convert the annual flow of bequests to a stock amount (i.e., the stock of transfer wealth). Life-cycle wealth is then obtained by subtracting transfer wealth from total wealth.

The results of the various studies are summarized in table 7.7, and as this table shows, there is considerable disagreement about the share of transfer wealth, with estimates ranging from 3 to 49 percent. However, a majority of the estimates lie in the lower end of this range (3 to 28 percent).

The result for countries other than Japan are shown in table 7.8, and as a comparison of tables 7.7 and 7.8 shows, the share of transfer wealth in Japan

Table 7.7 Estimates of the share of transfer wealth in Japan

Author of study	Year	Definition	Methodology	Share of transfer wealth (percent)
Campbell (1991)	1974–84	KS	1	At most 28.1
	1974–84	M	1	At most 23.4
Dekle (1988, 1989b)	1968–83	KS	1	3–27
Hayashi (1986)	1969–74		1	At least 9.6[a]
Barthold and Ito (1991) (benchmark case)	–	KS	2	At least 27.8–41.4
Dekle (1988, 1989b)	1983	–	2	At most 48.7[b]

KS = Kotlikoff and Summers (1981)
M = Modigliani (1988)
Methodology 1: "Cumulation of life-cycle saving" approach
Methodology 2: "Flow of bequests" approach
Refer to the text for details.

[a] The annual flow of transfers was converted to a stock amount using the same blow-up factor as that used by Barthold and Ito (1991) – namely, 25.
[b] This figure represents a flow ratio (i.e., the ratio of the annual flow of intergenerational transfers to the annual flow of household saving).

appears to be roughly comparable to the corresponding figures for the United States and the United Kingdom and possibly lower than those for Canada and France.

As pointed out by Ando (1986, p. 218) and Dekle (1989b, p. 404), the fact that the share of transfer wealth is relatively small in a rapidly growing economy like that of Japan is not surprising because, in such an economy, "assets accumulated by the currently living generation at their higher level of income are much larger than the assets accumulated by the deceased generation at their much lower level of income" (Ando, 1986, p. 218). Indeed, for this same reason, the fact that the share of intergenerational transfers in total wealth is low in a rapidly growing economy does not necessarily imply that the bequest motive is weak. As discussed by Kotlikoff and Summers (1981) and Modigliani (1988, p. 32), the elasticity of total wealth with respect to the flow of bequests is a far better measure of the contribution of bequests to society's total wealth, but unfortunately, the value of this parameter has not been estimated for the case of Japan. Moreover, as pointed out by Modigliani (1988, pp. 36–7), even this parameter is not an adequate measure of the strength of the bequest motive because it does not distinguish between intended and unintended or accidental bequests (the latter arising from risk aversion in the face of uncertainty about future

Table 7.8 Estimates of the share of transfer wealth in other countries

Author of study	Year	Definition	Methodology	Share of transfer wealth (percent)
Canada				
Davis and St Hilaire	–	KS	3	53
(1987)	–	M	3	35
France				
Babeau (1988)	1984	KS	2	22–35
	1984	M	2	16–23
Kessler and Masson	1975	KS	2	46
(1979)	1975	M	2	35
Masson (1986)	–	KS	3	50–5
	–	M	3	40
United Kingdom				
Royal Commission on the Distribution of Income and Wealth	1973		2	18.5[a]
United States				
Ando and Kennickell (1987)	1960–80	M	1	15.0–41.2
Kotlikoff and Summers	1974	KS	1	67[b]
(1981)	1974	M	1	20
Barthold and Ito (1991)	–		2	At least 25
Kotlikoff and Summers	1974	KS	2	46
(1981)	1974	M	2	17
Menchik and David (1983)	1946–64		2	18.5
Projector and Weiss (1964)			2	15.5
Barlow et al. (1966)	1964	–	4	14.3
Barlow et al. (1966)	1964	–	4	less than 20
Morgan et al. (1962)	–		4	less than 10
Projector and Weiss (1964)	–		4	16

Methodology 3: Simulation analysis
Methodology 4: Survey information

[a] Adjusted for interspousal transfers by assuming that they account for one-quarter of all bequests, the same share as in the United States.
[b] Adjusted for the error in the treatment of expenditures on consumer durables (see Modigliani, 1988).
Also see the notes to table 7.7.

Sources: Ando and Kennickell (1987), Barthold and Ito (1991), Kessler and Masson (1989), and Modigliani (1988).

medical and nursing home expenses, the timing of death, etc. (Abel, 1985; Kotlikoff, 1989; and Yaari, 1965)), or among different types of bequest motives.

At least four types of bequest motives can be distinguished (Kotlikoff, 1988, pp. 53–4):

1	An altruistic bequest motive whereby the utility level of one's descend-ants enters one's utility function (intergenerational altruism) (Barro, 1974, and Becker, 1974).

2	A bequest per se motive whereby parents derive utility from the amount of the bequest per se (Yaari, 1964, 1965).

3	An implicit annuity contract between aged parents and their children whereby the children agree to finance their parents' living expenses until death in return for a fixed payment (the bequest) Horioka, 1984, and Kotlikoff and Spivak, 1981).

4	A strategic bequest motive whereby the parents use the threat of dis-inheritance to induce their children to look after them (i.e., provide in-kind services) (Bernheim, Shleifer, and Summers, 1985).

Note, moreover, that only type 1 is consistent with the dynasty model and that types 3 and 4 are fully consistent with the life-cycle model inasmuch as, in both cases, the bequest is ultimately used to finance living expenses during old age.

Thus, the evidence on the shares of life-cycle and transfer wealth is not very helpful in determining the degree of applicability of the life-cycle and dynasty models in Japan. The range of estimates is very broad, and even if tighter bounds could be established, the results would not necessarily shed any light on the strength or the nature of the bequest motive in Japan.

Evidence from Public Opinion Surveys

In this subsection, I review the evidence from public opinion surveys on people's attitudes towards saving, bequests, etc.

Data on saving motives and income sources during old age   A full 27 to 47 percent of Japanese households cite preparation for old age as one of their motives for saving, and moreover, this figure has increased over time and also increases with age. Furthermore, the saving target for old age is also very large (five times annual income, on average), and as a result, the aggregate saving target for old age accounts for more than one-half of the aggregate saving target for all motives. Finally, the flow of life-cycle-related saving accounts for 13 to 48 percent of total household saving and for two to seven percentage points of the household saving rate.[14,15]

All of these figures suggest that the life-cycle model is highly applicable in the case of Japan, but data on the income sources of the aged appear to tell a very different story. Only 7 to 15 percent of those aged 60 to 69 and only 11 to 19 percent of those aged 70 and over rely on dissaving as one of their income sources, and moreover, the degree of reliance on dissaving is considerably lower in Japan than it is in Italy and the United States, although it is comparable to what it is in Denmark and the United Kingdom and higher than it is in France and Thailand.

There are at least three possible explanations for the failure of the data to show more extensive dissaving by the aged despite the importance of preparation for old age as a motive for saving. First, it could be that dissaving begins at a more advanced age than the age groups for which figures are available. The proportion of respondents relying on dissaving as one of their income sources is much higher in the 70 and over age group than in the 60–9 age group, and it would presumably be even higher if separate data were available for the 80–9 age group and above.[16]

Second, it could be that the aged to not dissave or do so only at a moderate pace because of risk aversion in the face of uncertainty about future medical expenses, the timing of death, etc. (Davies, 1981).

Third, it could be that the aged have an implicit annuity contract with their children, in which case their wealth is indirectly used to finance their living expenses during old age even though it is left behind as a bequest.

Thus, the failure of the data to show more extensive dissaving by the aged does not necessarily constitute evidence against the life-cycle model.

Data on family support of the aged In Japan, 22 to 30 percent of the aged receive support from their children, and this proportion is far higher than it is in the United States and Europe (though lower than it is in Thailand) (Horioka, 1990a, and Horioka et al., 1990). Moreover, a much higher proportion of the aged in Japan live with (and presumably receive financial and/or in-kind support from) their children than in the United States and Europe (Horioka, 1984). This evidence suggests (but does not prove) that, in Japan, it is far more common for children to look after their aged parents and that bequests are motivated by implicit annuity contracts to a greater extent than in the West.

Data on the incidence of bequests The data in table 7.10 (to be discussed in more detail below) show that a substantial proportion of respondents plan to leave a bequest to their children, etc. (views 1 and 2). 51.5 (44.2) percent of all respondents planned to leave a bequest in 1989 (1990), and moreover, this proportion increases with age (to 62.9 (62.4) percent in the case of the 70 and over age group in 1989 (1990)).

Moreover, Noguchi, Uemura, and Kito's (1989) data on people's actual behavior are broadly consistent with the above data on people's intentions. They find, for example, that either or both parents of the husband had left a

Table 7.9   People's attitudes toward bequests in Japan: 1

View		Percent of respondents
View 1:	Leave everything to our eldest son	43.2
View 2:	Leave everything to physically weak children and/or children with no earning power	4.3
View 3:	Divide equally among our children	12.1
View 4:	Leave more to children who take care of us	35.1
Other		2.8
No reply		2.6

The figures represent the percent of respondents holding each view. The data refer to males and females aged 60 and older.

Source: "Shisan Sōzoku ni tsuite no Ishiki Chōsa" (Opinion Survey on Bequests), conducted in October–December 1979 by the Zenkoku Shakai Fukushi Kyōgikai (All-Japan Social Welfare Council).

The results are reproduced in Sōridaijin Kanbō Rōjin Taisaku-shitsu (Office for Policy towards the Aged, Prime Minister's Secretariat) (ed.), Kōreisha Mondai Sōgo Chōsa Hōkoku (Comprehensive Research Report on the Aged) (Tokyo: Zenkoku Shakai Fukushi Kyōgi-kai (All-Japan Social Welfare Council), 1982), p. 222.

bequest in 74.6 percent of the cases in which both parents of the husband were already deceased and that 29 percent of such husbands had received a bequest. (The reason for the discrepancy between the two figures is that bequests are often divided unequally, with many children getting nothing.) Thus, the incidence of bequests is very high whether one looks at figures on people's intentions or on their actual behavior.

Data on people's attitudes towards bequests   Tables 7.9 and 7.10 present data from two different surveys on people's attitudes toward bequests in Japan. Looking first at table 7.9, views 1 ("Leave everything to our eldest son") and 4 ("Leave more to children who take care of us") correspond to the bequest motive motivated by an implicit annuity contract and/or the strategic bequest motive since, in Japan, it is traditionally the eldest son and his family that lives with, and looks after, the parents. These two views are by far the most dominant, with a full 43.2 and 35.1 percent of respondents adhering to them, respectively, for a total of 78.3 percent. The bequest per se motive (view 3: "Divide equally among our children") and the altruistic bequest motive (view 2: "Leave everything to physically weak children and/or children with no earning power") lag far behind, applying to only 12.1 and 4.3 percent of respondents, respectively.

Table 7.10 People's attitudes towards bequests in Japan: 2

Year	Age group	View 1	View 2	View 3	View 4	Other	No reply
1989	All ages	19.7	31.8	23.0	9.8	13.2	2.5
	20–9	10.4	30.5	23.2	15.9	17.7	2.3
	30–9	11.2	34.4	27.0	10.7	13.9	2.8
	40–9	16.1	30.9	25.5	11.5	14.3	1.7
	50–9	22.8	30.6	23.3	9.6	11.7	2.0
	60–9	28.8	31.6	18.7	7.2	11.0	2.7
	70 and over	27.5	35.4	12.0	4.8	15.5	4.8
1990	All ages	15.7	28.5	18.9	7.7	10.7	18.5
	20–9	7.9	33.9	18.9	8.7	11.0	19.6
	30–9	8.3	27.8	21.0	7.7	12.2	23.0
	40–9	12.6	23.8	21.2	8.4	9.7	24.3
	50–9	16.4	28.0	17.3	7.0	10.5	20.8
	60–9	25.4	35.2	18.0	7.1	10.1	4.2
	70 and over	27.6	34.8	9.6	9.2	14.0	4.8

View 1: We want to leave as large a bequest as possible to our children, etc., if they take care of us in our old age.

View 2: We want to leave as large a bequest as possible to our children, etc., regardless of whether they take care of us in our old age.

View 3: We don't plan to leave a bequest to our children, etc., because we want to enjoy our own lives.

View 4: We don't plan to leave a bequest to our chilren, etc., because we are afraid that our children, etc., will lose their will to work if they count on receiving a bequest from us.

The figures represent the percent of respondents holding each view.

The data refer to households with two or more members from throughout Japan.

Source: Chochiku Kōhō Chūō Iinkai (Central Council for Saving Information) (ed.), Chochiku ni kansuru Seron Chōsa (Public Opinion Survey on Saving), (Tokyo: Chochiku Kōhō Chūō Iinkai (Central Council for Saving Information), 1990), p. 144.

The survey whose results are shown in table 7.10 obtains somewhat different results. For example, the bequest motive motivated by an implicit annuity contract and the strategic bequest motive (view 1) are relatively less important even though their absolute as well as relative importance increases sharply with age. By contrast, the bequest per se and altruistic bequest motives (view 2) are relatively more important. Unfortunately, however, the results of the two surveys cannot be compared directly because the option of not leaving a bequest is included as one option in the survey whose results are shown in table 7.10 but not in the other survey and because the bequest per se and altruistic bequest motives are differentiated in the survey whose results are shown in table 7.9 but not in the other survey.[17]

Noguchi, Uemura, and Kitō (1989) obtain data on people's actual behavior, and these data are broadly consistent with the above data on people's attitudes. They find, for example, that children who live with their parents are much more likely to receive a bequest than those who live apart from their parents (63.3 percent vs. 20.5 percent) and that the probability of receiving a bequest increases sharply with the amount of financial assistance providing (from 29.2 percent in the case of a small amount of assistance to 66.7 percent in the case of a large amount of assistance). Since children who live with their parents are more likely to be providing financial and in-kind assistance, both results strongly imply the presence of an implicit annuity contract or a strategic bequest motive.

Empirical Evidence on the Nature of the Bequest Motive

In this subsection, I review a number of empirical studies that shed light on the nature of the bequest motive in Japan.

The Dekle study   Dekle (1990) uses the number of living children as a proxy for the strength of the bequest motive and finds that it has a positive and significant impact on the wealth holdings of the independent aged but that its impact on the wealth holdings of the dependent aged is positive but insignificant. The former result suggests that the bequest motive is present in Japan and that bequests are motivated by the altruistic bequest motive or the strategic bequest motive. By contrast, the latter result may have arisen (as Dekle himself points out) because the dependent aged are likely to leave most or all of their wealth to the child with whom they live. If this interpretation is correct, it suggests that bequests are motivated by an implicit annuity contract between aged parents and their children.

The Ohtake studies   Ohtake (1991a, 1991b) conducted a number of ingenious tests designed to shed light on the nature of the bequest motive in Japan.

The determinants of the wealth, saving, and labor supply of the aged
In one test, Ohtake (1991a, 1991b) uses the presence of living children as a proxy for the strength of the bequest motive, following Hurd (1987, 1990). Ohtake (1991a) finds that the presence of living children has a negative and significant impact on the aged's holdings of total tangible assets and of housing assets (especially the latter) but that its impact on the aged's financial net worth is negative but insignificant. This finding is contrary to expectation and suggests that the bequest motive in Japan is weak or nonexistent. However, a cross-tabulation of wealth data from the same data source by age group and the

absence or presence of living children shows that, although wealth holdings (whether defined as financial assets, financial net worth, housing assets, or total tangible wealth) are (with one exception) somewhat lower for those with living children than they are for those without living children in the 60–4 and 65–9 age groups, wealth holdings are (with two exceptions) much higher for those with living children than they are for those without living children in the 70–4 age group and above. Moreover, Ohtake (1991b) finds that the same pattern is observed even when the employment status of the aged is controlled for.

With respect to the decumulation of wealth holdings, Ohtake (1991a) finds (unlike Hurd, 1987) that the rate of decumulation is slower for the aged with living children than it is for the aged without living children and that the difference is significant in the case of total tangible assets and housing assets (especially the latter) though not in the case of financial net worth.

Finally, Ohtake (1991b) finds that, in the 70–4 age group and above, the labor force participation rate is significantly higher for those with living children than it is for those without living children, and his regression results show that this pattern holds up even when other factors are controlled for: the coefficient of the no-child dummy is found to be negative and significant in a labor supply equation for the aged.

These findings suggest that bequests are important in the case of Japan and that they are intended bequests. However, the results do not shed any light on the exact motivation for bequests; they are consistent with the altruistic bequest motive and implicit annuity contracts as well as the strategic bequest motive.[18]

Fortunately, Ohtake (1991a) conducts a number of additional tests that shed some light on this very question, and I now turn to a discussion of these.

The determinants of transfers from children to their aged parents
In one test, Ohtake (1991a) finds that transfers (support payments) from children to their aged parents increase with the parents' holdings of bequeathable wealth (financial net worth and housing assets) but not with the parents' holdings of non-bequeathable wealth (social security benefits and labor income). This finding suggests that bequests in Japan are motivated by an implicit annuity contract between aged parents and their children.

The determinants of co-residence
In another test, Ohtake (1991a) finds that the holdings of bequeathable wealth of the aged have a positive and highly significant impact on the probability that they live with their children, whereas the impact of their social security benefits is positive but insignificant and the impact of their labor income is positive but only marginally significant. Since co-residence facilitates the provision of in-kind services by children to their aged parents, this finding suggests that bequests are motivated by a strategic bequest motive or perhaps by an implicit annuity contract.

Thus, taken collectively, the Dekle and Ohtake studies suggest that the various types of bequest motives coexist in the case of Japan but that the implicit annuity contract and the strategic bequest motive (both of which are consistent with the life-cycle model) are perhaps the most dominant types.

The Verdict

My verdict, based on the foregoing evidence, is that the life-cycle model is far more applicable in Japan than the dynasty model.

First, the survey evidence shows that preparation for old age is the top or one of the top motives for saving whether the motives are ranked by the proportion of households saving for each motive, the saving target for each motive, or by the contribution of saving for each motive to the household saving rate (pp. 262–6).

Second, the evidence from micro-data is somewhat inconclusive but shows that the aged dissave in Japan, at least after they reach their eighties (pp. 253–8). The survey evidence shows that only a small proportion of the aged dissave, but this result could be due to defects with the data or other causes and is not necessarily inconsistent with the life-cycle model, as noted earlier (pp. 262–6).

Third, life-cycle-related factors (the age structure of the population and social security) have the hypothesized effects on saving and on the labor supply of the aged (pp. 258–9).

Fourth, bequests appear to be relatively prevalent in Japan, with about one in two people planning to leave a bequest (pp. 262–6), but the bulk of these bequests appear to be unintended or accidental, arising from risk aversion in the face of uncertainty about future medical expenses, the timing of death, etc., or intended bequests motivated by implicit annuity contracts between aged parents and their children or by a strategic bequest motive, all of which are fully consistent with the life-cycle model (pp. 262–8). Only a relatively small proportion of bequests appear to be motivated by intergenerational altruism in Japan (pp. 262–8), which suggests that the dynasty model has only limited applicability.

Note, moreover, that the fact that bequests are prevalent does not, necessarily mean that their contribution to total saving is large. First, if an asset is simply passed on from one generation to the next, with each generation consuming all of its income, bequest-related saving will be zero no matter how great the value of the asset being bequeathed (Hayashi, 1986, p. 197). Second, bequests of land, equities, and other assets whose value is largely the result of capital gains will necessitate little, if any, out-of-pocket saving. As noted by Hayashi, Ando, and Ferris (1988, p. 454), a very large fraction of bequests take the form of land in Japan, and "the high value of land passed by the older generation to the younger one is mostly the result of capital gains, not accumulated savings." Third, even if older individuals are saving for the purpose of leaving a bequest, younger individuals receiving bequests will be spending (dissaving) all or part of the bequests they receive. The contribution of bequest-related saving to total saving equals the bequest-related saving of the former minus the bequest-related dissaving of the latter and hence will not necessarily be large or even positive no matter how prevalent bequests are.

Note, finally, that bequests (even those motivated by intergenerational altruism) can be readily incorporated into the life-cycle model without changing its basic implications, provided the leaving of bequests satisfies two reasonable assumptions (Modigliani, 1988, p. 16).

Thus, even though bequests are relatively prevalent in Japan, they are motivated primarily by life-cycle-related reasons, they do not necessarily make any contribution to total saving, and they do not necessarily change the basic implications of the life-cycle model.

Hayashi (1986, 1989b) concludes that the dynasty model (in particular, the standard neoclassical growth model) has greater applicability in the case of Japan and that bequests are the main cause of Japan's high saving rate, but I have shown that a proper interpretation of the evidence (including that of Hayashi himself) points towards the opposite conclusion — namely that the life-cycle model has greater applicability in the case of Japan and that the bulk of saving is directly or indirectly for life-cycle purposes.

SUMMARY AND CONCLUSIONS

This paper has found that Japan's saving rate remains high even after conceptual differences and deficiencies have been eliminated but that the gap relative to other countries is not as wide as the official figures suggest, and that Japan's saving rate has shown a downward trend since at least 1976 (with the exception of the national saving rate during the 1983–8/9 period).

In addition, it has found that the life-cycle model is far more applicable in Japan than the dynasty model. Bequests are relatively prevalent in Japan, but they appear to be primarily unintended or accidental bequests caused by risk aversion in the face of uncertainty about future medical expenses, the timing of death, etc., or intended bequests motivated by implicit annuity contracts between aged parents and their children or by a strategic bequest motive, all of which are fully consistent with the life-cycle model. Altonji, Hayashi, and Kotlikoff (1989) decisively reject the dynasty model for the case of the United States, and this chapter does likewise for the case of Japan. This is a significant and somewhat surprising conclusion because it is often asserted that Japan is a society in which the family unit is close-knit and in which individuals care about the continuity and prosperity of the families to which they belong.

Turning finally to the implications of this chapter, my finding that the life-cycle model is applicable in Japan implies that the decline in her saving rate since the 1970s can be explained in large part by the ageing of her population and that it can be expected to become even more precipitous in the coming decades as population ageing accelerates.[19] This, in turn, has important implications for both the Japanese and world economies – especially for Japan's current account surplus and the world supply of capital.[20]

NOTES

1 More comprehensive surveys can be found in Blumenthal, 1970, Hayashi, 1986, Horioka, 1990c, 1992, Kanamori, 1961, Komiya, 1966, Mizoguchi, 1988, Sato, 1987, and Shinohara, 1982, 1983.

2 National disposable income (NDI) can also be calculated as net national product (NNP) – statistical discrepancy + other current transfers from abroad (net). Since both the statistical discrepancy and other current transfers from abroad (net) are relatively small, NDI and NNP are virtually identical. For example, NNP was 99.6 percent of NDI in 1989, and the gap was even smaller in most years.

3 The sectoral composition of saving becomes even more heavily dominated by the saving of the household sector narrowly defined when depreciation is valued at replacement cost (see p. 246 below). The average shares of the household sector narrowly defined, private non-profit institutions serving households, the business sector, and the government sector for the 1970–89 period are 63.3 (77.5), 0.9 (1.6), 14.8 (5.3), and 20.9 (15.7) percent, respectively, when depreciation is valued at historical cost (replacement cost). Whether or not capital transfers are included in saving has relatively little impact on the sectoral composition of saving (see pp. 246–8 below).

4 Canada values housing, agricultural, and government capital at replacement cost but all other capital at historical cost.

5 Ando (1985), Ando, Yamashita, and Murayama (1986), Blades (1983, 1988), Blades and Sturm (1982), Horie (1985), Takagi (1988), Takayama (forthcoming), Takayama, et al. (1989), and Takenaka and Ogawa (1987) also account properly for consumer durables: note, however, that Blades, Blades and Sturm, and Horie calculate only gross saving.

6 Note that this downward bias in depreciation is in addition to the downward bias caused by the valuation of depreciation at historical cost rather than at replacement cost.

7 Blades (1983), Blades and Sturm (1982), and Takagi (1988) also try including capital gains (holding gains) in saving; note, however, that Blades, and Blades and Sturm, include only capital gains on non-equity financial assets and liabilities due to data limitations.

8 The saving rate is positive for the aged without living children in the 90 – 4 age group,

but the small number of observations in this cell (3) casts doubt on the reliability of this finding.

9   Their saving rate again becomes positive for those living in households in which the younger generation is 70–4 and the older generation is 88, but the small number of observations in this cell (5) casts doubt on the reliability of this finding.

10   Ohtake controls for the cohort effect by including two proxies for lifetime income (pension income and labor income) in his regression equation.

11   Their wealth increases anew in the case of those living in households in which the younger generation is 70–4 and the older generation is 88, but the small number of observations in this cell (5) casts doubt on the reliability of this finding.

12   Ando (1985), Ando, Yamashita, and Murayama (1986), Ando, and Kennickell (1985), and Hayashi (1986) analyze earlier data from the same survey and obtain broadly consistent results.

13   Both financial wealth and total wealth are gross of liabilities because data on liabilities are not available in the data source used by Dekle.

14   All of the figures in this and the following paragraph are taken from Horioka (1990a) and Horioka et al. (1990).

15   This is far more than the amount of saving for educational expenses (Horioka, 1985, and Horioka, Mochizuki, Nakagawa, and Toyosawa, 1990a), marriage expenses (Horioka, 1987a, 1987b, and Horioka, Mochizuki, Nakagawa, and Toyosawa, 1990b), housing purchase (Horioka, 1987c, 1988, and Horioka, et al., 1991), and precautionary purposes (Ogawa, 1991b, and Ohno, 1991).

16   The finding in pp. 253–8 that the aged in Japan begin dissaving only after reaching their eighties supports this explanation.

17   The data from these two surveys and possible reasons for the divergent results are discussed in more detail in Ohtake (1991a).

18   The only exception is that the finding concerning the labor force participation rate of the aged is not consistent with implicit annuity contracts. The reason is as follows. If the aged are motivated by an implicit annuity contract, their bequests are ultimately used to finance their living expenses during old age and their labor income is also ultimately used for this purpose. Since the presence or absence of children should not affect the amount of funds needed to finance living expenses during old age, it should also not affect the labor supply of the aged if the aged are motivated solely by an implicit annuity contract.

19   See Horioka (1991a) for an analysis of the impact of the age structure of the population on past trends in Japan's saving rate and Horioka (1991b) for a survey of attempts to forecast future trends therein.

20   See Horioka (1991b) for a survey of attempts to forecast future trends in Japan's current account surplus.

REFERENCES

Abel, Andrew B. 1985: 'Precautionary Saving and Accidental Bequests'. *American Economic Review*, 75, no. 4 (September), 777–91.

Altonji, Joseph, Hayashi, Fumio, and Kotlikoff, Laurence 1989: Is the Extended Family Altruistically Linked? Direct Tests Using Micro Data. *Working Paper* No. 3046 (July). Cambridge, Massachusetts: National Bureau of Economic Research, Inc.

Ando, Albert 1985: The Savings of Japanese Households: A Micro Study Based on Data from the National Survey of Family Income and Expenditure, 1974 and 1979. Mimeo., Department of Economics, University of Pennsylvania: Philadelphia, Pennsylvania.

Ando, Albert 1986: Comment. In Stanley Fischer (ed.), *NBER Macroeconomics Annual 1986*. Cambridge, Massachusetts: The MIT Press, 1, 211–220.

Ando, Albert, Guiso, Luigi, Terlizzese, Daniele, and Dorsainvil, Daniel 1991: Saving, Demographic Structure and Productivity Growth: The Case of Japan. Presented at the Conference on "Saving Behaviour: Theory, International Evidence and Policy Implications" sponsored by the Savings Banks Research Foundation, May 26–29, 1991, in Hanasaari, Espoo/Helsinki, Finland.

Ando, Albert and Kennickell, Arthur B. 1987: How Much (or Little) Life Cycle is There in Micro Data? The Cases of the United States and Japan. In Rudiger Dornbusch, Stanley Fischer, and John Bossons (eds), Macroeconomics and Finance: Essays in Honor of Franco Modigliani. Cambridge, Massachusetts: The MIT Press, pp. 159–228.

Ando, Albert, Yamashita, Michiko, and Murayama, Atsuyoshi 1986: Raifu Saikuru Kasetsu ni motozuku Shōhi/Chochiku no Kōdō Bunseki (An Analysis of Consumption and Saving Behavior based on the life cycle model). *Keizai Bunseki*, Keizai Kikakuchō, Keizai Kenkyū-sho (Economic Research Institute, Economic Planning Agency), (ed.), no. 101 (January), pp. 25–139 (in Japanese).

Asō, Yoshifumi and Noguchi, Yukio 1988: Kōteki Nenkin ga Chochiku/Rōdō Kyōkyu ni Ataeru Eikyō (The Impact of Public Pensions on Saving and Labor Supply). Mimeo., Faculty of Economics, Hitotsubashi University, Kunitachi, Tokyo, Japan (in Japanese).

Barro, Robert J. 1974: Are Government Bonds Net Wealth? *Journal of Political Economy*, 82, no. 6 (November/December), 1095–117.

Babeau, André 1988: *Le Patrimoine Aujourd'hui*. Paris: Nathan.

Barlow, Robin, Brazer, H. E. and Morgan, J. N. 1966: *Economic Behavior of the Affluent*. Washington, DC: The Brookings Institution.

Barthold, Thomas A. and Ito, Takatoshi 1991: Bequest Taxes and Accumulation of Household Wealth: US–Japan Comparison. *Discussion Paper Series A* No. 233 (March), The Institute of Economic Research, Hitotsubashi University, Kunitachi, Tokyo, Japan.

Becker, Gary S. 1974: A Theory of Social Interactions. *Journal of Political Economy*, 82, no. 6 (November/December), 1063–93.

Bernheim, B. Douglas, Shleifer, Andrei, and Summers, Lawrence H. 1985: The Strategic Bequest Motive. *Journal of Political Economy*, 93, no. 6 (December), 1045–76.

Blades, Derek 1983: Alternative Measures of Saving. *OECD Economic Outlook*, Occasional Studies (June), pp. 66–84.

Blades, Derek 1988: Household Saving Ratios for Japan and Other OECD Countries. Mimeo., Organization for Economic Cooperation and Development, Paris, France.

Blades, Derek W. and Sturm, Peter H. 1982: The Concept and Measurement of Savings: The United States and Other Industrialized Countries. In Federal Reserve Bank of Boston (ed.) Saving and Government Policy. Boston, Massachusetts: Federal Reserve Bank of Boston, pp. 1–30.

Blumenthal, Tuvia 1970: *Saving in Postwar Japan*. Cambridge, Massachusetts: East Asian Research Center/Harvard University Press.

Boskin, Michael J. and Roberts, John M. 1988: 'A Closer Look at Saving Rates in the United States and Japan. In John B. Shoven (ed.), *Government Policy towards Industry in the United States and Japan*. Cambridge, England, Cambridge University Press, pp. 121– 43.

Campbell, David William 1991: Transfer and Life Cycle Wealth in Japan, 1974–84. Doctoral dissertation, Department of Economics, University of Michigan, Ann Arbor, Michigan.

Davies, James B.1981: Uncertain Lifetime, Consumption, and Dissaving in Retirement. *Journal of Political Economy*, 89, no. 3 (June), 561–77.

Davies, James, and St-Hilaire, France 1987: Reforming Capital Income Taxation in Canada, Ottawa: Ministry of Supply and Services of Canada.

Dekle, Robert 1988: Changing Age Structures and Bequest Motives in Japanese Saving: A Household and Aggregate Analysis. Doctoral dissertation, Department of Economics, Yale University, New Haven, Connecticut.

Dekle, Robert 1989a: A Simulation Model of Saving, Residential Choice, and Bequests of the Japanese Elderly. *Economic Letters*, 29, no. 2, 129–33.

Dekle, Robert 1989b: The Unimportance of Intergenerational Transfers in Japan. *Japan and the World Economy*, 1, no. 4 (November), 403–13.

Dekle, Robert 1990: Do the Japanese Elderly Reduce Their Total Wealth? A New Look with Different Data. *Journal of the Japanese and International Economies*, 4, no. 3 (September), 309–17.

Dekle, Robert and Summers, Lawrence 1991: Japan's High Saving Rate Reaffirmed: *Working Paper* No. 3690 (April) National Bureau of Economic Research, Inc., Cambridge, Massachusetts.

Feldstein, Martin 1974: Social Security, Induced Retirement, and Aggregate Capital Accumulation. *Journal of Political Economy*, 82, no. 5 (September/October), 905–26.

Hayashi, Fumio 1986: Why Is Japan's Saving Rate So Apparently High? In Stanley Fischer (ed.), *NBER Macroeconomics Annual 1986*. Cambridge, Massachusetts: The MIT Press, 1, 147–210.

Hayashi, Fumio 1989a: Is Japan's Saving Rate High? *Quarterly Review*, Federal Reserve Bank of Minneapolis, 13, no. 2 (Spring), 3–9.

Hayashi, Fumio 1989b: Japan's Saving Rate: New Data and Reflections. *Working Paper* No. 3205 (December), National Bureau of Economic Research, Inc., Cambridge, Massachusetts.

Hayashi, Fumio, Ando, Albert, and Ferris, Richard 1988: Life Cycle and Bequest Savings. A Study of Japanese and US Households Based on Data from the 1984 NSFIE and the 1983 Survey of Consumer Finances. *Journal of the Japanese and International Economies*, 2, no. 4 (December), 450–91.

Homma, Masaaki, Atoda, Naofumi, Iwamoto, Yasushi, and Ohtake, Fumio 1987: Nenkin: Kōreisha Shakai to Nenkin Seido (Pensions: An Aging Society and the Pension System). In Kōichi Hamada, Masahiro Kuroda and Akiyoshi Horiuchi (eds), *Nihon Keizai no Makuro-bunseki* (Macroeconomic Analysis of the Japanese Economy).

Tokyo: Tōkyō Daigaku Shuppankai (University of Tokyo Press), pp. 149–75 (in Japanese).

Horie, Yasuhiro 1985: *Gendai Nihon Keizai no Kenkyū: Kakei Chochiku/Shōhi Kōdō no Jisshō Bunseki* (Research on the Contemporary Japanese Economy: An Empirical Analysis of Household Saving/Consumption Behavior). Tokyo: Tōyō Keizai Shinpōsha (in Japanese).

Horioka, Charles Yuji 1984: 'The Applicability of the Life-Cycle Hypothesis of Saving to Japan: *The Kyoto University Economic Review*, 54, no. 2 (October), 31–56.

Horioka, Charles Yuji 1985: The Importance of Saving for Education in Japan. The *Kyoto University Economic Review*, 55, no. 1 (April), 41–78.

Horioka, Charles Yuji 1987a: The Cost of Marriages and Marriage-related Saving in Japan. *The Kyoto University Economic Review*, 57, no. 1 (April), 47–58.

Horioka, Charles Yuji 1987b: Nihonjin no Kekkon Hiyō to sono tame no Chochiku ni tsuite (On Marriage Costs and Marriage-related Saving in Japan). *Keizai Ronsō* (Kyōto Daigaku Keizai Gakkai (Kyoto University Economic Society), 140, nos. 1–2 (July–August), 17–31 (in Japanese).

Horioka, Charles Yuji 1987c: Nihon ni okeru Jūtaku Kōnyū to Kakei Chochiku to no aida no kankei ni tsuite (On the Relationship between Housing Purchase and Household Saving in Japan). *Jūtaku Mondai Kenkyū* (Housing Review) (Zaidan Hōjin Jūtaku Kin'yū Fukyū Kyōkai/Jūtaku Mondai Chōsakai), 3, no. 4 (December), 1–19 (in Japanese).

Horioka, Charles Yuji 1988: Saving for Housing Purchase in Japan. *Journal of the Japanese and International Economies*, 2, no. 3 (September), 351–84.

Horioka, Charles Yuji 1989: 'Why Is Japan's Private Saving Rate So High?' In Ryuzo Sato and Takashi Negishi (eds.), Developments in Japanese Economics. Tokyo: Academic Press/Harcourt Brace Jovanovich Japan, Inc., pp. 145–78.

Horioka, Charles Yuji 1990a: 'The Importance of Life Cycle Saving in Japan: A Novel Estimation Method. *Discussion Paper* No. 225 (August), The Institute of Social and Economic Research, Osaka University, Ibaraki, Osaka, Japan.

Horioka, Charles Yuji 1990b: 'Nihonjin no Seikatsu wa Hontō ni Yutaka ka?' (Do the Japanese Really Lead Affluent Lives?). *Nihon Keizai Kenkyū* (JCER Economic Journal) (Nihon Keizai Kenkyū Senta (Japan Economic Research Center), 20 (May), 45–55 (in Japanese).

Horioka, Charles Yuji 1990c: 'Why Is Japan's Household Saving Rate So High? A Literature Survey. *Journal of the Japanese and International Economies*, 4, no. 1 (March), 49–92.

Horioka, Charles Yuji 1991a: The Determinants of Japan's Saving Rate: The Impact of the Age Structure of the Population and Other Factors. *Economic Studies Quarterly* (The Journal of the Japan Association of Economics and Econometrics), 42, no. 3, September, 237–53.

Horioka, Charles Yuji 1991b: 'Future Trends in Japan's Saving Rate and the Implications Thereof for Japan's External Imbalance. *Japan and the World Economy*, 3, no. 4, 307–30.

Horioka, Charles Yuji 1992: Consumption and Saving. In Andrew Gordon (ed.), *Postwar Japan as History*. Berkeley, California: University of California Press, forthcoming.

Horioka, Charles Yuji et al. 1990: 'Mokuteki-betsu ni mita Chochiku no Jūyōdo ni tsuite, sono 3 (On the Importance of Saving for Specific Motives, Part 3). *Finansharu Rebyū* (Ōkura-shō, Zaisei Kin'yū Kenkyū-sho (Institute of Fiscal and Monetary Policy, Ministry of Finance) 18 (December), 162–221 (in Japanese).

Horioka, Charles Yuji et al. 1991: 'Mokuteki-betsu ni mita Chochiku no Jūyōdo ni tsuite, sono 4 (On the Importance of Saving for Specific Motives, Part 4). *Finansharu Rebyū* (Ōkura-shō, Zaisei Kin'yū Kenkyū-sho (Institute of Fiscal and Monetary Policy, Ministry of Finance)), 20 (March), 84–104 (in Japanese).

Horioka, Charles Yuji, Mochizuki, Tohru, Nakagawa, Kazuaki, and Toyosawa, Satoshi 1990a: Mokuteki-betsu ni mita Chochiku no Jūyōdo ni tsuite, sono 1 (On the Importance of Saving for Specific Motives, Part 1). *Finansharu Rebyū* (Ōkura-shō, Zaisei Kin'yū Kenkyū-sho (Institute of Fiscal and Monetary Policy Ministry of Finance)), 16 (March), 89–110 (in Japanese).

Horioka, Charles Yuji, Mochizuki, Tohru, Nakagawa, Kazuaki, and Toyosawa, Satoshi 1990b: 'Mokuteki-betsu ni mita Chochiku no Jūyōdo ni tsuite, sono 2' (On the Importance of Saving for specific Motives, Part 2). *Finansharu Rebyū* (Ōkura-shō, Zaisei Kin'yū Kenkyū-sho (Institute of Fiscal and Monetary Policy, Ministry of Finance)), 17 (August), 204–39 (in Japanese).

Hurd, Michael D. 1987: Savings of the Elderly and Desired Bequests. *American Economic Review*, 77, no. 3 (June), 298–312.

Hurd, Michael D. 1990: Wealth Depletion and Life Cycle Consumption by the Elderly. *Working Paper* No. 3472 (October), National Bureau of Economic Research, Inc., Cambridge, Massachusetts.

Ishikawa, Tsuneo 1987: Chochiku: Kakei Chochiku no Kōzō Yōin to Kin'yū Zeisei (Saving: Structural Determinants of Household Saving and the Financial and Tax Systems). In Kōichi Hamada, Masahiro Kuroda, and Akiyoshi Horiuchi (eds), Nihon Keizai no Makuro Bunseki (Macroeconomic Analysis of the Japanese Economy). Tokyo: Tōkyō Daigaku Shuppankai (University of Tokyo Press), pp. 177–210 (in Japanese).

Ishikawa, Tsuneo 1988a: 'Kōrei-sha Setai no Shūgyō Kōdō to Chochiku Kodo (The Labor Supply and Saving Behavior of Elderly Households). In Kikuo Iwata and Tsuneo Ishikawa (eds), *Nihon Keizai Kenkyū* (Research on the Japanese Economy). Tokyo: Tōkyō Daigaku Shuppankai (University of Tokyo Press), pp. 181–200 (in Japanese).

Ishikawa, Tsuneo 1988b: Saving and Labor Supply Behavior of Aged Households in Japan. *Journal of the Japanese and International Economies*, 2, no. 4 (December), 417–49.

Ishikawa, Tsuneo 1991: *Shotoku to Tomi* (Income and Wealth). Tokyo, Japan: Iwanami Shoten (in Japanese).

Kanamori, Hisao 1961: Nihon no Chochiku-ritsu wa Naze Takai-ka (Why Is Japan's Saving Rate So High?). *Keizai Geppō* (Keizai Kikaku-chō, Chōsa-kyoku (Research Bureau, Economic Planning Agency) (ed.)), 11 (October 30), 89–96 (in Japanese).

Kessler, Denis, and Masson, André 1979: Les Transferts Intergénérationnnels: l'Aide, la Donation, l'Heritage. CNRS Report. Paris.

Kessler, Denis, and Masson, André 1989: Bequest and Wealth Accumulation: Are Some Pieces of the Puzzle Missing? *Journal of Economic Perspectives*, 3, no. 3 (Summer), 141–52.

Komiya, Ryūtarō 1966: The Supply of Personal Savings. In Ryūtarō Komiya (ed.), *Postwar*

Economic Growth in Japan (Robert S. Ozaki, trans.). Berkeley, California: University of California Press, pp. 157–86.

Kotlikoff, Laurence J. 1988: Intergenerational Transfers and Saving. *Journal of Economic Perspectives*, 2, no. 2 (Spring), 41–58.

Kotlikoff, Laurence J. 1989: Health Expenditures and Precautionary Savings. In Laurence J. Kotlikoff, *What Determines Saving?* Cambridge, Massachusetts: MIT Press, pp. 141–62.

Kotlikoff, Laurence J. and Spivak, Avia 1981: The Family as an Incomplete Annuities Market. *Journal of Political Economy*, 89, no. 2 (April), 372–91.

Kotlikoff, Laurence J. and Summers, Lawrence H. 1981: 'The Role of Intergenerational Transfers in Aggregate Capital Accumulation. *Journal of Political Economy*, 89, no. 4 (August), 706–32.

Masson, André 1986: A Cohort Analysis of Age-Wealth Profiles Generated by a Simulation Model in France (1949–1975). *Economic Journal*, 96, no. 381, March.

Menchik, Paul L. and David, Martin 1983: Income Distribution, Lifetime Savings, and Bequests. *American Economic Review*, 73, no. 4, September, 672–90.

Mizoguchi, Toshiyuki 1988: Nihon no Shōhi Kansū Bunseki no Tenbō (Prospects for Consumption Function Analysis in Japan). *Keizai Kenkyū* (The Economic Review), 39, no. 3 (July), 253–76 (in Japanese).

Modigliani, Franco 1988: The Role of Intergenerational Transfers and Life Cycle Saving in the Accumulation of Wealth. *Journal of Economic Perspectives* 2, no. 2 (Spring), 15–40.

Modigliani, Franco and Sterling, Arlie 1983: 'Determinants of Private Saving with Special Reference to the Role of Social Security – Cross-country Tests. In Franco Modigliani and Richard Hemming (eds), *The Determinants of National Saving and Wealth*. London: The Macmillan Press Ltd pp. 24–55.

Morgan, J. N., David, M. H., Cohen, W. J. and Brazer, H. E. 1962: Income and Welfare in the United States. New York: McGraw-Hill.

Noguchi, Yukio 1982: Wagakuni Kōteki Nenkin no Shomondai (Aspects of Public Pensions in Japan). *Kikan Gendai Keizai*, 50 (Autumn), 18–33 (in Japanese).

Noguchi, Yukio 1983: Problems of Public Pensions in Japan. *Hitotsubashi Journal of Economics*, 24, 43–68.

Noguchi, Yukio, Uemura, Kyōko, and Kitō, Yumiko 1989: 'Sōzoku ni yoru Sedai-kan Shisan Iten no Kōzō: Shuto-ken ni okeru Jittai Chōsa Kekka (Inheritance and Intergenerational Transmission of Wealth: The Results of a Survey of the Tokyo Metropolitan Area). *Kikan Shakai Hoshō Kenkyū* (The Quarterly of Social Science Research), 25, no. 2 (Autumn), 136–44 (in Japanese).

Ogawa, Kazuo 1991a: Kakei no Shisan Keisei to Kōteki Nenkin (The Wealth Accumulation of Households and Public Pensions). *Discussion Paper* No. 9101 (May), Faculty of Economics, Kobe University, Rokko, Kobe, Japan (in Japanese).

Ogawa, Kazuo 1991b: Shotoku Risuku to Yobi-teki Chochiku (Income Risk and Precautionary Saving). *Keizai Kenkyū* (The Economic Review), 42, no. 2 (April), 139–52 (in Japanese).

Ohno, Masanori 1991: Shotoku Hendō to Kakei Chochiku (Income Fluctuations and Household Saving). Mimeo., Graduate School of Economics, University of Tokyo, Bunkyo-ku, Tokyo, Japan (in Japanese).

Ohtake, Fumio 1991a: Bequest Motives of Aged Households in Japan. Mimeo., Institute of Social and Economic Research, Osaka University, Ibaraki, Osaka, Japan.

Ohtake, Fumio (1991b): Isan Dōki to Kōreisha no Chochiku/Rōdō Kyōkyū (The Bequest Motive and the Saving/Labor Supply of the Aged). *Keizai Kenkyū* (The Economic Review), 42, no. 1 (January), 21–30 (in Japanese).

Projector, Dorothy and Weiss, Gertrude, S. 1964: *Survey of Financial Characteristics of Consumers.* Washington, DC: Board of Governors of the Federal Reserve System.

Sasaki, Motohiko and Tachibanaki, Toshiaki (1985): Kōteki Nenkin Seido ga Sedai-betsu Chochiku-ritsu to Shisan Keisei ni Ataeta Eikyō (Effects of Public Pensions on Saving Ratio and Asset Formation by Generation). *Kikan Shakai Hoshō Kenkyū* (The Quarterly of Social Security Research), 21, no. 1 (Summer), 59–71 (in Japanese).

Sato, Kazuo 1987: Saving and Investment. In Kozo Yamamura and Yasukichi Yasuba (eds.) *The Political Economy of Japan*, vol. 1: *The Domestic Transformation.* Stanford, California: Stanford University Press, pp. 137–85.

Shafer, Jeffrey R., Elmeskov, Jorgen and Tease, Warren 1991: Saving Trends and Measurement Issues. Presented at the Conference on Saving Behaviour: Theory, International Evidence and Policy Implications, sponsored by the Savings Banks Research Foundation, May 26–9, 1991, in Hanasaari, Espoo/Helsinki, Finland.

Shinohara, Miyohei 1982: *Industrial Growth, Trade, and Dynamic Patterns in the Japanese Economy.* Tokyo: Tōkyō Daigaku Shuppankai (University of Tokyo Press).

Shinohara, Miyohei 1983: The Determinants of Post-war Savings Behaviour in Japan. In Franco Modigliani and Richard Hemming (eds), *The Determinants of National Saving and Wealth.* London: The Macmillan Press Ltd pp. 201–18.

Takagi, Shintaro 1988: Trends of Saving and Assets and the Future Tasks of National Accounts. Presented at the International Symposium on "A Global Role of the Japanese Economy with Affluent Savings and Accumulated Wealth," sponsored by the Economic Research Institute, Economic Planning Agency, October 13–14, 1988, in Tokyo, Japan.

Takayama, Noriyuki (forthcoming): *Greying Japan: An Economic Perspective on Public Pensions.* Tokyo: Kinokuniya Co., Ltd/Oxford University Press.

Takayama, Noriyuki et al. 1989: Nihon no Kakei Shisan to Chochiku-ritsu (Household Assets and the Saving Rate in Japan). *Keizai Bunseki* (Keizai Kikaku-chō, Keizai Kenkyū-sho (Economic Research Institute, Economic Planning Agency)), 116 (September), 1–93 (in Japanese).

Takayama, Noriyuki et al. 1990a: 'Jinteki Shisan no Suikei no Kōteki Nenkin no Saibunpai Kōka (The Estimation of Human Capital and the Redistributional Effects of Public Pensions). *Keizai Bunseki* (Keizai Kikaku-chō, Keizai Kenkyū-sho (Economic Research Institute, Economic Planning Agency), 118 (March), 1–73 (in Japanese).

Takayama, Noriyuki et al. 1990b: Kakei no Chochiku to Shūrō-tō ni kansuru Keizai Bunseki: Kōteki Nenkin to no Kankei ni Shōten o Atete (An Economic Analysis of Household Saving, Labor Supply, Etc.: With Emphasis on the Impact of Public Pensions). *Keizai Bunseki* (Keizai Kikaku-chō, Keizai Kenkyū-sho (Economic Research Institute, Economic Planning Agency), 121 (November), 1–159 (in Japanese).

Takayama, Noriyuki et al. 1990c: Kakei Shisan Hoyūgaku no Nenji Suii to Kakei Chochiku no Nijiten-kan Hikaku (Yearly Trends in the Wealth Holdings of Households and a Two-point Comparison of Household Saving). *Keizai Bunseki* (Keizai Kikaku-chō,

Keizai Kenkyū-sho (Economic Research Institute, Economic Planning Agency)), 118 (March), 75–121 (in Japanese).

Takenaka, Heizō and Ogawa, Kazuo 1987: *Taigai Fukinkō ńo Makuro Bunseki: Chochiku/ Tōshi Baransu to Seisaku Kyōchō* (A Macroeconomic Analysis of External Disequilibrium: Saving/Investment Balances and Policy Coordination). Tokyo: Tōyō Keizai Shinpōsha) (in Japanese).

Yaari, Menahem E. 1964: On the Consumer's Lifetime Allocation Process. *International Economic Review*, 5, no. 3 (September), 304–17.

Yaari, Menahem E. 1965: Uncertain Lifetime, Life Insurance, and the Theory of the Consumer. *Review of Economic Studies*, 32, no. 2 (April), 137–50.

Yamada, Tetsuji 1987: Social Security, Savings, and Labor Supply of the Elderly in Japan. Doctoral dissertation, Department of Economics, City University of New York, New York, N.Y.

Yamada, Tetsuji 1990: The Effects of Japanese Social Security Retirement Benefits on Personal Saving and Elderly Labor Force Behavior. *Japan and the World Economy*, 2, no. 4 (December), 327–63.

Yamada, Tetsuji, Yamada, Tadashi, and Liu, Guorn 1990: Determinants of Saving and Labor Force Participation of the Elderly in Japan. *Working Paper* No. 3292 (March), National Bureau of Economic Research, Inc., Cambridge, Massachusetts.

Yoshikawa, Kaoru 1982: Kōteiki Nenkin wa Kojin Chochiku o Genshō saseru ka? (Do Public Pensions Lower Personal Saving?). *ESP* (Keizai Kikaku-chō (Economic Planning Agency)), 120 (April), 70–6 (in Japanese).

APPENDIX

National Income Accounts data for Japan were taken from the following sources:

(1) For 1955–69 data:
Keizai Kikaku-chō (Economic Planning Agency) 1988: *Kokumin Keizai Keisan Hokōku (Chōki Sokyū Suikei) (Shōwa 30-nen – Shōwa 44-nen)* (Report on National Accounts from 1955 to 1969). Tokyo: Ōkura-shō Insatsu-kyoku (Ministry of Finance Printing Bureau).

(2) For 1970–87 data:
Keizai Kikaku-chō (Economic Planning Agency) 1991: *Shōwa 60-nen Kijun Kaitei Kokumin Keizai Keisan Hōkoku* (Report on Revised National Accounts on the Basis of 1985). Tokyo: Ōkura-shō Insatsu-kyoku (Ministry of Finance Printing Bureau), vols 1 and 2.

(3) For 1988–9 data:
Keizai Kikaku-chō (Economic Planning Agency) 1991: *Kokumin Keizai Keisan Nenpō* (Annual Report on National Accounts), 1991 edition. Tokyo: Ōkura-shō Insatsu-kyoku (Ministry of Finance Printing Bureau).

The data in (2) and (3) incorporate the October 1990 benchmark revision, which is based on 1985 prices (benchmark revisions are conducted once every five years).

Part III

Policy Conclusions

8

Towards an International Savings Policy[*]

W. F. Duisenberg and A. H. E. M. Wellink

".... it is important to keep in mind that, while central banks can create money, they cannot create savings"

E. G. Corrigan (1990), p. 464.

INTRODUCTION

In recent years the subject of saving has been a focus of increasing interest, both in the scientific literature and in discussions about economic policy. This is not surprising, since, in proportion to national income, savings in the 1980s were considerably lower than in earlier decades, as indeed they still are, while the global pattern of saving has been subject to major changes. Interest is strengthened further as it may be expected that saving will be sorely needed in the coming years as a result of major world political developments such as those in Eastern Europe, the former Soviet Union and the Middle East. Given this situation, it is understandable that various agencies, including international organizations, are highlighting the increasing global scarcity of capital, urging national governments to encourage saving. The principal instrument which is available to governments in this respect is a reduction of budget deficits. Another highly important factor is the structure of tax systems, not so much for the level of savings as for their allocation, since unequal fiscal treatment of unearned income induces tax arbitrage, thus eroding tax revenues and disturbing the domestic and international allocation of savings. It is these aspects which form the subject of the present chapter.

This chapter has been organized as follows. The first section outlines the development of saving in the past few decades and discusses the factors influencing saving. The next sections deal with the global demand for capital as it

* The authors owe a debt of gratitude to Dr J. A. Bikker and Dr P. Buitelaar for their contributions.

may be expected to develop in the coming years, attention being paid to the possibility of increasing scarcity, review the manner in which governments influence the development and allocation of saving, centering on the budget deficit, the share of national income claimed by the public sector, the influence of taxation on the level and allocation of saving, and the consequences which financing methods for old-age pension schemes have for saving. The chapter concludes by presenting some policy recommendations.

DEVELOPMENT OF SAVING

World Saving and Investment

In the 1980s, the savings ratio declined in most countries. As is evident from table 8.1, the national savings ratio in the 1980s in the combined industrialized countries was about four and a half percent of GNP below the average for the period 1967–73. This decrease was largely attributable to public sector savings, as the fall in private sector savings was only limited. Also, investment in these countries in the 1980s was below the levels of prior years, but its decline was less pronounced than the fall in national savings. Consequently, in the 1980s the surplus on the current account of the combined balance of payments of the industrialized countries as it had been recorded in the 1960s and 1970s gave way to a deficit.

For the period 1991–6 the International Monetary Fund (IMF) has made a forecast for the industrialized countries (table 8.1). In this forecast it has been assumed that government savings will increase vigorously as a result of further reductions of budget deficits. With the private sector savings ratio expected to go down, the total savings ratio is still anticipated to increase slightly. The one percentage point fall in the aggregate private sector savings ratio is underlain mainly by a decrease in the private sector savings ratio in the vast majority of the countries, notably the United States, Japan and Italy. The IMF ascribes this decrease in part to the continuing ageing of the population. The investment ratio of the combined industrialized countries in expected to increase in the 1990s, but the high level of the 1960s and 1970s will not be matched. The combined savings deficit will increase, so that these countries will demand external savings, as they also did in the 1980s.

Table 8.2 shows the movements in savings, investment and current account balances outside the OECD. Here, too, a fall in national saving in the 1980s is evident, especially in Africa and the Middle East. In the 1990s these areas are expected to record a deficit on the current account, so that they will continue to require external saving to finance domestic investment. Especially in the Middle East, 1991/2 is anticipated to see a substantial drop in the current account balance, resulting from a strong upsurge of investment for reconstruction following the Gulf War.

Table 8.1 Saving and investment in the industrialized countries (percent of GNP/GDP)

	Savings			Investment	Current account balance
	private	*public*	*total*		
All industrialized countries[a]					
1967–73	21.5	3.5	25.0	24.4	0.5
1974–9	21.8	1.3	23.1	23.1	0
1980–90	20.3	0.3	20.6	20.9	−0.3
Forecast for:					
1991–6	19.3	2.1	21.4	22.0	−0.5
United States					
1967–73	16.6	−0.6	16.0	15.9	0.1
1974–9	17.8	−1.2	16.6	16.6	0
1980–90	16.1	−2.5	13.6	15.5	−1.9
Japan					
1967–73	30.3	7.7	38.0	36.9	1.1
1974–9	29.0	4.0	33.0	32.7	0.3
1980–90	26.3	5.6	31.9	29.9	2.0
France					
1967–73	21.3	4.8	26.1	26.8	−0.7
1974–9	21.7	2.9	24.6	24.7	−0.1
1980–90	18.8	1.4	20.2	20.8	−0.6
West Germany					
1967–73	21.5	5.3	26.9	25.5	1.4
1974–9	20.1	2.4	22.5	21.5	1.0
1980–90	20.8	1.9	22.7	20.6	2.2
Italy					
1967–73	28.3	−1.2	27.1	25.6	1.5
1974–9	30.9	−5.3	25.5	25.8	−0.2
1980–90	28.1	−6.4	21.7	22.6	−0.9
United Kingdom					
1967–73	13.3	6.9	20.2	19.9	0.3
1974–9	16.9	2.2	19.1	20.0	−0.9
1980–90	15.4	1.9	17.3	17.5	−0.2

[a] EC, Norway, Sweden, Finland, Austria, Iceland, Switzerland, United States, Japan, Canada, Australia, New Zealand.

Source: IMF (1991a), Table 10.

Table 8.2 Saving and investment in non–OECD regions (Annual averages in percent of GNP)

	National saving	National investment	Current account balance
	All developing countries		
1975–82	25.7	26.6	−0.9
1983–90	24.7	25.2	−0.5
Forecast for:			
1991–2	23.2	24.7	−1.5
1993–6	24.5	25.2	−0.7
	Africa		
1975–82	22.2	26.4	−4.2
1983–90	17.4	19.4	−2.0
	Eastern Europe and USSR		
1975–82	–	–	–
1983–90	31.3	30.5	0.8
Forecast for:			
1991–2	22.6	24.2	−1.6
1993–6	22.8	24.1	−1.3
	Middle East		
1975–82	38.2	26.3	11.9
1983–90	21.0	22.6	−1.6
Forecast for:			
1991–2	20.5	25.8	−5.3
1993–6	22.8	23.4	−0.6

The figures shown in this table have been derived from table 12 in IMF (1991a, 1991b) by analogy with Aghevli et al. (1990), table 2, p. 36. National investment as shown in the table is "domestic investment:" the sum total of fixed investment (excluding dwellings) and stockbuilding. The current account balance has been derived from the items "gross external saving" and "investment abroad." The national savings ratio is determined as a residual item.

Factors Determining Saving

The literature lists numerous factors which determine saving, notably household saving. A central position is help by the life-cycle hypothesis, economic agents dividing consumption and saving over their lifetime on the basis of the present value of anticipated future income. In a stationary economy (without capital formation and net saving) and with the demographic composition of the population remaining unchanged, saving from earned income is wholly offset by dissaving by the elderly running down their wealth. Economic growth leads to increased saving by the elderly, so that personal sector savings go up. A relative increase in the number of elderly leads to a decrease in saving. Thus, three major determinants of household saving have been identified: income growth, the demographic composition of the population, and wealth. In empirical studies, the demographic element is often represented by the share of old-age pensioners in the population.[1] It is expected that in many Western countries, the share of the elderly will increase in the future, leading to a decrease in saving, notably in Japan; see Auerbach (1989) and Horioka in chapter 7.

It is also argued on occasion that an increase in the participation rate of women adversely affects saving, because of the resulting reduced need for pre-cautionary balances and easier access to consumer credit. Wealth also plays a role in the life-cycle theory. With increasing wealth, households need to save less in order to maintain a certain level of wealth. In many countries property and equity prices have gone up vigorously in the 1980s. The impression is that this increase in wealth has contributed considerably to the decrease in house-hold saving in Japan, the United Kingdom and the United States (Aghevli et al., 1990, and Kauffmann, chapter 1 above). Another determinant of savings is the rate of interest; it must be noted, though, that the direction of this effect is not unambiguously clear in the theory. A higher rate of interest encourages saving (positive substitution effect), but also causes unearned income to grow faster, thus lessening the need to save (negative income effect). In empirical studies, the rate of interest is often found to have a positive effect on saving, but there are also studies showing a negative effect or a non-significant outcome of interest rates (Smith, 1990).

The level and the structure of taxes may also affect household saving. Taxes levied on unearned income reduce net interest receipts and thus discourage saving. Tax deductibility of interest payments in respect of consumer credit and mortgage loans may also lead to a decrease in saving. In this respect; there is a connection with the liberalization of capital markets in the 1980s, which eased access to credit, and with the increase in wealth, which may have encouraged consumption. These factors may have played a role in the decrease in saving in the United States and Japan in the past decade, but their effect is most evident in the Scandinavian countries. Not long ago, in Sweden and Norway, for instance, household saving was even negative for a number of years.

The government's budget deficit may also affect personal sector saving. According to the Ricardian equivalence theorem, a tax cut leading to an in-crease in the budget deficit will prompt economic agents to increase their saving correspondingly so as to be able to meet future tax increases. This theorem has been a major subject of discussion in recent years. The empirical literature often finds only partial compensation; see Nicoletti (1988, 1990) and Den Broeder and Winder (1991). It is noteworthy that, according to Nicoletti, the connection is most pronounced in the cases of Italy and Belgium. As it is these very countries where public sector deficits have run most conspicuously out of control, this finding could indicate that the connection between household saving and public sector deficit is mainly dependent on the longer-term sustainability of fiscal policy. Once the deficit exceeds a certain threshold value, households, fearing future tax increases, tend to step up saving because of tax discounting.

Yet another factor is the rate of inflation. Inflation reallocates real wealth: the public debt decreases in real terms at the expense of government bond holders. If the Ricardian equivalence hypothesis holds, no additional savings of households are necessary to restore the eroded value of its government bonds. As the hypothesis generally only holds in part, it seems plausible to assume that inflation positively influences saving of households. In addition, a higher rate of inflation creates uncertainty, encouraging saving on account of the precautionary motive. On the other hand, the uncertainty about the return on saving may discourage saving (Modigliani, 1990). The decrease in the savings ratio in the 1980s has been associated with the reduction in inflation rates during this period (OECD, 1989).

The final factor in this context is constituted by group pension schemes and the social security system. They may reduce saving because – at any rate in the case of a pay-as-you-go system – they will lessen the need for households to save from the motive of countering future loss of income as a result of illness or old age (Feldstein, 1980).

The influence of these factors on saving is not, of course, exactly specifiable. However, an attempt is made below at quantifying the relationships, as an illustration of the above enumeration of determinants. The equation used is based on Kramer and Mourik (1990) and concerns the personal sector savings ratio. It is a pooled-regression equation, underlain by annual figures for the estimation period 1961–88 for each of eight representative industrialized countries (United States, United Kingdom, Japan, Belgium, Germany, France, the Netherlands, and Sweden) and estimated with ordinary least squares. The influence of the individual countries has been weighted by the size of the population.

$$S/GDP = 0.22\ \bar{y}d + 0.15\ rrl + 0.39\ \bar{p}c + 0.31\ \frac{G-T}{GDP}$$

$$(4.76) \qquad (2.21) \qquad (7.29) \qquad (3.52)$$

$$+\ 0.18\ pe + 0.35\ p^{15/64} + 0.51\ pa^{65} - 0.21\ pa^{vr} - 22.74$$

$$(10.65) \qquad (5.45) \qquad (13.72) \qquad (-10.93) \qquad (-4.86)$$

$$\bar{R}^2 = 0.94 \qquad \text{estimated period:} \quad 1961–88$$

The t-values are given under the estimated coefficients. A dash over a symbol indicates a percentage change. The model variables are:

S	= net household savings
GDP	= gross domestic product
yd	= per capita disposable income in real terms
rrl	= real long-term interest rate
pc	= cost of living
G	= government current expenditure
T	= direct taxes paid by the personal sector
pe	= per capita public pension scheme payments in real terms
$p^{15/64}$	= share of the population aged 15–64 in total population
pa^{65}, pa^{vr}	= participation rate of persons over 64 and of women, respectively.

The coefficients for income growth and the share of persons aged 15–64 in the total population are significant and have the sign which was to be expected on the basis of the life-cycle hypothesis. Considering the sign found for the real rate of interest, the substitution effect proves to prevail over the income effect, the net effect being small: a one percentage point increase in the real rate of interest leads to an increase in the household savings ratio of over 0.1 to 0.2 percentage point. The results show that, given the effect of the real rate of interest, an acceleration of the rate of inflation leads to an increase in the household savings ratio of 0.4 percentage point. The coefficient found for the balance of government current expenditure and direct taxes indicates that compensatory household saving behavior (Ricardian equivalence) is evident in part. The sign of the term for public pension schemes is the net result of positive and negative influences. As such schemes are usually financed by a pay-as-you-go system, a decrease in saving might be expected: in that case, households can reduce their own saving. On the other hand existing provisions might cause attention to be shifted to related desiderata such as early retirement, so that there still continues to be a need for employees to save, the so-called induced retirement effect. Apparently, the latter, positive effect predominates. According to the life-cycle hypothesis, lower participation rates of the elderly may increase personal savings because the provision for old age needs has to be saved during the shorter working period. On the other hand, lower participation rates imply, given the present pension schemes, an increase in the number of people who dissave. The latter effect appears to be dominating. As to the participation rate of women, a negative effect was found. This finding is supported by empirical research by Lau in chapter 4 and by Graham (1987, 1989).

The regression results are, of course, presented with due reservation. None the less, it is striking how significant most of the determinants are.[2] At 94 percent, the descriptive power is fairly high. Yet, closer analysis of the residuals shows that not all differences among the countries have been explained. It is possible that the unexplained differences are related to socio-cultural factors, which vary from one country to the next.[3]

THE IMPORTANCE OF INCREASING NATIONAL SAVING

Saving and Economic Growth

In the growth model of Harrod and Domar, the rate of economic growth is governed by the quotient of the savings ratio and the capital output ratio, so that there is a direct relationship between saving and economic growth. In the neoclassical growth models, the long-run growth of production is governed by technological progress and the growth of the working population. As both determinants are regarded as exogenous, there is no relationship with saving. More recently, models have been developed in which technological progress in endogenous and is influenced by such factors as fixed investment, investment in human capital and expenditure on research and development (Ford and Poret, 1990). Such models have already been discussed in chapter 2 by Buiter. New investment, incorporating state-of-the-art technology, speeds up the growth of total factor productivity and, hence, economic growth. The financing of investment requires saving, bringing out the relationship between saving and economic growth.

In reality it can be perceived that countries with high savings and investment ratios are often also marked by high rates of economic growth, such as Japan, Taiwan, and Korea. Developing countries with high savings ratios also prove to have higher investment ratios, higher growth rates and lower inflation rates (IMF, 1991a). In these countries capital as a factor of production contributes more to economic growth as the savings ratio is higher. Recent empirical investigations thus concluded that the level of the saving ratio is a major determinant of the growth performance of the developing countries. On the other hand, significant differences in the level of national savings ratios are not invariably reflected in economic growth differentials (United States versus continental Europe). It might be noted in this context that the increased liberalization of capital movements has weakened the relationship between national saving and economic growth in individual countries, since investment can also be financed from external savings. This will, however, not apply to the same extent to the developing countries as, owing in part to their high levels of external indebtedness, their access to the international capital market is much more restricted, so that their national saving may impose a ceiling for investment.

The foregoing apart, the direction of causality between economic growth and savings ratio is not unambiguously clear, as, according to the life-cycle hypothesis, the reverse causality is also conceivable, economic growth being a determinant of the savings ratio.

Capital Requirements and Available Savings

On occasion, the question arises at what level the savings ratio in a country permits balanced economic development. As explained above, an analysis by country is less relevant in an environment of liberalized international capital movements. If, none the less, an individual country is to be taken as the starting point, use might be made of the golden rule of saving developed by Phelps (1961) and others. This permits the optimal level of the savings ratio to be derived on the basis of the neoclassical growth theory. In its most simple form, the rule tells us that consumption per head is maximized in an economy growing at that steady rate where the savings ratio equals the capital income ratio. Comparison between the actual savings ratio and the optimal ratio thus determined provides an indication of the savings surplus or deficit. For a large number of industrialized countries, Abel et al. (1989) have presented calculations showing that the actual savings ratio is lower than the calculated optimum. Increasing the savings and investment ratios would make it possible to achieve a higher level of economic growth. On the basis of similar calculations, Evans (1990) has concluded for the United States that the optimal net national savings ratio is 8 to 12 percent of net national product, a value of which the actual US ratio falls far short. There is a problem in respect of this sort of calculation in that the results vary widely depending on the assumed values of a number of crucial variables, such as the capital output ratio and technological progress, leading to such a broad range of values for the optimal savings ratio that it gives little to go on.

If, by analogy with the analysis by country, the optimal savings ratio for the world is to be determined, the level of the capital output ratio and the rate of technological progress are in fact unknown. As a result, calculating the optimal world savings ratio by Phelps's method is still problematic.

If nonetheless an attempt at quantification is to be made, a much lower level of abstraction must be chosen and some general relationships between saving, investment and economic growth at the global level must be taken as the basis. As noted above, the link between saving and investment in individual countries is increasingly being severed, but at the global level the two are equal. This means that, at the world level, a less 'ambitious' approach poses fewer problems than an analysis by country.

It must be noted, incidentally, that a detailed consideration of an optimal or

Table 8.3 Estimated additonal demands for external saving (billions of US dollars)

	1990	1991	Annual Averages 1992–6
German unification	35	70	55
Reconstruction in the Middle East	–	17	12
Eastern Europe and the USSR	–	10	33
Total	35	97	100

Source: IMF (1991b), table 7.

desired world savings ratio is beyond the scope of this chapter. Hence, a more pragmatic approach has been chosen in terms of the supply of and demand for saving at the global level. Below, the various factors which govern the demand for capital will be reviewed, such as demand from Eastern Europe and the former Soviet Union, from the Gulf area and from the developing countries.

The restructuring and the transition to a market-based economy in the countries of Eastern Europe and the former Soviet Union calls for renewal of production plant and infrastructure.[4] This will have to be financed from savings. It is not simple to approximate even the order of magnitude of these capital requirements. Shortly after the changes in Eastern Europe, the European Commission[5] mentioned an amount of $23 billion per annum for the coming five to ten years for the Eastern European countries excluding the former Soviet Union. The IMF has also made an estimation; it assesses the annual demand for savings from Eastern Europe and the Soviet Union at over $30 billion; see table 8.3.

It is not clear to what extent the Eastern European countries could themselves meet part of their capital requirements from domestic saving. As set out by Ickes in chapter 6, national savings in these countries originate largely from the public sector and are made up of elements such as retained earnings of state enterprises. Personal sector savings are at a relatively low level, not least because the precautionary motive (loss of income owing to unemployment or illness) is weak. The often negative real rate of interest does not encourage saving either. Ickes expects that, during the switch to a market-based economy but also later, the personal sector savings ratio will rise since uncertainty as to income will increase. It might be noted in this context that calculations as to capital requirements are usually underlain by macro–economic data and desiderata (target per capita income, high investment ratio) rather than on–the–spot observation. This means that for the time being the actual capital requirements will remain uncertain; moreover, it is not clear whether there will be sufficient projects in practice to absorb the many billions of dollars. Thus, the absorptive capacity of the countries concerned would appear to require as much attention as the supply of capital itself.

The developing countries, too, require capital to finance their development; to this end, they use both domestic savings and imported capital. There are various countries, such as Singapore and Korea, where capital imports in combination with domestic savings have raised investment and pushed up economic growth.[6] However, there are also indications that a relatively large part of the capital thus imported has ultimately been used for consumption rather than investment. Available research suggest a strong relationship between domestic saving and economic growth, but a much weaker link between inflows of external savings and domestic economic performance. In view of the often limited level of national saving, the developing countries may be expected to continue to require external savings in the years ahead.

In the area where the Gulf War was fought in 1991, major damage has been inflicted upon the available production potential. For the coming years the IMF expects annual capital market borrowing of $12 billion for the reconstruction of the Gulf region (table 8.3). Thus, it is likely that in the short and medium term, this region's demand for savings will be considerable.

All in all, it may be concluded that, in the medium term, both the Gulf region and the Eastern European countries will claim a greater share of world saving. This constitutes, as it were, additional demand, over and above the 'normal' demand from the industrialized and the developing countries.

A review of savings shows that at present about three-quarters of world savings are generated in the OECD area.[7] As noted above, pp. 282–4, the savings ratio in the combined industrialized countries in the 1980s was about four and a half percent of GNP lower than it had been in the period 1967–73. As a group, these countries incurred a deficit on the current account of the balance of payments in the 1980s, resulting in imports of capital. As to expectations for the development of savings in the somewhat longer run, it must be noted that in the 1990s the share of the elderly in the total population will show a steady increase in Europe and Japan, depressing saving. For Japan in particular, this process is expected to accelerate markedly during this decade. Horioka has already discussed this subject in chapter 7. Calculations show that this will substantially reduce both savings and the current account balance (IMF, 1990b). As Japan generates about one-quarter of world saving, this may have far-reaching consequences. On the other hand, counterweight might be provided by an increase in public sector saving resulting from a reduction in budget deficits. In its forecasts for the 1990s the IMF assumes such an increase in public sector saving that the aggregate savings ratio of the industrialized countries will show an increase, despite a fall in the private sector savings ratio (see table 8.1).

A Global Saving Deficit?

The foregoing suggests that in the (near) future, additional demand for world saving may be expected. The question arises whether this will be offset by a matching increase in world saving. As outlined above, the aggregate private sector savings ratio in the industrialized countries is expected to decrease rather than increase in the years ahead. Given the policy intentions in the various countries, some reduction in budget deficits may be anticipated, but whether its magnitude will be such as to lead to a rise in the overall savings ratio remains to be seen. Hence, it must not be ruled out that in the short or medium term, world saving will prove insufficient to finance world investment. Ultimately, a possible *ex ante* disequilibrium between national saving and national investment will be remedied by the normal interplay of market forces, notably through higher real interest rates. For the industrialized countries, this could mean that sustained not-inflationary growth will be hampered by capacity bottlenecks. For the developing countries an increase in interest rates would further complicate the financing of necessary new investment and the fulfilment of their payment obligations. In the light of an increased and further increasing *ex ante* savings deficit, it is desirable that saving should be stepped up worldwide. As Eastern Europe and the developing countries cannot be expected to make any significant contribution to increased saving, it is the industrialized countries which must boost saving. International organizations have rightly urged this course. (IMF, 1990a, OBCD, 1990, Bank for International Settlements, 1991).

Viewed globally, higher savings contribute to a reduction in the savings deficit, thus lessening the upward pressure on the real rate of interest and easing the financing of investment.[8] However, with the increasing freedom of capital movements, this effect will be much less pronounced for individual countries. With savings flowing across national frontiers in search of the highest yields, the relationship between national saving and domestic investment has become much looser. Under such conditions, it is quite possible that increased saving will not be used to finance domestic investment but will be exported for the benefit of investment in other countries. Consequently, a measure of international coordination of policies aimed at increasing savings is desirable, focusing notably on fiscal policies.

Table 8.3 showed an IMF estimate of the additional demand for capital averaging $100 billion per annum for the period 1992–6. Using the macroeconomic world model MULTIMOD, the IMF (1991b) has calculated the consequences of this extra demand for capital. The results are presented in table 8.4 which shows clearly that the extra demand for capital has its price in terms of higher inflation and a higher real rate of interest. The additional capital requirements may be met by means of increased saving at the global level. Below, the effects of an increase in savings on the world economy are simulated;

Table 8.4 Effects of increased investment demands (deviations from baseline, in percent unless stated otherwise)

	1990	1991	1992–6[a]
United States			
Real GDP	0.1	0.2	−0.1
GDP deflator	0.2	0.5	0.8
Real long-term interest rate[b]	0.3	0.5	0.3
Private investment[c]	−0.1	−0.2	−0.2
Current account balance[c]	0.0	0.2	0.2
Japan			
Real GDP	0.1	0.1	−0.2
GDP deflator	0.2	0.5	0.8
Real long-term interest rate[b]	0.3	0.6	0.4
Private investment[c]	−	−0.1	−0.2
Current account balance[c]	−	0.2	0.3
(West) Germany[d]			
Real GDP	0.6	1.8	0.4
GDP deflator	0.2	1.1	1.9
Real long-term interest rate[b]	0.6	1.0	0.9
Private investment[c]	−0.3	−0.6	−0.8
Current account balance[c]	−1.2	−2.4	−1.8
Other industrialized countries			
Real GDP	−0.1	−	−0.3
GDP deflator	−	0.1	0.1
Real long-term interest rate[b]	0.6	0.9	0.6
Private investment[c]	−0.2	−0.5	−0.4
Current account balance[c]	0.2	0.6	0.7
Net debtor developing countries			
Real GDP	0.2	0.3	−
Current account balance[c]	0.0	0.2	0.1

[a] Annual averages.
[b] Percentage points.
[c] Percent of GNP.
[d] Data for Germany are for West Germany, except the current account balance, which is for both East and West Germany and is expressed as a ratio of their combined GNP.

German unification, reconstruction in the Middle East, and economic transformation in Eastern Europe and the USSR.

Source: IMF (1991b), table 8.

the calculations have been made with the INTERMOD model (Meredith, 1989). INTERMOD is a world model which has been developed at the Canadian Treasury and derived from the IMF's MULTIMOD model. It consists of interlinked, highly stylized country models for the G7, a model for the aggregate of 11 smaller industrialized countries and two Rest of the World models representing the oil-producing countries and the developing countries, respectively.

The simulation conducted with the model concerns an autonomous decrease in personal consumption in the United States by 2 percent of GNP, corresponding to about $70 billion in 1990. Table 8.5 shows the short- and medium-term effects. In the short run, the growth of US gross national product decelerates. In all countries both prices and the real rate of interest (nominal rate less expected inflation) decrease. After some time, this decrease in the real rate of interest leads to an expansion of the volume of investment in all countries. The increase in the current account balance in the United States finds its counterpart elsewhere in the world, notably in Japan. All in all, this increase in saving has favorable economic effects all over the world, especially in terms of the real rate of interest and the level of prices. This serves to illustrate that an increase in saving may considerably help to mitigate the upward pressure on interest rates and prices exerted by the increasing global demand for capital (see table 8.4).

THE EFFECT OF POLICY ON SAVING

The desirability of boosting saving worldwide gives rise to the question as to what instruments are available to that end. This section reviews the efficacy of a number of instruments, namely the budget deficit, the share of the national income claimed by the public sector and the composition of expenditure and taxes; the review was conducted in part with simulations using the INTERMOD model discussed above. Subsequently, taxation of unearned income is discussed, as well as public and private pension schemes. Finally, attention is paid to the influence of policy on the composition of saving, centering on the neutrality of taxation of unearned income.

Reducing Budget Deficits

The most direct manner in which governments can increase saving is by reducing budget deficits. The worldwide fall in the savings ratio in the 1980s is usually ascribed in large measure to the decline in public sector saving,

Table 8.5 Effect of an autonomous decrease in personal sector consumption in the United States by 2% of GDP (percentage changes unless stated otherwise)

	US	Japan	Germany	France	UK	Italy	Canada	G7
1990								
Volume of GNP	-2.6	-0.6	-0.4	-0.3	-0.7	-0.3	-1.3	-1.4
Volume of investment	-2.1	-0.3	0.4	0.2	0.0	0.1	-1.1	-0.9
Price level	-0.3	-0.2	-0.3	-0.2	-0.2	-0.3	-0.2	-0.2
Current account balance ($ billions)	2.9	-0.1	2.6	-1.0	-6.2	-0.4	-1.6	-3.8
Real long-term interest rate (percentage points)	-1.0	-0.6	-0.6	-0.6	-0.7	-0.6	-0.9	-0.8
1992								
Volume of GNP	-1.1	-0.8	-0.3	-0.3	-0.2	-0.3	-0.6	-0.8
Volume of investment	-0.6	-0.1	1.1	1.2	0.9	0.8	0.0	0.1
Price level	-1.3	-1.0	-1.9	-1.5	-1.7	-1.6	-1.3	-1.3
Current account balance ($ billions)	44.9	-15.9	-3.1	-5.9	-7.8	-4.3	-3.4	5.4
Real long-term interest rate (percentage points)	-1.2	-0.9	-1.0	-1.0	-1.0	-0.9	-1.1	-1.0
1994								
Volume of GNP	0.0	-0.6	-0.3	0.2	0.2	0.3	0.2	-0.2
Volume of investment	1.3	0.7	1.5	2.3	1.6	1.6	1.3	1.2
Price level	-2.8	-2.1	-2.8	-2.8	-2.9	-2.9	-2.7	-2.6
Current account balance ($ billions)	71.5	-28.0	-8.5	-7.9	-8.3	-6.6	-3.7	8.5
Real long-term interest rate (percentage points)	-1.4	-1.2	-1.3	-1.3	-1.3	-1.2	-1.4	-1.3

Source: Authors' own simulations using INTERMOD.

especially in the United States and several large European countries. During the past few years, the tend has been reversed, thanks in part to a favorable cyclical development. An increase in the world savings ratio will consequently have to be achieved, mainly by putting public finance in order, as we will see from the rest of this chapter.

A reduction of the budget deficit also has indirect effects on, among other things, private sector saving. According to the Ricardian equivalence theorem, an increase in public sector saving is offset by a decrease in private sector saving (see pp. 284–8). For the greater part, empirical research indicates that Ricardian equivalence applies only partly. The regression equation presented on pp. 284–8 for eight industrialized countries suggests that the compensating reaction of private sector saving is approximately one-third, so that deficit reduction turns out to be a powerful method of stimulating saving.

The budget deficit can be reduced both by decreasing public expenditure and by raising taxes. The effects of these forms of deficit reduction are shown below on the basis of simulations made with the world model INTERMOD. The simulated changes relate to the economy of the United States. The fact that the simulations are based on a policy change in a specific country is not meant to suggest that this country is responsible for the global savings deficit.

We begin by taking a look at the findings for a deficit reduction achieved by means of a decrease in public spending. Table 8.6 shows the results of a non-recurring, lasting reduction in public expenditure in the United States by 2 percent of GDP, corresponding to about $70 billion. The figures show that the reactions make themselves felt worldwide. Real interest rates in the United States fall by 0.8 percentage point, those elsewhere by about 0.5 percentage point. In later years the effects on interest rates are even larger, real interest rates worldwide eventually undergoing a decline of nearly 1 percentage point. In the course of the years, higher savings mean more investment everywhere. The current account of the balance of payments in the United States also undergoes a favorable development. Although the effects are positive world-wide, they are the most favorable for the United States.

Table 8.7 presents the outcomes of a deficit reduction attained through a rise in taxes on wage income by 2 percent of GDP in the United States. A similar picture emerges as in the case of the reduction of expenditure, but the effects have been more or less halved. Real interest rates and prices worldwide are substantially lower and, after several years, investment has expanded. It must be noted that the model used does not make allowance for a situation where a higher tax burden is shifted to wages. If allowance had been made for this factor, the outcome would probably have been less favorable.

All in all, a reduction of the US budget deficit generally has a positive impact on the world economy, the effects being strongest when the deficit reduction is achieved through a decrease on public spending.

Table 8.6 Effect of a reduction in public spending in the United States by 2% of GDP (percentage changes unless stated otherwise)

	US	Japan	Germany	France	UK	Italy	Canada	G7
1990								
Volume of GNP	-2.2	-0.5	-0.3	-0.2	-0.6	-0.3	-1.1	-1.1
Volume of investment	-1.6	-0.2	0.3	0.2	0.0	0.0	-0.8	0.7
Price level	-0.3	-0.1	-0.2	-0.1	-0.2	-0.2	0.1	-0.2
Current account balance ($ billions)	4.3	-0.7	1.6	-0.9	-4.9	-0.3	-1.6	-2.5
Real long-term interest rate (percentage points)	-0.8	-0.5	-0.4	-0.5	-0.5	-0.4	-0.6	-0.6
1992								
Volume of GNP	-0.7	-0.6	-0.2	-0.2	-0.1	-0.2	-0.4	-0.5
Volume of investment	-0.2	0.1	0.8	1.0	0.8	0.6	0.1	0.2
Price level	-1.2	-0.8	-1.4	-1.1	-1.3	-1.2	-1.1	-1.1
Current account balance ($ billions)	33.4	-12.2	-2.5	-4.2	-5.5	-2.9	-2.4	3.7
Real long-term interest rate (percentage points)	-0.9	-0.7	-0.7	-0.7	-0.7	-0.7	-0.8	-0.8
1994								
Volume of GNP	0.2	-0.4	-0.2	0.2	0.2	0.3	0.2	0.0
Volume of investment	1.3	0.6	1.1	1.7	1.2	1.2	1.0	1.1
Price level	-2.3	-1.6	-2.1	-2.1	-2.2	-2.2	-2.1	-2.0
Current account balance ($ billions)	51.8	-20.4	-6.4	-5.6	-5.8	-4.6	-2.6	6.4
Real long-term interest rate (percentage points)	-1.0	-0.9	-0.9	-0.9	-0.9	-0.9	-1.0	-0.9

Source: Authors' own simulations using INTERMOD.

Table 8.7 Effect of tax rise in the United States of 2% of GDP (percentage changes unless stated otherwise)

	US	Japan	Germany	France	UK	Italy	Canada	G7
1990								
Volume of GNP	-0.7	-0.2	-0.1	-0.1	-0.2	-0.1	-0.4	-0.4
Volume of investment	-0.7	-0.1	0.3	0.1	0	0.1	-0.4	-0.3
Price level	-0.1	-0.1	-0.1	-0.1	-0.1	-0.1	0.1	-0.1
Current account balance ($ billions)	-0.7	0.4	1.0	-0.2	-1.9	-0.1	-0.3	-1.8
Real long-term interest rate (percentage points)	-0.4	-0.2	-0.2	-0.2	-0.3	-0.2	-0.3	-0.3
1992								
Volume of GNP	-0.4	-0.3	-0.1	-0.1	-0.1	-0.1	-0.2	-0.3
Volume of investment	-0.3	0	0.5	0.5	0.4	0.3	0	0
Price level	-0.3	-0.3	-0.7	-0.5	-0.6	-0.6	-0.4	-0.4
Current account balance ($ billions)	15.4	-5.4	-1.0	-2.1	-2.9	-1.5	-1.3	1.2
Real long-term interest rate (percentage points)	-0.5	-0.4	-0.4	-0.4	-0.4	-0.4	-0.4	-0.4
1994								
Volume of GNP	-0.1	-0.3	-0.1	0.1	0.1	0.1	0	-0.1
Volume of investment	0.2	0.3	0.7	0.9	0.6	0.6	0.4	0.4
Price level	-0.8	-0.8	-1.1	-1.1	-1.1	-1.1	-1.0	-0.9
Current account balance ($ billions)	26.5	-10.4	-3.1	-3.1	-3.3	-2.5	-1.5	2.6
Real long-term interest rate (percentage points)	-0.6	-0.5	-0.5	-0.5	-0.5	-0.5	-0.5	-0.5

Source: Authors' own simulations using INTERMOD.

Parallel Reduction of Public Spending and Receipts

Next to a deficit reduction, there is also the policy option of simultaneous decreases in public spending and receipts. If the budget deficit remains the same, this means that the public sector claims a smaller share of national income.

Table 8.8 shows the results of such a parallel decrease in public spending and taxation by 2 percent of GDP in the United States. It turns out that the general contraction of the public sector causes a fall in real interest rates and prices everywhere. Notably in the United States investment and gross national product undergo a marked expansion after a few years. Apparently the space released by a shrinking public sector is eventually filled by the private sector. It must be pointed out that the reduction in expenditure and taxation may have behavioral effects which have not been included in the model, such as an improvement in the impact of economic incentives on the supply side of the economy, which could make the effects on investment and gross national product even more favorable in reality.

Changes in the Composition of Public Spending and Receipts

Saving may be influenced not only by the level of the budget deficit and the size of the public sector, but also by the *composition* of public expenditure and taxes. For example, a larger proportaion of budget expenditure on interest leads to higher income for investors, who add much of it to their capital. The distribution of public expenditure into capital expenditure and current expenditure is, however, of fundamental importance from the point of view of savings. As public sector savings equal the balance of current receipts and current expenditure, an increase in capital expenditure, coupled with a corresponding decrease in current expenditure, means a rise in public sector saving by the same amount. Although there may be some decrease in household saving, the net effect on national saving will probably be positive. Savings are also affected by the composition of taxes, a matter dealt with in the next section in greater detail. Let it suffice here to say that a decrease in taxes on profits, combined with an increase in taxes on wage incomes, leads to an increase in national saving because more savings are made from profits than from wage income. Greater emphasis on indirect taxation instead of direct taxes can also have a favorable effect on saving as unearned income is not subject to indirect taxes.

Thus the government can (if the budget deficit and total expenditure and taxes remain unchanged) influence national saving through changes in the composition of spending and taxation. The following sections will deal with two aspects: taxation on unearned income and public and private pension schemes.

Table 8.8 Effect of a reduction in public spending and taxes in the United States by 2% of GDP (percentage changes unless stated otherwise)

	US	Japan	Germany	France	UK	Italy	Canada	G7
1990								
Volume of GNP	-1.5	-0.3	-0.3	-0.2	-0.4	-0.2	-0.8	-0.8
Volume of investment	-0.9	-0.1	0	0.1	0	0	-0.5	-0.4
Price level	-0.2	-0.1	-0.1	-0.1	-0.1	-0.1	0.1	-0.1
Current account balance ($ billions)	5.0	-1.3	0.5	-0.8	-2.9	-0.3	-1.3	-1.1
Real long-term interest rate (percentage points)	-0.4	-0.2	-0.2	-0.2	-0.2	-0.2	-0.3	-0.3
1992								
Volume of GNP	-0.3	-0.3	-0.2	-0.1	-0.1	-0.1	-0.1	-0.2
Volume of investment	0.2	0.1	0.3	0.4	0.4	0.3	0.1	0.2
Price level	-0.9	-0.4	-0.7	-0.6	-0.7	-0.6	-0.7	-0.7
Current account balance ($ billions)	17.7	-6.7	-1.5	-2.1	-2.7	-1.5	-1.2	2.0
Real long-term interest rate (percentage points)	-0.4	-0.3	-0.3	-0.3	-0.3	-0.3	-0.4	-0.3
1994								
Volume of GNP	0.4	-0.2	-0.2	0.1	0.1	0.1	0.2	0.1
Volume of investment	1.1	0.3	0.4	0.8	0.6	0.6	0.6	0.7
Price level	-1.5	-0.8	-1.0	-1.0	-1.1	-1.1	-1.2	-1.2
Current account balance ($ billions)	25.6	-10.4	-3.4	-2.5	-2.6	-2.1	-1.0	3.6
Real long-term interest rate (percentage points)	-0.5	-0.4	-0.4	-0.4	-0.4	-0.4	-0.5	-0.4

Source: Authors' own simulations using INTERMOD.

Taxation on Unearned Income

Taxation and the level of savings   Taxation on unearned income makes it less attractive to have capital and thus to save. In fact such taxation often has the same impact in saving as a reduction in interest rates. Because, as we saw on pp. 284–8 interest-rate adjustments have both income and substitution effects, which have opposite signs, their theoretical effect on saving is uncertain. A definitive pronouncement cannot be found in the empirical literature either. The regression equation presented above indicated that a rise in real interest rates makes household savings expand significantly (see also Fase et al., 1990). This positive link between real interest rates and savings implies that, in principle, taxing interest earnings has a slightly discouraging effect on saving.

The presumably negative impact of taxation of unearned income on private sector savings is to some extent undone by the effect of the resulting revenues. Being part of public sector receipts, they contribute to public sector savings. However, in cases where these tax revenues are used for more public spending, the net effect of taxation on unearned income is probably negative. It is clear that we do not know the magnitude, nor even the sign, of the total effect which taxes on unearned income have on saving and that this form of taxation is not an efficient way of stimulating saving. On the contrary, saving will on average sooner decrease.

In practice, receipts from various wealth components are taxed differently. This non-neutral character of the taxes involved, which has both a national and an international dimension (see pp. 303–4), exercises an influence on both the size of the tax receipts and the allocation of saving. This will be discussed in greater detail below.

Tax structure and allocation of saving   The allocation of saving is affected by the circumstance that taxation on unearned income is far from uniform. For an overview, the reader is referred to Kauffmann and Owens in chapters 1 and 3, respectively. Dividends, for example, are treated differently from interest receipts, and in most countries profits are taxed twice: first through the corporation tax payable by the enterprise in question and once more through the income tax payable by shareholders. In addition, various components of unearned income are eligible for divergent tax allowances, while owner-occupied houses are treated differently again. Taxation on stock exchange profits also varies from country to country. Some countries do not impose such taxes at all, whereas others tax the entire capital. Another complication is formed by the total exemption from taxation of certain categories of taxpayers. For example, in nearly all countries, life assurance companies, in respect of the provision for insurance liabilities, and pension funds need not pay taxes. Furthermore, non-residents are partly treated differently from residents. Finally, there are investment constructions which make it possible to avoid taxation partly or entirely, such as interest growth funds and investment schemes in low-tax countries.

Diverging tax rates, allowances and exemptions make investors adjust the allocation of their saving so that the effective tax burden on unearned income is reduced. The arbitrage by investors does not so much concern pre-tax investment yields as determined by the market, as post-tax yields. The decision of the fiscal authorities to regard unearned income as taxable income has the consequence that in a number of countries interest paid on borrowed funds is treated as negative income. This leads to a considerable expansion of the possibilities of arbitrage. In these countries, investors with a portfolio of debts and investments can deduct the entire negative income from interest payments, the positive income being taxed only partly or not at all. Thus one can benefit from an asymmetry in taxation, in the sense that interest receipts are, to some extent, treated differently from interest payments. The progressive nature of the income tax system only strengthens possible arbitrage. Taxpayers subject to a low marginal rate are stimulated relatively more to invest in heavily taxed debt instruments, while those subject to a high marginal rate are encouraged to take up loans.

Another asymmetrical aspect is that not all forms of unearned income are reported to the tax authorities. Taxes on unearned income can be avoided much easier than other taxes by transferring capital to other countries, thus concealing any income earnings on that capital. It must be kept in mind that data on interest transfers to other countries are not broken down by individual. The size of the total tax leak can be estimated by comparing the dividends and interest payments figuring in the National Accounts with the aggregate of the corresponding variables in the tax returns. For the Netherlands, the discrepancy comes out at a very substantial percentage of total income from interest and dividends.

Such legal and illegal forms of arbitrage encouraged by the tax system may cause the net tax receipts from unearned income to become nil or negative; see, for example, Gordon and Slemrod (1988). Lower or no tax revenues from unearned income lead to relatively higher tax rates on labor income and profits. In addition, the asymmetrical tax structure makes the budget more vulnerable to interest rate changes (Bikker, 1991). A more serious matter is that the prevailing tax systems disturb the allocation of saving, and more in general, the composition of portfolios. Investment activities are, after all, based not only on individual preferences and market conditions, but also on fiscal rules. From the point of view of society, this implies a distortion of optimal allocation and of the optimal use of the factors of production. In practice, a large number of fiscal rules discriminate against risk-bearing investments. This makes it difficult for the business sector to obtain finance, a situation which could have a negative impact on investment and thus in the longer term on prosperity. Applying especially to young firms, this impairs the competitiveness and resilience of the economy (Bovenberg, 1991).

Allocation among risk-avoiding and risk-bearing investments   The tax systems of many countries contain unintended incentives to hold savings in the form of risk-avoiding rather than risk-bearing assets. This goes particularly for the double taxation on dividends and the special treatment of savings for pensions. The double taxation makes it unattractive to invest in shares. There are, incidentally, numerous ways of easing this double burden, limiting tax receipts as well as the adverse effects. One of these is to retain profits in the expectation that this will show up in the share prices. The disadvantage of favoring financing by retainment of profits is that it discriminates against young and thus more risk-bearing enterprises. After all, they have not yet begun to make profits. Eliminating double taxation would therefore restore equal chances for risk-bearing investments.

Pension funds and life assurance companies accumulate large amounts of capital. Savings made to finance old age schemes are favored in comparison to other savings because pension premiums and life annuity premiums are wholly or partly tax deductible and because payments under capital sum insurance are tax-exempt in most countries. Although life annuities and pension benefits are subject to taxation, it can be ascertained that the accrued interest is in fact untaxed owing to this particular fiscal treatment (Bikker, 1991). The favoring of these savings may take place an even larger scale, if the marginal rate at which premiums have been deducted is higher than the marginal rate at which benefits are taxed. This is in fact subsidizing,[9] so that savings in the form of pension premiums are favored above alternative investment possibilities.

Pension funds and, to a lesser degree, life assurance companies are strongly inclined to invest the funds entrusted to them in non-risk-bearing assets, especially in cases where they guarantee benefits in the form of nominal amounts. There may also be institutional reasons for such cautious investment behavior. Given the large amounts at stake, this means a considerable allocation disturbance. The most effective way of remedying this disturbance is not necessarily a reduction of the fiscal favoring of savings in the form of pension premiums. An alternative could be to exercise an influence on the funds' investment behavior, for example, by stimulating competition between them or decreasing their institutional limitations.

International allocation   In recent years, the liberalization of the international capital market made a substantial contribution to the international reallocation of savings, which is expected to yield major advantages in terms of efficiency. The continuing process of economic integration in the European Community also makes for this development, as the exchange rate risks diminish further and legislation in the various countries converges, leading to greater competition in the financial markets. The degree to which fiscal legislation, which varies over the different countries, distorts the international allocation of savings consequently increases markedly. For instance, a withholding tax applicable both to residents and non-residents (which is not imposed in all countries) will chase savings out of the country (Gérard, 1991), as happened in West Germany in 1987 after the announcement of proposals to introduce a withholding tax on interest income. In many countries, such a capital flight is prevented in part, where foreign savings are concerned, by distinguishing between residents and non-residents (taxing and non-taxing, respectively). It must be noted that there are treaties which prevent taxes being levied both in the capital market involved and in the country of residence. Taxation of unearned income in the countries of residence is frustrated by the lack of sufficient information: no data are supplied to foreign public authorities on payments of interest and dividends, which are broken down by individual. International differences with regard to the levying of income and corporation tax and tax avoidance form serious threats in that they distort the international allocation of saving and because the base of taxation on unearned income is impaired by arbitrage. In addition, tax rate competition may compel countries to lower their rates to less than optimal levels.[10] Within the framework of these problems, the international reduction of marginal rates of income tax was only a modest step in the right direction.

If withholding tax is chosen as the way of taxing unearned income of individuals, greater uniformity of both a withholding tax and a corporation tax is of major importance, especially within the EC, even though international coordination in this field will prove far from easy. So long as unearned income is taxed on the principle of country of residence, international reporting of payments of interest and dividends broken down by individuals will be needed to prevent tax avoidance.

Conclusions on tax structures, saving and allocation   The above clearly shows the overwhelming influence which taxation on unearned income has on saving. It is not so much the level of saving which is affected. The numerous possibilities of reducing the actual burden of taxation in this area imply that saving is discouraged only to a limited extent, while the possible revenues could benefit public sector saving. The non-neutral character of tax systems, which disturbs the allocation of saving, would seem to be a much more serious matter. The recent tax reforms in most OECD countries have led to considerably lower marginal rates for income tax in particular and to a broader tax base, thus reducing the distorting nature of taxation. In many countries, one of the reforms involved an expansion of the tax base for income tax so as to include capital gains. On the other hand, the liberalization of capital movements have led to greater possibilities for arbitrage and thus to greater disturbances ensuing from diverging fiscal regimes.

It is therefore important to look into the possibilities of more uniform tax systems, which impose comparable taxes on all components of unearned income in all countries. Such convergence could be effected in the system of income taxes existing in many countries, where interest receipts are taxed and interest payments are tax deductible. In this case, uniform taxation of unearned income would mean that the accumulation of accrued interest in savings at pension funds and life assurance companies would also be subjected to taxation. An alternative is a system aimed more at taxation of consumption, interest not being taxed (Bradford, 1980; Bovenberg, 1991). This would imply that unearned income is exempt from taxation, but also that the tax deductibility of interest – on for example mortgage loans – would be scrapped. Such a shift towards taxation of consumption has been made in, among other countries, the United Kingdom, where income tax was reduced and indirect taxation expanded.

Public and Private Pension Schemes

Where pension schemes are concerned, a distinction can be made between public pension schemes (basic pensions) and the obligatory pension schemes included in labor contracts. The influence on saving in both cases will be dealt with below.

If an employee falls under an obligatory pension scheme operated on the funding principle, non-contractual household savings are replaced by compulsory savings in accordance with the life-cycle hypothesis mentioned earlier. It is doubtful whether this substitution is complete. Owing to insufficient information, lagged adjustment and transactions costs, not everyone will act entirely in accordance with the rational life-cycle hypothesis. In addition, the capital market does not function as perfectly as the life-cycle hypothesis assumes. Furthermore, it must be remembered that employees have no say in what happens to their savings in the form of pension premiums, so that there may continue to be a need for funds with a certain degree of liquidity. Moreover, the existing provisions might cause attention to be shifted to related desiderata such as early retirement, so that there still continues to be a need for employees to save – the so-called induced retirement effect. Finally, the literature points to the phenomenon where individuals come to realize the importance of sufficient savings for old age (recognition effect) as a result of their taking part in a compulsory pension scheme. These factors may contribute to less than complete substitution between compulsory and voluntary saving, on balance exercising a positive influence on saving. It is, incidentally, also possible that the substitution concerned is larger than unity. After all, individuals will have to save more to attain the security of an old age income which is comparable to that offered by pension funds, especially if those pension funds offer index-linked or even wage-linked pensions. Empirical research into the degree of substitution between compulsory and voluntary saving shows diverging results (Feldstein, 1978; Kuné, 1981; Pitelis, 1985). Munnel (1987) concludes in a survey that in a group pension scheme, non-contractual household savings decrease by about two-thirds of savings. This means that the positive effect in saving is around one-third.

In most countries, public old-age pension schemes are based on a pay-as-you-go system. In some countries, that also goes for compulsory pension schemes for employees.[11] If there are such systems, then there is a decreasing need for voluntary saving for old age, at least if the public and private schemes suffice. The measure in which voluntary saving decreases depends on the uncertainty about the magnitude of future benefits. In a pay-as-you-go system, these may be negatively dependent on the increasing ageing of the population. If a smaller or relatively less growing working population has to take care of an ever-increasing group of old-age pensioners, there is a considerable risk that the public benefit per capita will decrease. It must be noted though that empirical research has not unequivocally shown the expected negative effect of a scheme based on the pay-as-you-go system on saving (Kuné, 1981; Jafari-Samini, 1984). Munnel (1987) concludes that "most experts agree that no evidence exists to support the contention that social security had reduced saving." Bernheim (1987) states, however, that the negative effects are seriously underestimated because future income effects of basic pension schemes are measured inappropriately. Be that as it may, the negative influence of the pay-as-you-go system on saving is apparently too small to show up clearly.

In the funding system, the factors which determine the level of the premium are the growth of prosperity and real interest rates. In a pay-as-you-go system, these are the growth of prosperity and the expansion of the working population. A role is also played by the degree to which old-age pensioners receive a share of the growth of prosperity. The well-known condition of Aaron (1966) states that the funding system leads to greater prosperity (i.e., a smaller premium burden (than the pay-as-you-go system, if the sum total of the growth of the population and income is smaller than the real interest rate, and *vice versa*. In practice, applying this formula poses problems as variables such as the real growth of income and the real interest rate fluctuate sharply in the course of time. Another complication is the ageing of the population which is manifesting itself in many countries. Here a major factor is not only the lower growth rate of the working population figuring in the Aaron condition, but also the relative increase in the number of old-age pensioners. Assuming a situation where the sum total of the expansion of the population and of income more or less equals the real interest rate, the funding system leads to a more favorable distribution of the premium burden over time in an economy where the population is ageing rapidly. The capital is formed in a period when the working population is relatively large, and may be used for consumption in a period that the working population will be comparatively small. For an ageing population, the funding system leads to an intertemporal redistribution which is comparable to that of individuals in accordance with the life-cycle hypothesis.

The observation that the funding system is to be preferred in economies with ageing populations may, incidentally, for practical reasons not lead to the recommendation to replace the pay-as-you-go system by a funding system. The costs for the present working population would be disproportionately high. There is, however, much to be said for keeping the basic schemes founded on the pay-as-you-go system modest or – in countries where the basic scheme is generous – to reduce it, or in the longer term to accept the contraction of these schemes which ensues from the maximization of the premium burden, and to place the emphasis on furthering supplementary provisions on the basis of the funding system. In many countries steps have been taken to reduce the public basic schemes or there are plans for such a reduction. There is, however, no general trend towards stimulating the compulsory private schemes; on the contrary, these are also subject to pressure in some countries. In a number of countries, such as the United States and the United Kingdom, this is the result of the tendency to individualize supplementary pension schemes.

We may conclude that old-age pensions based on a pay-as-you-go system probably have a negative effect on saving to a moderate extent, whereas pension schemes based on a funding system probably affect saving positively to a considerable degree. From the viewpoint of saving, the funding system is to be preferred. In an economy with an ageing population, there are other welfare economic arguments, which are in favor of a shift from a pay-as-you-go to a funding system.

This can be achieved by reducing or limiting the public schemes and furthering private schemes on the basis of a funding system.

CONCLUSIONS

From this chapter's discussion of world savings, the following conclusions may be drawn:

• Owing to the increased liberalization of capital movements, the link between national saving and investment has slackened in individual countries, as recourse can also be had to foreign saving to finance investment. As a result, it has become more difficult as well as less relevant for individual countries to form an opinion of the desired level for the national savings ratio, as far as the financing of fixed investment of enterprises is concerned. On a global scale it is of crucial importance for continuing economic growth that sufficient saving be generated.

- The coming years are expected to see an increasing need for saving, notably on the part of Eastern Europe, the former Soviet Union and the Middle East. Ex ante, world savings are probably insufficient for that purpose, a situation which will be reflected in high real interest rates. Model calculations indicate that an expansion of world savings may mitigate the upward pressure on real interest rates. Policy should therefore be aimed at raising the international savings ratio.

- The most powerful and direct instrument for increasing saving is lowering the budget deficit. Model calculations show that deficit reduction through a decrease in expenditure is considerably more effective than that achieved through an increase in taxation. A second policy option is a parallel reduction of expenditure and receipts, leading to a situation where a smaller share of national income is claimed by the public sector. The budget deficit then remains the same, but, due to the decreased pressure on the private sector, more savings can be generated indirectly. Changes in the composition of public spending and receipts may also affect saving.

- The third instrument for stimulating saving are measures aimed at augmenting the neutrality of the tax system, both nationally and internationally. This has a more indirect effect, and is aimed much more at the *allocation* of saving. The national and international lack of uniformity characterizing taxation of unearned income offers investors numerous possibilities of reducing individual tax burdens by arbitrage. As a consequence, the negative effects on the volume of savings are probably slight. As the revenues boost public sector saving – at least when public spending remains unchanged – the ultimate effect is even unknown. It is clear that the tax structure is not an effective way of augmenting saving.

- The fourth instrument is the level of public and private pension schemes. The public provisions consist of a basic pension scheme founded in most countries on a pay-as-you-go system. It may be assumed that such a provision will reduce the tendency on the part of individuals to save for their old age themselves. The private schemes provide for supplementary pensions for employees, which are mostly based on a funding system. This provision will lead to an expansion of savings. There is much to be said for stimulating supplementary schemes and thus expanding the element of funding. As the government has only limited influence on supplementary pensions, the efficacy of this instrument is comparatively feeble.

- The unequal treatment of unearned income from different sources per country and the differences between countries give investors, as already pointed out, many possibilities of reducing individual burdens of taxation. This leads to lower tax receipts for the government and distorts the allocation of saving, leading to less than optimal use of the factors of production. Risk-bearing investments are disadvantaged by the various fiscal structures, while the international allocation is also impaired. The threat of disturbances to international allocation and the tax rate competition between different countries have been considerably augmented by the increased liberalization of capital movements and, within the EC, by the gradual completion of the internal market. It is therefore of great importance to strive for uniform tax treatment of unearned income from different sources and in different countries. At the same time, it is necessary that data on individual unearned income be reported internationally, so as to be able to counter tax avoidance, while maintaining the home-country principle.

- As a result of the advanced liberalization of the capital market, policy aimed at stimulating saving has gained a worldwide dimension. However, it is still being conducted at a national level. The question arises whether this will suffice, as national savings may flow away to other countries. On the one hand, international coordination would seem unnecessary, because countries with a systematic savings surplus are rewarded by factor income on foreign capital, which is paid by countries with cumulated saving deficits. However, as disequilibria can last longer once capital movements have been liberalized, some international coordination would seem to be desirable. That goes especially for limiting budget deficits and imposing greater uniformity of tax systems.

NOTES

1 For a survey of a number of major studies, see Aghevli et al. (1990).
2 The large spread of the values of the explanatory variables across countries and the large number of observations contribute to high t-values.
3 Such differences may also occur over time; see the results of Lau in chapter 4. They show that in the United States persons who were born before 1939 and have felt the depression of the 1930s have a considerably higher savings ratio than later generations.
4 See IMF (1990a) and IMF, World Bank et al. (1991).
5 Financial Times, January 18, 1990 and United Nations (1990), p. 13.
6 For further details, the reader is referred to IMF (1991a).
7 European Economy, Supplement A, no. 8/9, 1990.
8 For a discussion of the causes of the rise in real interest rates in the 1980s, the reader is referred to the contribution of Fitoussi and Le Cacheux in chapter 5.
9 The particular treatment also leads to the situation where part of what is in fact public sector saving is imputed to private sector saving. After all, savings in the form of pension premiums are subject to a deferred tax claim (Bovenberg, 1991). An advantage of this is that while the working population is still relatively large, the government builds up a tax claim which can be collected when the proportion of old age pensioners in comparatively high.

10 Calculations of the OECD (1991) indicate that the allocation disturbances are considerable.
11 For an overview, the reader is referred to Owens's contribution in chapter 3, as well as to Mercer (1990).

REFERENCES

Aaron, H. J. 1966: The social insurance paradox. *Canadian Journal of Economics and Political Science*, 32, 371–6.

Abel, A. B., Mankiw, N. G., Summers, L. H. and Zeckhauser, R. J. 1989: Assessing dynamic efficiency: theory and evidence. *Review of Economic Studies*, 56, 1–20.

Aghevli, B. B., Boughton, J. M., Montiel, P. J., Villanueva, D. and Woglom, G. 1990: The role of national saving in the world economy. *Internationale Monetaire Fonds*, Occasional Paper no. 67, Washington DC.

Auerbach, A. J., Kotlikoff, L. J., Hagemann, R. P. and Nicoletti, G. 1989: The economic dynamics of an ageing population: the case of four OECD countries. *OECD Economic Studies*, Spring, no. 12.

Back for International Settlements, 1991: *61st Annual Report, April 1990–Maart 1991*, Basle.

Bernheim, B. D. 1987: The economic effects of social security. *Journal of Public Economics*, 33, 273–304.

Bikker, J. A. 1991: Reële rente en sectorale verdeling van inkomen uit vermogen (Real interest rate and the sectoral distribution of unearned income). *Report for the Royal Netherlands Economic Association*, Stenfert Kroese, Leiden/Antwerpen.

Bovenberg, A. L. 1991: Overvloed en welbehagen: sparen en investeren in Nederland (Abundance and well-being: saving and investment in the Netherlands). *Economisch Statistische Berichten*, pp. 144–8.

Bradford, D. F. 1980: The economics of tax policy toward savings. In G. M. von Furstenberg (ed.), *The government and capital formation*. Cambridge.

Corrigan, E. G. 1990: The US savings gap and global imbalances. *De Economist*, 138, 464–70.

Den Broeder, C. and Winder, C. A. A. 1991: Financing government spending: an analysis from the Ricardian perspective. *De Economist* (forthcoming).

Evans, O. 1990: National Savings and Targets for the Federal Budget Balance in the United States. *IMF Staff Studies*.

Fase, M. M. G., Kramer, P. and Boeschoten, W. C. 1990: *MORKMON II*: the Nederlandsche Bank's quarterly model of the Netherlands' economy. *Economic Modelling* (forthcoming).

Feldstein, M. 1978: Do private pensions increase national savings? *Journal of Public Economics*, 10, 227–93.

Feldstein, M. 1980: International differences in social security and saving. *Journal of Public Economics*, 12, 225–44.

Ford, R. and Poret, P. 1990: Business investment in the OECD economies: recent performance and implication for policy. Working Paper no. 88, Department of Economics and Statistics OECD.

Gérard, M. 1991: The European cummunity tax game: a Bertrand approach. Paper presented at the European Meeting of the Econometric Society, Cambridge.

Gordon, R. H. and Slemrod, J. B. 1988: Do we collect any revenue from taxing capital income? In L. H. Summers (ed.), *Tax policy and the economy*. Cambridge (Mass).

Graham, J. W. 1987: International differences in saving rates and the life cycle hypothesis. *European Economic Review*, pp. 1509–29.

Graham, J. W. 1989: International differences in saving rates and the life cycle hypothesis: Reply and further evidence. *European Economic Review*, pp. 1499–1507.

IMF 1990a: *Annual Report*.

IMF 1990b: *World Economic Outlook*, May.

IMF 1991a: *World Economic Outlook*, May.

IMF 1991b: *World Economic Outlook*, August.

IMF, World Bank, OECD, and European Bank for Reconstruction and Development 1991: *The Economy of the USSR*.

Jafari-Samini, A. 1984: Social security and private savings. *Journal of Public Economics*, pp. 226–45.

Kramer, P. and Mourik, T. J. 1990: De Nederlandsche besparingen in internationaal verband (Dutch savings in an international setting). *Economisch Statistische Berichten*, pp. 768–72.

Kuné, J. B. 1981: The impact of social security on personal saving: evidence for the Netherlands, 1952–1978. *Het Verzekerings-Archief*, 58, 33–41.

Mercer, W. (ed.) 1990: *1990 International Benefit Guide Lines*, Brussels.

Meredith, G. 1989: INTERMOD 2.0: model specification and simulation properties. *Department of Finance Working Paper*, no. 89–7, Ottawa.

Modigliani, F. 1990: Recent declines in the saving rate: a life cycle perspective. *Revista di Politica Economica*, pp. 5–42.

Munnel, A. H. 1987: The impact of public and private pension schemes on saving and capital formation. *ISSA Studies and Research*, 24, 219–36.

Nicoletti, G. 1988: A cross-country analysis of private consumption, inflation and the "debt neutrality hypothesis." *OECD Economic Studies*, no. 11.

Nicoletti, G. 1990: Consumption and government debt in high deficit countries: is tax-discounting stable over time? The case of Italy and Belgium. *OECD, Department of Economics and Statistics*.

OECD 1990: *Economic outlook*, June.

OECD 1991: The future of capital income taxation in a liberalised financial environment. *Working party no. 1 of the Economic Policy Committee*, ESD/CPE/WP1(91)8.

Phelps, E. S. 1961: The golden rule of accumulation: a fable for growthmen. *American Economic Review*, pp. 638–43.

Pitelis, C. 1985: The effects of life insurance and pension funds on other savings: the postwar UK experience. *Bulletin of Economic Research*, 37, 213–29.

Smith, R. S. 1990: Factors affecting saving, policy tools and tax reform: a review. *IMF Staff Papers*, 37, no. 1.

United Nations 1990: Economic survey of Europe in 1989–1990. *Economic Commission for Europe*, New York.

Index

Compiled by M. J. Heary